Hiking Virginia

Help Us Keep This Guide Up to Date

Every effort has been made by the authors and editors to make this guide as accurate and useful as possible. However, many things can change after a guide is published—trails are rerouted, regulations change, techniques evolve, facilities come under new management, etc.

We would love to hear from you concerning your experiences with this guide and how you feel it could be improved and kept up to date. While we may not be able to respond to all comments and suggestions, we'll take them to heart and we'll also make certain to share them with the authors. Please send your comments and suggestions to the following address:

The Globe Pequot Press
Reader Response/Editorial Department
P.O. Box 480
Guilford, CT 06437

Or you may e-mail us at:

editorial@GlobePequot.com

Thanks for your input, and happy travels!

A **FALCON** GUIDE®

Hiking Virginia

A Guide to Virginia's Greatest Hiking Adventures

Second Edition

Bill and Mary Burnham

FALCON GUIDE®

GUILFORD, CONNECTICUT
HELENA, MONTANA
AN IMPRINT OF THE GLOBE PEQUOT PRESS

A FALCON GUIDE ®

Copyright © 2004 by Morris Book Publishing, LLC
The previous edition of this book was published in 2001
by Beachway Press Publishing, Inc.

All photos are by the Bill and Mary Burnham.

ISSN: 1547-3406
ISBN-13: 978-0-7627-2747-6
ISBN-10: 0-7627-2747-0

Manufactured in the United States of America
Second Edition/Third Printing

To buy books in quantity for corporate use
or incentives, call **(800) 962–0973, ext. 4551,**
or e-mail **premiums@GlobePequot.com.**

The Globe Pequot Press assumes no liability for accidents happening to, or injuries
sustained by, readers who engage in the activities described in this book.

Contents

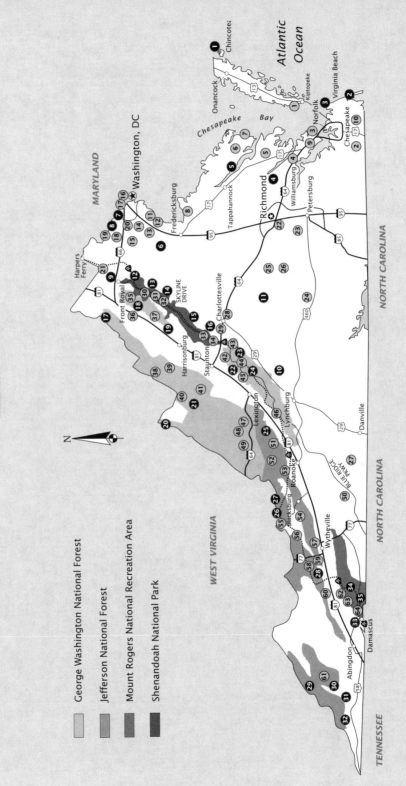

Virginia

George Washington National Forest

Jefferson National Forest

Mount Rogers National Recreation Area

Shenandoah National Park

The Art of Hiking

Acknowledgments

Family and friends have been our constant trail companions. We are privileged to have shared many trails and many miles with them. Bill especially recognizes Terry Fairbanks, who led his first backpacking trip. It planted the seed of a changed life. Mary sends out special recognition to the Burnham girls—Julie and Mary Rose—who taught her no matter how far she might wander from civilization, always bring a compact. As Julie uttered, memorably: "Just because we're in the woods, doesn't mean we have to look like we're from the woods."

Mary Rose Burnham and Dwayne Henderson hiked with us on many trails for this book, served as our models, and even snapped a photo or two. Their companionship made trail research an adventure. Mary and I especially commend them for reaching an amicable solution to the water problem on Mount Pleasant.

To Emily, Ben, Kathleen and Matt, Mary, Dennis, Allen and Joanne, Dahr, Marcy, and Geoff: Happy Trails! Let's plan a trip!

Forest Service rangers, geologists, historians, and plain everyday folks have provided us with advice, guidance, and education. John Stallard in the Clinch Ranger District of the Jefferson National Forest went to extraordinary lengths to assist us. Don Sawyer in the Lee Ranger District of the George Washington National Forest and Bob McKinney at Mount Rogers National Recreation Area provided trail advice. Ben Morgan and Avery Drake of the USGS provided geologic maps and literature on Virginia's complicated geology, as did John Marr and Palmer Sweet with the Virginia Division of Mines & Minerals.

Frank Kilgore of St. Paul helped open our eyes to the wonders of southwest Virginia. Shad Baker of the Pine Mountain Trail Association aided our navigation of what ranks as the most difficult trail we ever hiked. Thanks also to Henry Mullins, who showed us the route up Birch Knob and gave us much-needed beverages once we got there. Jim Jordan of Longwood College shared his knowledge of central Virginia, an often overlooked region for outdoor recreation.

Our dog Sasha is grateful to the staff of the Shenandoah Animal Hospital in Woodstock.

We would like to thank our parents. Mr. and Mrs. B's unwavering, unchanging advice was simply: "Get it done." Matt and Fran Kubick stepped in to run the household while we traveled. Without that help, we could not have written this book, which received a National Outdoor Book Award Honorable Mention in 2001. Thank you.

—Bill Burnham

Preface

People collect stamps. People collect antiques. We collect special places. We pursue them as vigorously as a hobbyist does his or her passion. In doing so, we subscribe to the theory Richard Nelson eloquently expressed in *The Island Within:* "What makes a place special is the way it buries itself in the heart, not whether it is flat or rugged, rich or austere, wet or arid, gentle or harsh, warm or cold, wild or tame." In this spirit, we welcome you to *Hiking Virginia*.

Our book is about more than destinations. It is about experiences set amid Virginia's natural beauty. More and more, people seek out culture and history where they travel. Walking, whether up a mountain or down a quaint city street, offers a traveler no better way of achieving this (admittedly, we're biased—we LOVE hiking). A walk slows the world so sights, smells, and sounds may leave a mental imprint. *Hiking Virginia* is a trail of bread crumbs you can use time and time again to enjoy Virginia's beautiful landscapes, rich history, and kind people.

Virginia lends itself to the foot traveler. Higher mountains and larger expanses of preserved land may be found elsewhere, but in Virginia, the best parts of many worlds exist. Flat, low-lying coastal areas enjoy temperate ocean breezes. The Piedmont unfolds westward, one gentle hill after another, up to the steep flank of the Blue Ridge, an ancient mountain range of billion-year-old granite and prehistoric lava flows. Beyond the Blue Ridge and great valley lies the Allegheny chain of mountains, with distinct valleys and ridges tending northeast-southwest. In the state's far southwest corner, the land rises to its highest peaks of nearly 6,000 feet.

In Virginia, hikers find endless possibilities. They might walk beneath the broad sky of a high-altitude meadow, inhale the spruce scents of a remnant boreal forest, delight in the natural richness of an Appalachian cove forest, walk along tidal marshes, or play in the ocean surf. The sun rises over an Atlantic barrier island, while hundreds of miles inland in a mountain valley, sunlight creeps, inch by inch, down a forested ridge until it alights on the deepest, coolest parts of the earth. From coast to mountain, Virginia beckons. Answer her call, find your place, and make it special.

Thank you for purchasing *Hiking Virginia*.

—Bill and Mary Burnham

How to Use This Book

Take a close enough look and you'll find that this little guide contains just about everything you'll ever need to choose, plan for, enjoy, and survive a hike in Virginia. We've done everything but load your pack and tie up your bootlaces. Stuffed with useful Virginia-specific information, *Hiking Virginia* features 40 mapped and cued hikes, 64 honorable mentions, 25 unique day hikes along the Appalachian Trail, and everything from advice on getting into shape to tips on getting the most out of hiking with your children or your dog. And you get the best maps man and technology can render. With so much information, the only question you may have is: How do I sift through it all? Well, we answer that, too.

We've designed our guidebook to be highly visual, for quick reference and ease-of-use. What this means is that the most pertinent information rises quickly to the top, so you don't have to waste time poring through bulky hike descriptions to get mileage cues or elevation stats. They're set aside for you. Yet *Hiking Virginia* doesn't read like a laundry list. Take the time to dive into a hike description and you'll realize that this guide is not just a good source of information; it's a good read. Here's an outline of the book's major components.

To aid in quick decision making, we start each hike chapter with a short summary to give you a taste of the hiking adventure to follow. You'll learn about the trail terrain and what surprises the route has to offer. If your interest is piqued, read on; if it isn't, skip to the next hike.

The hike specifications that follow are fairly self-explanatory. Here you'll find the quick, nitty-gritty details of the hike: where the trailhead is located, the nearest town, hike distance, approximate hiking time, difficulty rating, type of trail terrain, what other trail users you may encounter, trail contacts (for updates on trail conditions), trail schedules and use fees, and available maps. **Finding the trailhead** provides dependable directions from a nearby city right down to where you'll want to park. **The Hike** is the meat of the chapter. Detailed and honest, it's our carefully researched impression of the trail. While it's impossible to cover everything, you can rest assured that we won't miss what's important. **Miles and Directions** provides mileage cues to identify turns and trail name changes, as well as points of interest. The **Hike Information** section at the end of each hike is a hodgepodge of information. Here we'll tell you where to stay, what to eat, and what else to see while you're hiking in the area.

The **Honorable Mentions** for each section detail hikes that didn't make the cut. In many cases it's not because they aren't great hikes, but they may be overcrowded or environmentally sensitive to heavy traffic. Be sure to read through these. A jewel might be lurking among them.

We don't want anyone to feel restricted to just the routes and trails that are mapped here. We hope you'll have an adventurous spirit and use this guide as a platform to dive into Virginia's backcountry and discover new routes for yourself. One of the simplest ways to begin this is to just turn the map upside down and hike the course in reverse. The change in perspective is often fantastic and the hike should feel quite different. With this in mind, it'll be like getting two distinctly different hikes on each map.

For your own purposes, you may wish to copy the directions for the course onto a small sheet to help you while hiking, or photocopy the map and cue sheet to take with you. Otherwise, just slip the whole book in your backpack and take it all with you. Enjoy your time in the outdoors and remember to pack out what you pack in.

How to Use These Maps

Regional Location Map

This map helps you find your way to the start of each hike from the nearest sizable town or city. Coupled with the detailed directions at the beginning of the cue, this map should visually lead you to where you need to be for each hike.

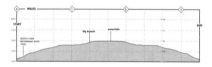

Elevation Profile

This helpful profile gives you a cross-sectional look at the hike's ups and downs. Elevation is labeled on the left, mileage is indicated on the top. Road and trail names are shown along the route with towns and points of interest labeled in bold.

Route Map

This is your primary guide to each hike. It shows all of the accessible roads and trails, points of interest, water, towns, landmarks, and geographical features. It also distinguishes trails from roads, and paved roads from unpaved roads. The selected route is highlighted, and directional arrows point the way. Shaded topographic relief in the background gives you an accurate representation of the terrain and landscape in the hike area.

Map Legend

Interstate Highway	
U.S. Highway	
State Road	
County Road	
Township Road	
Forest Road	
Paved Road	
Paved Bike Lane	
Maintained Dirt Road	
Unmaintained Jeep Trail	
Singletrack Trail	
Highlighted Route	
Nat'l Forest/County Boundaries	
State Boundaries	
Railroad Tracks	
Power Lines	
Special Trail	
Rivers or Streams	
Water and Lakes	
Marsh	

✝ Airfield   𝆏 Hiking Trail

✈ Airport   Lighthouse

🚲 Bike Trail   Mine

🚳 No Bikes   Overlook

Boat Launch   Ⓟ Parking

)(Bridge   Picnic

Bus Stop   ✕ Quarry

▲ Campground   ((Ⓐ)) Radio Tower

Campsite   Rock Climbing

Canoe Access   School

Cattle Guard   Shelter

† Cemetery   Spring

Church   Swimming

Covered Bridge   Train Station

Direction Arrows   Wildlife Refuge

Downhill Skiing   Vineyard

Fire Tower   ◆◆ Most Difficult

Forest HQ   ◆ Difficult

4WD Trail   ☐ Moderate

Gate   ● Easy

Golf Course

Introduction

Virginia Weather

Virginia's climate is a seasonal mixed bag. In winter, storms arrive from the west. In fall, tropical weather arrives from the Atlantic or, occasionally, from the Gulf of Mexico. When severe enough, these tropical storms become hurricanes. During summer, warm air settles over the state, resulting in hot days punctured by thunderstorms. Late fall and winter are wet-weather seasons, while summer and early fall are generally dry.

Along the coast—the state's warmest region—the Atlantic winds exert a moderating influence on temperatures, making highs and lows less extreme. Back Bay Wildlife Refuge, a coastal barrier island, averages 86°F in July. By contrast, the southern Piedmont city of Danville experiences an average temperature of 90°F in July. Likewise, in winter, temperatures on the coast average above freezing. Inland, on the Piedmont, temperature averages dip to the mid-20s.

Virginia's mountains and valleys produce wildly fluctuant temperatures and levels of precipitation. Virtually every state record—high and low temperature, high and low rainfall and snowfall—has occurred in the Blue Ridge Mountains and points west. Summer temperatures range from the mid 80s into the 90s. In winter, temperatures dip into the teens. Snow is common in the mountains, with average accumulations between 6 and 7 inches December through February.

When storms arrive from the west, the Allegheny Mountains cast a rain shadow over eastern mountain slopes and the Shenandoah Valley. When storms originate from the east, the Blue Ridge reverse the pattern, wringing moisture out on eastern slopes, leaving the western slopes and valleys dry. As a result, the Shenandoah Valley is the driest region of the state, averaging only 33 inches of rain annually. To the east, across the Blue Ridge, the city of Charlottesville averages 47 inches. And in far southwest Virginia, annual rainfall totals more than 60 inches.

Tropical storms and hurricanes deserve special mention in Virginia. They occur August through October and bring with them threats of high winds and flooding. A hurricane is defined as a storm with sustained wind gusts of 74 mph, but a tropical storm can be as harrowing an experience. Hurricanes are often thought of as coastal weather events, but Virginia's worst twentieth-century storm, Hurricane Camille in 1969, devastated Nelson County in the eastern Blue Ridge region. More recently, in 1996, Hurricane Fran caused mudslides and widespread flooding near Front Royal.

Virginia Flora and Fauna

Virginia's forests are comprised primarily of broadleaf, deciduous trees. Under this forest blanket exist plant communities specially adapted to the state's varying climates.

1

Grasses, saltmeadow hay, and hearty shrubs such as wax myrtle populate coastal fringes of Virginia. These are some of the most resilient plants in the world, able to withstand harsh winds and saltwater conditions. Inland from the beaches and dunes, lagoons mix a daily tidal wash with mainland runoff. Fish spawn here and crustaceans such as fiddler crab live out early years on a nutrient-rich diet. On the mainland, forests of pines and oak typify the flat coastal region. In swampy areas, bald cypress and live oak are often draped with Spanish moss.

Besides cushioning a daily onslaught of waves and wind, the Atlantic barrier islands of Virginia support breeding and migratory birds. From Assateague to False Cape, the arrival and breeding of songbirds, raptors, shorebirds, and wading birds of all shapes and sizes mark every season. As many as 400,000 birds of prey, representing twelve species, have been observed at Kiptopeke State Park on the Eastern Shore during a single fall count.

Virginia's Piedmont has traditionally supported agriculture. By the twentieth century, generations of farming left large swaths of barren land. Where forests returned, they are primarily black and white oak and Virginia and loblolly pine. In Virginia's state forests, oak and poplar are managed for harvest. Willow oak, river birch, hickory, and ash grow as well. Cumberland State Forest near Farmville marks the extreme western reach of the loblolly pine in Virginia. Turkey, fox, deer, raccoon, and squirrel populate these pockets of rejuvenated woodlands. Hunting has long been permitted, but state forests are a popular spot for hikers, horseback riders, mountain bikers, and campers as well.

The Appalachian oak-hickory forest rises to dominance within the Blue Ridge. Hickory is the successor of American chestnut. In the early twentieth century, it was estimated one of every four trees in the Appalachians was a chestnut. Today, few grow taller than 6 feet before succumbing to the Chestnut Blight. In the absence of chestnuts, oaks have assumed primacy in Virginia's western regions. Chestnut oaks are found on dry, rocky ridges, while white and red oak populate mountain slopes. In the forest understory, scrub oak and chinquapins grow.

In moist pockets below 4,500 feet elevation, the Appalachian cove forest holds more than twenty species of trees—beech, sugar, maple, and yellow poplar noticeable among these. Stands of eastern hemlock once made for impressive viewing. However, damage from the invasive woolly adelgid is now widespread in Virginia. Evidence of its handiwork is especially striking in Shenandoah National Park, where entire stands of hemlock are defoliated and dying. Even so, quiet, cool pockets of this venerable evergreen may still be found along isolated mountain streams. In the forest understory, dogwood and redbud bring colorful spring blossoms. Mountain laurel and rhododendron seem omnipresent on both dry, rocky ridges and in wet stream valleys. Wildflowers are profuse, from the common purple violets and white toothworts to the infrequently-spotted Turks caps lily. G. R. Thompson Wildlife Management Area, on the eastern slope of the northern Blue Ridge, is thought to hold the largest population of trillium wildflowers in North America. At Mount

Rogers and Laurel Fork, the state's highest elevations, spruce and fir trees indicate a remnant boreal forest more typical of Canada.

Deer have rebounded from overhunting and habitat destruction of one hundred years ago to rank as almost a nuisance throughout Virginia. Black bears are found primarily in the western regions of the state, but may be spotted in the Great Dismal Swamp in southeast Virginia. Otherwise, Virginia's forests support small-game wildlife. A hiker's footsteps may flush turkey or grouse from the woods. Raccoon and other nocturnal animals make hanging food a necessary part of any camping trip. Bobcat and coyotes are found statewide, but generally in larger areas of preserved forest.

The river systems of Virginia host a wide range of life, from the common brook trout to endangered freshwater mussels. The Clinch and Powell Rivers, flowing southwest to the Tennessee River, support a variety of the hard-shelled animals, many threatened or endangered due to sediment buildup and past toxic chemical spills. Salamander and crayfish are present in Virginia's mountain streams. Throughout Virginia, there are 210 species of freshwater fish. Wild trout streams include Big and Little Wilson Creeks in Mount Rogers National Recreation Area to North Fork Moormans River in Shenandoah National Park. In the coastal regions, crabs, clams, and other crustaceans inhabit muddy flats in the James, York, Rappahannock, and Potomac Rivers. Seasonal runs of rockfish, sea bass, croaker, and other fish have made sport fishing a popular pastime in the Chesapeake Bay and Atlantic Ocean.

Virginia has witnessed many successes under the federal Endangered Species Act, perhaps none as stirring as the return of a viable bald eagle population. Virginia is home to more than 225 active bald eagle nests. Mason Neck Wildlife Refuge, Caledon Natural Area, and other preserves along the lower Potomac River are renowned nesting and viewing areas for this bird of prey. Likewise, on the James River between Richmond and Isle of Wight County, more than 300 bald eagles have been counted in summer months. Best viewing times in any location are June through August and November through January.

Virginia Wilderness Restrictions/Regulations

In northern and southeast Virginia, public lands fall under three broad categories: federal parks, forests, and refuges; state parks and forests; and municipal parks. Keep in mind that wildlife refuges exist for the benefit of animals, not humans. Sections may be closed off to the public during breeding seasons. Conversely, federal, state, and municipal parks exist for humans, a fact reflected in their sometimes crowded conditions.

Virginia's two national forests cover 1.8 million acres of mountain forestland. The George Washington National Forest stretches from north of Winchester to just south of Lexington and Covington. The adjacent Jefferson National Forest continues southwest to the Virginia-Tennessee border. Both are managed out of a single forest headquarters in Roanoke. While it is tempting to think the forests exist for hikers' enjoyment, they are in fact multiuse, with trails for horseback riders, cyclists, and all-terrain vehicles. Developed campgrounds and recreation areas are suitable for a tenter or a motor home. Hunting is permitted in season, and timber harvests are conducted regularly.

Virginia's national forests are divided into nine ranger districts, and each district is responsible for fire prevention, maintenance, and ecology within its boundary. Rangers and their assistants make excellent resources for hikers and can provide information on trails and weather. Mount Rogers National Recreation Area, which covers 117,000 acres of high country in southwest Virginia is a specially managed component of the national forest and was created in 1965 with the intent of serving recreational needs of East Coast urban dwellers. Within it are 95 miles of trails for hikers, horseback riders, and cyclists.

Contained in Virginia's two national forests are seventeen wilderness areas—including the Priest and Three Ridges areas, which President Clinton designated in November 2000. The intent of wilderness is to allow land to return to a primitive state without interference from people. Motorized traffic and tools are not allowed and trails may be unblazed and unmaintained. There are exceptions to every rule, however. In cases of emergencies, the Forest Service or local emergency company may use vehicles, helicopters, chain saws, and other mechanical apparatus when responding in a wilderness area. Surprisingly, the wilderness designation does not automatically translate to remote. St. Mary's Wilderness Area, south of Staunton and Charlottesville, is blessed with an abundance of beautiful waterfalls; yet, because it's so easily accessed from Interstate 81, it's more heavily used than some nonwilderness areas. That said, just as many of these areas feel truly remote. Many hikers have never heard of Beartown Wilderness, on the edge of Burke's Garden near Tazewell, or Kimberling Creek Wilderness, near Wytheville.

Shenandoah National Park is Virginia's—and one of the nation's—most visited parks. There is an entrance fee; annual passes are available. Most visitors simply cruise Skyline Drive, a beautiful highway with scenic views that traces the ridgeline of the Blue Ridge. (South of the park, the road continues as the Blue Ridge Parkway, a scenic highway that ends in Great Smoky National Park in Tennessee.) It is said that a majority of travelers on Skyline Drive stray no more than a half mile from parking areas and pull-offs. Still, Shenandoah's backcountry receives a healthy number of visitors. Every hiker should be aware of the park's backcountry regulations, which govern issues from pets to fires to how to dispose of waste.

Getting Around Virginia

Area Codes: Virginia currently has seven area codes: 276 serves Martinsville, Bristol, Abingdon, and the rest of southwest Virginia; 434 serves Charlottesville, Lynchburg, and central Virginia; 540 covers Roanoke and western and northern Virginia excluding Arlington; 571 overlays with 703 to serve the Washington, D.C. suburbs and Arlington area; 757 serves Hampton, Norfolk, and southeastern Virginia; and 804 covers Richmond east to the Williamsburg area.

Roads: For current information on statewide weather and road conditions and closures, call the Virginia Department of Transportation (VDOT) 24-hour Highway Helpline at (800) 367–7623 or visit www.vdot.state.va.us. (TTY users, call 800–432–1843.)

By Air: Dulles International Airport (IAD) is 23 miles northwest of downtown Washington, D.C. **Ronald Reagan Washington National Airport** (DCA) is in nearby Alexandria. For full services, visit www.metwashairports.com. **Richmond International Airport** (RIC) is located 7 miles east of downtown Richmond. For full services, visit www.flyrichmond.com. **Norfolk/Virginia Beach International** (ORF) serves the Tidewater Region. For full services, visit www.norfolkairport.com.

Other major airports in Virginia include **Roanoke Regional Airport** (ROA), www.roanokeairport.com or www.roanoke.org/air.html; **Shenandoah Valley Regional Airport** (SHD), www.flyshd.com; **Charlottesville Albemarle Airport** (CHO), www.gocho.com; and **Newport News–Williamsburg International** (NNW), www.nwairport.com.

To book reservations on-line, check out your favorite airline's Web site or search one of the following travel sites for the best price: www.cheaptickets.com, www.expedia.com, www.flycheap.com, www.priceline.com, travel.yahoo.com, www.travelocity.com, or www.trip.com—just to name a few.

By Train: Virginia is well served by **AMTRAK.** For information and/or reservations, visit them on-line at www.amtrak.com or call (800) 872–7245.

Virginia Railway Express (VRE) operates commuter rail service weekdays along two lines from Fredericksburg and Manassas to Union Station. For more information, call (800) RIDE–VRE or visit www.vre.org. **Maryland Rail Commuter** (MARC) operates commuter rail service weekdays along the Potomac River in Maryland. (An important stop for hikers is Harpers Ferry, West Virginia, where the Appalachian and C&O Canal Trails converge.) For more information, call (800) 543–9809 or visit www.mtamaryland.com.

By Bus: Greyhound serves most larger towns and cities in Virginia along with Dulles Airport several times a day. For information and/or reservations, visit them on-line at www.greyhound.com or call (800) 231–2222. Links to local transit operators in Virginia are available on-line at www.apta.com/sites/transus/va.htm.

Visitor Information: For visitor information or a travel brochure, call the **Virginia Tourism Corporation** at (800) 321–3244 or visit their Web site at www.virginia.org.

Eastern Virginia

W ater, not the land, defines Virginia's eastern region. It washes up onto Atlantic barrier islands and rolls into the Chesapeake Bay, forming and shaping the coastline. It runs along a vast network of upland streams, molding river bluffs and carving small inlets and bays. It pours forth from western regions of the state, bursting into the estuarine lower reaches of the James, York, Rappahannock, and Potomac Rivers, giving shape to three large peninsulas that jut out into the Chesapeake Bay.

Water also redefines the landscape, as dramatically evidenced by Hurricane Isabelle in September 2003. One of the state's worst all-time storms in terms of damage inflicted, Isabelle hit state and city parks particularly hard, none more so than York River State Park. There, an 8-foot storm surge destroyed footpaths and boardwalks and forced the closure of trails. Elsewhere, in Newport News Park and on the Eastern Shore's Chincoteague Wildlife Refuge, trails remained closed six months after the storm.

Over the long reach of geologic time, the influx and regress of water—sometimes gradual, sometimes dramatic—has been Eastern Virginia's legacy. The Chesapeake Bay itself is the drowned mouth of the Susquehanna River. In glacial times, when the ocean levels dropped some 400 feet, what we know today as the Chesapeake Bay was a wide river valley. The coastline stood 60 miles out into the present-day ocean. The sand beaches and brackish lagoons of today were, millions of years ago, forests and freshwater ponds.

Images of colonial Virginia ring out in accounts written by early explorers. The English, seeking permanent settlement of North America, came ashore in Virginia Beach, present-day Cape Henry. After months at sea, they were awestruck by an abundance of trees, plants, and animals. They saw dense swamps, where sheets of Spanish moss dangled from trees standing in knee-deep black water. Discarded oyster shells littered the beaches. Fish were abundant. Inland, near Tidewater, the Algonquin Indians had cleared only a fraction of the forest for their crops. Trees were tall and thickly trunked, and sheltered an abundance of wildlife.

Eastern Virginia today harbors bits and pieces of this once-resplendent nature. Rare migratory birds winter over in the Dismal Swamp. Endangered turtles live in the swamps of First Landing State Park. In the harsh beach and dune environments, piping plovers struggle against predators large and small. Behind barrier islands, marshes perform the critical job of filtering land runoff while supporting a nursery of fish and shellfish. In hidden, secluded spots, rare orchids bloom and old-growth

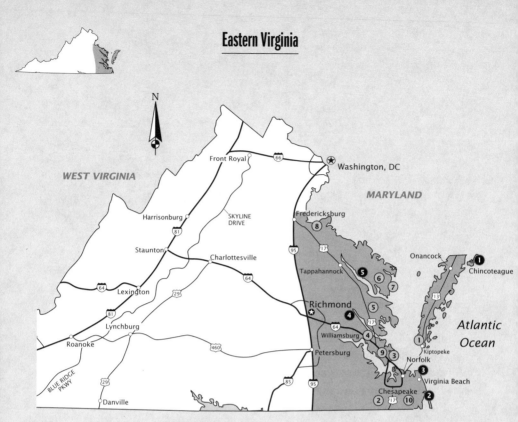

Eastern Virginia

trees spread their branches, inviting you to rest in their shade. Bald eagles nest and roost on stretches of the James River between Richmond and Isle of Wight County.

Wherever you choose to explore, bring a pair of waterproof boots. Because no matter where you hike in eastern Virginia, you're bound to hit water.

1 Chincoteague National Wildlife Refuge

Every spring and fall, millions of birds migrate between cold, northern environs and temperate and tropical homes in Central and South America. En route, their needs are simple: an occasional place to rest and food to nourish. Wildlife biologists at Chincoteague National Wildlife Refuge, on the southern tip of Assateague Island, have engineered a deluxe ornithological wayside for the winged travelers. Entire sections of beach are closed during nesting season for the endangered piping plover. On small, man-made earthen mounds rising in the middle of bayside lagoons, waterfowl perch and feed, protected from predators. As the human hand tinkers with wildlife balance, real drama plays out in the daily life of birds and land animals—and it's on display for all to see.

Start: From the Refuge Visitor Center on Beach Road.
Distance: Wildlife Pond/Beachfront Loop: 9.1 miles; Beachfront Backpack: 22.8 miles.
Approximate hiking time: 10 hours (shorter option is 5 hours).
Difficulty rating: Moderate due to length.
Trail surface: Wildlife Pond/Beachfront Loop: A network of paved roads, dirt roads, and sand jeep trails lead hikers to a wide ocean beach, maritime forest of oak and pine, low dunes, and saltwater marsh. *Beachfront Backpack:* Sand and surf along a wide ocean beach.
Land status: National wildlife refuge.
Nearest town: Chincoteague, VA.
Other trail users: Cyclists, anglers, and hunters (in season).
Canine compatibility: Dogs not permitted.

Trail contacts: Chincoteague National Wildlife Refuge, Chincoteague, VA, (757) 336-6122, chinco.fws.gov.
Schedule: Open daily, dawn to dusk. Access to "The Hook," a section of beach along Tom's Cove, is closed mid-March through August for piping plover nesting. Deer hunting is allowed for two weeks in October, and one week prior to Christmas through January.
Fees/permits: Entrance fee: $10.00 per vehicle; bikers and pedestrians free. Backcountry permit: $5.00. Register at the Tom's Cove Visitor Center at least 24 hours before starting your hike. Backpackers must depart Tom's Cove Visitor Center four hours before sunset to reach the State Line backcountry campsite in Maryland. Visit www.nps.gov/asis for camping rules and regulations.
Maps: USGS maps: Chincoteague East, VA.

Finding the trailhead: From Chincoteague: *Wildlife Pond/Beachfront Loop:* Turn left onto Main Street (Virginia Route 175) from the island bridge. In 0.5 mile, turn right onto Maddox Boulevard (Virginia Route 2113). Drive 1.2 miles to a traffic circle and follow Maddox Boulevard through the circle. In 0.8 mile, enter the refuge. In 0.3 mile, turn left into the parking area for the Refuge Visitor Center. *Beachfront Backpack:* After entering the refuge, continue past the Refuge Visitor Center. In 2 miles, enter Beach Parking Lot No. 1. *DeLorme: Virginia Atlas & Gazetteer:* Page 63, A5.

Snowy egret in a wildlife pond.

The Hike

Screams and cries rise off the oceanfront as hungry gulls and terns scavenge for food along the surf. Beyond Assateague Island's low sand and inland pine, snow geese float restlessly in a freshwater pool. Suddenly, on some silent, unseen signal, a single goose, then two, three—then the entire flock rises in flight. Their *whonk-whonk* joins with cries of shorebirds in a resounding cacophony.

An explosion of snow geese off the water draws the birder's eyes skyward. Here, a broad-winged raptor swoops high above the pond. Its brown wings tilt slightly left, then right in a jittery act of balance. The telltale white head and yellow, hooked bill soon come into focus. This bald eagle, its search for a meal frustrated, soars out of sight behind crowns of loblolly pine.

This winter struggle between prey and predator will end when snow geese fly north in spring. Closer to the ocean, a different life struggle begins in spring when piping plover descend upon Chincoteague National Wildlife Refuge on the southern tip of Assateague Island. After a brief courtship, breeding pairs build a nest in the sand. Four eggs will hatch within a month of being laid. For five critical days, the young chick's life consists of dodging predators and finding enough food to survive. Days turn to weeks, and the handful of chicks that survive face new dangers. Camouflage, the tiny, sand-colored plover's best defense, leads to unintended consequences: Humans inadvertently step on nests. Off-road vehicles run them over. Gulls

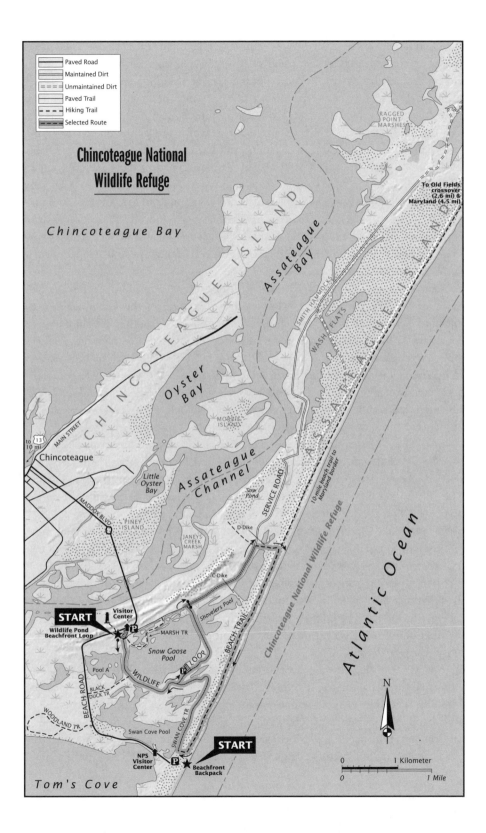

harass adult plovers and carry away chicks. Other predators, raccoons and foxes among them, raid nests. Storms send tidal surges crashing over protective dunes—violent weather has destroyed entire nesting seasons at Chincoteague.

Animals fend for themselves on a daily basis in a never-ending search for an advantage—and a meal. Humans represent an interference in this delicate balance. The side of the scale on which we place our weight makes all the difference. In the case of the Delmarva fox squirrel, farming and homes had, by 1900, destroyed habitat in all but a tiny spot in Maryland. The balance tipped in the squirrel's favor in 1945, however, when Maryland set aside land for its protection. In 1971 it became illegal to hunt the large fox squirrel, which can weigh up to three pounds and measure 30 inches in length. On reserves in Virginia, Maryland, and Delaware, squirrel populations increased. From a population of 30 squirrels in 1970, Chincoteague now keeps its numbers around 350, shipping out squirrels to other suitable habitats if their numbers exceed this level.

Human intervention, often the cause of ailing animal populations, is just as often the cure. Wildlife biologists maintain intensive tracking of the fox squirrel, even injecting electronic transponders into a small sampling of the population. The tiny device works like a scanner at a grocery store checkout. Activated remotely, it allows more thorough tracking of the squirrel. Piping plover benefit from management as well. When plover chicks hatch in late May, refuge staff begin a sixteen- to eighteen-hour vigil over nesting sites. Nesting areas are signed and roped off, and occasionally beach roads are closed to vehicular traffic. In the fall of 1999, after the first year of intensive monitoring, 43 plover chicks reached maturity in the refuge.

In 1998 the Chincoteague refuge welcomed back a female peregrine falcon that two years earlier staff had found underweight and injured from an attack. By the 1960s, breeding peregrine falcons had disappeared from the eastern United States. The falcons had suffered a fate similar to the bald eagles'—contamination from the pesticide DDT. Weakened eggshells broke, and chicks hatched prematurely. DDT was banned in 1972. In the late 1970s scientists began releasing pairs of peregrines in Virginia, both in coastal and mountain regions. In 1982 they hit gold when a pair of peregrine falcons was found nesting on Assateague Island. By 1996 all but one of the sixteen nesting pairs of peregrines were located in coastal Virginia. A delisting of the peregrine from an *endangered* species to a *threatened* species reflects national success in reintroducing breeding populations. In 2000, hawk watchers recorded 1,428 sightings of migrating peregrine falcons at Kiptopeke State Park, on the southern tip of the Eastern Shore.

And yet even in a managed environment, disaster strikes. When several storms inundated the maritime forest of lower Assateague Island—which encompasses the whole of the Chincoteague refuge—volumes of salt water weakened the resident loblolly pines. The stress caused by a lack of freshwater made the pines susceptible to the Southern pine beetle. Casualties are visible today along the Wildlife Loop Trail—you'll undoubtedly notice the large piles of deadwood gathered in clearings. Low shrubs and grass now grow where a mixed forest of loblolly, oak, and maple once stood. The open space has proved ideal for pine saplings, which are making a vigorous comeback—so much so that refuge staff are now thinning them to avoid overcrowding.

A 9-mile hike north from the Chincoteague refuge ends at the Maryland border. Assateague Island continues under protection of Maryland State Parks and the National Park Service (which operates backcountry campsites in the dunes). For years, protection of Assateague extended to correcting nature itself. After every major storm, the park service rebuilt dunes with the goal of keeping an ocean ecology from slipping away. Littoral drift, the term for a shift in barrier islands westward, moves Assateague, on average, 30 feet every decade. But not everything needs protecting. Park managers have decided against rebuilding dunes. Whatever conditions a storm leaves the barrier island, staff will leave untampered. Instead of permanent structures, the park service is buying temporary cabanas that can be torn down in just hours. Humans, and not the environment, will adapt to conditions. Briefly, balance tips back to Mother Nature.

Miles and Directions–Wildlife Pond/Beachfront Loop

0.0 **START** from the parking lot for the Refuge Visitor Center. Opposite the visitor center, a boardwalk trail leads away through a pine forest. (Note: Avoid a paved path that leads away from the parking lot left of the boardwalk trail.)

0.1 Turn right onto the paved Wildlife Loop. (FYI: Views of Snow Goose Pool, a freshwater impoundment, open up on the left. This road is open to vehicles from 3:00 P.M. to dusk.)

0.6 Continue straight, past the Black Duck Trail, which exits to the right. (FYI: The Black Duck Trail leads a half mile to paved Beach Road.)

1.3 Continue straight, past Swan Cove Trail, which exits to the right. (FYI: Swan Cove Trail leads 1.3 miles to Beach Parking Lot No. 1.)

1.6 Turn left onto the short Boardwalk Trail, which leads to an observatory overlooking a freshwater marsh. After completing the Boardwalk Trail, turn left and resume hiking on the paved Wildlife Loop.

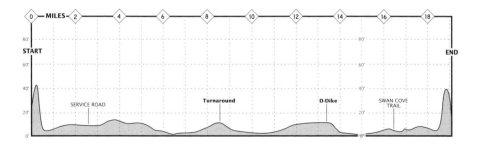

2.6 Cross Snow Goose Pool on a dike and turn right onto a gated dirt road, which is closed to public vehicle traffic except between Memorial Day and Labor Day, when sightseeing trams operate. (**Option:** To return to the Refuge Visitor Center, turn left at this T junction and follow the paved Wildlife Loop Road.)

3.2 Continue straight on the gravel road past C-Dike. (FYI: This earthen embankment is closed and may not be used to access the beach.)

3.6 Turn right onto D-Dike and hike 0.3 mile to the oceanfront.

3.9 Emerge from the dunes onto the beach, turn right and head south along the beachfront.

6.4 Look for railings across four dunes. Follow the walkway to Beach Parking Lot No. 1 on the landside of the dunes. In the northwest corner of this parking lot, turn right onto Swan Cove Trail. (FYI: This trail may be closed during periods of high rainfall.)

7.8 Swan Cove Trail ends at Wildlife Loop. Turn left to return to the Refuge Visitor Center.

9.1 Arrive back at the visitor center.

Miles and Directions–Beachfront Backpack

0.0 **START** from Beach Parking Lot No. 1. Cross the dunes on a walkway and descend to the beachfront. Turn left and walk north.

1.9 Pass a dune crossover to C-Dyke on the left. Continue straight. (FYI: This dyke is closed and may not be used to access the refuge's interior service road.)

2.6 Pass a dune crossover to D-Dyke on the left. Continue straight.

4.6 An unmarked road breaks through the dunes on the left. Continue straight. (FYI: This road is closed to foot traffic and may not be used to access interior roads.)

9.2 Pass Old Fields crossover, a route leading left through the dunes to an interior service road. Continue straight.

10.9 Cross the Maryland state line and enter Assateague Island National Seashore. Continue straight.

11.4 A tent sign in the dunes to the left indicates State Line campsites, primitive sites with no running water and chemical toilets. Camping is permitted amid dunes only.

22.8 Hike ends at Beach Parking Lot No. 1.

Hike Information

Local Information

Chincoteague Chamber of Commerce, Chincoteague, VA, (757) 336-6161, www.chincoteaguechamber.com.

Local Events/Attractions

Annual Pony Swim and Penning, July, Chincoteague, VA, (757) 336-6161. An event of national renown, wild Chincoteague ponies are driven off the refuge across a small water passage and penned on Chincoteague Island for auction.

International Migratory Bird Celebration, May.

Eastern Shore Birding Festival, October, Chincoteague NWR, VA, (757) 336-6122. Two major birding events held in conjunction with other wildlife refuges and state parks on the Eastern Shore.

Lodging

Driftwood Motor Lodge, Chincoteague, VA, (800) 553-6117.

Refuge Inn, Chincoteague, VA, (888) 831-0900.

Backcountry camping is allowed only at Assateague National Seashore in Maryland. Commercial campgrounds are located in and around the village of Chincoteague.

Restaurants

More than twenty Chincoteague restaurants serve up fare ranging from seafood to the standard burger and fries.

Tours

Refuge staff lead walking tours throughout the year. Call (757) 336-6122 for information.

Organizations

Chincoteague Natural History Association, Chincoteague, VA, (757) 336-3696, www.assateague.org/plover.

Other Resources

United States Lighthouse Society, San Francisco, CA (415) 362-7255.

2 False Cape State Park/Back Bay Wildlife Refuge

Barrier islands serve as an ecological first line of defense for our shores. Storms batter them, waves wear them down, wind strips them clean. Tucked out of harm's way behind the islands lie sheltered bays and marshes teeming with grasses, shellfish, birds, and small animals. False Cape State Park and Back Bay National Wildlife Refuge showcase just one of Virginia's many barrier island and lagoon ecosystems, albeit a critical one. The preserves stand within striking distance of Hampton Roads' two million residents and all the incumbent pressures (pollution, development, overcrowding). Sprawl stops at the park boundaries, and hikers and bird-watchers are assured a quiet afternoon with space to walk and think, or watch and listen.

Start: From Little Island Recreation Area.

Distance: 14.7-mile loop.

Approximate hiking time: 5 hours.

Difficulty rating: Moderate due to length of hike.

Trail surface: All aspects of seashore ecology are present, from the beach to dunes to maritime pine and oak forests. Between the barrier islands and mainland lie salt marshes and shallow bays replete with waterfowl.

Land status: National wildlife refuge and state park.

Nearest city: Virginia Beach, VA.

Other trail users: Cyclists, anglers, and bird-watchers.

Canine compatibility: Leashed dogs permitted in False Cape State Park. Dogs not permitted in Back Bay National Wildlife Refuge from April 1 to September 30.

Trail contacts: False Cape State Park, Virginia Beach, VA, (757) 426-7128, www.dcr.state.va.us/parks/falscape.htm. Back Bay National Wildlife Refuge, Virginia Beach, VA, (757) 721-2412, backbay.fws.gov.

Schedule: Back Bay National Wildlife Refuge, interior trails closed November 1 through March 31. Certain interior trails are closed in summertime to protect birds; hiking is allowed on the beach during this period.

False Cape State Park, closed for one week beginning the first Saturday in October for a game-management program.

Fees/permits: There are twelve backcountry sites in False Cape State Park; the closest is a 5-mile walk from Little Island Recreation Area. Drinking water is available at three locations: near the contact station and near two campsites in the Barbour Hill section. Call (800) 933-7275 for a permit. When you arrive, place one copy of the permit on your car dashboard and carry a duplicate with you. There is a $4.00 fee to park at Little Island Recreation Area on weekends. It costs $9.00 to camp. Hikers also must pay $2.00 to pass through Back Bay NWR.

Maps: USGS maps: North Bay, VA; Knott Island, VA.

Finding the trailhead: From Virginia Beach: Take the Indian River Road exit off I-64. Proceed east on Indian River Road for 13.4 miles, then turn left onto Newbridge Road. In 1.1 miles, turn right onto Sandbridge Road. After 3.1 miles, turn right onto Sandpiper Road. Drive south on Sandpiper for 3.8 miles to Little Island Recreation Area, where overnight parking is permitted. (There is a parking fee Memorial Day to Labor Day.) *DeLorme: Virginia Atlas & Gazetteer:* Page 35, C7.

A flock of royal terns in the surf.

The Hike

Barrier islands are a habitat of extremes. The same beach where sunbathers flock for relaxation also harbors some of the earth's harshest living conditions. Waves beat upon it unceasingly, but those same waves bring ashore food that nourishes microorganisms, shellfish, birds, and small animals. Unfettered wind reduces shrubs and trees to bonsai proportions; wind also spreads beach grass and sea oat seeds, two species that help prevent sand-dune erosion. Then there is sand itself, barren of most nutrients, yet it creates the very reefs and dunes that preserve our coast.

A hiker must adapt to False Cape State Park and Back Bay National Wildlife Refuge (the park and refuge share a common border and, combined, stretch 20 miles down the coast to the North Carolina border). Forget mountain grandeur. Forget tall hemlocks or yellow poplar trees. Here, wind-lashed holly, oak, and pine eek out a precarious living. Deer, raccoon, opossum, and fox rustle the shrubby thickets.

Migratory birds capture the imagination—shorebirds in the spring, songbirds in spring and fall, and nesting birds in summer; in winter, it's the ducks and geese.

Plant and animal life here have had more time to adapt than humans. Wax myrtle has a coating on its leaves that protects it against the relentless sun and moisture loss from high winds. Marsh grass are able to overcome both the presence of salt water—which would kill less hardy plants—and a severe lack of oxygen in the dense marsh soil. The problem of salt water is solved by reverse osmosis, whereby salt water is allowed into the plant's cells. Oxygen, meanwhile, is pulled from the air and transported down the stem to the roots. If you find an uprooted piece of salt grass, look for red mud clinging around the roots. This is rust, a by-product of oxygen mixing with iron sulfide.

Every dune, especially on the lagoon or *wash* side, features plants whose progression reveals their place in the ecology of the island. On the fringe grows sea rocket, a member of the mustard family. Higher on the dune, beachgrass, native to northern barrier islands, and sea oats, commonly found on dunes from Virginia southward, coexist. In areas flooded daily by the tide, saltmarsh cordgrass grows almost exclusively. In the afternoon, at low tide, on a clear day, the sun will glint off oxidized salt particles clinging to tall stems of grass, giving the impression of light bouncing off thousands of mirrors. Beneath the sludge and puddles of brackish water, juvenile blue crabs reach maturity and fish spawn.

FYI The organic matter produced by decaying saltmarsh cordgrass (*Spartina alterniflora*) is comparable to the world's average production of corn, wheat, or sugarcane.

Plants that seem withered and dead during dry spells spring to life after rain. False heather jumps to life under moist conditions. Looking something like a small cedar, the heather's yellow flowers coat the oceanside of dunes. Because it grows low to the ground and spreads, heather helps stabilize the sand.

Down on the beach, sanderlings dart hither-and-dither, first chased by a crashing wave, only to turn and pursue it back into the ocean. This small bird pecks at the spongy sand, digging deep for shellfish. During the summer, as many as 30 million clam larvae will occupy one square meter of surf. There are snails beneath the sand, too, and small crabs. At nighttime, sandhoppers (small crabs) emerge from holes by the thousands to pick food from shells and seaweed coughed up by waves. Luminescent and quick, the sandhopper has startled more than a few nighttime beach strollers. Rest assured, by the time you've figured out it's an animal and not a ghost, the critter is out of harm's way. It digs a hole in the sand at a speed of 6 feet in ten minutes, putting it well out of reach of prying eyes and bird beaks.

Given this diversity and complexity, it's worth considering how the wilds of False Cape and Back Bay might have developed were it not for the park and refuge. A few

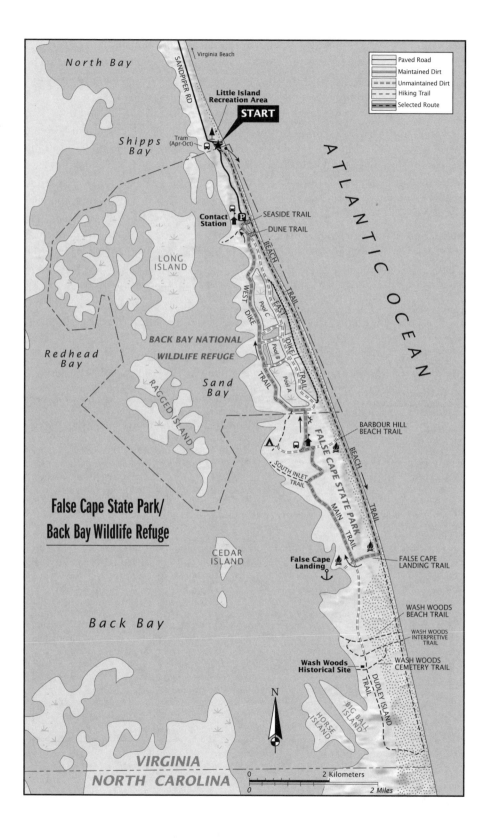

North Bay

Virginia Beach →

SANDPIPER RD

**Little Island
Recreation Area**

START

*Shipps
Bay*

Tram
(Apr-Oct)

**Contact
Station**

P

SEASIDE TRAIL

DUNE TRAIL

A T L A N T I C   O C E A N

LONG
ISLAND

BEACH TRAIL

WEST DIKE TRAIL

Pool C

EAST DIKE TRAIL

*BACK BAY NATIONAL
WILDLIFE REFUGE*

Pool B

*Redhead
Bay*

RAGGED ISLAND

Pool A

*Sand
Bay*

BARBOUR HILL
BEACH TRAIL

FALSE CAPE STATE PARK

SOUTH INLET
TRAIL

**False Cape State Park/
Back Bay Wildlife Refuge**

BEACH TRAIL

MAIN TRAIL

CEDAR
ISLAND

**False Cape
Landing**

FALSE CAPE
LANDING TRAIL

WASH WOODS
BEACH TRAIL

WASH WOODS
INTERPRETIVE
TRAIL

Back Bay

**Wash Woods
Historical Site**

WASH WOODS
CEMETERY TRAIL

DUDLEY ISLAND TRAIL

BIG BALL ISLAND

N

HORSE
ISLAND

VIRGINIA

NORTH CAROLINA

	Paved Road
	Maintained Dirt
	Unmaintained Dirt
	Hiking Trail
	Selected Route

0   2 Kilometers

0   2 Miles

miles up the beach, Virginia Beach's boardwalk teems with humans on hot summer days. Sunbathers, surfers, and beach strollers crowd miles of white Atlantic beach. The city spends millions to preserve this, fighting nature with "beach replenishment projects," a process of pumping sand from offshore back onto shore.

The process they're fighting is the gradual drift of barrier islands (and our coast, generally) to the south and west. Left to its own devices, the white sands of Virginia Beach would, in a couple hundred years, move, shifting south along the coast in the fashion of all barrier islands. Scientists call this littoral drift. Each wave picks up sand and transports it down the shoreline. A calm day or two will see tons of sand displaced. A hurricane or nor'easter will move those same tons in a few hours. The inlet below Ocean City, Maryland, which separates that resort town from Assateague Island, was carved by a single hurricane in 1933.

There was no dramatic event responsible for Back Bay and False Cape. In the 1800s, some 300 people lived in the Wash Woods, a section of False Cape State Park. They fished for a living. A few raised livestock and farmed. (Interestingly, Wash Woods settlers were survivors of a shipwreck off the coast; their first homes and church were built from what they could salvage from the ship.) Like the island itself, they lived at the mercy of the ocean. Over hundreds of years, farmland turned to marsh. Sand replaced fertile soil. Soon, sportsmen outnumbered inhabitants. Hotels and sporting clubs sprang up. Four-legged game was slim pickings. The waterfowl, on the other hand, were plentiful.

It can be taken as a sign of progress, then, that in time, Virginia has moved from hunting wildfowl on this small barrier island to protecting them. Like other barrier islands up and down the East Coast, this island hosts neo-tropical birds migrating to Central and South America. Waterfowl nest here. In September, vireos, yellowthroats, and warblers arrive. By October, yellow-rumped warblers have alighted to spend winter. In all, bird spotters have recorded 288 bird species in the Back Bay refuge. (This is typical of barrier islands lining the East Coast; Chincoteague National Wildlife Refuge on Virginia's Eastern Shore lists 300 bird species spotted.)

On these slivers of sand, the equivalent of an interstate highway rest stop, birds find the amenities they need: nesting spots, food, and, quite frankly, a spot to rest weary wings. And they seem to be more than willing to share it with hikers.

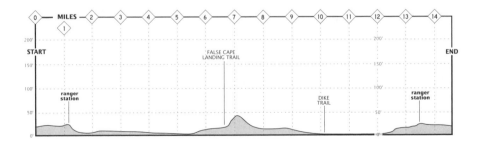

Miles and Directions

0.0   **START** at Little Island Recreation Area. Walk to the south end of the parking lot. At a picnic pavilion, turn toward the beach and surf.

1.2   Hike straight along the beach, past a boardwalk that leads up into the dunes on the right. (FYI: The boardwalk leads to a ranger station and visitor center.)

4.3   Reach the boundary of False Cape State Park. Continue straight on the beach.

4.9   Continue along the beach past the Barbour Hill primitive campsites, marked on the left by a small metal post with a yellow tent. (FYI: There's a pump at the campsite that provides drinkable water. There are also toilets. Camping is permitted for four to six people.) The campsites also mark a junction with Barbour Hill Beach Trail, which leads 0.7 mile across the island to the bay.

6.7   Turn right onto False Cape Landing Trail. (FYI: If you're walking in the surf far below the dune line, keep an eye peeled for a wood-and-wire fence and a metal post with a tent sign. There are primitive campsites in dunes after you turn onto False Cape Landing Trail.)

7.1   Turn right onto False Cape Main Trail, a wide dirt road. (FYI: The ocean is now on your right, out of sight over the dunes. Back Bay is on your left. Straight on False Cape Landing Trail, there is a boat landing in 0.3 mile, as well as bay-side campsites.)

8.4   False Cape Main Trail arcs right at a junction with Smith Inlet Trail. Follow the road right. (FYI: Smith Inlet Trail leads left for 0.4 mile to a sheltered reach of water with scenic views.)

9.0   Turn left onto Barbour Hill Beach Trail. There is a ranger station on the right side of the road. Past the ranger station, turn right onto Barbour Hill Interpretive Trail.

9.6   Pass an observation deck on the right side of the trail.

9.8   Leave False Cape State Park and enter Back Bay National Wildlife Refuge. Turn left onto the Dike Trail, which is a gravel and dirt road. (FYI: The Dike Trail is a loop that runs alongside wildlife impoundments, large pools of water that attract waterfowl and migrating birds. This hike follows the western leg of the Dike Trail.)

10.1   Where the trail forks, bear right onto the Dike Trail. (FYI: The left-bearing trail is a short spur to the bay.)

10.9   Hike straight past a road that turns right and leads between two impoundments.

11.4   Follow the trail as it jogs left then right and continues its northward route. A road branches right, leading between impoundments. Within two-tenths of a mile, hike past a third road that branches right.

13.2   The Dike Trail merges with its eastern leg. Continue on past a pool on the right side of the trail.

13.4   Reach the Back Bay visitor center and ranger station. At the station, turn right onto the Seaside Trail boardwalk.

13.5   Descend off the boardwalk and dune and turn left. Head north along the beach.

14.7   Arrive back at the Little Island Recreation Area.

Hike Information

Local Information

Virginia Beach Department of Convention & Visitor Center, Virginia Beach, VA, (800) 822-3224, www.vbgov.com.

Local Events/Attractions

International Migratory Bird Celebration, May, False Cape State Park, VA, (757) 426-7128.
The Pungo Strawberry Festival, May, Virginia Beach, VA, (757) 721-6001.
The Virginia Marine Science Museum, Virginia Beach, VA, (757) 425-FISH. More than 800,000 gallons of aquariums with sharks, sea turtles, and dolphins.

Restaurants

Blue Pete's Seafood & Steak Restaurant, Virginia Beach, VA, (757) 426-2005. Specialties include fresh seafood, sweet potato biscuits, and homemade deserts.

Tours

False Cape State Park, Virginia Beach, VA, (757) 426-7128. Conducts canoe, hiking, birding, and astronomy tours.

③ First Landing State Park

The ultimate *surf-and-turf* park, First Landing State Park is great for a tan—and far less crowded than the Atlantic beaches a few miles south. The "surf" is the mouth of the Chesapeake Bay, where it flows into the Atlantic Ocean; the "turf" is a trail network through an ecosystem that mixes tropical plants with Northern, temperate species. Spend an afternoon here among bald cypress swamps decked with Spanish moss, towering loblolly pines, and swamp marsh. High, forested dunes offer great views of the water. Boardwalks take you safely through blackwater swamps, but at high tide be prepared to get your feet wet and muddy on some other trails.

Start: From the visitor center off Shore Drive.
Distance: 6.5-mile loop.
Approximate hiking time: 2–3 hours.
Difficulty rating: Easy due to flat terrain and a well-marked trail, with some difficult stretches along eroded trails and wet riverside routes.
Trail surface: Dune trails, gravel roads, and boardwalks lead through marsh, beach, cypress swamp, and forested dunes with views of the bay.
Land status: State park.
Nearest town: Virginia Beach, VA.
Other trail users: Cyclists, bird-watchers, and joggers.

Canine compatibility: Leashed dogs permitted (leashes can be no more than 6 feet long).
Trail contacts: First Landing State Park, Virginia Beach, VA, (757) 412-2300, www.dcr.state.va.us/.
Schedule: Open year-round, 8:00 A.M. to dusk. The Trail Center and Chesapeake Bay Visitor Center are open April through November.
Fees/permits: Admission is free, but there's a $2.00 parking fee during the week, $3.00 on weekends and holidays; it's just $2.00 to park in the off-season, on the honor system.
Maps: USGS maps: Cape Henry, VA.

Finding the trailhead: From Norfolk: Take exit 282 (Northampton Boulevard) off I-64 and drive 4.5 miles north on U.S. Highway 13. Follow signs for U.S. Highway 60 East (Shore Drive). Drive 4.5 miles on US 60 to the park entrance. At the traffic light at the park entrance, turn right into the park and follow the main park road straight into the parking lot for the Trail Center, where you can get information on park trails and what you can expect to see. If you turn left at the light, it's another 0.5 mile to the parking lot at the Chesapeake Bay Visitor Center, which offers camping-related assistance and information on Virginia Beach. *DeLorme: Virginia Atlas & Gazetteer:* Page 35, A6.

The Hike

The 6th and 20th of April, about four o'clock in the morning, we described the land of Virginia...There we landed and discovered a little way, but we could find nothing worth the speaking of, but fair meadows and goodly tall trees, with such fresh waters running through the woods as I almost ravished at the first sight thereof.

Observation deck on Long Creek Trail.

So wrote George Percy, a Jamestown settler, recounting his first steps on North American soil in 1607. After a rough few days at sea, terra firma no doubt thrilled Percy's group, even if the landscape did not. They would name this point Cape Henry, christening forever present-day Virginia Beach's northernmost tip, where the Chesapeake Bay meets the Atlantic Ocean. Today the land inland from Cape Henry Lighthouse and Fort Story is called First Landing State Park, in their honor. Here hikers will find riches Percy and company found commonplace: maritime forest and Southern swamp and beach ecology, all preserved for a walker's enjoyment.

By Percy's account, the landing at Cape Henry was rough. Native Americans attacked and two men were injured, one fatally. It was an inauspicious welcome that might have chased lesser men back to the Caribbean. There, at least, they had enjoyed hot spring baths, fish, and fowl to their satisfaction.

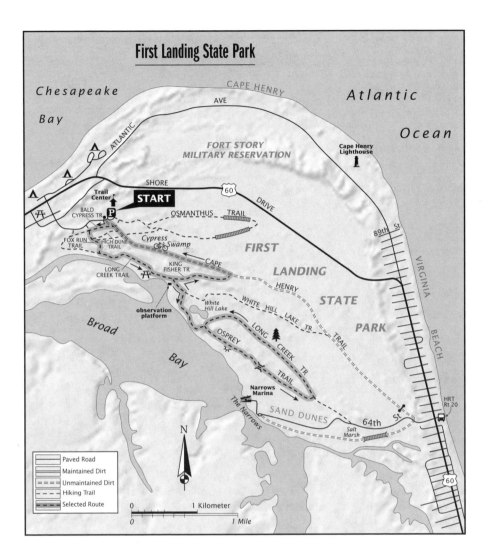

First Landing State Park

But these privateers, commissioned by the England-based Virginia Company, had other plans. Explorations by foot carried them inland from Cape Henry, through land entangled in vines as thick as a man's thigh. They chased Native Americans off a pile of oysters roasting in a fire, and tasted a delicacy that would make the Chesapeake Bay famous around the world. By boat, they traveled to Hampton, Virginia, which they dubbed Point Comfort, met up with Powhatan Indians, and, instead of fighting, exchanged gifts.

When it came time to leave, the explorers staked a small cross to mark Cape Henry. Left behind were the "fair meadows and goodly tall trees," and for one reason or another, this coastal area never saw permanent settlement (save the military reservation occupying land around the lighthouse). As colonial Virginia grew in the

1600s, fishermen claimed it as common ground, launched boats, built small shelters, and laid out nets. In 1936 the state created Seashore State Park here. It was renamed First Landing in 1996.

What has been preserved? An ecology that mixes subtropical and temperate-zone plants for a species diversity one would normally find farther south. Loblolly, eastern, and pitch pines tower 100 feet and higher. Broad bald cypress stand in oily blackwater swamps, their small knees poking through primordial-like ooze. White sand dunes topped with clingy grasses. And bones. Archeologists unearthed remains of twenty-six Chesapean Indians here, predecessors of the Powhatan tribe that attacked Percy's group. The Smithsonian Institute housed the artifacts until 1998, when they were returned and reburied in a ceremonial mound near the park's visitor center.

FYI First Landing's beach offers more than sunbathing, and summer isn't the only time to visit. Bird-watchers with binoculars flock to Cape Henry in winter for views of Northern gannets that winter offshore in the Mid-Atlantic region. During feeding, gannets tuck their wings and narrow themselves for a plunge of 100 feet or more into ocean depths.

Also here, the chicken turtle ranks as a critically endangered species in Virginia, with five or fewer known to be in existence.

You can start on an incredibly diverse hike at the Trail Center parking lot. The Bald Cypress/Long Creek/Osprey Trail loop takes you from cypress swamp through tidal marsh, bayside beach, dune forest, and back to swamp. Bring your binoculars. In one afternoon you're likely to see osprey nests, snowy egrets, and great blue heron.

On Bald Cypress Trail, Spanish moss hangs from the cypress. (This is the northernmost reach of the moss, a parasitic plant.) Larger specimens of this tree may date from 500 years ago. Around it, water lilies float on still water that reflects rainbow patterns—not from pollution, but from oils secreted by trees. It's possible, park interpreters say, that Captain John Smith and others replenished their casks of water here for a long return trip to England. The water, which colonists say tasted like strong ice tea, was so tannic it could last six to eight weeks at sea.

Long Creek Trail takes you to the edge of Broad Bay and a view of large homes on the opposite bank—reminders of development this park escaped. Virginia Beach is the state's most populated city; First Landing is the state park system's most visited, attracting more than one million visitors annually. Yet it can handle the load. Solid trails built by Civilian Conservation Corps crews are well maintained, a considerable feat given the constant erosion. It helps that most people hike short interpretive trails near the visitor center, or hike and bike the wide Cape Henry Trail.

Hikers will find quieter moments on the hiker-only Long Creek Trail. Where the trail skirts White Hill Lake—more of a marsh than a true lake—snowy egrets and great blue herons wade in relative peace. Look for an osprey's huge nest atop dead loblolly and oak trees at the junction with the Osprey Trail. You might see muskrat and mink lodges in the tidal marshes. (You can identify muskrat by their flat, naked-looking tail.) If you're hiking early in the morning, sit for a while on the shore of Long Creek, near shallow or marshy water. A slick head will break the water's surface, swivel left and right, then disappear beneath the water. Each time it surfaces, it emits a hasping noise, as if it's clearing its nostrils. The muskrat survives primarily on aquatic vegetation, but its morning feeding ritual may yield clams, frogs, or an occasional fish. Back on the trail, look for the partridgeberry, a trailing evergreen common in the park. The white pairs of tubular flowers bloom in June and July; the red berries and shiny green leaves are visible all winter. Curiously, partridges don't eat them, but Native American women drank a partridgeberry tea during the last weeks of pregnancy to lessen the pain of childbirth.

You can link again with Long Creek Trail by hanging a left at the end of Osprey Trail. This section gains a little elevation as you hike giant sand dunes covered with vegetation. It's the primary landform in the park—and it's constantly shifting, if ever so slowly.

Heads up: In warm months be prepared for ticks, mosquitoes, and snakes. During high tide, portions of the Osprey Trail may be messy, or even impassable. Be sure to stay on the trails, and ignore the bushwhacked side trails.

Miles and Directions

0.0   **START** from the Trail Center parking lot. Walk down a wide gravel path that parallels the park entrance road. Walk straight past a footpath that breaks left. (The trail bearing left is a shortcut to the Cape Henry Trail.)

0.05   Turn left onto the Cape Henry Trail. (Note: This wide multiuse trail is popular with bicyclists and joggers.)

0.08   Turn right onto Bald Cypress Trail. (Note: The fence across the trailhead indicates this is a hiker-only trail.)

0.1   (FYI: Across the trail lies a nurse log, noteworthy for the shoots growing from the mossy, rotted lumber—shoots growing into small trees themselves. On your left is a sand dune thick with holly and pine. To your right is a cypress swamp. The chicken turtle

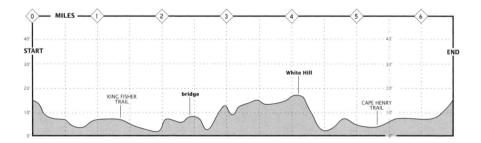

Deitrochelys reticularia, an endangered species, lives here, as do more common frogs and wading birds.)

0.15 (Note: An unmarked path climbs the dune on your left. This is the first of many unmarked trails that spread like a spiderweb throughout the park. Hiking them might provide adventure, but it also contributes to erosion. Stay on the marked trails.)

0.2 The Bald Cypress Trail makes a hard left. Climb five wooden steps, then turn left onto the Fox Run Trail. (A right turn leads to the park entrance road.)

0.6 Cross a sand dune and come to a T intersection with the Long Creek Trail. Turn left onto Long Creek Trail.

0.7 Pass by a wide opening in the trees and underbrush with views onto Broad Bay.

0.8 Ignore two unmarked trails that split left off the Long Creek Trail. Long Creek Trail follows the riverside, separated from water by only marsh grass.

1.1 Top out on a sand dune with views over Broad Bay. (FYI: This is a good spot for a picnic.)

1.35 Stay straight on Long Creek Trail as King Fisher Trail enters on the left.

1.4 (FYI: An observation deck on the right side of the trail allows for great views over the tidal wetlands that buffer Broad Bay. This structure marks the beginning of a series of boardwalks spanning sensitive habitat.)

1.5 At a fork in the trail, bear right on Long Creek Trail. Cross a concrete spillway and skirt the south side of White Hill Lake.

1.8 Begin a brief steep climb to the top of the "white hill" sand dunes that lend the lake its name. Broad Bay is to the right.

2.0 Turn right and descend on the Osprey Trail. (Note: The Osprey Trail skirts the water's edge. During high tide, it may be washed out. In all cases, prepare for wet hiking.)

2.4 Cross a small wooden bridge.

2.7 Trail leaves behind its wet portions and climbs onto a low, wooded finger of land bounded by marsh.

3.1 Turn left onto Long Creek Trail.

4.3 Pass the Osprey Trail on the left.

4.5 Turn right onto King Fisher Trail. (Note: Numerous unmarked paths lead off in different directions from this trail. Use the white blazes to keep you on track.)

5.1 (FYI: On the hillside to your left, notice the series of enormous loblolly pines. This species is a valuable commercial lumber. Native Americans called it the loblolly—meaning "mud puddle"—for the environment in which it grows well.)

5.4 Turn left onto Cape Henry Trail.

6.3 A portion of the Bald Cypress Trail crosses the Cape Henry Trail. Continue straight on the Cape Henry Trail.

6.45 Reach the junction with the parking lot access trail. Turn right to return to the parking lot.

6.5 Hike ends at the parking lot.

Hike Information

Local Information

Virginia Beach Department of Convention and Visitor Development, Virginia Beach, VA, (800) VA BEACH, www.vbfun.com or www.virginia-beach.va.us.

Local Events/Attractions

March for Parks, held at the park in spring, (757) 412-2300. Hikers obtain pledges to help support trail maintenance.

The Chesapeake Bay Center (located on the Chesapeake Bay side of the park), Virginia Beach, VA, (757) 412-2316. The center was completed in 1999 and houses exhibits on the First Landing in 1607, natural resource displays, the park's visitor information, and a Virginia Beach tourism information office.

Fort Monroe, Hampton, VA, (757) 788-3391. A half-hour drive from the park, this active U.S. Army installation houses the Casemate Museum. In it is a definitive history of the Coastal Defense System, a now-defunct branch of the military once dedicated to protecting America's coast. Videos and a lighted display board explain what role Fort Story, which occupies the beach near First Landing State Park, played in protecting the mouth of the Chesapeake Bay.

Lodging

The park has more than 222 campsites, open March to December, and 20 cabins, open year-round. For reservations and information, call (800) 933-7275.

Restaurants

Duck-In, Virginia Beach, VA, (757) 481-0201, www.duck-in.com. A Virginia Beach landmark since 1952, the restaurant features a sandy beach and a gazebo jutting out into the Chesapeake Bay.

Organizations

Friends of First Landing, Virginia Beach, VA, (757) 412-2320.

4 York River State Park

The worm-eating warbler, common to Virginia's Blue Ridge province, is also found in the coastal environment of York River State Park. After walking through the park's forests, thick with mountain laurel and holly, shaded by chestnut oaks and American beech, hikers will agree with the songbird: This park looks a lot like Virginia's mountain regions. Most paths here lead to the York River. Land underfoot holds evidence—pottery shards, arrowheads—of settlement dating from tens of thousands of years ago. Perhaps the park's most interesting story is still being recorded—that of the Taskinas Creek Estuary, a vital marsh and hardwood swamp monitored by scientists as a gauge of the Chesapeake Bay's health. (Note: In September 2003, Hurricane Isabelle rampaged through Eastern and Central regions of Virginia, leaving in its wake widespread destruction. York River State Park was particularly hard-hit, experiencing an 8-foot tidal surge that destroyed boardwalks and dams and washed away sections of beach and footpaths. Hikers should call ahead for a more up-to-date status of trails than is possible here. Patience and understanding will help the dedicated staff focus on rebuilding one of Eastern Virginia's most recreation-friendly parks.)

Start: From the visitor center parking lot.
Distance: 7.5-mile loop.
Approximate hiking time: 1 to 4 hours.
Difficulty rating: Easy due to flat terrain, well-marked trails, and options for shorter hikes.
Trail surface: Wooded paths, boardwalks, and gravel and dirt roads lead through marsh, fields, hardwood swamps, and upland forests.
Land status: State park.
Nearest town: Williamsburg, VA.
Other trail users: Cyclists and equestrians.
Canine compatibility: Leashed dogs permitted (leashes must be 6 feet or shorter).

Trail contacts: York River State Park, Williamsburg, VA, (757) 566-3036, www.dcr.state. va.us/parks/yorkrive.htm.
Schedule: Open year-round, 8:00 A.M. to dusk. The visitor center is open year-round, but the visitor center office is open April through October, 8:00 A.M. to 6:00 P.M. It operates on a limited schedule from November to March.
Fees/permits: April through October: $2.00 per vehicle (Monday through Friday); $3.00 for adults (weekends and holidays). Parking is $2.00 during the off-season.
Maps: USGS maps: Gressitt, VA.

Finding the trailhead: From Croaker: Take the Croaker exit 231B off I-64 and go 1 mile north on Virginia Route 607. At the intersection of VA 607 and Virginia Route 606, turn right onto VA 606—also called Riverview Road—and drive 1.7 miles to Virginia Route 696. Turn left onto VA 696 (also called York River State Park Road). The fee station is in 2 miles. Parking lots for the visitor center, picnic area, and trails are just beyond the fee station. *DeLorme: Virginia Atlas & Gazetteer:* Page 50, A1.

The Hike

Offshore of Taskinas Creek Trail, saltmarsh cordgrass sways with a stiff breeze. On the creek's muddy flats, spotted sandpipers and black-bellied plovers dart in earnest

The winding Taskinas Creek.

pursuit of food. A cluster of fiddler crabs scuttle for shelter. As you climb away from the creek on a trail beneath oak and beech trees, a great blue heron, startled, lumbers toward open water, letting loose a *gaaaak* as a parting shot.

How much, you might wonder, can these scenes differ from those of 300 years ago? The Native Americans of eastern Virginia were a *riverine* people; their lives revolved around what the rivers provided. Men hunted meadow and wood for white-tailed deer, turkey, and other prey, but the water provided all things necessary for life: food, fertile soil, shells for ornaments and tools, reeds for mats and baskets, and even transportation. At low tide, women foraged in freshwater marsh for arrow arum, whose root, tuckahoe, is edible when boiled. Thick-stemmed saltwort, pickled or preserved, made a tasty delicacy.

English settlers called it a "hand-to-mouth" existence, and yet their survival, too, depended on it. On a monthly—sometimes biweekly—basis, Native Americans sent gifts of food to the James Island fort in 1607–08, sustaining settlers during spring "starving times," when the previous fall's harvest had run out and new forest growth made hunting more difficult. When English farmers spread beyond fort walls onto the James/York River Peninsula, they found why the Native Americans could afford generosity: Chiskiack Indians planted maize, beans, and squash among burned tree stumps, remnants of field clearing. It was a high-yield, if not terribly efficient, farming system.

York River State Park's Powhatan Forks Trail crosses high peninsula meadows, then enters the shade of hardwood forest. A person who has spent time in Virginia's mountain woods may sense something familiar. The trees—chestnut oak, American beech, green ash—and a forest understory of mountain laurel, holly, and berry-producing shrubs thrive here thanks to soil conditions normally found in western Virginia. York River State Park soil contains marl, a limestone-heavy clay similar to soils of the Shenandoah Valley. Elsewhere in the park, the Yorktown rock formation sinks as deep as 150 feet or more underfoot. This is a calcium-rich soil, thick with deposits of ancient seashell and sand. Prehistoric seas washed over Virginia's coastal region several times. Erosion along the York River constantly churns up fossils pointing to past aquatic life. Unearthing five-million-year-old shells and whalebones is not an uncommon occurrence here.

Where the north branch of Powhatan Forks Trail drops into a marshy area, an expansive view of the river opens up. This approach is much gentler than the Riverview Trail's abrupt ending on high river bluffs a half mile downstream, yet both permit an unobstructed view of Purtan Bay on the opposite shore. Captain John Smith, hoping to save a struggling colony, took in a similar vista in the fall of 1608. (Today, homes dot that far shoreline and recreation boats bob in the water.) In Captain Smith's time, Purtan Bay was one home of Powhatan, chief of the eastern Native American empire that bore his name. His tribe, the Werowocomoco, built huts along the shallow bay and its three tributaries and used fragile bridges strung across tidal flats as links with each other.

FOSSIL HUNTING Near the visitor center, a short walk up the Mattaponi Trail, lies Fossil Beach. Erosion has exposed the ragged roots of trees that hang precariously off the edge of the river bluffs. Underfoot, troves of fossils lie for the taking. Prize finds include a piece of whale ear—the tympanic bone. Visitors have recorded finding whalebones, dolphin bones, and shark teeth as well. Park rules: You can take one fossil with you.

In what must have been an embarrassing moment for the adventurous John Smith, he and a party of men crossed the York River to meet Powhatan, but landed in the wrong spot. Some men disembarked and tried crossing a stream by way of a bridge made of forked stakes and planks. It defeated the heavily clad men, and the Werowocomoco ferried them, a few at a time, across the creek. Later, after negotiating for corn, Smith and company tried returning to their ship, but his canoe ran aground on a mud flat. Powhatan's men trudged out to retrieve them; Smith asked instead for "some wood, fire, and mats to cover me." He spent the night thusly, waiting for the tide to return and float his boat off its hang-up.

York River State Park

Despite initial feebleness, the expanding colony soon had Powhatan's empire in retreat. Nathaniel Bacon Jr., a settler, led a group of armed, discontented landowners against the Native Americans in the summer of 1676. Miffed by the colonial governor William Berkeley's inability to keep Indian raiders in check, Bacon's men soon hounded the governor into hiding. Given virtually free reign, Bacon used outposts throughout the Tidewater to launch attacks. As a result, travelers today will see his name attached to innumerable homes, old forts, back roads, and "hideaways" throughout the region. York River State Park is no different. Near the park stands the Stonehouse site, a seventeenth-century military outpost during Bacon's Rebellion, now listed on the National Register of Historic Places. The Occoneechee tribe fell in May 1676, and the Pamunkey fell in August of that same year.

Bacon died of natural causes in October 1676 and Berkeley regained control of the Virginia colony. In February 1677, English settlers and Native Americans struck the Treaty of Middle Peninsula. Besides war reparations—prisoners, land, weapons, tools—the treaty made remnants of a once-powerful Indian empire formal subjects to the king of England. It called for an annual tribute of three arrows and twenty beaver pelts in exchange for reservation land near West Point. More than 300 years later, the Treaty of Middle Peninsula remains in force. Every March, Mattaponi (*matta-PO-ni*) and Pamunkey Indians trek to the governor's mansion to pay their rent for reservation land—twenty beavers strung on a pole, with tribesmen dressed in full regalia supporting either end of the stick.

Miles and Directions

0.0 **START** from the parking lot near the park contact and fee station. From the bathrooms located here, turn away from the visitor center and walk down a paved path.

0.1 Turn left onto Woodstock Pond Trail, a wide gravel path that leads down a small hill. (There are signs for people who use the pond loop as a fitness trail.)

0.16 Pass the Beaver Trail on the left. **Option:** Beaver Trail is a 0.6-mile alternative for circling Woodstock Pond. It ends near the York River at a junction with Woodstock Pond Trail. Use Beaver Trail to complete a shorter loop around the pond that will return you to the park visitor center.

This boardwalk across a marshy slough of the York River once linked Powhatan Forks Trail and Majestic Oak Trail. Hurricane Isabelle destroyed a section of it, making the route impassable for now.

0.2 (FYI: Notice the terrain on the left side of the trail. There is a deep ravine carved by a drainage that supplies Woodstock Pond with runoff. It's the first of several examples of how the park topography defies the stereotype of coastal landscapes as flat and sandy.)

0.5 At the junction of Woodstock Pond Trail and Backbone Trail, turn right onto Backbone Trail. (FYI: Backbone Trail is a dirt road that runs 1.3 miles to the park's south boundary. Both cyclists and hikers use this trail. The Me-Te-Kos bridle path (for horses) intersects it at numerous points.) **Option:** Following Woodstock Pond Trail left leads to the visitor center in 0.8 mile.

0.6 Follow the Backbone Trail past the Laurel Glen mountain bike trail on the left. (Note: This is a bike-only route for beginner riders.)

0.7 Continue straight on Backbone Trail. On your right, you'll begin seeing unmarked paths entering the grassy fields. (The park service maintains these fields for horseback riders.) A park service road on the right leads to a maintenance and storage facility.

0.9 Pass the Marl Ravine trailhead on your right. (Note: This is a bike-only trail for intermediate and experienced riders.)

1.2 Walk past the Pamunkey Trail, which branches left off Backbone Trail. (Note: At this intersection, a power line cuts across Backbone Trail. Stick to the roadway bearing right.)

1.5 Follow Backbone Trail past Majestic Oak Trail, which forks left into the woods.

1.6 The Whitetail Trail heads right into the woods, leading to views of the York River. Turn left onto Riverview Trail. (FYI: There's a picnic table here.)

1.7 At the split log fence, turn right. Riverview Trail becomes a narrow footpath.

2.1 Bear right on Riverview Trail, past an unmarked trail that exits left.

2.8 The trail, which has kept a fairly straight course since the junction with Powhatan Forks, begins descending. (FYI: Yellow marsh grass is visible at lower elevations off the side of the trail. There's a strong smell of brackish water—that mix of freshwater and salt water. Songbirds may be drowned out here by the occasional helicopter making its way to Cheatham Annex naval installation and the Yorktown Naval Weapons Depot, both located on the York River south of this park.)

3.1 Riverview Trail ends on a high, sandy bluff overlooking the York River. Turn and retrace your steps along the Riverview Trail.

4.1 Turn right onto a dirt footpath marked with red-letter signs. Immediately after this right turn, you'll make another right turn onto Powhatan Forks Trail.

5.0 The Powhatan Forks Trail ends at the York River. Turn and retrace your steps to a three-way junction with Majestic Oak Trail and the Spur Trail. (Note: A boardwalk appears to

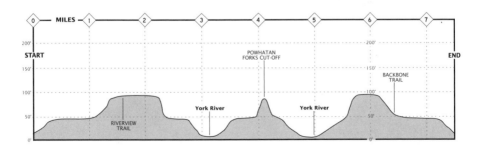

cross the marsh at the foot of this bluff, a section of which was blown away during Hurricane Isabelle in September 2003. The structural integrity of this bridge is in question and hikers should not attempt to walk on it.)

6.0 Powhatan Forks Trail ends at a three-way junction with Majestic Oak and Spur Trail. Turn right on Majestic Oak for another river view reached in 0.9 miles. Or, continue straight on the Spur Trail to its junction in 0.1 miles with Pamunkey Trail. (Note: The Majestic Oak Trail is notable for its woodland environment that seems more typical of mountain Virginia. Generally, forests along the coast are pine-oak forests, with an open canopy and grassy forest floor. Oak-hickory forests, like that through which Majestic Oak Trail winds, are deeply shaded by American beech, yellow poplar, red and white oak, and hickory. The forest understory is crowded with mountain laurel and berry bushes and shade-tolerant trees like hornbeam, maple, and redbud. It is a beautiful and refreshing change of pace.)

6.1 Spur Trail intersects with Pamunkey Trail. Turn right.

6.2 At the T intersection, turn left onto Pamunkey Trail.

6.3 Turn right onto Backbone Trail.

7.0 Bear left downhill on Woodstock Pond Trail to return to the parking lot.

7.5 Hike ends at the parking lot near the park contact and fee station.

Hike Information

Local Information
Williamsburg Area Convention & Visitors Bureau, Williamsburg, VA, (757) 253-0192, (800) 368-6511, www.visitwilliamsburg.com.

Local Events/Attractions
Estuaries Day, late September. Displays, demonstrations, boat tours, and other programs centered around Taskinas Creek. Contact the park for specfic dates and times.
Yorktown Victory Weekend, third weekend of October, Yorktown, VA, (888) 593-4682.

Lodging
Williamsburg & Colonial KOA Resorts, Williamsburg, VA, (800) 562-1733, www.WilliamsburgKOA.com.

Tours
Contact the park for information about canoe trips on Taskinas Creek.

Organizations
Friends of York River State Park, Williamsburg, VA, (757) 566-3036.

Other Resources
Virginia Department of Conservation & Recreation, (800) 933-7275.

5 Belle Isle State Park

Since colonial times, farmers have tilled the fields of Belle Isle; parts of this state park are farmed even today. Bird-watchers, hikers, horseback riders, and cyclists in the mood for wide-open spaces find this an ideal destination. Trails trace cornfields, cross tidal marshes, and wind through pine and hardwood *filter strips*—ribbons of woodland that separate fields from sensitive wetlands. Well-marked and easy to follow, trails feature interpretive boards explaining Chesapeake Bay ecology. Depending on the season, there's a better-than-average chance of spotting a bald eagle or two, flocks of wintering tundra swan, and in summer, maybe a dolphin cruising the wide Rappahannock.

Start: From the Mud Creek boat launch parking lot.
Distance: 3.3-mile out-and-back.
Approximate hiking time: 1 hour.
Difficulty rating: Easy due to flat terrain, short distance, and well-marked trails.
Trail surface: Gravel roads and dirt woodland paths through farmland, marsh, and swamp-fringe forest leading to river views.
Land status: State park.
Nearest town: Lancaster, VA.
Other trail users: Cyclists and equestrians.

Canine compatibility: Leashed dogs permitted (but leashes must be no longer than 6 feet).
Trail contacts: Belle Isle State Park, Lancaster, VA, (804) 462-5030, www.dcr.state.va.us/parks/belleisle.htm.
Schedule: Open year-round, sunrise to sunset.
Fees/permits: $3.00 parking fee in summer on weekends; $2.00 during week and off-season.
Maps: USGS maps: Lively, VA.

Finding the trailhead: From Lancaster Courthouse: Take Virginia Route 3 west for 3 miles and turn left onto Virginia Route 201 in the village of Lively. Drive 3.3 miles and turn right onto Virginia Route 354 at St. Mary's White Chapel. Head west for 3.2 miles and turn left onto Virginia Route 683. The park office is 2 miles down the road, where you turn right for the boat launch parking lot. The Mud Creek Trail starts on the wood's edge, behind a trail board. *DeLorme: Virginia Atlas & Gazetteer:* Page 60, B2.

The Hike

On a cold, moonless winter night, a boat circles in the black mist rising off the Rappahannock River. A bushel basket floats upside down in the water and underneath it, a light flickers. The pilot deftly navigates while two shadows operate a dredge. There's a sureness in their movements, though hardly a word passes between them.

Still, it's hard to stay hidden. Wind carries sounds ashore. A spotlight blasts through the fog, freezing the crew in its bright gaze. Momentarily stunned, the men snap to attention. Harsh words drift out of the darkness: "Cut your engines." Instead, the pilot revs his motor and swings toward deep water. Noise and wind drown out the *snap, snap, snap* of rifle shots. Nighttime swallows the poachers and their stash of oysters.

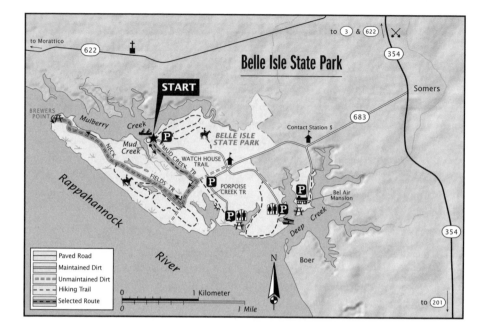

On land, the spotlight refocuses on the abandoned bushel basket; the wide beam also illuminates tall, skinny sticks marking an oyster bed. The light stays trained on this spot until dawn. A watchman, awake and alert, sits in a house on shore, rifle across his knee, ready for the next raider.

Starting after the Civil War, turning violent first in the 1880s and 1890s, and again in the 1940s and 1950s, the *oyster wars* of the Chesapeake Bay pitted Virginia and Maryland watermen against each other, vying for what was then the Chesapeake Bay's most sought-after resource. Along the Northern Neck and Eastern Shore, in alleys and saloons of tough water towns such as Crisfield, Maryland, and Colonial Beach, Virginia, Marylanders fought Virginians over the oyster. In the shallow waters of the Eastern Shore sounds, tongers—watermen who collected oysters using long-handled tongs—resisted dredgers, whose large scoops raped the bay bottom, and everyone, it seemed, fought the marine police, whose vigilance ebbed and flowed like the ocean tides—strict and trigger happy one moment, indifferent the next.

Belle Isle State Park, in Lancaster County on Virginia's Northern Neck, was—if not a hot spot in this war—a lukewarm spot, at least. On this spit of land, Thomas Powell staked out the original 500 acres for a farm and plantation in 1650. The period marked a population boom of sorts for the Northern Neck. In the 1650s, settlers were gobbling up land on this northernmost of Virginia's peninsulas. Ancestors of three presidents—George Washington, James Monroe, and James Madison—settled farther up this strip during this period. Farms soon became plantations, modest homes turned into manor houses, and Belle Isle thrived as a tobacco-producing estate, with cotton, flax, wheat, and corn grown as well.

Yet Belle Isle's envious perch on the Rappahannock River could not be ignored. Native Americans called the Rappahannock the "quick-rising" river. Narrow and shallow, it's brackish mix of salt water and freshwater extends upriver for miles, making it ideal for growing oysters—especially in tidal flats at the mouth of Mulberry and Deep Creeks, which create Belle Isle's distinctive landform.

Watermen jealously guarded these beds. For good reason, too. By one estimate, as many as 170 poachers operated in the Chesapeake Bay in the 1940s and 1950s. Worsening matters, after decades of overharvesting, oyster production was in decline. At a peak in 1880, watermen caught 125 million pounds of oysters. By 1958–1959, a mere four million bushels were harvested. (There was a temporary rebound in the late 1970s, when the harvest jumped to 25 million pounds, but numbers dropped to 138,000 pounds by 1998.) Scarcity drove up price; suppliers paid $3.25 cents a bushel in 1958–1959 (up from 60 cents a bushel in the 1880 heyday).

NOTE As the state has built up the park infrastructure, Native American artifacts—mainly arrowheads and pottery—have been discovered at Belle Isle. There are no formal archeological sites, however, and it's illegal for visitors to collect the artifacts for personal use. The class-one misdemeanor carries a maximum punishment of one year in jail and a $2,500 fine.

As overharvesting depleted natural oyster beds, seed beds like those off Belle Isle became a tempting target. To guard against poachers, watermen built shacks on elevated platforms overlooking tidal flats. Scattered along riverbanks and sounds of the Chesapeake Bay, the buildings-on-stilts formed a rag-tag line of defense, akin to outposts on a distant frontier.

Across from Belle Isle State Park's offices, a wide, dirt and gravel trail passes by a field of corn, to your right. (This is the only state park that also operates as a farm. The state leases the land to a Lancaster County farmer for $50 an acre.) Fields soon drop away and the trail enters a narrow strip of pine and hardwoods. Fringe forests like these act as a barrier between field runoff and fragile wetlands. Continuing on, the path crosses a neck of land bounded by tidal marshes. On your left, you'll see where waterfowl flock to Porpoise Creek, and where its marsh grass segues into the deeper, blue waters of Deep Creek, look for wintering tundra swan in spectacular white groups numbering from ten to one hundred. (They arrive in December and leave in March.) Although a bit removed from the Atlantic Flyway—the north-south route for migrating birds that traces Virginia's Eastern Shore—migratory birds still flock to Belle Isle.

Finally, the trail meets the lapping shores of the Rappahannock River. Look closely around you for clues to a chapter in this plantation-turned-park's history. Overgrown with grass, decaying wood pilings, and riprap mark the site of an old watch house. You've hiked only a short distance, but you've witnessed at least 350 years of history.

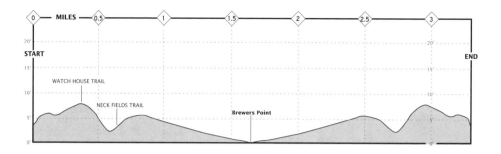

Miles and Directions

0.0 **START** from the Mud Creek boat launch parking lot. Take Mud Creek Trail southeast, back toward the park office.

0.1 Mud Creek Trail passes between two thick-trunk oaks whose branches, high overhead, entwine to create a natural arbor.

0.2 Mud Creek Trail turns sharply left and emerges from the woods, then bears right to follow the edge of a cornfield. A red barn is visible across the field. (FYI: As you emerge into the open, look for the round, spindly fruit of the sweet gum.)

0.3 Mud Creek Trail ends at a T intersection with Watch House Trail, a wide gravel and dirt road that heads left and right. Turn right. (Turning left onto Watch House Trail will lead you to a picnic area and the park office, as well as a trailhead for horseback riders.)

0.6 Arrive at a T intersection with Neck Fields Trail, another wide dirt and gravel road. Turn right onto Neck Fields Trail and continue your hike to Brewers Point.

1.5 The trail detours around a small pond hidden behind a tangle of small shrubs, vines, and trees. (FYI: Peek through for a sighting of merganser and canvasback, two types of ducks that call Belle Isle home.)

1.65 The trail ends at Brewers Point on the Rappahannock River. There is a picnic table here. Retrace your steps back to the boat launch parking lot.

3.3 Hike ends at the parking lot.

Hike Information

Local Information
The Northern Neck Tourism Council, Warsaw, VA, (800) 393-6180, www.northernneck.org.

Local Events/Attractions
Rappahannock River Waterfowl Show, White Stone, VA, held one weekend in March by the Decoy & Carver's Guild, (804) 435-6355.
Stratford Hall Plantation, Stratford, VA, (804) 493-8038, www.stratfordhall.org. Robert E. Lee's ancestral home.
St. Mary's White Chapel, Lancaster, VA, (804) 462-7371. George Washington's mother, Mary

Ball Washington, was from Lancaster County, and many of her ancestors are buried in the churchyard.

Lodging
The Bel Air Mansion and **Guest House** are located on the park grounds, (800) 933-7275. The mansion is a 1942 Georgian-style house that was built to resemble a colonial plantation house; the guest house sits 15 feet off a cove on Deep Creek. Www.dcr.state.va.us/parks/bellisle.htm.

Honorable Mentions

Eastern Virginia

Here is an index of great hikes in Eastern Virginia that didn't make the A-list this time around but deserve recognition. Check them out and let us know what you think. You may decide that one or more of these hikes deserves higher status in future editions or, perhaps, you may have a hike of your own that merits some attention.

1 Kiptopeke State Park

A bayside beach near the tip of the Eastern Shore, minutes from U.S. Highway 17. From the Chesapeake Bay Bridge-Tunnel, turn left onto Virginia Route 704. Short hiking trails lead along the beaches and through a maritime forest. Kiptopeke is best known as an observatory for migrating hawks. There are fees for both admission and reserved-site camping. For more information, call (757) 331–2267. *DeLorme: Virginia Atlas & Gazetteer:* Page 51, C5.

2 Great Dismal Swamp National Wildlife Refuge

Located on the Virginia/North Carolina border, 4.5 miles east of Virginia Route 32. The 4.5-mile Washington Ditch Road leads to Lake Drummond, one of only two natural lakes in Virginia. Trails begin on Washington Ditch off Virginia Route 642 (White Marsh Road). Hike through a Southern swamp forest of maple, tupelo, bald cypress, and pine. Spanish moss drips from the trees and the distinctive knees of the cypress jut from inky swamp water. The swamp harbors species of migratory, song, and marsh birds. Day-use only. Call (757) 986–3705. *DeLorme: Virginia Atlas & Gazetteer:* Page 34, C2.

3 Grandview Preserve

Located in the city of Hampton off Beach Road. Take exit 263 off I–64 onto Mercury Boulevard; turn left onto Fox Hill Road (Virginia Route 169) and left again onto Beach Road. Hike the 6-mile beach path around a windswept point on the Chesapeake Bay, featuring a trove of seashells and lots of privacy. *DeLorme: Virginia Atlas & Gazetteer:* Page 50, D4.

4 Newport News Park

A large, accessible city park just minutes off I–64; take exit 250B and follow the signs. The park surrounds Lee Hall Reservoir. The trails and dirt roads spread throughout this 8,000-acre park make possible a remote hike in the middle of a large city. Whiteoak Trail leads away from the visitor center, across marshes, and past Civil War battle sites. Highlights include old Confederate breastworks ruins and a detour into the adjoining Yorktown Battlefield. Reserved-site camping allowed. Call (757) 888–3333. *DeLorme: Virginia Atlas & Gazetteer:* Page 50, C2.

5 Beaverdam Park

Located minutes from Gloucester Court House on Virginia's Middle Peninsula. From Business U.S. Highway 17, turn left onto Virginia Route 616; the road dead-ends at the park entrance. The main hiking trail passes along marshy fringes of the reservoir and through an upland hardwood forest. There are plans to greatly expand trail offerings, adding as much as 25 miles of trails and overnight camping. Call (804) 693–2107. *DeLorme: Virginia Atlas & Gazetteer:* Page 50, A2.

6 Hickory Hollow

Located on the Northern Neck near Lancaster Court House, on Virginia Route 604, 0.3 mile east of Virginia Route 3. This is a special hike along the wooded bluffs overlooking Western Branch. Spur trails plunge off the hillside into the stream's marshy backwaters. Lancaster County once considered developing this 254-acre spot into an industrial park—bird-watchers and nature lovers fought off the proposal with the aid of the Northern Neck Audubon Society. For a map brochure, write the Audubon Society at P.O. Box 991, Kilmarnock, VA 22482. *DeLorme: Virginia Atlas & Gazetteer:* Page 60, B3.

7 Hewlett Point/Dameron Marsh Natural Area Preserves

Located on the tip of the Northern Neck, east of Virginia Route 200 and 6 miles northeast of Kilmarnock. These two closely situated preserves bound Ingram Point to the north and south, sticking out like fingers into the Chesapeake Bay. Hiking is on dirt roads and boardwalks. Hewlett Point harbors the endangered Northeastern beach tiger beetle. *DeLorme: Virginia Atlas & Gazetteer:* Pages 60, B4.

8 Caledon Natural Area

Located in King George County. From U.S. Highway 301, follow Virginia Route 206 to Virginia Route 218, and then head east on VA 218 for 1.5 miles to the entrance. Created to provide nesting and roosting spots for bald eagles, Caledon has five short trails that lead to bird-watching spots along the Potomac River. Some trails may be temporarily closed to protect nesting birds. Sandy bluffs in the Horsehead Cliff area are imbedded with fossils. Day-use only. Guided tours are conducted mid-June through Labor Day. Call (540) 663–3861. *DeLorme: Virginia Atlas & Gazetteer:* Page 71, B5.

9 Sandy Bottom Nature Preserve

Located off the Hampton Roads Center Parkway in Hampton. From exit 261A off I–64, follow the Parkway west to the nature preserve entrance, a half mile past the intersection of Big Bethel Road. There are eleven trails in the park. Old Crystal Trail around a former sand pit-turned-lake is the longest, at 2.1 miles. Boardwalks cross wetland habitat, while graded dirt paths pass through hardwood forest. Fishing, recreational boating, and primitive camping are allowed. Contact the park at (757) 825–4657. *DeLorme: Virginia Atlas & Gazetteer:* Page 50, D-3.

10 Northwest River Park

Located in Chesapeake. Take the Battlefield Boulevard (Virginia Route 168) exit off I–64 and drive south 15 miles to Indian Creek Road. Turn left onto Indian Creek Road, and it's 4 miles to the entrance. This 764-acre park is situated on a point of land where Indian and Smith Creeks empty into the Northwest River. Park trails pass through a riverine environment, alternating between marsh areas and hardwood forests. Indian Creek Trail is the longest at 2.5 miles. Use it to link with Otter Point, Wood Duck Slough, and Molly Mitchell Trails for a 5-mile walk. Other recreational activities include boating, horseback riding, and camping. Contact the park at (757) 421–7151. *DeLorme: Virginia Atlas & Gazetteer:* Page 35, D-5.

Northern Virginia

What is Northern Virginia? Is it coastal or Piedmont? Urban or suburban? Could it even be rural? Northern Virginia is, in fact, all of these. First and foremost, it is a metropolis, with all the baggage this carries: highways, pollution, sprawl. Such conditions do not, however, negate quality outdoor experiences. This region—which encompasses the pastoral hills of Fauquier County, the ragged 90-foot cliffs at Great Falls, and the calm estuaries around Pohick Bay and Mason Neck—ranks as wildly diverse as any in the state. Absent the mountains of western regions, the region features streams that, over centuries, have carved out channels through granite, schist, and metagraywacke. Healthy forests of hardwoods crown river bluffs. Microcosms of Appalachian cove forest—with its stunning array of flowers, trees, mosses, and animals—pop up along quiet, secluded streams. Virginia's fall line bisects the region, creating picturesque waterfalls and cascades that transport you hundreds of miles away.

Northern Virginians work hard for these special environments. They work hard to find them, and they work hard to protect them. Difficult Run, a tumbling, tree-sheltered stream, has long been the focus of conservationists' efforts to preserve a greenway along its banks. Preserved tracts of land on the Potomac, below Washington, D.C., are recognized as top spots in the East for nesting and roosting bald eagles. Even land that has been logged, farmed, mined, and left to waste away—as was the case with Prince William Forest Park—has rebounded to a state of natural and scenic beauty. Years of preservation work in Northern Virginia have made possible just about every type of outdoor pursuit, from walking to rock climbing, bird watching to hunting.

Whatever natural wonders await the explorer in Northern Virginia, history makes doubly rewarding. More than a few chief executives have left their mark. Roosevelt Island, a vacation spot for Theodore Roosevelt, is prominent among them. James Madison fled a burning Washington, D.C., during the War of 1812, stashing the Declaration of Independence in an old gristmill now preserved as a museum. Less prominent, but just as intriguing, are Civil War raiders who prowled eastern foothills of the Blue Ridge. Archeologists have unearthed the garbage heaps of prehistoric residents who encamped along the Potomac. And on the shores of America's river, the Potomac, Chicocoan Indians watched Captain John Smith sail as far as the waterfalls at Georgetown.

The paths of our history are today the paths of hikers, bird-watchers, and nature lovers. The stories behind place names and old buildings are as much a part of the outdoor experience in Northern Virginia as the flowers, birds, and trees.

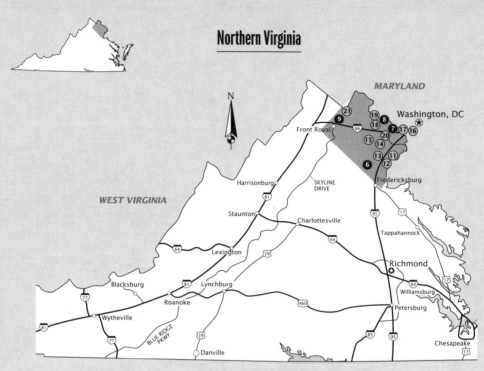

Northern Virginia

MARYLAND

Washington, DC

Front Royal

SKYLINE
DRIVE

WEST VIRGINIA

Harrisonburg

Staunton

Charlottesville

Tappahannock

Fredericksburg

Lexington

Richmond

Blacksburg

Lynchburg

Williamsburg

Roanoke

Petersburg

Wytheville

BLUE RIDGE
PKWY

Chesapeake

Danville

NORTH CAROLINA

6 Prince William Forest Park

Roughly 100 miles inland from Virginia's coast, a geologic boundary called the *fall line* marks a change in the landscape. Here, the sandy soil of Virginia's coastal plain segues into the bedrock underlying the Piedmont. The effect is pronounced on rivers, where waterfalls and rapids form. Historically, these acted as barriers to ocean-faring vessels. Towns formed up and down the fall line to handle commerce between inland farmers and coastal traders. Prince William Forest Park, a small national park straddling the fall line in Prince William County, is tied to this history through the tobacco farmers and miners who used the nearby port town of Dumfries to ship their goods. Today, the park still receives heavy use, but now hikers, cyclists, and nature lovers are drawn by the cascades, wildlife, rare plants, and historic ruins.

Start: From Parking Area A on Scenic Drive, 1.6 miles from the intersection with Park Headquarters Road.
Distance: 6.8-mile loop.
Approximate hiking time: 3 hours.
Difficulty rating: Easy due to well-graded, clearly marked trails and only a moderate elevation change.
Trail surface: A combination of dirt forest paths, dirt roads, and paved roads lead through hardwood forests and along streams to small cascades, rock outcrops, and waterfalls.
Land status: National park.
Nearest town: Dumfries, VA.
Other trail users: Joggers, cross-country skiers, and mountain bikers.
Canine compatibility: Dogs permitted.

Trail contacts: Prince William Forest Park, Triangle, VA, (703) 221-7181, www.nps.gov/prwi.
Schedule: Park is open daily, sunrise to sunset. Campsites are open February 1 through October 15 (one cabin is open for winter camping).
Fees/permits: Entrance fee: $5.00 (good for three days); annual pass: $20.00. Individual camping is $10, groups are $40. Chopawamsic Backcountry Area is a small primitive camping area south of Virginia Route 619. Open mid-April through mid-October. There is no fee, but campers must register at the park visitor center. Cabins and group sites are available; call (703) 221-4706.
Maps: USGS maps: Quantico, VA; Joplin, VA.

Finding the trailhead: From I-95: Take exit 150 and turn west onto VA 619 (a left turn if you're traveling I-95 northbound; a right turn if you're traveling I-95 southbound). Stay in the left lane. In 0.4 mile from the exit, turn right into Prince William Forest Park. A left turn 0.5 mile from the park entrance station puts you on Scenic Drive. Parking Area A is 1.6 miles ahead on the left. There are two more parking areas on Scenic Drive within 0.2 mile of Parking Area A. *DeLorme: Virginia Atlas & Gazetteer:* Page 76, D3.

The Hike

High Meadows Trail covers some rough, broken-up terrain between the Quantico Creek and South Fork Quantico Creek stream valleys. Mountain-laurel slicks coat steep hillsides. Stream water flows over bedrock slate, which, where exposed, creates small rapids and riffles. Fossils of a prehistoric sea lily *(crinoid)* found in this rock formation bear strong resemblance to European fossils. Geologists think this slate and related rocks evolved thousands of miles distant from the prehistoric North America continent, and was "abducted" here. This means North America's first imports were prehistoric invertebrate fossils that predate the well-known Jamestown settlers by roughly 500 million years. Quantico slate is also super-resistant—water simply bounces over it and flows on its merry way. Here in Prince William Forest Park, it's a last hurrah of sorts. Within a mile or so, the small streams of Prince William Forest Park empty into Quantico Creek. The descent over Virginia's fall line is complete.

WHY TO LEASH YOUR DOG

· Leashes protect dogs from becoming lost and from wilderness hazards such as porcupines, mountain lions, bears, and sick, injured, or rabid animals.

· Unleashed dogs harass, injure, and sometimes kill wildlife.

· A leashed dog's keen senses can enhance your awareness of nearby wildlife or visitors.

· Unleashed dogs increase the probability of dogs being banned from public lands.

· Failure to leash may cost you a fine.

—Adapted from American Dog Owners Association of Castleton, New York

Climbing out of the South Fork stream valley on High Meadows Trail, young trees of a third- and fourth-generation forest fall away, replaced by old fields. Tobacco was the cash crop of choice throughout colonial Virginia, and the men who tilled land along Quantico Creek were no different. These farmers had the added benefit of being close to Dumfries, Virginia's oldest continually chartered municipality, established in 1749. Town fathers drew up the boundaries and voted the town into creation a mere three hours before Alexandria, a few miles north. Unlike Alexandria, however, Dumfries' usefulness as a port declined soon after the Revolutionary War. Relentless tilling on land surrounding the town, including Prince William Forest Park, caused massive soil runoff. Dumfries' harbor filled with silt and ocean ships could not sail into port.

The Taylor family was the last to farm inside the park proper. High Meadows Trail passes through their old lands between the South Valley Trail and Turkey Run Ridge.

Prince William Forest Park in full mountain laurel splendor. ▶

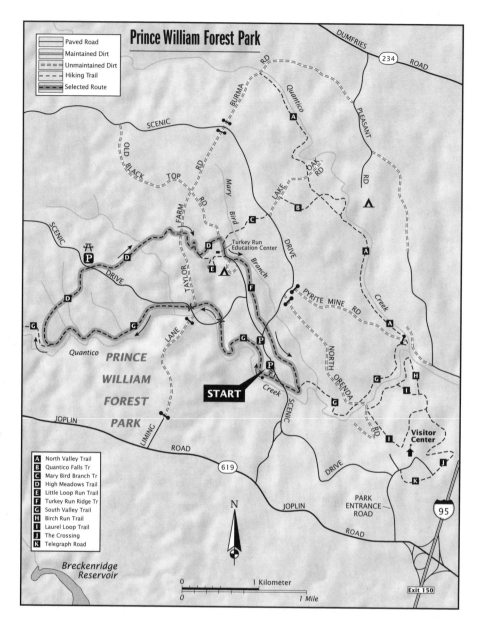

Prince William Forest Park

Legend:
- Paved Road
- Maintained Dirt
- Unmaintained Dirt
- Hiking Trail
- Selected Route

Trail Index:
- **A** North Valley Trail
- **B** Quantico Falls Tr
- **C** Mary Bird Branch Tr
- **D** High Meadows Trail
- **E** Little Loop Run Trail
- **F** Turkey Run Ridge Tr
- **G** South Valley Trail
- **H** Birch Run Trail
- **I** Laurel Loop Trail
- **J** The Crossing
- **K** Telegraph Road

PRINCE
WILLIAM
FOREST
PARK

START

Turkey Run Education Center

Visitor Center

Breckenridge Reservoir

0   1 Kilometer
0   1 Mile

An off-trail detour leads to two tombstones in the family plot, surrounded by sun-dappled woodland. There are no marked trails, only vague animal paths. Dry leaves crackle underfoot. Hidden amid the leaf debris are small green stems. Somewhere, behind a shrub or camouflaged by other spring flowers, might grow a small whorled pogonia, an endangered species.

Since it's the commonwealth's most urban region, Northern Virginia seems the last place to look for a rare plant. Loudon, Fairfax, and Fauquier Counties, however, are among the fastest growing in the country. Development, then, is the biggest single threat to the small whorled pogonia. The U.S. Fish & Wildlife Service lists it as threatened; Virginia ranks it as endangered.

This woodland orchid's bloom lasts a preciously short time. Within two weeks of the first yellow-green sepals, an entire colony will flower and lose its bloom. Following this, the flower reverts to a modest green-stemmed plant, with five or six slender leaves arranged in a whorl midway up the stem.

There's a perplexing aspect to all this. The flower, when it reproduces, stores upwards of 1,000 seeds in a small capsule. Despite the potential, it's rare for a community to number more than twenty-five plants. Scientists can't say why.

Three regions in the eastern United States harbor stable populations of small whorled pogonias. One is in New Hampshire. Another is in North Carolina. The third is in the coastal and Piedmont counties of Virginia, places such as Prince William Forest Park. A look at how one pogonia perished in King & Queen County, a rural area southeast of Prince William Forest Park, illustrates why the small flower is endangered. In 1997, a U.S. Fish & Wildlife biologist found a solitary whorled pogonia on a wooded slope between two small streams. Surveys in two consecutive years reaffirmed the plant's health. The next year, a survey found the habitat clear-cut and trammeled by heavy machinery. Later that summer, the land was burned. Presently, it is managed for timber harvests. "The site no longer provides suitable habitat for pogonia," a biologist's report stated. Its cold, matter-of-fact tone only heightens this small flower's vulnerability.

Prince William Forest Park shelters not only the rare, but the common as well. A logbook at the visitor center lists sightings of deer, raccoon, turkey, and falcons, a diversity of wildlife that stands in sharp contrast from when the federal government took over the area. After the last farmer pulled up stakes here, and after a pyrite mine closed in the 1920s amid labor strife and strikes, the federal government took over as protector of the waters that flow into Quantico Creek. The area was first used as a demonstration site for land reclamation methods such as tree planting and erosion control. Gradually the emphasis shifted to recreation and protecting the Quantico Creek watershed.

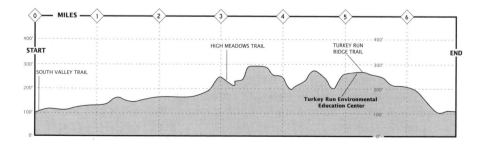

The process of recovery is ongoing. The boundaries of old tobacco fields are still visible. Thistle and milkweed grow in them now. Ecologically, these weeds prove a better return for wildlife than tobacco ever did for humans. A threatened butterfly, the regal fritillary, prefers the thistle for food. Like the small whorled pogonia, this is a minor threatened species whose plight rarely receives notice. In Virginia, sightings have been recorded from Prince William Forest Park to mountainous regions of far southwest Virginia. There are, however, five or fewer confirmed population clusters of the regal fritillary in Virginia; biologists have had more success reintroducing this insect in Midwest states, where the tallgrass prairies make an ideal habitat. Pennsylvania is believed to have the only viable population of these orange and black butterflies in the East.

From a distance, the butterfly looks like a Monarch. A female is distinguishable by the off-white circles on its rear, or hind, wings. A better way of identifying one is to watch mating rituals. A female regal fritillary signals her displeasure with a male suitor by flying straight up, as much as 100 feet, then entering a nosedive that scares away the unlucky male.

Like the pogonia, commercial and residential development threaten the regal fritillary. And like the pogonia, the regal fritillary seems to have a built-in destruct button. Butterflies, for the most part, follow an established breeding pattern. Females lay eggs in a host plant, and the larvae eat the plant as they grow. Regal fritillary defy this routine. Females lay eggs just about anywhere. And they lay a lot of eggs—upwards of 2,400 in a season. After hatching in fall, larvae lie dormant for the winter. They awaken in spring and seek out their preferred food, violet leaves (bird's-foot violet is a favored plant). Taken together, the dormant period and the search for food kill off all but a fraction of this large insect.

With such varied terrain and so much room to explore, it's easy to imagine seeing a regal fritillary, or a small whorled pogonia, as you hike about Prince William Forest Park. Finding either would be considered an accomplishment—they aren't endangered or threatened because they're plentiful. But half the fun is knowing they're there, somewhere. That, and appreciating the sanctuary that can harbor them.

Miles and Directions

0.0 **START** at Parking Area A on Scenic Drive. From the back of the parking lot, follow a set of wooden stairs downhill. A narrow dirt footpath leads to white-blazed South Valley Trail. Turn right onto South Valley Trail and walk alongside South Fork Quantico Creek.

0.4 Cross a wooden footbridge over a feeder stream.

0.6 Past a second wooden footbridge, the trail forks. Follow the right path up a set of wooden stairs. The trail climbs steeply, switchbacks twice, and tops out on a hill overlooking the river. It then descends to meet the riverside trail.

1.0 (FYI: The trail passes by several falls on South Fork. Large, flat rocks crop up in the middle of the river. The stream valley narrows considerably. Across the water, mountain laurel covers the steep stream bank. Downed trees and wood chips indicate beaver activity.)

1.2 Pass under a road bridge and continue straight along the dirt streamside path.

1.4 Proceed straight on white-blazed South Valley Trail. (FYI: Taylor Farm Road branches right here and leads 0.2 mile to Scenic Drive.)

1.6 Pass beneath a road bridge and continue straight along the dirt streamside path.

2.2 Climb steeply up a hill. The trail will descend again to the river. It repeats this pattern once more, climbing the right stream bank and then descending to the river.

3.1 Reach a trail junction and follow orange-blazed High Meadows Trail to the right. (FYI: South Valley Trail turns left and descends to the river.)

3.7 A double orange blaze marks a hard right turn in High Meadows Trail.

3.9 Cross Scenic Drive at Parking Area H. The area has picnic tables for resting or lunch. Re-enter the woods on the right side of Parking Area H and follow orange blazes.

4.2 Cross a series of boardwalks across a marsh loaded with ferns.

4.6 Trail rises out of a streambed and passes a clearing on the right. (FYI: This is the Taylor family cemetery and an old apple orchard.)

4.7 Cross Taylor Farm Road and re-enter the woods on orange-blazed High Meadows Trail. (FYI: Following the gravel road right returns you to South Valley Trail in 0.6 mile. A left onto Taylor Farm Road leads to Old Black Top Road in 0.3 mile.)

4.9 Turn right and cross a footbridge.

5.1 Turn right onto Old Black Top Road, a dirt road overgrown with grass. (FYI: Within 0.1 mile, Mary Bird Branch Trail exits left. It connects with Quantico Falls Trail and leads to Quantico Creek in 1.3 miles.)

5.2 Pass by a chain across Old Black Top Road. Follow the paved road past Turkey Run Education Center. (FYI: There are tent campsites, bathrooms, and a ranger building in this area.)

5.3 Turn left off the paved road and enter the woods on blue-blazed Turkey Run Ridge Trail.

5.9 Cross Scenic Drive and re-enter woods on the opposite side on blue-blazed Turkey Run Ridge Trail. The trail is wide and strewn with pebbles.

6.5 The trail forks left and right. Turn right for a return along South Valley Trail to Parking Area A on Scenic Drive. (FYI: A left turn leads to the North Valley Trail.)

6.8 Turn right off South Valley Trail. Follow the cutoff trail up wooden steps to Parking Area A.

Hike Information

Local Information

Prince William County Visitor Information Center, Occoquan, VA, (703) 491-4045, www.visitpwc.com.

Local Events/Attractions

The Cherry Jubilee, February, Dumfries, VA, (703) 221-3346. Celebrates George Washington's birthday.

Occoquan Arts and Craft Show, September and June, Occoquan, VA, (703) 491-2168.

Old Mine Ranch, Dumfries, VA, (703) 441-1382, www.oldmineranch.com. Pony ranch and working farm. Offers guided hikes. Pumpkin patch and hay rides in October.

Lodging

Holiday Inn Express, Dumfries, VA, (703) 221-1141. Allows pets.

Restaurants

Tim's Rivershore, Dumfries, VA, (703) 441-1375. Seafood on the shores of the

Potomac. Follow Cherry Hill Road to the railroad tracks, cross, and turn left onto a gravel road. It's worth the effort to get there.

Hike Tours

Park rangers conduct nature programs during spring, summer, and fall. Prince William Forest Park's varied topography makes it ideal for the orienteering classes run by park staff. Call or visit the park Web site for information. (703) 221-7181, www.nps.gov/prwi.

Organizations

Friends of Prince William Forest Park, Burke, VA, (703) 591-0911.

Capital Hiking Club, c/o Susan Klein, Washington, D.C., (301) 229-5816, www. capitalhikingclub.org. Hikes and trips in Virginia, Maryland, and Pennsylvania.

Center Hiking Club, c/o Duncan Thompson, (703) 527-2349. Hikes and trips in Virginia, Maryland, and Pennsylvania.

Wanderbirds Hiking Club, c/o Herb Cooper, (301) 460-3064, www.wanderbirds.org. Hikes in George Washington National Forest and Shenandoah National Park.

Washington Women Outdoors, Germantown, MD, (301) 864-3070, www.washingtonwomenoutdoors.org. Outdoor adventures for women, including hiking, kayaking, rock climbing, and biking.

7 Scott's Run Nature Preserve

Scott's Run Nature Preserve offers Northern Virginians a relaxing way to spend some time in a deep-forest atmosphere of oaks, beech, and tulip poplar. The small streams that spill off high river bluffs nourish carpets of ferns, grasses, and wildflowers. The most spectacular stream is, of course, Scott's Run, with its multilevel waterfall that breaks just before the stream joins the Potomac River. Four out of five Beltway insiders agree: Scott's Run is the best place to leave politics behind and enjoy a walk in the woods.

Start: From the parking lot off Georgetown Pike (Virginia Route 193) at Swinks Mill Road.
Distance: 3.2-mile loop.
Approximate hiking time: 2 hours.
Difficulty rating: Moderate due to the narrow, eroded trails along Scott's Run and steep drops off Potomac River bluffs.
Trail surface: Rocky streamside paths, dirt footpaths, and dirt roads wind through hardwood forest with some stands of eastern hemlock, tall river bluffs, wildflowers, rock outcroppings, riverine flats, and upland forests.

Land status: County park.
Nearest town: McLean, VA.
Other trail users: Joggers, cross-country skiers, and mountain bikers.
Canine compatibility: Dogs permitted.
Trail contacts: Fairfax County Park Authority, River Bend Park, Great Falls, VA, (703) 759-9018, www.co.fairfax.va.us/parks/parks.htm.
Schedule: Open year-round, sunrise to sunset.
Fees/permits: No fees or permits required.
Maps: USGS maps: Falls Church, VA.

Finding the trailhead: From I-495: Take exit 13. If traveling north on I-495, turn left off the exit onto Georgetown Pike (VA 193). In 0.7 mile, at the intersection of Swinks Mill Road (on the left), turn right into Scott's Run Nature Preserve parking area. *DeLorme: Virginia Atlas & Gazetteer:* Page 76, A4.

The Hike

You work up quite the appetite exploring Scott's Run Nature Preserve, what with negotiating steep hills, narrow billy goat–like paths, and a nest of trails through the upland forest. So I was half expecting the pronouncement, delivered in no uncertain terms, that my assistants—my niece and nephew—were hungry. They demanded food, and I, sensing their growing resolve, made an executive decision. Lunch all around, I muttered.

On a rocky point near Stubblefield Falls, where mayflies swarm heavy off the marshy shoreline, we found shelter from both insect and sun under a scrubby tree. Out came sandwiches, drinks, cheese-on-cheese crackers. I stifled a mutiny over mustard (no one told me they didn't like mustard) by pointing to a cryptic rock carving—some long phrase, partly weathered, carved in neat block letters, referencing

Waterfall at the base of Scott's Run, on the Potomac River.

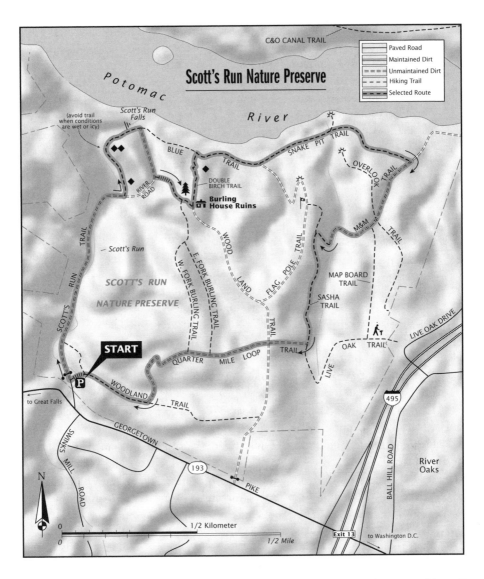

Scott's Run Nature Preserve

Potomac River

C&O CANAL TRAIL

Legend	
	Paved Road
	Maintained Dirt
	Unmaintained Dirt
	Hiking Trail
	Selected Route

Scott's Run Falls

(avoid trail when conditions are wet or icy)

BLUE TRAIL

SNAKE PIT TRAIL

OVERLOOK TRAIL

RIVER ROAD

DOUBLE BIRCH TRAIL

Burling House Ruins

SCOTT'S RUN TRAIL

Scott's Run

SCOTT'S RUN NATURE PRESERVE

W. FORK BURLING TRAIL

E. FORK BURLING TRAIL

WOODLAND TRAIL

FLAG POLE TRAIL

M&M TRAIL

MAP BOARD TRAIL

SASHA TRAIL

START

QUARTER MILE LOOP TRAIL

OAK TRAIL

LIVE OAK TRAIL

LIVE OAK DRIVE

WOODLAND TRAIL

to Great Falls

GEORGETOWN PIKE

193

495

SWINNS MILL ROAD

N

Exit 13

River Oaks

to Washington D.C.

BALL HILL ROAD

0   1/2 Kilometer

0   1/2 Mile

trade imbalances, nature, and logic (clearly *not* ancient Native American writings, I told my disappointed niece and nephew). While they busied themselves, I scraped mustard off the white bread. My cell phone chirped and I took the call. Ahhh, nature.

That's when she screamed.

When a child screams, instinct kicks in. "Her mom's gonna kill me," I panicked. Out loud, I yelled, "What's wrong? Are you OK?" She screamed again.

I followed her pointing finger and at first saw nothing. Then a rock about 50 yards offshore moved. Or, the rock didn't, but the snakes did. Five—no, six, seven, eight—black, oily water snakes adjusted their sun tanning positions on a rock dam. The rock dam where they lay stretched far downstream, but these snakes felt uncomfortably close. Quietly, one slipped from off its perch and moved closer.

It's not unusual, in springtime, for the common variety water snakes—the dark brown–banded water snake and its lighter-shaded cousin, the northern water snake—to siesta on exposed rocks, bridge abutments, even dams. These are nonpoisonous, members of the colubrid family. They give birth to live young in the spring and together the whole clan haunts rivers, lakes, and pond shorelines looking for food. Youngsters are skinny and harmless looking. Elders tend toward the heavy side, their thick heads, muscular jaws, and rows of sharp teeth conveying a slightly more sinister intent.

FYI You won't find Scott's Run Nature Preserve labeled on USGS topo maps. Look instead for its old name, Dranesville District Park.

At this point, it should be established that I am, for better or for worse, a tree and rock guy. I get excited about rocks folded and broken by violent collisions of continental plates. I think it's cool that shale, subjected to extreme heat hundreds of millions of years ago, turned first to slate, then schist. And how schist, so hard it withstands the steady flowing drumbeat of the Potomac River, comprises the bedrock underfoot at Scott's Run Nature Preserve. I thrill at identifying an Eastern hemlock along Scott's Run, at spying mountain laurel breaks on that same steep streamside hill. Wildflowers peaking through soggy ground rot in a cove forest make me downright giddy.

All of which is a roundabout way of saying I am *not* a snake guy. I'm barely an insect guy. For sure, though, snakes make me shudder.

That said, I understand leaders should wear a brave face. I regained some composure and made a mental checklist of snake facts and myths. Only about 10 percent of snake species worldwide are poisonous. One of them, unfortunately, *is* a water snake, the cottonmouth, or water moccasin. Fortunately, you'll find them no farther north than the Dismal Swamp in southeast Virginia, some 200 miles away. Even there, they're rare. Standing where I was, on the shore of the Potomac River, I reasoned I was relatively safe.

Snakes are nearly always smaller than you remember. Water snakes, in particular, average only about 3 feet in length. Naturally, the snakes I saw swimming against the current were 10 feet long. But maybe not.

Finally, snakes do not poison people with their breath. They can't charm prey to prevent flight. And snakes do not swallow little children whole. A water snake's diet consists of insects, crayfish, small fish, and, occasionally, small mammals.

That final thought jerked me back to reality and I quickly checked on my two small mammals. They weren't in immediate danger of being charmed, choked, breathed upon, coughed on, or sprayed (water snakes emit a foul, musky scent when handled), or—God forbid—swallowed whole, but I still played it safe. Saying a short prayer to St. Patrick, he who droveth the snakes from Ireland, I shepherded the kids off the rock. I may have even muttered "cool" once or twice to show I wasn't unhip.

I do recall declaring snake-viewing hour over. As I shoved lunch leftovers into a backpack, my nephew stated that a water snake would make a great pet. I tried distracting him.

"Look at this cool tree," I said. He ignored me. He'll probably grow up to be a snake guy.

Miles and Directions

0.0 **START** at the metal gate that spans across the gravel road known as Scott's Run Trail. Continue north on Scott's Run Trail. (FYI: Be prepared to cross Scott's Run three times before reaching the Potomac River.)

0.5 Cross Scott's Run. You may follow the dirt road, or follow a narrow footpath along the right stream bank. Both take you to the Potomac River, but the Scott's Run Trail is more rugged, cut into the steep-sided stream bank. (Note: There are many rock and tree hazards, and the trail is severely eroded in sections. The streamside trail is not a recommended route in wintertime, in times of inclement weather, or with young children.)

0.7 A scenic, 30-foot waterfall marks Scott's Run's confluence with the Potomac. From river's edge, walk away from the water, uphill on River Road. Midway up the hill, turn left and climb a clearly visible set of wooden steps.

1.0 A chimney and house foundation mark what's left of Edward Burling's home. (FYI: Burling once owned the land that comprises Scott's Run Nature Preserve.) Look left of the ruins for a double-trunked birch. Walk past the tree on an unmarked footpath. This trail drops steeply off the bluff, returning you to the Potomac River bottomland.

1.2 Cross a ditch, turn right onto a blue-blazed trail, and walk downstream. (FYI: The Potomac River is in view off to the left.)

1.5 Reach "The Snake Pit" (so dubbed for our exciting encounter with water snakes). (FYI: This a great place for lunch. Good luck deciphering the rock carvings.) Past this rocky point, the trail climbs a steep hill between two rock outcrops. Halfway up the hill, the trail bears left.

1.8 Reach a trail junction with M&M Trail, turn right, and hike uphill. **Sidetrip:** A left turn leads to the Potomac River in one-tenth of a mile. Another half mile downstream leads to the American Legion Bridge, the northern trailhead of the 10-mile Potomac Heritage Trail, which continues downstream to Theodore Roosevelt Island.

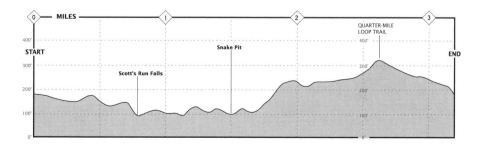

2.1 Pass straight through a four-way trail intersection.

2.2 Turn right onto an unmarked, clearly defined dirt footpath.

2.3 Cross a stream and arrive at a trail junction with Sasha Trail. Turn left and follow Sasha Trail along the stream.

2.5 Reach yet another trail junction and turn right. **Sidetrip:** A left turn takes you to Live Oak Drive on the park's eastern edge.

2.6 Turn right onto the Quarter-Mile Loop Trail. In the next two-tenths of a mile, you'll pass three trails that lead right to the Potomac River. Continue straight.

3.0 Turn right onto the Woodland Trail.

3.2 Descend a set of wooden stairs to the parking lot on Scott's Run.

Hike Information

Local Information

Fairfax County Convention and Visitors Bureau, Vienna, VA, (703) 790-3329, www. visitfairfax.org.

Local Events/Attractions

Fairfax Cross-County Hike, National Trails Day, (703) 821-0975 (evenings only), www. mindspring.com/~potomacgreenways/. Annual event raises awareness and support for a cross-county trail. Roughly 30 miles of a proposed 45-mile multiuse trail are completed.

Taste of the Town, fourth weekend in June, Reston, VA, (703) 707-9045. Features dozens of restaurants, food kiosks, and great eats.

Fairfax Chocolate Lovers Festival, first weekend in February, Old Town Fairfax, VA (703) 293-7120.

Lodging

The Arlington and Alexandria Bed & Breakfast Network, (703) 549-3415, www.aabbn.com. Assists with reservations for thirty area bed-and-breakfasts.

Restaurants

Old Brogue Irish Pub, Great Falls, VA, (703) 759-3309. Traditional Irish fare, including Guinness beef pie. Live entertainment.

Deli Italiano, Great Falls, VA, (703) 759-6782. Grab a sandwich before heading into the park, or a slice of pizza afterward.

Tavern at Great Falls, Great Falls, VA, (703) 757-4770. Daily specials, Tavern Southern Salad, and a to-die-for carrot cake.

Organizations

Friends of Riverbend Park, (703) 759-1657, www.forb.org.

Capital Hiking Club, c/o Susan Klein, (301) 229-5816, www.capitalhikingclub.org. Hikes and trips in Virginia, Maryland, and Pennsylvania.

Center Hiking Club, c/o Duncan Thompson, (703) 527-2349, www.centerhikingclub.org. Hikes and trips in Virginia, Maryland, and Pennsylvania.

Wanderbirds Hiking Club, c/o Herb Cooper, (301) 460-3064, www.wanderbirds.org. Hikes in George Washington National Forest and Shenandoah National Park.

Washington Women Outdoors, Germantown, MD, (301) 864-3070, www.washingtonwomen outdoors.org. Outdoor adventures for women, including hiking, kayaking, rock climbing, and biking.

Northern Virginia Hiking Club, Arlington, VA, (703) 440-1805, www.nvhc.com.

Other Resources

Potomac Appalachian Trail Club (PATC), Vienna, VA, (703) 242-0693, www.patc.net. The PATC Map D covers Scott's Run, as does the PATC guidebook *Hikes in the Washington, DC Area.* Call for maps and book orders, cabin rentals, scheduled hikes, and membership.

Public Transportation

Metro Bus, (202) 637–7000, www.wmata.com. Route 24T stops at the intersection of Swink Mill and Lewinsville Roads. It's a 1.5-mile walk to the trailhead.

8 Great Falls Park

Land and history are interwoven throughout Great Falls Park—the spot where George Washington championed a canal to skirt the Potomac River's 77-foot "great falls." This may be metropolitan D.C., but beyond the crowds, you can find small reminders of a time when our nation's capital was a tidal backwater and our country's survival wasn't assured. Stones in a restored canal wall bear inscriptions unique to the masons who built it. Ruins of old chimneys and homes in Matildaville mark the boomtown that lived and died on hopes that the Patowmack Canal would succeed. For a time it did succeed, ferrying farm goods from western lands to eastern seaports. Then it went bankrupt, leaving us with canal ruins, inspired views over Mather Gorge, wildflowers that bloom spring through fall, and a moment of solitude.

Start: From the park visitor center.
Distance: 3.4-mile loop.
Approximate hiking time: 2 hours.
Difficulty rating: Easy; well-traveled trails with a few short, steep sections along the Potomac.
Trail surface: Rocky cliff tops, dirt footpaths, dirt roads, riverside trails, hardwood forests, and marsh.
Land status: National park.
Nearest town: Great Falls, VA.
Other trail users: Joggers, cross-country skiers, equestrians, mountain bikers, and rock climbers.
Canine compatibility: Dogs permitted.
Trail contacts: Great Falls Park, Great Falls, VA, (703) 285-2966, www.nps.gov/gwmp/

grfa. Great Falls is one park in a series under the umbrella of the George Washington Memorial Parkway. Other spots worth visiting are Turkey Run Park, Theodore Roosevelt Island, Arlington National Cemetery, and Dike Marsh Wildlife Preserve.
Schedule: Open daily, sunrise to sunset, except Christmas.
Fees/permits: Entrance fee, $5.00 ($3.00 by means other than a vehicle, i.e., bike, horse, motorcycle, on foot) good for three days and access to Maryland's C&O Canal National Historical Park. A state fishing license is required to fish in the park.
Maps: USGS maps: Vienna, VA; Falls Church, VA.

Finding the trailhead: From I-495: Take exit 13 and turn left onto Georgetown Pike/Virginia Route 193. Go 4.3 miles and turn right onto Old Dominion Drive and enter the park. From the park boundary, drive 1.2 miles to the visitor center parking lot. *DeLorme: Virginia Atlas & Gazetteer:* Page 76, A3.

The Hike

Canal Cut, the final descent on the Great Falls skirting canal, drops 76 feet through solid rock in Mather Gorge. Considered an engineering marvel in its time, the canal—and especially this last passage—evolved painfully. Dynamite was a discovery some eighty years away, so workers on the Patowmack Canal hand-drilled bore-

Great Falls on the Potomac.

holes, poured in black powder, and ignited the volatile mix. If dust particles exploded prematurely, few within range survived. It took sixteen years to construct the canal around Great Falls; all but one year was spent blasting Canal Cut.

George Washington believed the Potomac River would serve as a great unifier for a young nation. He wasn't the first or the last to view it as a means to an end. From the day Captain John Smith ventured up the Potomac to Little Falls (near present-day Georgetown) Americans have had their way with this river. Explorers, canal-builders, farmers, miners, theme-park promoters—each has left a mark. Today various agencies, commissions, and nonprofits pursue watershed protection and monitor stream pollutants. Industries and farms situated in the Potomac's massive four-state, 15,000-square-mile river basin discharge pollutants into its tributaries daily. Along the southern shores of the middle Potomac, Northern Virginia grows an estimated 70 square miles every year. Housing subdivisions gobble up land on such small tributaries as Bullneck Run, Pimmit Run, and Difficult Run.

But as Washington's Patowmack Canal illustrates all too well, the river has the final say. Despite Herculean efforts, seasonal fluctuations in water levels made the canal operable only a few months during the year. It declared bankruptcy in 1828, some twenty-six years after completion.

On a spring afternoon, an eagle soars above craggy Potomac river rocks below Great Falls, a 70-foot vertical drop of thunder, mist, and frothing water. The raptor dips and alights on the south wall of Mather Gorge. Upended boulders show distinct layers of compressed rock that built the gorge millions of years ago. Spleenwort ferns grow thick here, where the River Trail cuts dangerously close to the cliff edge. Lined with pink spring beauties in May, this mile-and-a-half route follows an up-and-down course, eventually reaching river level at the far southern end of the park. It gets heavy use, with side trails leading to gorgeous overlooks of the waterfalls. Beyond these points, however, foot traffic dwindles and the River Trail becomes a nice conduit to the less crowded areas in the park's southern reaches.

It should be expected that a park 20 miles from the nation's capital attracts a large number of visitors. Kayakers frolic in the surf below the falls. Rock climbers dangle off Birds Nest, one of twenty-plus mapped climbs on the cliffs of Mather Gorge. Joggers use the wide Matildaville Trail and Old Carriage Road. Painters set up easel and palette along Falls Overlook Trail. Picnickers lounge in grassy fields under shady red oaks.

All the activity makes the Swamp Trail—in the southern section of the park—that much more attractive. It's a hiker-only path that branches off the Ridge Trail. From a slight hill, it drops through a forest of tulip poplar and beech and reaches a swampy confluence of unnamed streams. Sluggish and meandering, the streams support a lush undergrowth of wood fern and wildflowers. Concave green trillium leaves spread across a widening forest floor. It's unusual to see this wildflower in such great numbers east of the Blue Ridge, but it thrives in these wet conditions nonetheless. In fact, on this brief stretch of trail, plant life approaches the variety typical of an Appalachian cove—a forest type defined by its wet, sheltered climate and diversity of trees and plants. Eastern hemlock, white basswood, tulip poplar—with a little sleuthing, you'll find representatives of each tree along the Swamp Trail.

FYI Masons carved canal walls out of bedrock. To ensure payment, they inscribed finished blocks with a sign identifiable only to themselves.

The priceless scenery we enjoy today was viewd by James Rumsey as merely supplies. Rumsey came to Great Falls in 1785 as the overseer of construction on the Patowmack Canal, hand-picked by Washington and carrying tremendous expectations. From hophornbeam trees, workers fashioned tool handles. White oak trees fell to make planks for supply boats. Masons carved canal walls out of the bedrock. They inscribed finished blocks with a unique symbol to ensure they could document their work for pay. Unfortunately, money proved a sparse commodity during construction and the weather was unpredictable and uncooperative. It was a recipe for disaster.

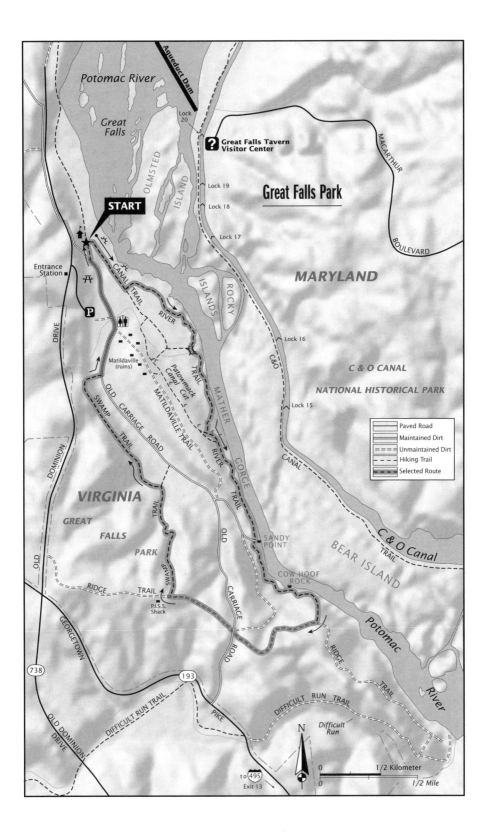

Potomac River

Great
Falls

Aqueduct Dam

Lock 20

? Great Falls Tavern
Visitor Center

OLMSTED ISLAND

Lock 19

Lock 18

START

Lock 17

Great Falls Park

MACARTHUR BOULEVARD

Entrance
Station

CANAL TRAIL

RIVER

ROCKY ISLANDS

MARYLAND

P

Matildaville
(ruins)

MATILDAVILLE TRAIL

Patowmack
Canal Cut

TRAIL

MATHER

RIVER

GORGE

C&O

Lock 16

Lock 15

C & O CANAL

NATIONAL HISTORICAL PARK

	Paved Road
	Maintained Dirt
	Unmaintained Dirt
	Hiking Trail
	Selected Route

DRIVE

OLD CARRIAGE ROAD

SWAMP TRAIL

TRAIL

TRAIL

OLD

VIRGINIA

GREAT

FALLS

PARK

SANDY
POINT

CANAL

C & O Canal

TRAIL

OLD DOMINION

OLD

RIDGE TRAIL

SWAMP

P.I.S.S.
Shack

COW HOOF
ROCK

OLD CARRIAGE ROAD

BEAR ISLAND

Potomac River

GEORGETOWN

738

193

DIFFICULT RUN TRAIL

PIKE

OLD DOMINION DRIVE

DIFFICULT RUN TRAIL

RIDGE TRAIL

Difficult
Run

N

to 495
Exit 13

| 0 | 1/2 Kilometer |
| 0 | 1/2 Mile |

Rumsey quit after only one year on the job (he would later resurface in a dispute over who "owned" the patent for the modern steamship). After Rumsey, six different men oversaw the Great Falls project before the canal opened in 1802.

For twenty-six years, the Great Falls Canal moved thousands of pounds of flour, corn, livestock, and farm goods from western territories to eastern ports. Each boat that passed through finished its journey by dropping through Canal Cut, past bore marks made by workers who blew solid rock away with black powder. This same passage today bears little resemblance to its heyday. Trees cling to the hard-hewn cliff walls. Weeds grow everywhere. And beyond it all, the Potomac, America's river, keeps on rolling.

Miles and Directions

0.0　**START** at the Great Falls Park visitor center. Follow a gravel sidewalk across restored parts of the Patowmack Canal, falls overlooks, and picnic area.

0.3　Bear left onto a dirt footpath, the start of blue-blazed River Trail. (Note: Use caution. Footing is tricky and the trail runs close to the edge of Mather Gorge, named in honor of Stephen T. Mather, director of the national park system from 1917 to 1929.)

0.7　Descend to a boardwalk that spans a stream. A footpath along the right cliff wall leads to an opening on the river.

0.8　Cross the Canal Cut.

1.2　Cross a paved road that sweeps left to a boat landing on the Potomac River at Sandy Point. Beyond the road, the trail passes through American beech, hophornbeam, oak, and pine as you climb and descend short, steep hills before topping out at Cow Hoof Rock. (FYI: American beech is a tree often recognizable for the initials folks carve in the tree's thin bark. Resist the temptation.)

1.6　River Trail ends at the Ridge Trail. Turn right onto the Ridge Trail. **Sidetrip:** A left turn onto Ridge Trail takes you to Difficult Run Trail in a half mile and, beyond that, another river overlook. Difficult Run follows its namesake stream outside park boundaries.

1.9　Cross over Old Carriage Road on the Ridge Trail.

2.0　Split rail fencing on the left, parallel to the Ridge Trail, marks an unblazed path that leads to the park boundary on Old Dominion Road. Continue straight on the Ridge Trail.

2.1　Turn right onto Swamp Trail. There is a fenced enclosure and metal shack here, part of the Potomac Interceptor Sewer system. (FYI: If you've noticed a particularly obnoxious

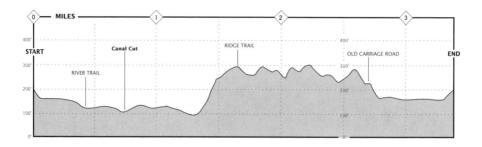

smell during any part of the hike, this intercept system is likely the culprit.) The Swamp Trail is a footpath through dense oaks, tulip poplar, and maple.

2.4 Bear left and continue walking along a flat, wet trail.

2.7 After a 90-degree turn, the Swamp Trail intersects with Old Carriage Road. Turn left onto Old Carriage Road to return to the visitor center.

3.0 Old Carriage Road and the Matildaville Trail meet in a forked intersection. Turn left to return to the visitor center. **Sidetrip:** A right turn brings you to the Matildaville ruins.

3.3 Veer right on the trail as it approaches the visitor center.

3.4 Hike ends at the Great Falls Park visitor center. (FYI: For an extended hike, follow the streamside path upriver to Riverbend Park.)

Hike Information

Local Information

Fairfax County Convention & Visitors Bureau, Vienna, VA, (703) 790-3329, www.visitfairfax.org.
Fairfax County Visitor Center, (800) 732-4732.

Local Events/Attractions

Reston Concerts on the Town, Saturday evenings in June, July, and August, Reston, VA, (703) 707-9045, www.restontowncenter.com. Sit back and enjoy a variety of musical entertainers under the stars.
Wolf Trap National Park for the Performing Arts, Vienna, VA, (703) 255-1860, www.nps.gov/wotr/. National park dedicated to performing arts. Three different facilities offer year-round performances. The Theater in the Woods is geared especially toward children.
Columbia Pike Blues Festival, May (the Sunday before Mother's Day), Columbia Pike, VA, (703) 892-2776, www.uptownarlington. com/thepike. A one-day free music festival featuring national and local blues acts, food, and vendors.

Lodging

The Arlington and Alexandria Bed & Breakfast Network, (703) 549-3415, (888) 549-3415, www.aabbn.com. Assists with reservations for thirty area bed-and-breakfasts.

Restaurants

Serbian Crown Restaurant, Great Falls, VA,
(703) 759-4150. Authentic Serbian and Russian food.
See also, Restaurants, page 60.

Hike Tours

Park staff lead nature and historical tours all year. Call (703) 285-2966 for information.

Organizations

Fairfax Trails & Streams, (703) 821-0975, www.fairfaxtrails.org. Champion of the Pimmit Run Trail and Fairfax Cross-County Trail, with links to other Northern Virginia hiking and preservation efforts.
Capital Hiking Club, c/o Susan Klein, (301) 229-5816, www.capitalhikingclub.org. Hikes and trips in Virginia, Maryland, and Pennsylvania.
Center Hiking Club, c/o Duncan Thompson, (703) 527-2349, www.centerhikingclub.org. Hikes and trips in Virginia, Maryland, and Pennsylvania.
Wanderbirds Hiking Club, c/o Herb Cooper, (301) 460-3064, www.wanderbirds.org. Hikes in George Washington National Forest and Shenandoah National Park.
Washington Women Outdoors, Germantown, MD, (301) 864-3070, www.washingtonwomen outdoors.org. Outdoor adventures for women, including hiking, kayaking, rock climbing, and biking.
Northern Virginia Hiking Club, Arlington, VA, (703) 440-1805, www.nvhc.com.

Other Resources

Chesapeake & Ohio Canal National Historical Park, Sharpsburg, MD, (301) 739-4200, www.nps.gov/choh. The C&O Canal along the Potomac River in Maryland succeeded where Washington's Patowmack Canal failed by linking farm markets west of the Appalachians to eastern seaports.

Potomac Appalachian Trail Club (PATC), Vienna, VA, (703) 242-0693, www.patc.net. PATC Map D covers Great Falls and vicinity. Call for maps, book orders, cabin rentals, scheduled hikes, and membership.

9 G. Richard Thompson Wildlife Management Area

Virginia's Department of Game & Inland Fisheries oversees thirty wildlife management areas around the state with the hunter and angler in mind. Fields are kept clear to attract grazing animals, and seed plots are sown to keep them plump and healthy. Streams and man-made lakes are stocked with trout and other fish. As the state makes these areas hiker-friendly as well, they'd do well to model the G. Richard Thompson Wildlife Management Area in Fauquier County, where hikers and naturalists stake as much a claim to the beautiful surroundings as outdoorsmen. There is an abundance of wildflowers—the area harbors one of the largest populations of large-flowered trillium in North America. Virginia's Native Plant Society lists the Thompson Wildlife Management Area on its register of important native plant sites.

Start: From Parking Area 4 (for the Ted Lake Loop) and Parking Area 7 (for the Stone Wall Loop).

Distance: Ted Lake Loop: 2 miles; Stone Wall Loop: 4.3 miles.

Approximate hiking time: 3–4 hours (to do both loops).

Difficulty rating: Easy along wide roads. Younger or inexperienced hikers may have difficulty with blowdowns on the unmaintained trail along the Stone Wall Loop to connect with the Appalachian Trail.

Trail surface: Dirt roads and woods paths wind through young second- and third-generation forests dominated by deciduous trees. This is the Blue Ridge, but the hills are more rolling than steep.

Land status: State wildlife management area.

Nearest town: Linden, VA.

Other trail users: Anglers, cyclists, equestrians, hunters (in season), and naturalists.

Canine compatibility: Dogs permitted.

Trail contacts: G. R. Thompson Wildlife Management Area, Sperryville, VA, regional office phone number (540) 899–4169, www.dgif.state.va.us. Good maps of the trail network.

Schedule: Open year-round. Deer-hunting season runs from November into January; turkey, grouse, and squirrel also attract hunters.

Fees/permits: No fees or permits required.

Maps: USGS maps: Linden, VA; Upperville, VA.

Finding the trailhead: From Linden: Turn north off Virginia Route 55 onto Virginia Route 638 (this is a left turn if you're traveling east on VA 55; it is a right turn if you are traveling west). Drive 5.3 miles to Parking Area 4 on the right. A signboard indicates this is public parking for the wildlife management area. A second parking area is up VA 638 in 0.2 mile. In 1.3 miles from the first parking area is Parking Area 7 on the right, at the intersection of Freezeland Road (0.1 mile past where VA 638 turns to gravel). *DeLorme: Virginia Atlas & Gazetteer:* Page 75, A5.

The Hike

It never received headlines the way taxes or elections seem to, but native plant lovers throughout Virginia still celebrated when the state declared purple loosestrife a

Waterfowl on Thompson Lake.

"noxious weed." The very word "noxious" showed how seriously botanists view alien species. "Harmful to health, injurious, corrupting or unwholesome" are a few of the descriptors now legally associated with loosestrife, which is especially damaging to freshwater wetlands.

The battle against invasive alien species seems never-ending; they outcompete native plants and disrupt the web of life—in which native plants play an irreplaceable role. Kudzu was, for years, enemy Number One. Virginia's Department of Transportation planted it as groundcover along roadways. Much later, they watched

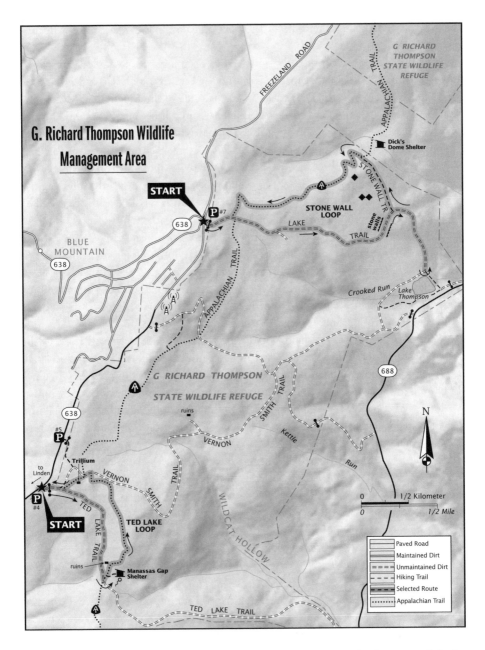

G. Richard Thompson Wildlife Management Area

this plant engulf entire stands of trees and shrubs. In Shenandoah National Park, rangers have watched as ailanthus (aka *tree of heaven*) replaces stands of oak killed by gypsy moth infestation. In coastal communities, the common reed spreads uncontrollably in wetland settings. The reed's root structure sinks 6 feet deep and deeper, making it impossible to extricate except through repeated burning and chemicals.

Worse, this alien grass outcompetes the hays and cordgrasses that make a healthy marsh ecosystem.

If all this ever gets too much, Virginia's native plant lovers and wildflower aficionados—and anyone else for that matter—can find respite in the G. Richard Thompson Wildlife Management Area. Draped across the east side of the Blue Ridge Mountains, this small patch of land in far-western Fauquier County hosts an array of wildflowers. Most noticeable in April through June are the large-flowered trillium (1996 Wildflower of the Year in Virginia) that grow in large swatches on the slopes of this preserve. Thompson Wildlife Management Area (WMA) is thought to have one of the largest concentrated populations of this wildflower anywhere in North America.

The Thompson WMA is not so much a destination as it is a place to wander. The easy 2-mile Ted Lake Loop leads through patches of mayapple, with blackberry bushes and sassafras filling the forest understory. Yellow poplar grows tall, as do the oaks that survived gypsy moth attacks in the mid-1980s. A tangle of wildflowers in a hedgerow alongside the trail sports delicate, white-petaled flowers with a sweet, applelike fragrance. The return on the Appalachian Trail leads past an old home foundation and a heap of scrap metal. The white flowers that cover blackberry bushes in May hold promise of trailside snacking come July.

Several large birch trees stand out on the unblazed path that leads back to the parking area. Where a large blowdown forces you to detour, the newly worn path leads not to brambles and frustration, but to large patches of trillium. Even when not in bloom, the flower is easily recognizable by its three broad leaves. Anyone familiar with the leaf appearance of garden-variety lilies will see the resemblance in trillium leaves. It's hard to imagine this flower is a cousin of the onion and asparagus, which are also members of the lily family.

The interaction between trillium and insects makes for a fascinating study of how various forms of life—plant, animal, and insect—rely on each other. The trillium's bright coloring attracts bees and butterflies, yet a nose-to-nose study of the flower proves it to have quite an offensive odor. That explains the presence of flies, which are the primary pollinators of trillium. In the matter of seed dispersal, plants generally rely heavily on birds ingesting then discharging seeds far afield. In the case of the trillium, its seeds excrete an oily substance that attracts ants, which come in droves and eat them.

If the Ted Lake Loop leaves you hungry for more hiking, follow a wide, grassy road leading out of Parking Area 7; it's the Stone Wall Loop. The old road ends at serene Lake Thompson, a man-made impound upon which ducks float and anglers cast their lines. There are plenty of distractions en route. A black snake slithers across the trail, and, a few minutes past it, rustling in the leaves leads to the discovery of a small, yellow-marked box turtle. Left unmolested, this reptile could live more than sixty years. If you're wondering how to tell its age, look at the shell. If it's 5 inches or smaller, the turtle is probably ten years old or younger.

Off either side of the trail, the surrounding forest shows signs of youth. The saplings are skinny and obstruct any clear view. The exception comes a half mile downhill from the parking area, where another overgrown road leads right, into the woods to a fire ring and a massive yellow poplar. Someone, a long time ago, had girdled the tree. A ring incised deep into the trunk would kill the tree slowly.

John Cahill, former president of the Nature Conservancy, once said: "Our society will be defined not only by what we create, but what we refuse to destroy." Staring at this old, grizzly tree, still standing despite repeated attacks to bring it down, brings that sentiment to mind. By saving small pockets of land like Thompson WMA, we acknowledge this is important. And every visit here makes us a community with others who have walked through the woods. As Shakespeare wrote: "One touch of nature makes the whole world kin."

Miles and Directions–Stone Wall Loop

0.0 **START** from Parking Area 7 at the intersection of gravel VA 638 and Freezeland Road. Hike down the chained-off road that drops off the left side of the parking lot. The road is gravel at first, then reverts to dirt and grass.

0.2 Walk straight past a junction with the Appalachian Trail (AT). **Sidetrip:** A right on the AT leads to Manassas Gap Shelter in 3 miles.

0.5 A grass road veers off on the right. Continue straight downhill on the main grass road.

0.6 Continue straight downhill past another grass road that turns right into a clearing. (FYI: There is a fire ring in the clearing and a huge yellow poplar tree that survived a girdling many years ago.)

1.3 The trail levels and on both sides, remnants of stone walls are visible. Within a tenth of a mile, the trail passes a large black locust tree on the right. Continue toward the right on the grass road as an overgrown, unblazed footpath known as Stone Wall Trail branches off to the left.

1.8 The road emerges from the cover of trees. Ahead is a nice view across a valley to a farm on the opposite hill. The trail has the width of a road, but there is only a narrow footpath through waist-high grass.

2.0 Reach Lake Thompson. Backtrack uphill. (FYI: Lake Thompson is stocked with rainbow trout and brown trout. White geese float on the small man-made impoundment. A multitude of butterflies flutter around milkweed. [Road access to the lake is via Virginia Route 688.])

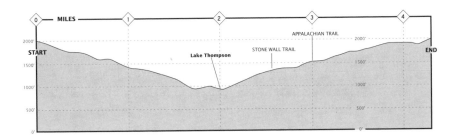

2.6 Turn right onto an overgrown, unblazed footpath known as Stone Wall Trail. Within a few feet, you will cross a stone wall. (FYI: As you climb from Lake Thompson, the black locust tree you passed at 1.3 miles makes a good landmark for where to make this right turn.)

2.7 Detour around the first of several blowdowns.

2.9 Pass by a set of large boulders in the woods to the left and climb steeply.

3.0 Emerge from the woods onto the AT. Walk straight ahead on the singletrack, white-blazed AT. **Sidetrip:** The AT downhill to the right reaches Dick's Dome Shelter in 0.3 mile.

4.1 Pass a huge oak tree on the left. In a few yards, the AT emerges onto a grass road. Turn right and head uphill to Parking Area 7.

4.3 Hike ends at Parking Area 7.

Miles and Directions—Ted Lake Loop

0.0 **START** at Parking Area 4 where a dirt road, the Ted Lake Trail, heads downhill in a southeast direction. The road is wide and clear of obstacles. Blue blazes are few and far between. A hiker should ignore the double-yellow slash marks that appear on trees to the right of the road.

0.7 Turn left onto the white-blazed AT. The trail is a narrow footpath. In a few feet, a spur trail exits right to Manassas Gap Shelter. (FYI: There is a spring near the shelter. Treat any water before drinking it.)

1.2 After a long, steady climb, the AT levels briefly, then undulates around rock outcrops. (FYI: The forest consists of young Eastern hornbeam, oak, and poplar. The large bushes alongside the trail are nannyberry, which flowers in May and June. The small blue-black berries hanging off the red, drooping stalk are edible.)

1.5 Turn left, as the AT intersects and runs concurrent with the Vernon Smith Trail.

1.6 At a three-way intersection, turn left and follow an unmarked road uphill in a southwest direction. Also at this intersection, the AT splits right and descends. The Vernon Smith Trail continues straight and reaches VA 638 at Parking Area 5 in 0.6 mile.

1.9 Emerge from the woods onto the Ted Lake Trail and turn right, uphill, to return to Parking Area 4.

2.0 Hike ends at Parking Area 4.

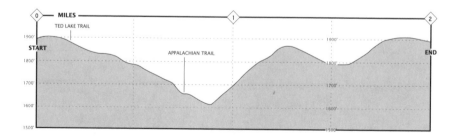

Hike Information

Local Information

Warrenton-Fauquier County Visitor Center, Warrenton, VA, (540) 347-4414, www.fauquierchamber.org.

Local Events/Attractions

The Virginia Gold Cup Races, May, The Plains, VA, (540) 347-2612, www.vagoldcup.com.

The Annual Festival of Virginia Wines, August, The Plains, VA, (410) 267-7205, www.greatmeadow.org.

The Flying Circus Airshow, May through October, Leesburg, VA, (540) 439-8661, www.flyingcircusairshow.com.

The Linden Vineyards, Linden, VA, (540) 364-1997.

The Naked Mountain Vineyard, Markham, VA, (540) 364-1609, www.nakedmtn.com.

Organizations

Virginia Native Plant Society, Boyce, VA, (540) 837-1600, www.vnps.org. Located at Blandy Experimental Farm in the Virginia State Arboretum.

Other Resources

Potomac Appalachian Trail Club (PATC), Vienna, VA, (703) 242-0693, www.patc.net. Call for maps and book orders, cabin rentals, scheduled hikes, and membership.

Honorable Mentions

Northern Virginia

Compiled here is an index of great hikes in Northern Virginia that didn't make the A-list this time around but deserve recognition. Check them out and let us know what you think. You may decide that one or more of these hikes deserves higher status in future editions or, perhaps, you may have a hike of your own that merits some attention.

11 Pohick Bay Regional Park

Conveniently located off I–95, exit 163 north of Woodbridge. Wooded trails, dirt paths, and boardwalks meander along bay inlets. Marsh birds and bald eagles are just two of the sights visible here. Admission charged. Reserved-fee camping available. Call (703) 339–6104. *DeLorme Virginia Atlas & Gazetteer:* Page 77, C5.

12 Mason Neck Wildlife Refuge/Mason Neck State Park

These two areas, nearly adjacent to one other on Virginia Route 242 (exit 163 off I–95), are among the best places in Virginia to see bald eagles. Each park has trails leading to marshes and viewing spots. Both are day-use only. The state park offers picnicking and rest rooms. National wildlife refuge, (703) 490–4979; state park, (703) 550–0362. *DeLorme Virginia Atlas & Gazetteer:* Page 76, C4.

13 Bull Run-Occoquan Trail

A 17.5-mile point-to-point trail along the Bull Run River and the Occoquan Reservoir. The northern trailhead is located off Virginia Route 28, south of I–66 near Manassas. The appreciable length of the trail, combined with stream crossings—some impassable after inclement weather—make this hike a real challenge. Bull Run Regional Park and Fountainhead Park, the county parks that anchor this hike, are open mid-March through mid-November. Call (703) 352–5900. *DeLorme Virginia Atlas & Gazetteer:* Page 76, B2, C3.

14 Burke Lake Park

Located off Virginia Route 123, accessible via exit 169B off I–95. This small park has one trail, an easy 5 miles along the shore of a man-made lake. Vesper Island, in the middle of the lake, is a state waterfowl refuge; bald eagles can sometimes be seen flying overhead. There's also a campground with 150 sites for tents and trailers. Call (703) 323–6600. *DeLorme Virginia Atlas & Gazetteer:* Page 76, B3.

15 Manassas National Battlefield Park

Located less than a mile from I–66; take exit 47 to Virginia Route 234. Park trails pass through the same fields where the North and South fought the first and second battles of Manassas during the Civil War. Scenery harkens back to nineteenth-century farmland. Open daily, dawn to dusk. Admission fee. Call (703) 361–1339. *DeLorme Virginia Atlas & Gazetteer:* Page 76, B1.

16 Rock Creek Park

Located entirely within the District of Columbia, exit 31B off I–495. Hike on a network of easy to moderate trails along Rock Creek, through Civil War battlements, and near old barns and buildings. The Potomac Appalachian Trail Club has produced maps and guidebooks on park trails. Call (202) 282–1062. *DeLorme Virginia Atlas & Gazetteer:* Page 77, A5.

17 Theodore Roosevelt Island

Accessed via a footbridge from a parking area on the northbound lane of the George Washington Memorial Parkway. Easy woodland paths pass rock outcrops on this Potomac River island within view of the nation's capital. Island trails link with two Potomac River trails: Mount Vernon Trail (southbound) and the Potomac Heritage Trail (northbound). Call (703) 285–2598. *DeLorme Virginia Atlas & Gazetteer:* Page 77, A5.

18 Difficult Run Trail

Begin at a parking area on the left side of Virginia Route 193, a half mile before reaching Virginia Route 738 (Old Dominion Drive). This hike follows a stream valley trail more reminiscent of Virginia's mountains than metropolitan Washington, D.C. Call (703) 759–9018. *DeLorme Virginia Atlas & Gazetteer:* Page 76, A3.

19 Riverbend Park

A large county park adjacent to Great Falls Park. There are 5 miles of riverside and wooded uplands trails, including a hillside trail that passes through Appalachian cove-like forest. The nature center is a worthwhile detour. Day-use only. Call (703) 759–3211. *DeLorme Virginia Atlas & Gazetteer:* Page 80, D3.

20 Fairfax Cross-County Trail

A 45-mile multipurpose trail open to walkers, bikers, joggers, and equestrians stretching from the town of Occoquan to the Loudoun County line beyond Riverbend Park. The trail utilizes two stream valleys, Difficult Run in northern Fairfax County and Accotink Creek in lower Fairfax County, and passes through Lake Accotink Regional Park and Colvin Run Mill Park. Portions remain under development, including a proposed extension to Algonkian Park in Loudoun County. Contact Fairfax Trails and Streams for trail updates and maps, (703) 821–0975 or www.fairfaxtrails.org. *DeLorme Virginia Atlas & Gazetteer:* Page 76, C4, B4, A4.

21 Sky Meadows State Park

Located on U.S. Highway 17 in Fauquier County, just south of U.S. Highway 50. At Sky Meadows, the rolling Piedmont meets the Blue Ridge. This former farm has a historic house, hike-in primitive campsites, and wonderful views. Call (540) 592–3556. *DeLorme Virginia Atlas & Gazetteer:* Page 75, A5.

Central Virginia

Aperson traveling west from the Atlantic Coast would, after 100 miles or so, encounter a significant change in the landscape of Virginia. Around Richmond and Fredericksburg, the topography shifts from the flat lowland of the Coastal Plain to the soft hills of the Piedmont. Along rivers, impressive waterfalls mark this line of demarcation, the spot where resistant Piedmont bedrock gives way to sand and clay. A few miles downstream, the largest waterways cease acting as real rivers and instead become estuaries, filled with brackish water and ruled by the ebb and flow of the ocean's tide.

Upland from the fall line—which roughly traces Interstate 95—Virginia's landscape begins a slow march to the Blue Ridge. The term *rolling* Piedmont borders on cliché, but remains the best description of the landscape, which dips and rises in ever-greater folds, until finally giving way to the mountains of western Virginia.

The landscape wasn't always so uniform. Piedmont bedrock shows signs of violent prehistoric mountain-building events. Large basins, some miles and miles in length and width, collected mud and silt that eroded from mountains to the west. This same material later, under intense heat and pressure, became Arvonian and Quantico slate, considered among the highest quality found worldwide. Today, a thick mantle of clay and sediment covers most of the bedrock in the Piedmont. The poverty of exposed rock makes outcrops visible along the Holliday River in Appomattox-Buckingham State Forest a rewarding experience.

Evidence of Native Americans in Virginia dates from 10,000 years ago. In central Virginia, ancestors of the Monacan Indians traveled and camped along the major rivers. The rise of the powerful Indian confederacies, the Powhatan in Tidewater and the Monacans west of the Blue Ridge, left central Virginia as a buffer between them. Both tribes hunted and traveled in this area, but archeologists have yet to identify large, permanent settlements on the scale that existed elsewhere in the state. Artifacts and stone piles near Willis Mountain point to the region possibly holding ritual or ceremonial significance for prehistoric Indians and their ancestors.

European contact in the 1600s brought the rise of the agricultural machine in central Piedmont. Planters grew tobacco. Bateaux laden with tobacco hogsheads, livestock, and grains plied shallow streams such as the Willis and Slate Rivers. With advances in technology came the large-scale mining of gold, iron-ore, coal, slate, and other minerals.

Today those rivers that were the lifeblood of central Virginia commerce serve as natural hiking corridors. Grass and weed-choked floodplains give way to hillsides

Central Virginia

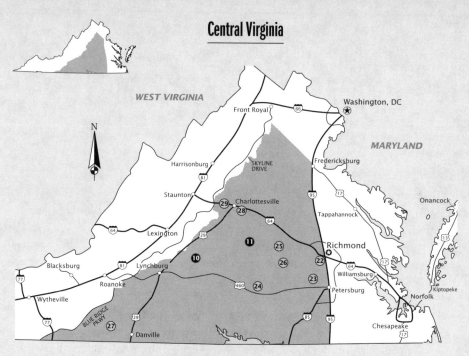

covered with mountain laurel. And where the landscape levels into fields, Virginia pine and black oaks dominate. Yet, due to this history of heavy farming, the overarching feature of central Virginia remains its wide-open landscape, a holdover from days when farmers planted acre after acre of tobacco until the soil failed, only to move west in search of fresh land. State forests created in the 1920s and 1930s have slowly rehabilitated depleted land by managing the growth of timber for commercial use. For people who enjoy the outdoors, this commercial-driven enterprise has a fortunate by-product: pockets of forest that offer quality recreation opportunities.

10 Trout Trail

Hikers are the latest folks to enjoy Holliday Creek in a line stretching back 8,000 years: Native Americans, gold miners, homesteaders, Confederate soldiers, scientists, foresters, and anglers—each found this beautiful stream suited their needs. Today, one of its greatest attributes—the scenery—enjoys protection within the largest of Virginia's state forests, the Appomattox-Buckingham. This prime Piedmont spot has mountain laurel bloom in spring, and the hills and a gorge near Holliday Lake dam defy anyone who equates Piedmont with pastoral. Throw in three unaided stream crossings and you've got an adventure that rivals any found in Virginia's mountains.

Start: From the Woolridge Wayside off Virginia Route 640.

Distance: 6-mile point-to-point.

Approximate hiking time: 4 hours.

Difficulty rating: Moderate due to three difficult stream crossings and occasional bushwhacks.

Trail surface: Dirt forest roads and woodland paths lead hikers along grassy stream banks, a pristine river, and steep slopes, as well as through marshes and a gorge.

Land status: State forest and state park.

Nearest town: Appomattox, VA.

Other trail users: Anglers.

Canine compatibility: Dogs permitted.

Trail contacts: Appomattox-Buckingham State Forest, Dillwyn, VA, (434) 983-2175. Free forest maps and a brochure with a drawing of the Trout Trail.

Holliday Lake State Park, Appomattox, VA, (434) 248-6308. Free brochures on hiking trails in the park.

Schedule: Park and forest open year-round. Hunting is permitted in the state forest. (Mid-November through the first weekend of January is the busiest season.) Holliday Creek is stocked in the fall, winter, and early spring. Catch-and-release rules are in effect October 1 through May 31. Open harvest extends from June 1 to September 30.

Fees/permits: No state forest fee. State park parking fee is $2.00 weekdays; $3.00 weekends per vehicle. Camping is $20.00. A statewide fishing license costs $12.00. A trout stamp, which is required when fishing June 1 to September 30, costs $12.00. Artificial lures only.

Maps: USGS maps: Holliday Lake, VA.

Finding the trailhead: Start Point From Appomattox Court House: Drive 11.8 miles east on Virginia Route 24 from the intersection of U.S. Highway 460 and VA 24. Turn right onto Virginia Route 636 and enter Appomattox-Buckingham State Forest. Pass the forest headquarters on the left. In 2.5 miles, turn right onto VA 640. In 0.8 mile, turn right into the Woolridge Wayside parking area. Park and walk 0.2 mile downhill on VA 640. The trailhead is across the bridge spanning Holliday Creek. *DeLorme: Virginia Atlas & Gazetteer:* Page 45, A7.

Shuttle Point

From Woolridge Wayside: Proceed to Holliday Lake State Park by driving past the trailhead on VA 640, turning right onto Virginia Route 692, and driving 3 miles into the state park. Park near the state park office or bathhouse. *DeLorme: Virginia Atlas & Gazetteer:* Page 45, A7.

Descending to the dam at Holliday Lake.

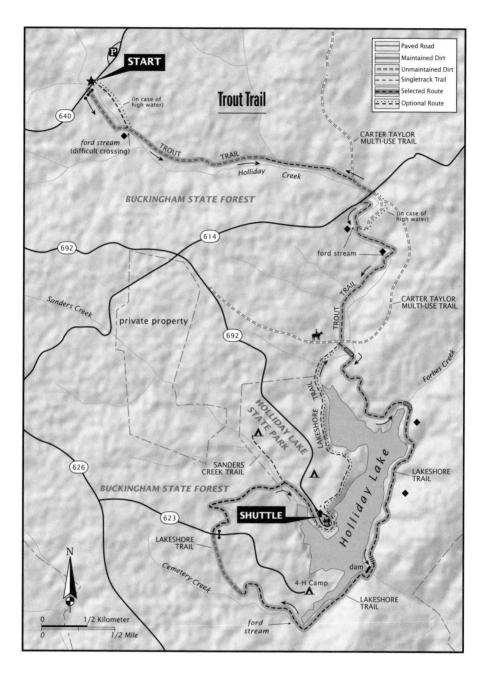

Trout Trail

The Hike

Virginia's Piedmont isn't exactly a hot spot for rocky gorges and deep stream valleys. Yet here you stand on the stream bank of Holliday Creek in Appomattox-Buckingham State Forest, watching water froth, twist, and turn through a narrow cleft between two steep hills. Stream boulders stir up rapids. Off one hillside, a small stream feeds the frenzy with spring runoff.

Watching the water tumble over a small cascade, you might consider how a prospector would view this scenery. The base of a waterfall, it turns out, is a great place to find gold.

Virginia settlers were first in the nation to mine gold. A lode deposit in Spotsylvania County triggered a rush that faltered only when California gold lured miners west in 1848–1850. Around Buckingham County, gold ushered in some high times. Twenty or so mines operated, a few even into the 1900s. One near Dillwyn in Buckingham produced nuggets three pounds in weight, the largest found anywhere in the state. Up the road from Dillwyn, the name of the town Gold Hill speaks for itself—the precious metal was prospected here for a number of years.

Early miners focused on streams such as Holliday Creek, using a technique called *placer* (plas-ser) mining, whereby they panned up sandy streams for gold dust until the trail ran cold. Then they scouted surrounding hillsides, looking for the vein that produced the stream residue. If they found one, they sunk a shaft. Mine sizes varied. The Buckingham Mine in Dillwyn dug 183 feet. The Burnett Mine, also near Dillwyn, needed only 58 feet before hitting gold. After striking a vein, the difficult work of extracting gold began. Workers at the Buckingham Mine crushed 20 tons of ore a day to produce 130 hundredweight (or 208,000 ounces) of gold per year.

Local historians say two placer mines operated on Holliday Creek. No one knows exactly where, although one site holds promise. On a triangle of land where Holliday Creek and the Appomattox River meet, several hand-dug ditches run about 40 yards long. It's consistent with a mining method that excavated old streambeds in search of black sand. This sand "showed color," a prospector's term for indicating gold dust. Today, this possible mine site is valuable, not for undiscovered gold, but rather as a historical and archeological record of this little-publicized era of Virginia history. Unfortunately, both potential mine sites are on private property outside the boundaries of Holliday Lake State Park and the state forest. The closest you'll get to them is when you cross Holliday Lake dam, which stands less than a mile upstream from Holliday Creek's confluence with the Appomattox.

Gold is just one mineral among many Virginia's Piedmont has yielded over the course of European settlement. Upstream from the confluence of the Appomattox River and Holliday Creek, the lake dam marks one end of a long, low ridge. Contained in the bedrock is another rock worth mining—Buckingham slate, considered in the slate industry to be among the highest quality produced in the United States today. Much of the activity centers around Arvonia, a village settled by immigrants of a Welsh town of the same name. Slate carving in Arvonia, Virginia, is an art. Eaves of some homes are trimmed in decorative slate. Tombstones in the cemetery, carved out of slate, are in the shape of household furniture, like beds, couches, and baby cribs. Also in the vicinity of Holliday Lake stands the privately owned Willis Mountain, which is mined for kyanite, a mineral used in heat-absorbing products—like the white ceramic on a motor spark plug. Some people believe wearing a piece of this bluish-white mineral on a necklace or holding it in your hands induces a calm feeling during times of distress and aids meditation. (Kyanite also flakes and crumbles into tiny, sharp points and shards that may cause splinters. This, in turn, will produce a sensation quite opposite that of calm. So be careful if you handle it.)

If crystals aren't your thing, the clear waters of Holliday Lake produce a calming sensation as well. Works Progress Administration (WPA) workers dammed Holliday Creek and formed the 150-acre lake in 1938. Similar public works projects at Bear Creek Lake State Park in Cumberland County, and Twin Lakes State Park in Prince Edward County, served as a source of work for unemployed men during the Great Depression and a means of reclaiming overfarmed, barren land for recreational uses. Conspiracy buffs will enjoy the rumor circulating in Buckingham County about the size and location of Holliday Lake. Some will have you believe this long lake was built as a practice landing strip for amphibious aircraft pilots-in-training. This is undocumented, but still interesting. What's certain is that pike, pickerel, largemouth bass, and blue gill thrive in its water, and anglers are welcome to cast their lines here.

IDENTITY CRISIS How do you spell Holliday? If you're the state park, it's Holliday Lake. If you're the state forest, it's Holliday Creek. If you're the USGS, however, the spelling for both is Holiday—one "l," not two. Even park staff aren't sure if the name derives from a local family or the fact that it's just a great place to spend a holiday.

For years, the United States Geologic Service (USGS) monitored stream flow from a station on Virginia Route 615. The tin shed on the stream's edge belongs to the USGS, as does the cable-and-pulley system that spans the creek. Researchers nicknamed this the *carnival ride*. To gather flow data, workers rode in a small bucket, connected to the cables, above the middle of the stream. From there, they gathered flow- and water-level readings by dipping instruments into the water. Time and again, water quality on Holliday Creek proved so consistently clean that scientists made it a benchmark stream for judging the health of other streams. For this pristine condition, credit goes to the state forest, which has kept the Holliday Creek watershed relatively unaffected by humans since the Great Depression.

An archeological dig at the mouth of Holliday Creek has unearthed Native American arrowheads and pottery shards dating from 8,000 years ago. Signs of permanent settlement—domestication of plants and animals—date back 500 years. Anthropologist Jim Jordan of Longwood College, who supervised excavation of the site, has focused his studies on the lateness of permanent human settlement here, compared with Tidewater Virginia and other regions of the state. Jordon believes that

Crossing Holliday Creek at the backwater of Holliday Lake.

prior to European colonization, the state was split between the Powhatans of eastern Virginia and the Monacans, who laid claim to land west of the James River headwaters. The region we call Central Virginia lay between them and acted as a kind of buffer zone between these sometimes-warring empires. Native Americans traveled regularly through the area, but did not settle the land. Instead, they treated it as a prehistoric *preserve* (or, in modern terms, a *demilitarized zone*) available to both for hunting and fishing. After 8,000 years and so many different uses, Holliday Creek has come full circle, enjoying status today as a preserve of the state.

Miles and Directions

0.0 **START** from a bridge across Holliday Creek on VA 640. The Trout Trail begins on the right side of the stream. A forest chain gate blocks vehicle traffic on the trail, which is an old grass and gravel road. Follow the road downstream. Trout Trail is not blazed, but follows old roadbeds for all but a short stretch.

0.2 The roadbed ends at Holliday Creek. A steep-sided hill on the right forces a stream crossing. Passage during periods of low water is aided by a sandbar that divides the stream into two shallow channels. **Option:** During high water, return to VA 640, cross Holliday Creek on the road, and drop down the embankment to the left stream bank. Thickets and swampy conditions will soon force you left onto a slope scarred by ice storms and beavers. Pick your way across fallen trees, always keeping the stream audible on your right. You'll cross a number of ditches and gullies that dissect the river floodplain before reaching the trail at 0.3 mile. You'll recognize the crossing by the sandbar in the stream. A well-defined roadbed bears left. The trail follows the roadbed.

0.4 (FYI: Easy hiking on a flat road permits some sight-seeing. There are broadleaf maples on this stretch. On the opposite river bank, mountain laurel and small trees cling dramatically to a sheer hillside.)

0.7 A road enters the trail from the left. Continue straight on the Trout Trail.

1.0 The trail reverts to a thin path as the hillside on your left steepens. (FYI: Moss and lichen cover exposed rock on your left.)

1.1 Cross a small tributary of Holliday Creek. (Note: This is a rugged section of trail. Use caution.)

1.3 (FYI: Look closely at exposed rock on your left. It's shot through with small dikes of a white, crystal-like rock. The gray mass is felsic volcanic rock that oozed through crevices

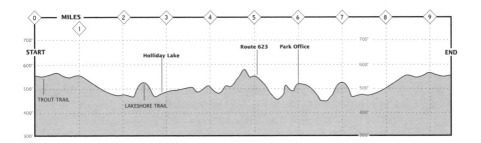

in the Piedmont landscape 800 million years ago. During ensuing periods of metamorphism, the white rock, called pegmatite, shot through the volcanic rock under incredible heat and pressure. Geologists consider this outcrop one of the finer examples of this region's underlying rock strata.)

1.5 Come to a junction with the Carter Taylor Multi-Use Trail. Turn right and walk a few feet to paved Virginia Route 614. Cross the stream on the road and turn left down a gravel road. Avoid a short left-arching spur trail, which leads to a metal shed.

1.7 The gravel road dead-ends at Holliday Creek, forcing another stream crossing. The water is deeper here and there are no sandbars to aid hikers. **Option:** Return to VA 614, cross to the left stream bank, drop off the road, and walk straight until you hit a wide dirt path. Turn right onto the dirt path and follow it back to the river. At the river's edge, turn left and hike downstream.

2.0 Reach the third and final stream crossing. There are no options for a bushwhack here given the steep hillsides on either side of the stream. After crossing, the Trout Trail follows the right bank of Holliday Creek to the backwater of Holliday Lake.

2.5 The Trout Trail ends at the Lakeshore Trail. Turn left onto the Lakeshore Trail and cross Holliday Creek on a wooden footbridge, then turn right. (Note: This junction requires some alert hiking, given that the Carter Taylor Multi-Use Trail passes close by. There are also trails to a fording spot for horses.)

2.9 Pass by a nature observation deck on Holliday Lake.

3.1 Cross a marsh on a boardwalk and climb a set of stairs up a steep hillside. Signs caution hikers of eroded trail conditions ahead. The trail from here is narrow and approaches water level several times.

4.0 Come around the steep side of a hill and drop to the lake dam on a set of very, very steep stairs. (FYI: Look closely on exposed rock for fish scale patterns. The dam is built on a fault where Holliday Creek, over millions of years, cut a path through Arvonian slate. This mica rock is softer than the volcanic rock known to exist in the hillsides around it. The effect is something like bookends. When the soft middle shifts, it creates the scale patterns.)

4.5 Reach the southern tip of Holliday Lake. The trail leaves the lakeshore, crosses Cemetery Creek, and runs up the right stream bank. A 4-H Camp is visible on the right side of the trail. (FYI: If you're interested in tree identification, take a moment to walk the 4-H Discovery Trail. The trailhead is just before you cross Cemetery Creek. Club members built the trail and identified trees typical of this region, such as green ash, bald cypress, American hornbeam, sweet gum, black gum, and willow oak.)

5.1 Reach Virginia Route 623 near the 4-H Camp gate. Walk straight across the road and re-enter the woods. The trail bears right and descends.

5.6 Cross Sanders Creek and turn right onto the orange-blazed Sanders Creek Trail. A right turn will lead you along the lakeshore to bath and shower huts, picnic facilities, and car parking.

6.0 Hike ends at the Holliday Lake State Park ranger office. **Option:** You can make this hike a 9.5-mile loop by continuing on the blue-blazed Lakeshore Trail, which climbs a hill across the road from the ranger station. The Lakeshore Trail intersects the Trout Trail 1 mile from the ranger station. It is another 2.5 miles up Holliday Creek to VA 640.

Hike Information

Local Information

Appomattox Visitor Information Center, Chamber of Commerce, Appomattox, VA, (434) 352-2621, www.appomattox.com. Located in an old train depot.

Local Events/Attractions

Historic Appomattox Railroad Festival, second weekend in October, Appomattox, VA, (434) 352-2621. Food, music, craft, and antiques festival commemorating the donation of the Appomattox train depot to the town by Norfolk Southern Railroad. Today the depot, at 5 Main Street, houses the chamber of commerce and visitor center.

Joel Sweeney Banjo Festival, each fall, Paradise Lake Family Campground, VA, (434) 352-2621. Appomattox native Joel Sweeney was a nineteenth-century banjo maestro—he reputedly added the fifth string on the banjo. He toured Europe extensively and played for England's Queen Victoria. Admission is $5.00.

Appomattox Court House National Historical Park, Appomattox, (434) 352-8987, www.nps.gov/apco/. Park preserves the site where General Robert E. Lee surrendered to General Ulysses S. Grant, an act that formally ended the Civil War. Walking tours, interpreters, and special events commemorate this small village's big role in the war.

Hike Tours

A park interpreter leads nature and history walks and boat trips during summer months. Call (434) 248-6308 for dates and times.

Other Resources

Virginia Department of Game & Inland Fisheries, Farmville, VA, (804) 367-1000, www.dgif.state.va.us. Information on fishing Holliday Creek and places to buy fishing stamps and licenses.

11 Willis River Trail

Cumberland State Forest is the second largest in the state forest system, and the Willis River Trail is the longest hiker–only trail in any state forest. From the flat land along the Willis River, the trail passes through oak and yellow poplar forest, under plantations of Virginia and loblolly pines, and past old farm sites. Beaver keep active in the swamps. There are also signs of turkey and fox in the sand along the river. State forest staff, in keeping with an evolving mission to provide not only harvestable timber but also recreational opportunities, built a primitive campsite in Rock Quarry Natural Area, an improvement that makes this hike a legitimate overnight excursion.

Start: From the dead end on Warner Fire Road, a half mile off Virginia Route 608.
Distance: 15.1-mile point-to-point.
Approximate hiking time: 9-10 hours.
Difficulty rating: Moderate due to length, frequent road crossings, and hard-to-follow stretches of trail along the Willis River.
Trail surface: Encounter woodland paths, dirt forest roads, paved roads, small streams, and hilly terrain with little in the way of high peaks or deep valleys. The river flats are overgrown with grass and shrubs; the hillsides are shaded by hardwoods. Most hillcrests host plantations of loblolly and Virginia pines.
Land status: State forest.
Nearest town: Cumberland Courthouse, VA.
Other trail users: Hikers only.
Canine compatibility: Dogs permitted.
Trail contacts: Cumberland State Forest, Cumberland, VA, (804) 492-4121, www.vdof.org/stforest/index-csf.shtml. Forest headquarters provides hand-drawn maps of the Willis River Trail, plus information on other forest uses. It's recommended you at least inform forest staff of your itinerary, if merely to alert them to the presence of cars at either end of the trail.
Bear Creek Lake State Park, (804) 492-4410, www.dcr.state.va.us/parks/bearcreek.
Old Dominion Appalachian Trail Club, www.odatc.org. This chapter of the Appalachian Trail Conference helped build the Willis River Trail in the early 1980s.
Schedule: Open year-round. Hunting is permitted within the forest, and foresters report heaviest use from mid-November through the first weekend in January. Wear orange blaze during hunting seasons.
Fees/permits: No fees or permits required for the state forest. Bear Creek Lake State Park charges a parking fee ($2.00 weekdays, $3.00 weekends per vehicle) and camping fees ($14.00; $20.00 with hookups per night). There's a $3.00 pet fee at the park.
Maps: USGS maps: Whiteville, VA; Gold Hill, VA.

Finding the trailhead: Start Point
From Cumberland Courthouse: Drive east on U.S. Highway 60 for 1.2 miles and turn left onto Virginia Route 622 (Trents Mill Road). Reach Bear Creek Market in 3.4 miles. Drive past the market and turn right onto Virginia Route 623, which turns from pavement to gravel. After 1.7 miles, turn left onto Virginia Route 624, a paved road, and drive 2.1 miles to the intersection of VA 608. Here, you turn left onto VA 608 and look on the right for Warner Fire Road in 2.2 miles. Turn right

onto the fire road, which is dirt, and drive a half mile to a dead end. You'll recognize the trailhead by the swinging bridge over the Willis River. *DeLorme: Virginia Atlas & Gazetteer:* Page 56, D3.

Shuttle Point

From Cumberland Courthouse: Drive east on US 60 for 1.2 miles and turn left onto VA 622 (Trents Mill Road). Reach Bear Creek Market in 3.4 miles and turn left onto Virginia Route 629. The southern trailhead is located at Winston Lake on VA 629, 1.2 miles past Cumberland State Forest headquarters. (Bear Creek Market, on VA 622, or Bear Creek Lake State Park, on VA 629, offer convenient mid-trail parking.) *DeLorme: Virginia Atlas & Gazetteer:* Page 56, D3.

The Hike

The first thing you should know about the Willis River Trail is this: It's never looked as good it does today. Not in our lifetime, at least.

Sycamores, easily identified by their thick, white-splotched trunks, tower in open, grassy fields along the Willis River. On wooded slopes, oaks, yellow poplar, and beech lend old farmland a shady, deep forest feel. Along old dirt roads, pink-petal mallows peek out of roadside ditches. Taken together, it's land changing from farm to forest, a process that's been under way for seventy years and counting in Cumberland State Forest.

Abusive best describes how farmers once treated the soil here and elsewhere in central Virginia. By the Great Depression, the farm economy of Cumberland and neighboring counties bottomed out. A condition called *plow pan* typified the problem: White clay was compacted into a cementlike state that prevented plow blades from penetrating its surface. Rain couldn't nourish plant roots. Deprived of water, crops and trees shriveled, choked, and died.

When the U.S. government paid pennies on the dollar for this land, it resembled the dust-bowl conditions of the nation's heartland. After Works Progress Administration (WPA) and Civilian Conservation Corps (CCC) workers built roads and dams, Virginia created state forests on the land. On the sides of roads, foresters planted farm and tree demonstration plots. Sleuthing by present-day rangers has revealed square, one-acre stands of oak, poplar, and pines. The plots were used to show landowners not only what trees they could plant, but also how to manage forestland for a sustainable timber harvest. Restoration had begun.

The full benefits of seventy-plus years of restoration are best appreciated on the Willis River Trail. Beavers have laid claim to land along the first mile of the trail. Notice the small channels that crisscross the landscape as it slopes toward the beaver swamp on the left side of the trail. As beavers range farther afield in search of their favorite food—hardwood saplings—they build canals for safe passage. That's one theory to explain the presence of these small drainages. A more likely explanation would be field furrows, planted and replanted so many times they've made indelible marks on the landscape.

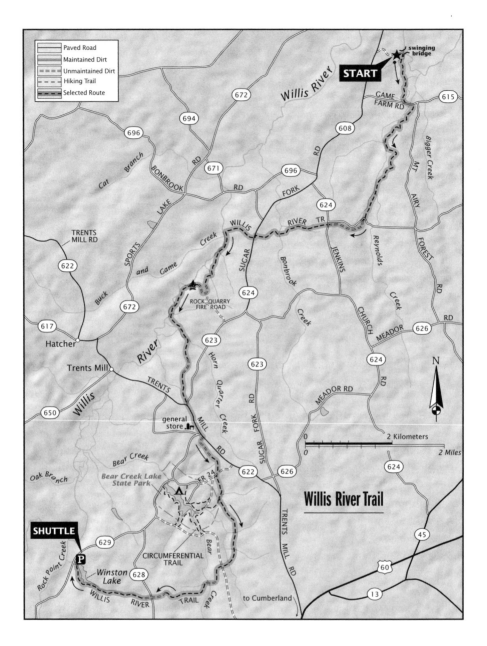

Human handiwork is evident farther along the trail, where plantations of Virginia pine are visible through the forest understory of sassafras and holly. Foresters currently manage pine plots for about thirty-five years and then harvest. Hardwood stands, by contrast, can take seventy to one hundred years to reach maturity. In the case of both types, the lumber is used in state building projects.

Eight miles in from the trailhead, more clues to the land's farming past emerge. In a clearing along the trail, just before you enter a cedar plantation, a large hole to the left indicates a collapsed farm well. Farther afield, weeds cover concrete blocks, once a farmhouse foundation.

Less evident along the Willis River Trail are signs of the river's busy past. At one time, flat-bottom riverboats (or *bateaux*) loaded with livestock and hogsheads of tobacco and/or flour congregated on this stream. The Willis River canal system, designed specifically for this shallow stream, worked most efficiently when four or five boats used a lock at once. Considered a pioneering form of navigation, the Willis River locks employed a wooden flash gate, which linked two stone jetties that stuck out into the river from either bank. Hinged at the bottom, this flash lock fell flat when opened. Boats coasted through the sluice and proceeded downstream. (Upriver navigation was a tad more difficult, relying on the brawn of bateau polers, rather than gravity.) The locks made the Willis River navigable for up to 50 miles from its confluence with the James River. Gristmills and inspection warehouses occupied strategic points on the water route, often near locks. Names of local roads, such as Trents Mill, a few miles past Bear Creek Market on VA 622, reference these long-ago points of commerce.

If you're looking for old locks, brush up on local history and prepare to bush-whack. (What looks like a promising clue near the primitive campsite downhill from Rock Quarry Fire Road is nothing more than a set of stone steps—not the ruins of a lock.)

For all the innovation, commercial use of the river was cyclical. When the channel filled with sediment or wooden flash locks rotted, traffic declined. It revived when local businessmen saw fit to pay for improvements—or petition the state to fund repairs. Yet even when the James River and Kanawha Canal—the main east-west commercial route in central Virginia to which the Willis River linked—was abandoned for railroads in 1880, Cumberland County farmers continued using parts of the Willis River to ship goods to railroad depots. Use declined only when the land could not sustain enough crops to make farming profitable.

Which brings us full circle, to land once misused, now protected and plentiful with trees and wildlife. Your footsteps can roust a turkey, partridge, or deer from pro-tected feeding areas managed by another state agency, the Department of Game & Inland Fisheries. You can walk through forests used by scientists and researchers as laboratories for cultivating genetically improved versions of loblolly pine, white pine, and Virginia pine. Or you can engage in amateur research: Rock Quarry Natural Area, midway along the trail, is one of four natural areas in Cumberland left untouched by forest personnel. Here, nature manages growth. To a forester, it repre-sents chaos, where less valuable hardwoods crowd valuable red and white oak and yellow poplar. For this hiker, it holds some of the wildest, most scenic portions of the Willis River Trail. You be the judge.

Miles and Directions

(FYI: A May 2003 tornado produced many blowdowns that may make hiking the trail a bit more difficult.)

0.0 **START** from the swinging bridge spanning the Willis River at the end of unpaved Warner Forest Road. The trail heads away from the river, entering the woods at the back of a vehicle turnaround. If grass and shrubs obscure the trail, look for yellow slash marks on trees in the woods left of the trail. These mark the forest boundary. The next half mile of trail runs up and down gentle bumps in the landscape and alongside a beaver swamp.

0.3 The trail crosses a small, wet ditch, the first of several.

0.5 The trail begins a run on level ground amid loblolly pines. (FYI: Cumberland State Forest marks the farthest west this pine will grow in Virginia.) On this level stretch, you'll cross four drainages in succession, which makes for some wet walking in spring.

0.7 Reach Virginia Route 615 and turn left, following white blazes on the right side of the road. After crossing Reynolds Creek, turn right to re-enter the woods. The trail runs alongside a beaver swamp on the right, before climbing sharply up to traverse hilly terrain around the marshy bottomland, formed by beaver dams on Reynolds Creek.

1.1 Pass over a very wet section of trail where you cross a small tributary of Reynolds Creek. The trail turns very narrow and eroded. A large log blocks the path. As the trail drops to the level of the stream, it practically disappears in a mess of mud and rocks. This lasts for about 30 yards, until the river floodplain provides more solid ground for walking.

1.2 Swing left away from Reynolds Creek up a cove created by a tributary. Cross the small drainage and turn back toward the river.

1.7 Cross Reynolds Creek. (Note: Steep, eroded stream banks make this a difficult passage during periods of high water. You can wade across or traverse a thick log that clears the river by 5 feet—quite a tightrope walk.)

1.9 Crest a small hill amid a plantation of Virginia pine. (FYI: The climb from the river is an ideal stretch to watch the forest transition from hardwoods [hornbeam, oak, and alder] at lower elevations to pines at the top.) The trail then drops to the river.

2.2 A beautiful, moss-covered log marks the spot where the trail climbs away from Reynolds Creek again. You'll return to the river once more, then depart it for good where the trail turns uphill near two large oak trees. As it climbs, the trail becomes an old forest road and the trees again change from hardwood to pine.

2.6 An old fire road branches off the left side of the trail. Stay straight on the white-blazed Willis River Trail. You'll see a barn and house through the trees on the right.

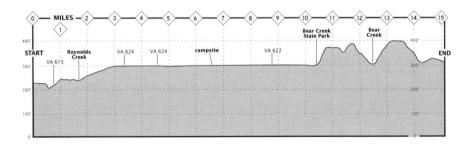

Bottomland along the Willis River.

2.8 Reach a gate and turn right onto a dirt forest road. You'll pass a clear-cut on the right, moments before reaching VA 624.

3.3 Walk straight across VA 624 and re-enter the woods. (The forest boundary is somewhere between the blue house on the right and the trail, so don't stray too far.) As you descend on a singletrack path, a small stream forms on the right, as the terrain, left, changes from field to wooded slope.

3.6 Cross a wet ditch and climb a small hill to avoid getting your feet wet where the stream cuts close to the base of the hill.

3.9 The trail turns sharply left, away from the stream. (FYI: Through the understory of sassafras and witch hazel, you'll make out the border of a pine plantation.) The trail almost reaches the pines, then turns to run parallel to the plantation in a narrow ditch.

4.1 Cross Bonbrook Creek. Look right for white blazes and follow the trail around the base of a hill.

4.5 Barbwire and yellow blazes on trees right of the trail mark the forest boundary. Through the woods on the right is a long white barn.

4.6 Walk straight across VA 624, turn left, and walk up the right side of the road. At a gated forest road with a stone apron, turn right onto a dirt road. In 0.1 mile, turn left and enter the shelter of the woods. Avoid following the forest road straight into a field.

5.1 The trail reaches the Willis River amid a field of tall grass and wildflowers. (FYI: Here, the stream runs a wide, flat course. Its arrowstraight banks suggest it may have been straightened for commercial navigation. Cutting the bends out of the river allowed easier passage for bateaux, which measured 60 feet long and 8 feet wide.)

5.3 Walk on the muddy bottomland along the Willis River. Keep a sharp eye out for the trail as it crosses wet ditches and passes through heavy vegetation. If you lose the trail, tend to the riverbank. You're on the mark if you see a large tree leaning out over the river.

5.5 A blue stripe on a tree marks the boundary of the Rock Quarry Natural Area. (FYI: It's one of four in the Cumberland State Forest. Natural areas are left wild and untouched. The trees here are larger, more mature species than you'll see elsewhere on the trail. The forest subcanopy is also overgrown, an appearance that results if the forest is not thinned.)

5.7 The trail turns left away from the Willis River to climb hilly upland forest in Rock Quarry Natural Area. En route, you'll cross two streams that feed the Willis.

6.1 Enter a clearing and turn left. This old road climbs through plantations of Virginia and loblolly pines.

6.3 Turn right onto Rock Quarry Fire Road. After a few paces, an old road goes left. Continue straight on Rock Quarry to where it dead-ends in a clearing. Here, the trail bears left and takes a steep drop to the Willis River.

6.6 Reach the Willis River and a primitive campsite, comprised of a plywood outhouse and fire ring. If you're passing through, continue past the outhouse and rejoin the trail as it rides a ledge with a steep drop off the right side down to the river flats.

7.0 Pass by a large, dead tree as you descend onto the river floodplain.

7.1 Without the convenience of a double blaze, the trail takes a hard left and the trail widens. This is confusing because a wide path also continues straight ahead. If you miss the left turn, you'll know soon enough—the riverside path peters out in a blaze of vegetation.

7.2 A double white blaze marks the spot where you turn right and the trail reverts to a single-track woods path.

7.4 Reach Horn Quarter Creek and turn left to follow it upstream along the left bank. (FYI: Good spot for lunch or photos or just a quick swim.)

7.6 Cross the stream and climb the opposite bank. The trail will soon convert to a wide road. (FYI: Where the land levels, look for signs of an old farm. There's a crater on the left side of the trail that's likely a collapsed well. In an overgrown field on the right side of the trail, there are piles of concrete blocks, indicating that a house or outbuilding once stood here. The stones are covered in vinca violets.)

7.9 Enter a pine plantation on a wide road. (FYI: Clear-cut ten years ago, this area now hosts 20-foot-tall Virginia pines, which gives you an idea of how fast they grow.) Blazes are scarce here. As you walk out of the woods, continue straight down a corridor through the pines.

8.1 Turn right onto a dirt forest road. In 0.1 mile, another road cuts into the pines on the right. Stay straight. The condition of the road deteriorates into a mess of rocks and mud.

8.4 Turn left off the road onto a singletrack woods path. You're following a stream on the left side of the trail as you climb a gentle hill.

A DICKENS MYSTERY

THIS IS THE GRAVE of a little Child whom God in his goodness called to a Bright Eternity when he was very young. Hard as it is For Human Affection To reconcile itself To Death In any shape (and most of all, perhaps at First In This) HIS PARENTS can even now believe That it will be a Consolation to them Throughout their lives and when they shall have grown old and grey always to think of him as a Child IN HEAVEN and Jesus Called a little Child unto him, and set him in the midst of them. He was the son of ANTHONY AND M.I. THORTON Called CHARLES IRVING. He was born on the 20th day of January 1841, and he died on the 12th day of March 1842. Having lived only 13 months and 19 days.

As you know, Charles Dickens wrote *Oliver Twist, David Copperfield,* and *A Tale of Two Cities*—all literary classics. But did you know he also wrote two tombstone epitaphs? This one is located in Cumberland State Forest.

The deceased was thirteen-month-old Charles Irving Thorton. Dickens was traveling in America at the time of the child's death. Why Dickens wrote the memorial is a mystery. Was he inspired by the death of such a young child? Or, perhaps, was he smitten with the child's mother, as Randolph W. Church speculated in a 1971 article in the *Virginia Cavalcade?* A less romantic and probably more likely theory suggests that Dickens's friend Washington Irving (of "Rip Van Winkle" fame) was close to the mother, and, perhaps, Dickens wrote the epitaph in consideration of this mutual friendship.

All that's known for certain is that the physician who attended the dying child requested that Dickens write the epitaph. Dickens mailed it back from Cincinnati, Ohio, where he was visiting. The marble headstone etched with Dickens's words is located in the state forest on the grounds of Oak Hill, the Thorton family's former homestead.

8.8 Emerge from the woods onto VA 622 and turn left. Cross dirt VA 623 and continue walking up the left side of VA 622 in the corridor cut for the power lines.

9.3 At the intersection of VA 622 and VA 629, cross the road and enter the woods opposite Bear Creek Market. (Look for the right turn into the woods amid loblolly pines.)

9.5 After winding through forest thick with the smell of pine, the trail widens into a road. It will revert to a woods path again after you cross an unmarked forest road running left to right.

10.0 Walk straight across Forest Road 24. A sign at this junction points right to Bear Creek Lake State Park, which is about 0.7 mile downhill. The Willis River Trail re-enters the woods and heads downhill along a stream that cuts a surprisingly deep groove in the Piedmont countryside.

10.4 Pass by state park boundary markers on the right side of the trail. (FYI: After a few steps, a trail leads right to Bear Creek Lake State Park. This unmarked path curves up and around a hill, then drops into a nexus of state park trails. From it, you can access the park's Pine Knob, Lake Shore, and Lost Barr Trails. All lead to swimming and concession areas.)

11.3 Cross Little Bear Creek and head upstream. (FYI: You'll see paw-paw [aka the "false banana" tree] on this stretch of trail. Its peanut-shaped fruit is a food staple for squirrels, raccoons, and birds.)

12.4 Cross Bear Creek. (FYI: WPA work crews dammed the stream to create popular Bear Creek Lake State Park. It was one of seven lakes built in central Virginia between 1935 and 1937 for recreational use.) The trail on the opposite side climbs a hill and becomes an old road.

13.1 Turn left onto dirt Booker Forest Road.

13.3 Cross Virginia Route 628. On the opposite side, the trail descends, gently first, then more steeply, to a small stream. Cross it and bear right to circumvent a hill.

13.7 Cross another stream. (FYI: Both this and the previous stream feed the backwaters of Winston Lake. From this point until you climb a hill and circle Winston Lake, you'll see signs of beaver activity everywhere, namely marsh and felled trees with telltale wood chips piled around the base.)

14.4 Begin your climb out of the lowlands of Winston Lake's backwater to walk along a hillside overlooking the south side of the lake.

14.9 Turn right on a stone pathway constructed by WPA workers.

15.1 Cross a footbridge below Winston Lake Dam and enter a picnic and parking area. This is the southern terminus of the Willis River Trail.

Hike Information

Local Events/Attractions

James River Bateau Festival, mid-June, James River: Lynchburg to Richmond, (434) 528–3950, www.downtownlynchburg.com. A weeklong celebration of a bygone era. Replicas of the bateaux that transported commerce up and down central Virginia rivers and canals in the 1800s travel from Lynchburg to Richmond, powered by volunteers in period costume. Picnics and parties are scheduled along the route in towns such as Columbia and Cartersville.

Honorable Mentions

Central Virginia

Compiled here is an index of great hikes in Central Virginia that didn't make the A-list this time around but deserve recognition. Check them out and let us know what you think. You may decide that one or more of these hikes deserves higher status in future editions or, perhaps, you may have a hike of your own that merits some attention.

22 Belle Isle (Richmond)

This 54-acre island is part of the James River Park System, 450 acres of city-owned parks lining the James River, in the heart of downtown Richmond. From Main Street in downtown, follow signs for Belle Isle and the Valentine Museum. There is a parking lot on Tredegar Street past the museum. A footbridge crosses onto the island from the parking lot. A wide 1-mile loop runs past ruins of iron works and a Civil War prison. More narrow trails explore the interior woodlands. Park closes at nighttime. Call (804) 780–5733 or visit www.ci.richmond.va.us/department/parks_rec/james.asp. *DeLorme Virginia Atlas & Gazetteer:* Page 58, D2.

23 Pocahontas State Park

A Richmond-area park located 5.3 miles west of Chesterfield Courthouse by way of Virginia Route 655 and Virginia Route 780. Beaver Lake is the centerpiece of this 156-acre park. Using woodland hiking trails and paved bike tracks, you can make a 4-mile loop hike. Pocahontas State Forest, featuring the Swift Run Natural Area, surrounds the state park. Reserved-fee camping is available in the state park. Call (804) 796–4255. *DeLorme Virginia Atlas & Gazetteer:* Page 48, A1.

24 Twin Lakes State Park

Located at the heart of the Prince Edward–Gallion State Forest, Twin Lakes is accessed via Virginia Route 613 off U.S. Highway 360. The loop hike around Prince Edward Lake leads from high, forested hills into the marshy flow of Sandy River at the head of the lake. There are beaches and reserved-fee camping is permitted. Call (434) 392–3435. *DeLorme Virginia Atlas & Gazetteer:* Page 46, C2.

25 Powhatan Wildlife Management Area

Centrally located in Powhatan County, 3 miles west of Powhatan Courthouse on U.S. Highway 60. Powhatan WMA's 4,462 acres offer the greatest length and diversity of any preserve in the region. Call (804) 367–1000 or visit www.dgif.state. va.us/hunting/wma/powhatan.htm. *DeLorme Virginia Atlas & Gazetteer:* Page 57, D5.

26 Amelia Wildlife Management Area

Located between U.S. Highways 60 and 360, 25 miles southwest of Richmond. State-owned wildlife management areas cater to the hunters, but they also make nice areas in which to day hike. Amelia WMA has 2,200 acres of pine and hardwood forests set against the Appomattox River. The terrain is rolling and the hiking grade easy. Call (804) 367–1000 or visit www.dgif.state.va.us/hunting/wma/amelia.htm. *DeLorme Virginia Atlas & Gazetteer:* Page 47, A5.

27 Fairy Stone State Park

Located in the foothills of the Blue Ridge Mountains northwest of Martinsville on Philpott Reservoir. The park entrance is 9 miles west of Bassett on Virginia Route 57. Whiskey Run Trail offers a wide view of the parkland and reservoir. Use it to form a 4.7-mile loop with Stuart's Knob Trail and Iron Mine Trail. There's a beach on Fairy Stone Lake and picnic facilities. Fee camping. Call (276) 930–2424. *DeLorme Virginia Atlas & Gazetteer:* Page 26, B2.

28 Rivanna Trails

This emerging greenbelt will eventually circle the entire city of Charlottesville. As of this printing, the Rivanna Trails Foundation has completed more than 18 of the 20 miles planned. A good starting point is at Quarry Park. To get there, take exit 121 off I-64. Turn right onto Monticello Avenue, and take the first left onto Quarry Road. The park is on the left. Call the Rivanna Trails Foundation at (434) 923–9022 or visit monticello.avenue.org/rivanna. *DeLorme Virginia Atlas & Gazetteer:* Page 68, D1.

29 Ragged Mountain Natural Area

This 900-acre nature preserve is a wonderful surprise just west of the Charlottesville city limits. The Ivy Creek Foundation—which also maintains the Ivy Creek Natural Area—manages the area. The 4-mile hiking trail circles the Charlottesville Reservoir, rolling up and down the rugged and heavily forested Ragged Mountains. To reach the Ragged Mountain Natural Area, take exit 124 off I-64, then head north 0.5 mile on the Virginia Route 29 Bypass to the Fontaine Avenue exit. Turn away from Charlottesville onto Fontaine Avenue. After a quarter mile, turn right onto Reservoir Road, which is a narrow, curvy gravel road. Use caution, as the road is popular with local joggers. The parking lot is on the right, approximately 2 miles down the road, just before the entrance to Camp Holiday Trails. Dogs are not permitted on the trails. Visit on-line at monticello.avenue.org/RMNA.html. *DeLorme Virginia Atlas & Gazetteer:* Page 67, D7.

Shenandoah National Park

I n the 1920s, when the government proposed a national park along the spine of Virginia's Blue Ridge Mountains, wilderness purists scoffed. A century of farming and logging had left a legacy of barren soil and mountain slopes scarred with clear-cuts. Wildlife had dwindled to near extinction. It irked some that so much time and effort would be spent on such a depleted landscape.

Oh, if the skeptics could see Shenandoah National Park today.

In a testament to nature's healing power, scars of the park's past have all but disappeared. Shenandoah is rightfully counted as one of the crown jewels in our country's national park system. Long and thin, it measures 75 miles from Front Royal in the north to Rockfish Gap in the south. Within its boundaries are some of Virginia's finest forests. From overlooks, on a clear day, views stretch east to Washington, D.C., and west into West Virginia. You're as apt to see a bear or deer amble across Skyline Drive as you are another human. That's not incidental. Black bears are a park success story, having rebounded from near extirpation to more than 300 in number.

On the mountaintops, a new generation of oaks and hickories has replaced the oak-chestnut forest that provided a livelihood for so many mountain dwellers. Hemlocks rise out of deep stream valleys. Waterfalls come in all shapes and sizes, from the reckless fury of a spring run on Big Devil Stairs to the free-form drops along popular day hikes like Whiteoak Canyon.

Above all are the mountains. Approached from the east, the Blue Ridge sweeps skyward underlaid with granite that formed more than one billion years ago—before recorded life on earth—making the Blue Ridge one of the oldest mountain ranges on earth. Basalt lava flows and metamorphic Catoctin greenstone indicate a violent prehistoric past when, deep in the bowels of the earth, heat and pressure formed new rocks from old, then thrust them upwards to form the mountains we see today. So large a barrier did these mountains pose to colonists in Virginia that it bred two distinct cultures: a land-owning aristocracy on eastern Piedmont and Coastal Plains, and a Scots-Irish farm culture in the western valleys and ridges. Today, the only restriction to travel is your imagination and leg power. Hundreds of miles of trails spread through the park and its 93,000 acres of designated wilderness. Each trail invites the traveler to step from the car and explore what lies beyond what the eyes can see.

Shenandoah
National Park

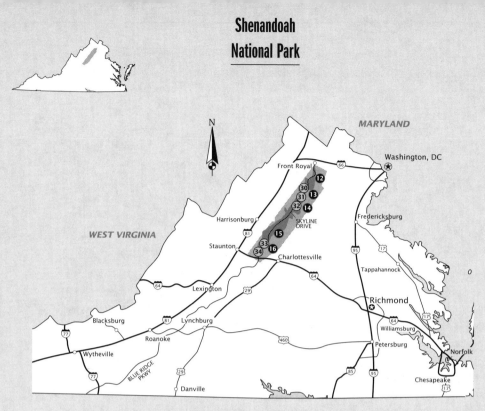

The Hikes	**Honorable Mentions**
Bluff Trail/AT Loop **12.**	30. Jeremy's Run
Hazel Mountain **13.**	31. Nicholson Hollow
Old Rag **14.**	32. Whiteoak Canyon
Rocky Mount/Gap Run **15.**	33. Big Run Portal–Rockytop Loop
North Fork Moormans River **16.**	34. Riprap Hollow–Appalachian Trail Loop

12 Bluff Trail/AT Loop

Like so many of the park's popular trails, the first—and most often visited—feature of this hike is a series of waterfalls within easy reach of Skyline Drive. Big Devil Stairs tumbles down Mount Marshall on rock shelves and outcrops worn out of ancient lava flows. Yet something bigger and a bit older on the geologic timeline awaits up the Bluff Trail, an enticing destination aptly named The Peak. This steep-sided mountain, crowned with billion-year-old granite, measures just under 3,000 feet in elevation. The rugged ascent—1,000 feet in just over a half mile, on a trail no longer maintained by the park service—makes it one of Shenandoah's lesser known, but more-demanding climbs.

Start: From the Gravel Springs parking area on Skyline Drive.

Distance: 15.4-mile loop.

Approximate hiking time: Overnight.

Difficulty rating: Difficult due to distance and the fact that the trail up The Peak is steep, unmarked, and overgrown.

Trail surface: Hike rocky singletrack paths, old forest roads, and abandoned trails through the cascades and falls of Big Devil Run and enjoy the breathtaking views approaching and from The Peak.

Land status: National park.

Nearest town: Front Royal, VA.

Other trail users: Cross-country skiers.

Canine compatibility: Leashed dogs permitted (leash can be no longer than 6 feet).

Trail contacts: Shenandoah National Park, Luray, VA, (540) 999–3500, www.nps.gov/shen.

Schedule: Open year-round. Campfires prohibited except in established fireplaces. Skyline Drive may close without advance warning due to inclement weather. Portions of this road may be closed at night from early November to early January to discourage poaching. All facilites open mid-May through October. Limited services rest of year.

Fees/permits: Entrance fee: $10 per vehicle, valid for seven days; annual pass: $20. Free backcountry permits, available at ranger stations between sunrise and one hour before sunset, are required. Before visiting, review backcountry regulations, which cover such issues as group size, where to camp, and waste disposal. Call (540) 999–3500 for regulations. To fish in Shenandoah National Park (SNP), anyone age sixteen or older must have a Virginia state fishing license. Five-day nonresident licenses cost $6.50 and are available at Panorama Restaurant, Big Meadows, and Loft Mountain. If you're a nonresident, age twelve or older, you must have a Virginia license.

Maps: USGS maps: Chester Gap, VA. PATC maps: Map #9. Shenandoah National Park Northern District ($5.00).

Finding the trailhead: From Front Royal: Travel south on U.S. Highway 340 from the intersection of Virginia Route 55 and US 340 in downtown Front Royal. In 0.3 mile, turn left onto Skyline Drive. In 0.5 mile, pass the park entrance booths. Drive south on Skyline Drive to the Gravel Springs parking area between mileposts 17 and 18, on the left (east) side of the road. There is parking for ten cars. If the lot is full, consider parking at Range View Overlook (0.6 mile north on Skyline Drive) or Gimlet Ridge Overlook (0.8 mile south on Skyline Drive). *DeLorme: Virginia Atlas & Gazetteer:* Page 74, B3.

The author on a rocky outcrop atop The Peak.

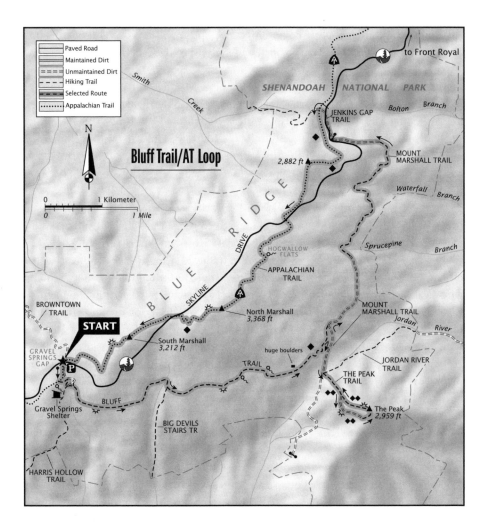

Bluff Trail/AT Loop

The Hike

Springtime in the Blue Ridge Mountains begins not with green leaves, but with flowering trees. Lavender, white, pink, and yellow buds overflow their small calyx and coat charcoal-shaded branches with color. Tree buds appear first on warmer, southwest facing hills and in moist creases in the mountain slopes. As April turns to May, the day lengthens and temperatures warm. The ornamental redbud—a tree preferred by George Washington over even Virginia's official tree, the flowering dogwood—strikes a note by filling its moist soil habitat with a mix of lavender, purple, and pink buds. Dogwoods, habitual to dry slopes, follow with showy white petals, cloven and red-tinged. Later in May, white and pink cups burst from the dark evergreen of mountain laurel. By June, this spring symphony will drop into anonymity. Sunlight-gobbling oaks, elms, and poplars will leaf out and overshadow all else. In these still-cold days of April and early May, though, the small trees shine as stars of the landscape.

The Bluff Trail along the east flank of Mount Marshall is hardly the only place in Shenandoah National Park to catch spring's colorful performance. The trail does, however, offer a side bonus in spring—great views down the Blue Ridge onto the small farms and crossroads of the Blue Ridge foothills. The narrow and sometimes uneven route rises to three distinct overlooks with vistas onto a wide, pastoral valley. Each view only whets the appetite for what lies ahead on top of The Peak (2,959 feet).

As seen first from the Bluff Trail, The Peak stands alone, separate from the main trunk of the Blue Ridge Mountains. The path to the summit fell off the park's list of maintained trails about a decade ago. USGS topographic maps still show the route, and a sharp-eyed hiker will find the trailhead a few paces southeast of the junction of Mount Marshall and Jordan River Trails. Just minutes into your climb up The Peak and the challenges are evident: First a steep pitch, without benefit of switchbacks, then fallen trees and overgrown trail; finally, poor or nonexistent trail markers. Locals nicknamed this mountain Little Bastard. From first glimpse to final weary steps, the name fits. The exposed rock at the summit is charnockite, a billion-year-old granite found the world over. Joseph Charnock, the Englishman for whom the rock is named, founded the city of Calcutta, India. His tombstone is a charnockite rock. Legend says the explorer died from injuries when he tripped over a large chunk of this rock and struck his head. True or not, it serves as a timely reminder as you pick your way over the rough, exposed charnockite boulders descending The Peak. Watch your step!

The Peak once belonged to a family, the Millers, who owned it as part of their 6,000-acre mountain estate. For a time, they worked the tanbark trade. Workers stripped bark off chestnut trees and, using the roads we hike on today, drove mule-pulled carts across Mount Marshall to a tannery in Browntown. The process of turning animal hides into leather required the tannin found in the bark of chestnut and oak trees (also found, in smaller doses, in acorns, coffee, and tea). Tanning was a smelly, dirty job. After grinding the chestnut bark, a tanner mixed bark with water and submerged animal hides in the concoction. Over a period of months, the tannic mixture cured the hide, making it leather. Until the blight of the early 1900s, the American chestnut was preferred for this process because of its high tannic content.

The road that runs along The Peak's south flank is a remnant of the tanbark trade, but today it's hard to imagine anything but foot traffic on it. Fallen trees impede progress at every turn. Thickets of mountain laurel grow off the steep-sided slopes and grass has overgrown the wheel ruts. As you climb through brush, violet pinwheeled periwinkle pokes through last fall's leaf debris, its roots spreading across the dry slope. Closer to the summit, bloodroot, great chickweed, and liverwort splotch the woods with white blossoms. The chickweed practically begs for attention, growing in large tufts that make it attractive to the butterflies that flock to its red-tipped stamens.

There are no chestnut trees left in Shenandoah National Park, or none that could produce bark in the quantity it once did. The chestnut blight stifles tree growth and young chestnuts die before they can grow more than head-high. There are, however, plenty of oak trees. Hickory has replaced chestnut as a companion tree. Mountain laurel is ever-present in the understory. There are dogwoods, witch hazel, and spice-bush as well. Witch hazel deserves mention, if only for how it reproduces. When the shrub's seedpods dry, they burst and release two seeds that can fly outward 30 feet. This not only explains why witch hazel seems omnipresent, but also confounds an old saying about seeds not falling far from the tree. Less reliable are claims that a forked witch hazel branch functions as a divining rod, leading a person to under-ground water sources. If by chance it does, credit luck, not witchcraft. The shrub takes its name from the Old English word wych, meaning "flexible."

The vistas off Bluff Trail spread east over the Blue Ridge foothills and Piedmont. Four mountains fill the horizon: Keyser, Jenkins, Wolf, and The Peak. Their presence illustrates just how complicated Blue Ridge geology can be. Here, within a few miles, stand mountains with marked differences in shape, not to mention rock. Mount Marshall is young—its bedrock is basalt lava, formed by a series of lava flows that oozed from the earth's crust about 550 million years ago. The Peak and its neighbors are old, weathered stubs of resistant granite that date from a billion years ago. The valley between them is more than the route of some picturesque stream. Beneath its crust lies a geologic fault. Faults, by their very nature, slip. That movement breaks rocks, and, over a period of millions of years, the land overlying them collapses. Water, seeking the easiest route downhill, finds the groove and contributes to fur-ther erosion. A crease becomes a valley. What's left? Mount Marshall and The Peak, standing like two prizefighters on either side of an imaginary line.

TIP Bring a shovel! Proper disposal of waste in SNP backcountry means depositing solid human waste in a hole at least 6 to 8 inches deep and 200 feet from water, camp, and park trails.

Miles and Directions

0.0 **START** from the Gravel Springs parking area on Skyline Drive. From the trail board, follow the white-blazed Appalachian Trail (AT). It parallels a yellow-blazed fire road on the left for about one-tenth of a mile.

0.1 Turn left at a concrete post and follow a narrow, blue-blazed dirt path.

0.4 Bluff Trail empties onto a fire road. Turn left and look immediately on the right side of the road for a concrete post and the yellow-blazed Bluff Trail. A huge oak tree helps mark the junction. (FYI: In this clearing stands the PATC's Gravel Springs Hut. A different concrete post marks Gravel Springs, a dependable, year-round water source. Treat any water you take from the spring.)

0.5 Pass a horse trail that enters Bluff Trail on the left.

0.6 Harris Hollow Trail intersects the Bluff Trail from the right. It descends to the Rush River and the park boundary, eventually reaching a parking area on Virginia Route 622.

1.2 As the trail arcs left following the contours of Mount Marshall, look to the right for views of The Peak.

1.6 Reach a junction with the new Big Devils Stairs Trail on the right. It follows a rocky, sometimes steep course for 0.8 mile to the park boundary. **Sidetrip:** For a bushwhack, retrace your steps along the Bluff Trail, recross Big Devils Stairs, and scan the woods downslope for an old trail. It is obscured by downed trees and may be hard to find, but it's well worth it. Rugged, steep, and wet, this old trail follows Big Devils Stairs to the park boundary; oftentimes, trail and stream are one route. Once at the park boundary, turn left and follow red paint slashes across the stream to the new trail. Turn left and head back up to the Bluff Trail. The new Big Devils Stairs Trail rises above the creek, following a ridge.

3.0 (FYI: Walk past boulders the size of small houses, remnant leftovers of a freeze-thaw cycle during past ice ages that loosened boulders and sent them crashing down the mountain slope.)

3.3 Begin a descent to Mount Marshall Trail over a series of steep switchbacks. Before the drop, look for some good campsites on the right side of the trail.

3.6 Junction with Mount Marshall Trail. This was once a wagon road rising from the Rush River to Jenkins Gap. Wagon wheel ruts are still noticeable. Turn right onto the Mount Marshall Trail and follow yellow blazes downhill.

4.0 The Jordan River Trail intersects with Mount Marshall Trail. Walk 18 paces past this junction, all the while scanning the woods on your left for the abandoned trail leading up The Peak. It helps if you avoid looking for any established trailhead, instead peering deeper into the woods to see signs of a fairly well-worn path. (Note: If you walk past a metal USGS sign on the left side of the Mount Marshall Trail, turn around—you've missed the trail.)

4.3 After a steep climb unaided by switchbacks, The Peak Trail splits. Bearing right, it follows an overgrown tanbark road thick with tall grass and blowdowns. Straight ahead, the trail continues its assault up the mountain slope. Both trails meet at the top, but the right trail offers respite and some good views. Turn right.

4.8 As you arc left around the mountain, notice the terrain on your left change from steep, nearly vertical, to a gentler slope. Begin looking for an orange flag on a tree branch, about eye height, on the left side of the trail. This is your best marker for a hard left turn

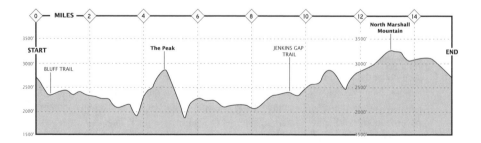

Hikers consult their map along the Bluff Trail.

that takes you off the road and back onto a singletrack woods path for the final 230 feet of climbing. This turn is not well marked, but blue blazes will reappear on trees as you climb. (FYI: The Peak is comprised of a 2,959-foot summit and a lesser peak to the south.) If you're still hiking on the road when it intersects a saddleback between two knobs, you've missed the turnoff. At this point, you can turn left and follow the ridgeline north to reach The Peak's true summit, or retrace your steps along the road and look for the turnoff.

5.1 The Peak summit.

5.5 The old tanbark road enters from the left. Continue straight downhill.

5.8 The Peak Trail junctions with Mount Marshall Trail. Turn right and pass the Jordan River Trail, which enters from the right side.

6.2 The Bluff Trail enters from the left. **Option:** A return on the Bluff Trail to Gravel Springs parking area makes a 9.8-mile hike. Continuing past the Bluff Trail, Mount Marshall Trail climbs in and out of two river drainages, Sprucepine Branch and Waterfall Branch.

9.5 Reach a red forest gate. Turn right onto yellow-blazed Jenkins Gap Trail. It descends along a steep slope through hardwood forest, then rises to meet Skyline Drive at Jenkins Gap Overlook. Cross Skyline Drive and follow the Jenkins Gap Trail, which is now a dirt road, to an intersection with the AT in 0.1 mile.

10.1 Turn left onto the white-blazed AT, which is a singletrack footpath. It climbs steeply for 1 mile to cross a 2,882-foot unnamed knob, then descends to the flat terrain of Hogwallow Flats.

11.7 Cross Skyline Drive.

12.3 Pass a piped spring on the left side of the trail. (FYI: Treat any water you take from this spring.)

13.2 Cross the highest point on North Marshall at 3,368 feet of elevation. (FYI: There are no views from the summit; vistas over the Shenandoah Valley present themselves as you hike down into a gap between North Marshall and South Marshall.)

13.8 Cross Skyline Drive.

14.3 Reach the top of South Marshall at 3,212 feet. As with North Marshall, views are limited until rock outcrops open on the right side of the trail as you make a steep descent.

15.4 Reach a junction of the AT and the Browntown Trail, which descends off the west flank of the Blue Ridge. Turn left and cross Skyline Drive to enter the Gravel Springs parking area.

Hike Information

Local Information
Front Royal Visitors Center, Front Royal, VA, (800) 338-2576, www.ci.front-royal.va.us.

Local Events/Attractions
Wildflower Weekend, May, Shenandoah National Park, Luray, VA, (540) 999-3582, www.snpbooks.org. Shenandoah National Park Association volunteers lead hikes from Big Meadows.

Lodging
Quality Inn-Skyline Drive, Front Royal, VA, (540) 635-3161, www.qualityinnfrontroyal.com.

Park lodges at Skyland (Mile 41.7) and Big Meadows (Mile 51) and cabins at Lewis Mountain (Mile 57.5) are seasonal. Skyland is open late March through October; Big Meadows opens in mid-May and closes in October. Call (540) 999-3500 for information.

Reserved campsites are located at Matthews Arm (Mile 22.1), Big Meadows (Mile 51), Lewis Mountain (Mile 57.5), and Loft Mountain (Mile 79.5). For campground reservations, call (540) 999-3500.

Backcountry trail huts (seven) and **cabins** (six) are operated by the PATC. For reservations, call (703) 242-0693. You must file a responsibility statement with the club before renting. Applications may be downloaded from their Web page and mailed to their Vienna headquarters.

Restaurants
Big Meadows Restaurant, Shenandoah National Park, VA, (540) 999-2221. Big Meadows (Mile 51.2) features a full-service

restaurant and is open mid-May through the first weekend in November.

Big Meadows Wayside, (540) 743-5108, is open late March through November.

Panorama Restaurant, Shenandoah National Park, VA, (540) 999-2265. At Thornton Gap, the Panorama Restaurant (Mile 31.5) serves breakfast, lunch, and dinner starting mid-May through the first weekend in November.

Skyland Restaurant, (Mile 41.7), Shenandoah National Park, VA, (540) 999-2211. Skyland features a full-service restaurant and is open late March through November.

Hike Tours

The PATC sponsors trips in the park. Call (703) 242-0693.

SNP's Education Office. Sponsors field seminars on fly-fishing, bird identification, land management, painting, butterfly identification, and environmental threats such as air pollution. Call (540) 999-3489.

Other Resources

Potomac Appalachian Trail Club (PATC), Vienna, VA, (703) 242-0693, www.patc.net.

Shenandoah National Park Association, Luray, VA, (540) 999-3582. Publishes guidebooks, maps, brochures, and CDs on the history, flora, and fauna of Shenandoah National Park. Co-sponsors events in the park, such as Wildflower Weekend and the Christmas Bird Count.

13 Hazel Mountain

Hazel Mountain and Sam's Ridge once offered a sizable mountain community all the tools and products for a decent living. Today, it draws people for its natural beauty. At Hazel River Falls, the stream drops 30 feet into a pool ringed by tall cliffs in the shape of a natural amphitheater. From here, a trail climbs to the heights of White Rocks, before dropping back to the river and more scenic cascades. Throughout the area, a sharp-eyed hiker will spy evidence of mountain settlers. Trails follow old roads used to transport farm products, and old fields, apple orchards, and home foundations are visible.

Start: From the trailhead at the Meadow Springs parking lot.

Distance: 10.0-mile loop.

Approximate hiking time: 5 hours.

Difficulty rating: Moderate due to steep climbs along White Rocks and unaided stream crossings across the Hazel River.

Trail surface: Dirt footpaths and old wagon roads lead to waterfalls and rock overhangs at Hazel Falls, views off White Rocks, streamside trails along the Hazel River, and an old homesite on Sam's Ridge.

Land status: National park.

Nearest town: Luray, VA.

Other trail users: Hikers only.

Canine compatibility: Leashed dogs permitted (leash can be no longer than 6 feet).

Trail contacts: Shenandoah National Park, Luray, VA, (540) 999-3500, www.nps.gov/shen.

Schedule: (See Hike 12: Bluff Trail/AT Loop.)

Fees/permits: (See Hike 12: Bluff Trail/AT Loop.)

Maps: USGS maps: Thornton Gap, VA; Old Rag Mountain, VA.
PATC maps: Map #10: Shenandoah National Park Central District ($5.00).

Finding the trailhead: From Luray: Drive east on U.S. Highway 211 for 8.8 miles. Turn left onto Skyline Drive access road at the Thornton Gap entrance station. Proceed south on Skyline Drive. Park at the Meadow Springs parking area on the left (east) side of Skyline Drive between mileposts 33 and 34. A concrete post at the back of the parking lot marks the start of Hazel Mountain Trail. *DeLorme: Virginia Atlas & Gazetteer:* Page 74, C2.

The Hike

To my considerable disappointment, Mr. Bear didn't stick around to answer questions about life on Sam's Ridge. He saw me before I saw him, and my view constituted his posterior ambling into the brush. A bear in the wild ranks as one of Mother Nature's more fleeting encounters (gaping at the bear from your car on Skyline Drive does *not* count). But what adrenaline!—my imagination worked overtime. Would the bear circle back and track us to our tent? Did bear reinforcements lie in waiting nearby? Mentally, I prepared myself for a late night banging pots around a bonfire.

Then I tripped. Rocks in the trail are a definite hazard if you're daydreaming. Abandoning the trail, I followed Mary past small shrubs and creeper vines toward a

Checking a map on the Hazel Mountain Trail.

patch of uneven ground. An iron stove and a blue-and-white specked pail lay partly buried. Faint markings of an old home foundation were visible. Glancing skyward, I commented that of all the homesites scattered around Hazel Mountain, this spot surely qualified as prime real estate. Views carried east across the Hazel River to White Rock's four distinct peaks. A thick mat of green broad-leafed plants crowded a nearby spring. Hazel Mountain Road, a main route across the Blue Ridge in the 1800s, passed just a half mile up the trail. Mary listened, then turned and said simply: "It feels like there's a ghost around here."

A hike around Hazel Mountain (you never actually *climb* this 2,880-foot mountain) runs with ghosts of mountain settlers from beginning to end. The initial descent to the Hazel River passes by hidden ruins of settler homes, and patches of apple trees indicate old orchards. As recently as 1900, the trail itself was a busy thoroughfare through Thornton Gap; a church and school stood at the junction of Sam's Ridge and Hazel Mountain Trails. White Rocks Trail and Sam's Ridge Trail were old roads as well. On White Rocks Trail—where it arcs right around a boulder field—the landscape to the right side looks suspiciously like an overgrown field. On Sam's Ridge, where we found a home foundation, there also stood a fruit tree, a twisted piece of metal stove, and a pile of rocks—each a ghostly sighting of a past life in the mountains.

In the black-and-white photos of that period, mountain settlers rarely smile. But to say theirs was a hardship is misleading. Certainly by our modern standards it was hard. Fireplaces provided the only heat during cold winter months. One personal recounting of a season spent on the Blue Ridge describes how blankets froze where the sleeper's breath touched it. Otherwise, life revolved around subsistence farming. Warmer months found men and women outdoors, working fields, cutting wood, planting garden plots. Kids attended school in between chores. Small garden plots supplied most of a family's organic food; larger fields were sown with corn, rye, or oats to be sold in town. Through the 1800s, Thornton Gap was a busy thoroughfare. A mill complex on the east side of the mountain ground corn and cut lumber. A blacksmith was located here, and a distillery, too. On the western flank of the Blue Ridge, leading to Luray, a tannery operated.

This was the age of the chestnut tree. Once the dominant tree of the Southern Appalachians, the American chestnut supplied wood for homes, nuts for eating, and bark for tanning. As the nuts ripened, kids would stand under the trees throwing rocks into the branches, trying to shake loose the round, burry fruit. Tea from the leaves, mixed with honey, made a natural cough syrup. In fall, dry leaves were gathered and stuffed in mattresses (they called these "talking beds" for the noise they made). The tree bark proved most profitable. Tanners chopped, ground, and mixed bark with water to form a thick, watery, acrid-smelling stew. Animal hides were layered in vats filled with this liquid. Over the course of a year or so, tannic acid—a harsh, bitter, yellowish substance plentiful in the chestnut tree bark—leached into the animal hide and cured it. As you climb through the gap between Hazel and Catlett Mountains on the Sam's Ridge Trail, it's hardly a stretch to imagine a wagon loaded with sheets of chestnut tree bark en route to the tannery near Luray, driver perched atop the running board.

Coincidence is sometimes unsettling. In 1900, plants imported from Japan to a New York City zoo contained a blight that would destroy the mature American chestnut population within forty years. In 1925, President Hoover proposed a national park along the Blue Ridge south of Front Royal. In the fall and winter of 1931–1932, the two events—the chestnut blight and construction of a national park—converged on the upper slopes of Hazel Mountain, Catlett Mountain, and other peaks in the northern Blue Ridge. For months, standing dead chestnuts shimmered ghostly, their bark stripped, the wood bleached white. At a time when mountain residents were facing displacement and relocation for a new national park, the tree that had provided sustenance in so many ways was dying as well.

Seventy-plus years later, Shenandoah National Park faces another tree crisis. This time, it's the Eastern hemlocks, a mighty tree visible near the junction of White Rocks and Hazel Mountain Trails. Exposure to years of air pollution and the

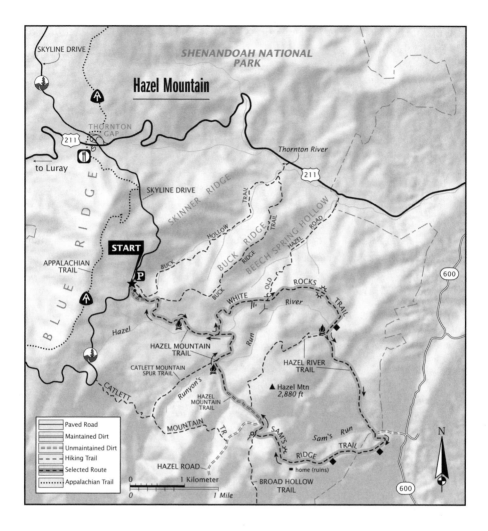

Hazel Mountain

SHENANDOAH NATIONAL PARK

droughts of the late 1980s have weakened hemlocks. This makes them vulnerable to blight, specifically to the hemlock woolly adelgid. The microscopic organism coats the underside of hemlock needles with millions of white sacs. Defoliation results, and, from that point, the tree's death is assured within a year or two. The rate of decline of the hemlock population in Shenandoah National Park is alarming. Ten years ago, 75 percent of all hemlocks in the park had 90 to 100 percent of their foliage. In 1995, only 4.8 percent met that threshold. Rangers at Shenandoah predict that without a deterrent, large stands of old-growth hemlock will be a thing of the past within several years. The current defense strategy is costly but effective. It involves spraying trees with an insecticidal soap, in tandem with using an injectable insecticide. Certain hemlocks have been targeted as significant—naturally, culturally, or historically—and the park's goal is to treat and protect six distinct stands of high-elevation hemlocks. These include ones at Skyland and Big Meadows, which will someday serve as seed sources for hemlock restoration.

Recent research has focused on a promising bio-control agent, *Pseudoscymnus tsugae,* a ladybird beetle that preys on the adelgid. This is not, however, a viable option at Shenandoah due to the late stages of infestation and tree mortality rates, park rangers say. Areas that are just now showing signs of adelgid infestation, like Great Smoky Mountains National Park, stand a better chance with this bio-control measure because there is still time to build the population of ladybird beetles needed in the wild to effectively combat the adelgid.

I don't believe in specters, but I had to agree with Mary as we climbed back to Skyline Drive: There was an unsettling feeling in the air on Sam's Ridge, in the vicinity of old homesteads, and along the Hazel River, where we stared at the old hemlocks. The ghosts of people and trees—not the haunting kind—just silent reminders of how time marches on.

Miles and Directions

0.0   **START** at the concrete post labeled HAZEL MOUNTAIN ROAD. Almost immediately, the blue-blazed Buck Hollow Trail branches off left. Continue straight on the yellow-blazed Hazel Mountain Trail, which is an old dirt road.

0.4   Buck Ridge Trail, marked by a concrete post, enters from the left. About 50 paces past here is an unmarked campsite on the right of Hazel Mountain Trail.

1.0   Hazel Mountain Trail begins paralleling the Hazel River, which is audible to your right. (FYI: This is not an open-harvest stream and all fish caught must be released.)

1.4   Hazel Mountain Trail junctions with White Rocks Trail. Turn left and follow the blue blazes of White Rocks Trail.

1.7   (FYI: White Rocks Trail begins a long curve right, skirting a spot that shows evidence of an old settlement or field. Trees are sparse or young growth. Shrubs and vines run riot here and dominate the understory. It was common for settlers, when clearing fields, to pile the rocks or make stone fences. Remnants of both are visible.)

2.1   **Sidetrip:** An unmarked trail breaks right through a wall of mountain laurel that has flanked the trail for the last three-tenths of a mile. Follow it, and you'll drop steeply to a waterfall on Hazel Creek with a rock overhang on the opposite bank. This is not the popular Hazel Falls, but it's a pretty spot that might be less crowded in summertime.

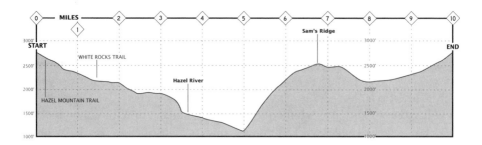

2.2 **Sidetrip:** Enter into a "four-corners" junction. Turn right and descend 0.1 mile down a steep, narrow footpath to the Hazel River. At the stream, turn right and hike upstream a few feet to a 30-foot waterfall. (FYI: Birds nest in the rock overhangs and the common blue violet peeks out from thin patches of soil amid the rock boulders.) To return to White Rocks Trail, follow the route you descended.

2.4 Turn right on White Rocks Trail. Follow blue blazes as the trail climbs to the first of four knobs whose exposed white rocks give this ridge its name.

3.0 Hike past an unmarked trail that leads right to a flat area with room for one tent amid the mountain laurel and pines. (FYI: To the southeast, the lush Hazel River valley unfolds. Look left for a nice view of the remaining White Rock knobs.)

3.5 Achieve the final knob and begin descent to the Hazel River. After a few hundred yards, the trail swings westerly and makes a sharp drop to the Hazel River.

3.7 Cross the Hazel River and turn left toward Hazel River Trail. (FYI: This is a good camping spot with several established sites marked by fire rings.)

3.8 Watch for—and ignore—a double yellow blaze that indicates a stream crossing that no longer exists. Instead of crossing, continue hiking downstream on the right bank. Roughly 100 feet beyond the double yellow blaze, you'll come to a T intersection with the Hazel River Trail. Turn left and follow the Hazel River Trail to the park boundary.

5.1 Turn right onto the blue-blazed Sam's Ridge Trail, begin a steep ascent, and exit the park. **Option:** An alternate starting point for this hike is straight ahead on the Hazel River Trail, which empties onto Virginia Route 600.

5.7 Re-enter the park. Boundaries are marked by red slashes on the trees.

6.5 The trail levels as you near the top of Sam's Ridge. (FYI: Around you, the vegetation changes from the hardwood-dominated ridge flanks to a lush mix of evergreens and scrub hardwoods. The woods thin and again you're entering an old settlement area. Metal stoves, pots, stone walls, and piles of rock all testify to the previous inhabitants, displaced when the federal government seized land to create this park. Spend some time and explore, but don't disturb the remains.)

7.1 Broad Hollow Trail exits on the left to access trails around Catlett Mountain and Nicholson Hollow. Continue straight on blue-blazed Sam's Ridge Trail. There is a spring just around the bend from this junction.

7.3 Turn left onto the Hazel Mountain Trail, marked by a concrete post. Within 0.1 mile, you'll pass the Hazel River Trail on the right, a footpath that skirts Hazel Mountain, descends to the river below the falls, then returns to the T intersection at Mile 3.8.

8.0 Follow Hazel Mountain Trail as it bears right at a junction with the Catlett Mountain Spur Trail. (FYI: Catlett Mountain Spur Trail follows Runyon's Run upstream 1.2 miles to Catlett Mountain Trail.)

8.6 Pass the trailhead for the White Rocks Trail.

10.0 Hike ends at the Meadow Springs parking lot.

Hike Information

Local Information

Luray-Page County Chamber of Commerce, Luray, VA, (888) 743-3915, www.luraypage.com.

Local Events/Attractions

The Virginia Mushroom & Wine Festival, third Saturday in May, Front Royal, VA, (800) 338-2576.

Christmas Bird Count, National Audubon Society, December, Page County, VA, (540) 999-3282.

Lodging

Hillside Motel, Luray, VA, (540) 743-6322, www.hillsidemotel-luray.com. Open mid-April through October.

Brookside Restaurant & Cabins, Luray, VA, (800) 299-2655, www.brooksidecabins.com. Cabin rentals year-round, plus motel and gift shop. (See Hike 12: Bluff Trail/AT Loop.)

Restaurants

The Mountainside Market, Sperryville, VA, (540) 987-9100. Sandwiches, pizza, fresh veggies, and dry goods, plus microbrews, wines, and veggie dog/cat food. The bulletin board out front is packed with notices for local events and services. (See Hike 12: Bluff Trail/AT Loop.)

Hike Tours

The PATC sponsors trips in the park. Call (703) 242-0693.

SNP's Education Office. Sponsors field seminars on fly-fishing, bird identification, land management, painting, butterfly identification, and environmental threats such as air pollution. Call (540) 999-3489.

Other Resources

Potomac Appalachian Trail Club (PATC), Vienna, VA, (703) 242-0693, www.patc.net.

Shenandoah National Park Association, Luray, VA, (540) 999-3582. Publishes guidebooks, maps, brochures, and CDs on the history, flora, and fauna of Shenandoah National Park. Co-sponsors events in the park, such as Wildflower Weekend and the Christmas Bird Count.

14 Old Rag

Old Rag is so popular the park has special rules for recreational use. There's a fee to park and use the trails on certain weekends and holidays during summer and fall. What's the attraction? Old Rag is a quick drive from Northern Virginia and offers day-trippers a craggy knob with eye-popping views. Beating the crowds on Old Rag means hiking in the off-season. Mountain laurel decorates the Saddle Trail with white and pink blossoms during spring. In fall, views from Old Rag across Weakley Hollow are filled with autumn colors. Whatever the season, carry a warm overshirt or jacket; wind and no tree cover can make Old Rag's summit feel positively alpine.

Start: From the parking lot at the end of Virginia Route 600, 1.3 miles west of Nethers. There is also an overflow parking lot on VA 600, 1.2 miles before the trailhead.

Distance: 7.4-mile loop.

Approximate hiking time: 6 hours.

Difficulty rating: Difficult due to the route's length and strenuous climbs.

Trail surface: Dirt roads and dirt trails meander through the mixed hardwood forest on lower slopes and along the trout stream at the foot of the mountain; the path is mostly exposed rock face along the cliffs and through the narrow passages between house-size boulders around the peak.

Land status: National park.

Nearest town: Sperryville, VA.

Other trail users: Hikers only.

Canine compatibility: Dogs not permitted.

Trail contacts: Shenandoah National Park, Luray, VA, (540) 999-3500, www.nps.gov/shen.

Schedule: (See Hike 12: Bluff Trail/AT Loop.)

Fees/permits: Entrance fee: The trailhead is outside the park, so you don't need to pay the $10 park fee. However, there is a $5.00 fee to hike Old Rug (younger than age 16 free); pay at the parking area. Free backcountry permits, available at ranger stations between sunrise and one hour before sunset, are required. Before visiting, review backcountry regulations, which cover such issues as group size, where to camp, and waste disposal. Call (540) 999-3500 for regulations. **Parking:** space for 14 cars at the trailhead; additional parking for 200 cars is 0.8 mile away near Nethers. When parking reaches its capacity, visitors will be turned away until space becomes available.

Maps: USGS maps: Old Rag, VA. PATC maps: Map #10: Shenandoah National Park Central District ($5.00).

Finding the trailhead: From Sperryville: Drive south on U.S. Highway 522 and in 0.3 mile, turn right onto Virginia Route 231. In 8 miles, turn right onto VA 600. Follow VA 600 through Nethers and reach a park service overflow parking lot 0.1 mile past Nethers. On summer weekends, park rangers man a booth here and collect a $5.00 parking fee. In another 1.2 miles, reach a parking area for fourteen cars at the trailhead. *DeLorme: Virginia Atlas & Gazetteer:* Page 74, B3.

Looking north from Old Rag to Corbin Mountain.

The Hike

The climb up Old Rag leads from mountain slopes thick with oak and tulip poplar to a rugged, exposed landscape of rock and straggly table-mountain pine. The forest floor, littered with dead leaves along Hughes Run near the trailhead, sports a thick mat of pine needles at higher elevations. Where you had once seen witch hazel growing in the forest subcanopy, now mountain laurel sinks its tenacious roots into thin, rocky soil. For the hiker, this is a noticeable change with a subtle, less noticeable effect on the mountain. Near the summit, those pine needles collect in puddles of water on open rock. Nitrates released from the needles mix with billion-year-old granite rock, and the erosion process begins. Bowl-shaped depressions form in rock boulders. And just like that, another piece of Old Rag wears away.

As sturdy a mountain as the Blue Ridge ever produced, Old Rag is nonetheless a still-evolving mountain. Still evolving is a curious description for a peak of such stature that, by park estimates, 100,000 people climb it annually. But it explains both how Old Rag's signature summit came to exist and how it continues to change. Millions of years of weathering led to the exposure of granite boulders at the summit.

More recently, rain-triggered rock slides reshaped the mountain's east slope (which is well known to only the most experienced bushwhackers and rock climbers). The exposed rock in the recent slides has triggered new interest in Old Rag among geologists. Carbon dating of rocks in the last few years debunked a long-held belief that Old Rag granite is the oldest rock in America's oldest mountain range. Samples of rock taken near

TIP Byrds Nest No. 1 and Old Rag Shelters are day-use only. If you're hiking on the weekend, arrive early to beat the crowds.

Mary's Rock on Skyline Drive date a few hundred million years earlier. This new information doesn't diminish or change Old Rag; it merely adds to a story that is being written in small ways every day.

Climbing the last mile on the Ridge Trail demands strength and balance. At one point, a narrow rock ledge is all that separates you from a long fall onto a pile of loose rocks. At another point, you may need a boost from behind to climb over a boulder. The trail negotiates steps made of Catoctin greenstone, rock pillars and boulders as large as a house, and short tunnels between the first false summit (where the trail emerges from the forest) and the true summit at 3,268 feet. The difficulty of the last mile, coupled with the crowds that flock here from June to October, will cause climbing delays.

Approaching Old Rag on the Saddle Trail is less popular, but it recommends itself for exactly that reason: Few people hike it. Hiking on Weakley Hollow Road, views open in the forest canopy and stretch all the way to the mountain. If you bushwhack off Weakley Hollow Road, it's possible to find relics of Old Rag village. In the 1780s there was a post office, school, church, and homes. (The post office stood at the junction of the Saddle Trail with Old Rag Road.) Local mountain men were employed by Skyland Resort to carry packs for the visitors climbing and camping out on Old Rag. Byrds Nest Shelter No. 1, a mountaintop picnic spot just shy of the peak, was donated by another well-heeled Old Rag climber: Virginia governor and senator Henry Flood Byrd Sr. climbed the mountain every year on his birthday.

Land at the foot of Old Rag was once one of the most populated and developed areas of Shenandoah National Park. Archeologists estimate 460 people lived in a network of hollows and coves, including Weakley Hollow. Recent surveys have identified nearly ninety sites that were once homes, gristmills, churches, or schools. It is from Weakley Hollow—and the communities in neighboring Nicholson and Corbin Hollows—that the image of Appalachian mountain folk as barefooted, moonshine-swilling hillbillies emerged. A 1933 sociological study called "Hollow

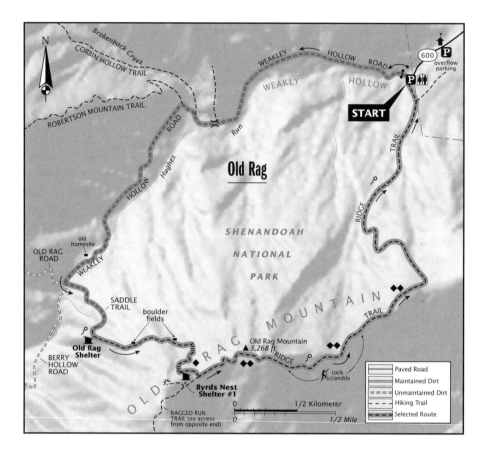

Folk" described residents of the Blue Ridge as "unlettered folk, sheltered in tiny mud-plastered log cabins and supported by a primitive agriculture." That description went a long way in swaying public and political opinion to evict residents in favor of building Shenandoah National Park.

Seventy years later, archeologists with the Colonial Williamsburg Foundation are revisiting these hollows and rewriting the history. Material recently collected, from calendars and watches to medicine bottles and music, paints a picture of inhabitants not as primitive people who lived hand to mouth. Rather, they were rural people who faced and overcame weather, soil, and social conditions that might have—and probably did—humble people of lesser character. Testament to the power of catalog marketing, the Sears Roebuck Company probably did more to bring the outside world to hollow folk as any technological advancement.

Climbing away from the remains of Old Rag village, the Saddle Trail passes by thick patches of blackberries. A shredded log shows where a bear ripped away soft, rotted wood hunting for grubs. Unlike deer, which were reintroduced to the park in 1935, bear returned to the park on their own. They now number between 250 and 300 (deer number in the thousands).

On a quiet day, the staccato of a woodpecker echoes through the woods. In winter, the source of sound may well be a yellow–bellied sapsucker, a bird species that extracts sap from tulip poplars. Nestled below a rock outcrop at lower elevations along Saddle Trail, dusk wraps around the mountain. Wind buffets the peak and drifts downslope. It whistles outside the tent. One gets the sense that the mountain is alive.

Miles and Directions

0.0 **START** from the parking lot at the end of VA 600 (Weakley Hollow Road). In the southwest corner of the parking lot, a yellow chain blocks vehicle traffic from passing. Follow the road as it drops to Hughes Run, crosses on a metal bridge, and begins a long, steady climb.

1.1 Continue straight on Weakley Hollow Road as Corbin Hollow Trail enters on the right. (FYI: Corbin Hollow Trail leads up Brokenback Creek and intersects with the Old Rag Road in just more than 2 miles.)

1.2 Continue straight on Weakley Hollow Road as Robertson Mountain Trail enters on the right. (FYI: Robertson Mountain Trail leads across the top of Robertson Mountain and intersects with Old Rag Road in 2.4 miles.)

2.1 Turn left onto Old Rag Road. In a few feet, turn left again onto the blue-blazed Saddle Trail, an old road overgrown with grass. The signboard has information on park fees and the "leave no trace" ethic.

2.5 Pass the Old Rag Shelter and a spring on the right side of the Saddle Trail. (FYI: The shelter is for day-use only. The spring is marked by a concrete post with yellow striping. If you drink water from the spring, make sure you treat it first.)

2.8 Saddle Trail narrows and crosses a boulder field.

3.1 Pass around a boulder the size of a small house. Steps lead uphill to a switchback in the trail.

3.5 Reach Byrds Nest Shelter No. 1. (FYI: An unmarked and unnamed footpath leads past the day-use-only shelter to a perch overlooking Weakley Hollow. Use caution when walking on exposed rock or near cliff edges. The views are beautiful, but they're not worth dying for. Another unmarked trail descends down the east slope of Old Rag. This trail is abandoned and ends at private property with no public access.)

3.7 Saddle Trail forks. Bear right and switchback to continue ascent of Old Rag.

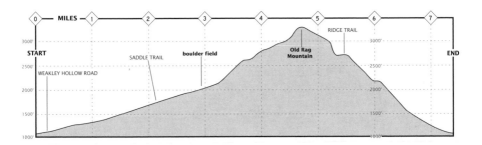

Dramatic rock formations on Old Rag.

4.0 Reach the top of Old Rag. A concrete post marks the end of the Saddle Trail and beginning of the Ridge Trail. (FYI: For views, turn left at the concrete post and climb the rocks. To descend on the Ridge Trail, return to the concrete post and turn left.)

4.5 Begin rock scrambling beneath boulders wedged in crevices. The next half mile brings steep drop-offs and tricky passages around and over the rocks.

4.7 Pass over the "false summit" of Old Rag. A look back up the trail nets a nice photo op of the Old Rag summit.

5.1 The Ridge Trail leaves Old Rag's exposed granite and re-enters the woods under a canopy of oak and yellow poplar.

7.4 Hike ends at the parking lot.

Hike Information

Local Information

Orange County Department of Tourism & Visitors Bureau, Orange, VA, (877) 222-8072, www.orangechamber.com.

Lodging

Quality Inn-Skyline Drive, Front Royal, VA, (540) 635-3161, www.qualityinnfrontroyal.com.

Park lodges at Skyland (Mile 41.7) and Big Meadows (Mile 51) and cabins at Lewis Mountain (Mile 57.5) are seasonal. Skyland is open late March through October; Big Meadows opens in mid-May and closes in October. Call (540) 999-3500 for information.

Reserved campsites are located at Matthews Arm (Mile 22.1), Big Meadows (Mile 51),

Lewis Mountain (Mile 57.5), and Loft Mountain (Mile 79.5). For campground reservations, call (540) 999-3500.

Backcountry trail huts (seven) and **cabins** (six) are operated by the PATC. For reservations, call (703) 242-0693. You must file a responsibility statement with the club before renting. Applications may be downloaded from their Web page and mailed to their Vienna headquarters.

Restaurants

Big Meadows Restaurant, Shenandoah National Park, VA, (540) 999-2221. Big Meadows (Mile 51.2) features a full-service restaurant and is open mid-May through the first weekend in November.

Big Meadows Wayside, (540) 743-5108, is open late March through November.

Panorama Restaurant, Shenandoah National Park, VA, (540) 999-2265. At Thornton Gap, the Panorama Restaurant (Mile 31.5) serves breakfast, lunch, and dinner starting mid-May through the first weekend in November.

Skyland Restaurant, (Mile 41.7), Shenandoah National Park, VA, (540) 999-2211. Skyland features a full-service restaurant and is open late March through November.

Hike Tours

The PATC sponsors trips in the park. Call (703) 242-0693.

SNP's Education Office. Sponsors field seminars on fly-fishing, bird identification, land management, painting, butterfly identification, and environmental threats such as air pollution. Call (540) 999-3489.

Other Resources

Potomac Appalachian Trail Club (PATC), Vienna, VA, (703) 242-0693, www.patc.net.

Shenandoah National Park Association, Luray, VA, (540) 999-3582. Publishes guidebooks, maps, brochures, and CDs on the history, flora, and fauna of Shenandoah National Park. Co-sponsors events in the park, such as Wildflower Weekend and the Christmas Bird Count.

15 Rocky Mount/Gap Run

Rocky Mount's western flank is a demanding climb of 1,000 feet in about 1 mile. If you're not breathless at the top, the view will steal what breath is left. A series of ridges and peaks intersect and rise in succession to the limitless horizon. A return hike on Gap Run Trail takes you from soaring heights into shaded forest. It's said trails in the south district of Shenandoah National Park get less use than other areas of the park. The Rocky Mount/Gap Run loop is proof of this. As a day hike, it is a strenuous, full-day trip. Overnighters will find that a quiet tent site along Gap Run allows time to tarry and enjoy the deep-woods scenery.

Start: From the concrete post on the west, or southbound, side of Skyline Drive, 0.1 mile north of Twomile Run Overlook.

Distance: 9.4-mile loop.

Approximate hiking time: 7 hours.

Difficulty rating: Moderate due to a steep climb up Rocky Mount.

Trail surface: Make your way along dirt and grass footpaths, rock slides, high-water washes, old streambeds, and rock outcrops on Rocky Mount to the old-growth chestnut oak forests and the dark, sheltered stream valley.

Land status: National park.

Nearest city: Staunton, VA.

Other trail users: Hikers only.

Canine compatibility: Leashed dogs permitted (leash can be no longer than 6 feet).

Trail contacts: Shenandoah National Park, Luray, VA, (540) 999-3500, www.nps.gov/shen.

Schedule: (See Hike 12: Bluff Trail/AT Loop.)

Fees/permits: (See Hike 12: Bluff Trail/AT Loop.)

Maps: USGS maps: McGaheysville, VA. PATC maps: Map #11: Shenandoah National Park South District ($5.00).

Finding the trailhead: From Staunton: Drive east on I-64. Take exit 99, the Afton Mountain exit, and turn right onto eastbound U.S. Highway 250. After passing under the interstate, turn right off US 250 and ascend to Skyline Drive/Blue Ridge Parkway. Turn left and drive north on Skyline Drive. From the Loft Mountain Visitor Center, Twomile Run Overlook is 3.3 miles north on the left side of the road. *DeLorme: Virginia Atlas & Gazetteer:* Page 67, B6.

The Hike

Gap Run can be a monster. That much was clear from tree limbs and other forest debris scattered across its floodplain. Rocks larger than a human head lay piled around the base of larger trees, some 20 feet removed from the actual stream bank. Thinking of the torrent that moved them made me reconsider the small, puddling, barely moving flow that trickled past my campsite. You see, in late July, Gap Run is anything but a monster: a puddle here and a puddle there, and not much else.

A few feet upstream, my nephew, Matthias, took advantage of summer's low-water conditions to scramble over streambed rocks in search of a crayfish or salamander. I had gone over with him proper streambed hunting techniques: Squat or

Climbing Rocky Mount.

hunch down on a rock, I said, and just stare at one spot in the stream. Then slowly, with two fingers, lift one stone at a time. Give the silt time to settle, then, if you don't see what you're looking for, replace the stone where you found it. A lot of critters call this stream their home, I said. And no one likes to come home and find his house rearranged.

These are the good times, I thought as I watched him explore. A few hours earlier, it was all about adjusting packs, lightening loads, tending to blisters and hot spots, and helping a struggling seven-year-old come to terms with carrying his food, water, and clothing for miles on end, all so we could sit in the woods, eat prepackaged food, and sleep on hard ground.

Leadership training, whether for business or wilderness adventure, preaches the importance of monitoring your group's morale. A happy camper interacts better with others and is more willing to help the group. With children, this is especially true. There usually comes a time, a critical moment—almost always after a difficult stretch of trail—when an uncomfortable thought settles in: This, they state plainly, is too much like work.

Our group—Mary, myself, and our niece and nephew, Sarah and Matthias—began the hike off Skyline Drive on Rocky Mount Trail. It started nicely on a dirt

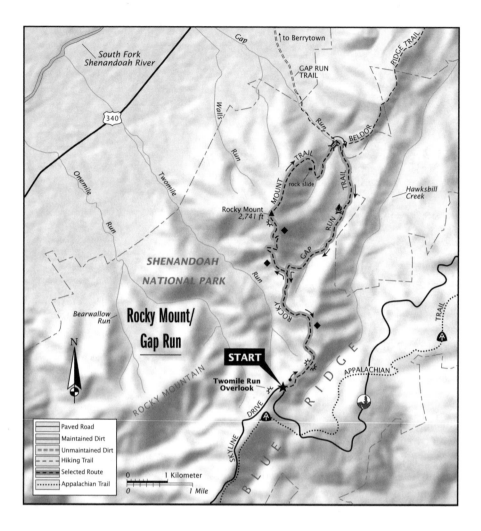

Map labels:
- to Berrytown
- Gap
- South Fork Shenandoah River
- GAP RUN TRAIL
- RIDGE TRAIL
- 340
- Walls Run
- Twomile Run
- BELDOR
- MOUNT TRAIL
- rock slide
- GAP RUN TRAIL
- Hawksbill Creek
- Rocky Mount 2,741 ft
- Onemile Run
- SHENANDOAH NATIONAL PARK
- Run
- GAP
- Bearwallow Run
- **Rocky Mount/ Gap Run**
- ROCKY MOUNTAIN
- ROCKY
- RUN
- TRAIL
- **START**
- APPALACHIAN
- Twomile Run Overlook
- N
- SKYLINE DRIVE
- BLUE RIDGE

Legend:
- Paved Road
- Maintained Dirt
- Unmaintained Dirt
- Hiking Trail
- Selected Route
- Appalachian Trail

Scale: 0 — 1 Kilometer / 0 — 1 Mile

footpath that posed little risk of injury, on a gentle slope with sporadic views south-west to Twomile Ridge. When the trail steepened and curved around the east side of a small knob, legs weakened. Complaints started drifting back my way and I heard someone say they were dizzy. All indicators pointed to a much-needed rest. The opportunity presented itself once the trail re-entered the shade of forest.

Every leader needs a bag of tricks and the next 2 miles exhausted my personal stash. We played "Trail-Wheel of Fortune." We set group challenges to hike a certain distance in a certain period of time. We sang songs. Every time a view opened on the trail, I used it as a topographic lesson by pointing out where we stood. We juggled loads, adjusted shoulder straps, medicated sore feet, and, before long, we hit a nice campsite on the Gap Run Trail. Three miles in six hours—the pace left a little to be desired, but a successful first day by all other measures.

Sigurd Olson, author of *Campfires,* wrote "anyone who has traveled in the wilds knows how much he looks forward to the time of day when he can lay down his burden and make camp." I'm not sure Olson ever hiked with children, because for them, camp means one thing: Work. Unpack your backpack. Help set up tents. Prep dinner. Get firewood. Get water. Then a chorus of *don'ts:* Don't go in the tent with shoes. Don't throw dirt at your sister. Don't touch that plant. Don't eat that bug . . .

At this delicate point, when commands are flying fast, it pays to remember: The poor kids have already completed a Herculean task just getting here. More importantly, if their needs aren't met, they can hardly be expected to meet someone else's.

With imagination, jobs can be fun. Matthias and I drew water duty, which led us to search Gap Run for some running water, which in turn led to not getting water at all. Instead, we moved up and down the dry wash, checking out small pools for aqua-critters. A snap-crackle brought us to the shoreline where, in dry oak leaves, a turtle the size of a half-dollar pumped tiny legs in a vain attempt to escape detection. We tracked it for ten minutes or so, until I remembered that without water, we wouldn't eat. We filtered and headed back to camp.

Anticipation motivates. Over breakfast the next morning, Mary and I announced the day hike would be without packs. That prospect sent Matthias and Sarah up the trail like shots. When we caught up, their flushed faces and panting told the story: It's hard to keep an excited kid down, but it's also difficult to run up Rocky Mount. As we approached the white outcrops of the summit, I told the kids to be on the watch. The Erwinian quartzite is pocked with small, fossil wormholes that date from a period when this incredibly hard rock was the beach of a prehistoric ocean. As amazing as that sounds, I witnessed something even more mind-boggling: two kids running uphill the last tenth of a mile, each trying to be the first to the summit.

Atop Rocky Mount, we stared across to Rocky Mountain and Twomile Ridge, each of us alone in our thoughts. Turkey vultures rode air currents, wings shifting to-and-fro as they held a tricky balance of speed and direction. "This," said eleven-year-old Sarah, "is the most awesome thing I've ever seen in my entire life."

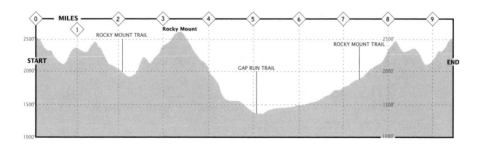

Miles and Directions

0.0 **START** at the Rocky Mount trailhead 0.1 mile north of Twomile Run Overlook on Skyline Drive.

0.6 The trail climbs briefly, then drops to an easy stretch along a footpath. (FYI: The trail shows signs of once being a road. In fact, this route once served as a fire road up from Berryville, a town at the foot of the Blue Ridge west of Rocky Mount. Occasional views open west to Twomile Ridge and east into the Hawksbill Creek river valley and Weaver Mountain.)

1.0 Hike along an exposed stretch of trail as you make a brief, 200-foot climb up over a small knob. The trail re-enters the woods as it descends the northwest side of this hill.

2.1 Come to the intersection of Gap Run Trail and Rocky Mount Trail; bear left to climb Rocky Mount. (FYI: Gap Run Trail heads off to the right and descends past the headwaters of Gap Run. It junctions with the opposite end of Rocky Mount Trail in 2.2 miles. There are good campsites along the stream, including a site 1 mile downhill from this junction.)

2.5 Begin a steep climb up Rocky Mount. Views of Twomile Ridge open up when the trail switches back to the right.

2.9 (FYI: Exposed chunks of chalky rock become more frequent. Close examination reveals fossilized wormholes in this Erwin quartzite.)

3.2 About 40 yards shy of the wooded peak on Rocky Mount are cliffs with views of Twomile Ridge and six ridges rising in succession beyond. (FYI: There is rocktripe lichen on the rocks at this summit. It appears brown, with folded-up edges, and is brittle to the touch. The Audubon field guide describes this lichen as "rarely seen," so take a minute to enjoy.)

3.5 A large slab of rock becomes increasingly visible on the left side of the trail as you descend. (FYI: Old-growth chestnut oaks line the trail on your right, and the forest under-story is a mix of blueberries, sassafras, and scrub oak. The sassafras has quite a history. Explorers and colonists treated it as a cure-all. It shrinks less than any southern hard-wood, thus was favored in building fences and boats, but its odor supposedly drove away bedbugs, which made it a favored wood for building a bed frame. It was once used widely as a flavor agent. Lately, scientists have found that safrole, a clear oil found in the roots of sassafras, is a cancer-causing agent. Its use in food and drinks is forbidden in the United States.)

4.0 Cross the first of several rock slides that have covered the mountain below and above the trail with boulders. (Note: Be careful when crossing the rock slides. There is no danger of further slippage, but footing is tricky.)

4.6 Cross a small stream and follow the right bank downhill. Within several hundred yards, you'll hop back across the stream and follow the left bank. The trail is clear; stream crossings are well marked.

5.1 Come to a T intersection where Rocky Mount Trail meets Gap Run Trail. Turn right onto Gap Run Trail. (FYI: To the left, Gap Run departs the park in 0.8 mile and reaches Virginia Route 630 near Berrytown in 1.7 miles.)

5.3 Come to an intersection with the Beldor Ridge Trail; continue straight on Gap Run Trail. (FYI: Beldor Ridge Trail exits on the left to climb 2,300-foot Beldor Ridge in 1.2 miles. Small metal tags in the vicinity of this trailhead are part of a black bear study by the park. Biologists place the tags every mile or so, depending on terrain. Near them, they place an attractant—scents or bait—and record the number of "hits" it receives. Black bear have rebounded from single-digit tallies when the park was opened in the mid-1930s, to number more than 300.)

6.2 Cross Gap Run and hike up the right stream bank.

6.5 After running at a gentle uphill pace, the trail crosses Gap Run for the last time and the grade steepens. This marks the approach to Rocky Mount Trail.

7.3 Gap Run Trail ends at Rocky Mount Trail. Turn left to return to Skyline Drive.

9.4 Hike ends at Skyline Drive. Turn right and head downhill 0.1 mile to parking at Twomile Run Overlook.

Hike Information

Local Information

Staunton/Augusta County Travel Information Center, Staunton, VA, (540) 332-3972, www.augustachamber.org.

Local Events/Attractions

Fall Foliage Celebration, Waynesboro, VA, (540) 949-8203. Craft show, theater, gem and mineral show, and a 10K run.

North American Butterfly Association Annual Count, July, Page County, VA, (540) 999-3282.

Lodging

For lodging outside the park, Charlottesville and Staunton feature a number of chain hotels, and a fair number of rather exclusive inns. (See Hike 12: Bluff Trail/AT Loop.)

Restaurants

Purple Foot, Waynesboro, VA, (540) 942-9463. Lunch every day from 11:00 A.M. to 2:00 P.M.

Depot Grille, Staunton, VA, (540) 885-7332. Located in downtown Staunton's old train depot.

Big Meadows Restaurant, Shenandoah National Park, VA, (540) 999-2221. Big Meadows (Mile 51.2) features a full-service restaurant and is open mid-May through the first weekend in November.

Big Meadows Wayside, (540) 743-5108, is open late March through November.

Panorama Restaurant, Shenandoah National Park, VA, (540) 999-2265. At Thornton Gap, the Panorama Restaurant (Mile 31.5) serves breakfast, lunch, and dinner starting mid-May through the first weekend in November.

Skyland Restaurant, (Mile 41.7), Shenandoah National Park, VA, (540) 999-2211. Skyland features a full-service restaurant and is open late March through November.

Hike Tours

The PATC sponsors trips in the park. Call (703) 242-0693.

SNP's Education Office. Sponsors field seminars on fly-fishing, bird identification, land management, painting, butterfly identification, and environmental threats such as air pollution. Call (540) 999-3489.

Other Resources

Potomac Appalachian Trail Club (PATC), Vienna, VA, (703) 242-0693, www.patc.net.

Shenandoah National Park Association, Luray, VA, (540) 999-3582. Publishes guidebooks, maps, brochures, and CDs on the history, flora, and fauna of Shenandoah National Park. Co-sponsors events in the park, such as Wildflower Weekend and the Christmas Bird Count.

16 North Fork Moormans River

North Fork Moormans River runs a modest path down the foothills of the Blue Ridge along Shenandoah National Park's east boundary. Fly fishermen work the stocked waters. Hikers push upstream toward the waterfalls on picturesque mountain streams that feed the North Fork. Beyond the most popular day hikes lies rugged Shenandoah backcountry. From Sugar Hollow Reservoir deep into the park, the landscape shows scars of a 1995 flood that swelled the river and tributaries with water, rocks, trees, and mud. This is not only a great day hike, but also a firsthand account of earth-shaping events, and the process of recovery that follows.

Start: From the national park boundary north of the Sugar Hollow Reservoir on Virginia Route 614.

Distance: 3.2-miles out-and-back.

Approximate hiking time: 3 hours.

Difficulty rating: Easy due to short distance and level terrain. There are dangerous passages across rock slides and undercut stream banks, however.

Trail surface: Mostly dirt roads and occasional streambeds wind through an expansive stream valley hewn by flood waters and fed by numerous small mountain streams. One tributary, Big Branch, drops 50 feet off barefaced rock into a deep pool.

Land status: National park.

Nearest town: White Hall, VA.

Other trail users: Mountain bikers and cross-country skiers.

Canine compatibility: Leashed dogs permitted (leash can be no longer than 6 feet).

Trail contacts: Shenandoah National Park, Luray, VA, (540) 999-3500, www.nps.gov/shen.

Schedule: (See Hike 12: Bluff Trail/AT Loop.)

Fees/permits: (See Hike 12: Bluff Trail/AT Loop.)

Maps: USGS maps: Browns Cove, VA; Crimora, VA.

PATC maps: Map #11: Shenandoah National Park South District ($5.00).

Finding the trailhead: From White Hall: Drive 5.6 miles west on VA 614 to the Sugar Hollow Reservoir. Past the reservoir dam, the road turns to gravel. There is parking for fifteen cars on the left side of the road. Parking spaces fill quickly on weekends. Signs indicate where you may park along the shoulder. *DeLorme: Virginia Atlas & Gazetteer:* Page 67, C6.

The Hike

Geologists study materials that form the earth, and the elements that work on those materials, like wind, water, heat, and pressure. They work with history, but on a scale so much larger and longer than the human time frame, it's often difficult to fathom.

Not all geologic activity is ancient history, however. On the North Fork Moormans River, it appears uncomfortably recent. Stream banks look like a rogue bulldozer blew out banks 20 feet high. Trees, their exposed roots bleached by sun, lay

Cut-away banks caused by 1995 flooding on the North Fork Moormans River.

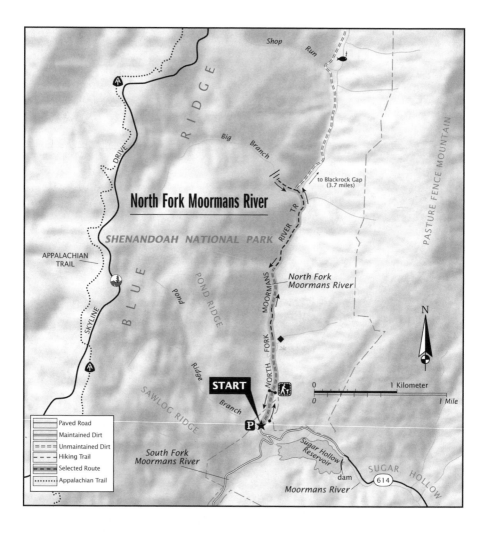

North Fork Moormans River

SHENANDOAH NATIONAL PARK

APPALACHIAN TRAIL

North Fork Moormans River

to Blackrock Gap (3.7 miles)

START

Paved Road
Maintained Dirt
Unmaintained Dirt
Hiking Trail
Selected Route
Appalachian Trail

South Fork Moormans River

Sugar Hollow Reservoir

dam

Moormans River

614

SUGAR HOLLOW

0   1 Kilometer
0   1 Mile

N

mixed in with piles of rock rubble. Vines drape over unstable stream banks underlain by a mud-clay-rock conglomerate. Loose boulders show a fresh, rough aspect, a marked difference from smooth, rounded shapes expected along streambeds. From uprooted logs to piles of boulders waist-high, all signs point to a great force that swept down the river valley.

The cataclysmic event that caused this began on June 22, 1995. Rain fell throughout Shenandoah National Park for six days. On June 27, an intense storm pocket formed over the North Fork. Nine hours of hard rain followed. In a two-hour period, the dam manager at Sugar Hollow Reservoir, which is fed by the North Fork, recorded 11.5 inches of water. A USGS report by geologists Benjamin Morgan and Gerald F. Wieczorek offers a chilling account of how quickly water rose.

At 7 P.M., Virginia Power had received reports of power failure in Sugar Hollow from residents below the dam. At 9–9:30 P.M., a lineman rearming a safety device on a pole near White Hall, Virginia, found that water had suddenly risen up to his knees within a few minutes. Rapidly rising water to chest level flooded his truck before he could drive to higher ground.

White Hall is 6 miles downstream from the reservoir. Above the lake, no one witnessed what occurred along the North Fork Moormans River. If they did, there is no saying they'd be alive to describe it.

Trouble started on the steep slopes rising out of the stream valley. In this area of Shenandoah National Park, a thick coating of saprolite overlays the Blue Ridge rock complex of billion-year-old granite, greenstone, and Chilhowee sandstone. Saprolite has a claylike consistency that, under proper conditions, can loosen and shift. When this happens, other surface elements—topsoil, block fields, and loose rocks—will join the flow and create a landslide. In June 1995, all elements coalesced in a single spot—the North Fork Moormans River. What followed is described as a once-a-millennium geologic event.

Geologists documented more than one hundred landslides in a 5-mile area upstream from Sugar Hollow Reservoir. Soil slips and debris flows turned hillsides into liquid, muddy concoctions that ripped trees from their roots and moved boulders by the ton. Transported downstream, this material pummeled stream banks. Evidence of its power is visible a mile and a half upstream from the reservoir, on the right bank, where water cut a stream bank 20 feet high.

Up on mountain slopes west of the river, small streams became channels 100 to 200 feet wide. Big Branch, a stream that discharges into the North Fork at a spectacular waterfall, experienced an estimated water flow rate of 6,200 cubic feet per second. Amazingly, this means flow down Big Branch equaled, for a time, the rate of water flowing over Great Falls on the Potomac River (when the Potomac's water level is at the low level of 3.5 feet above median). The National Park Service calls any flow rate a "guess," given that there are no gauges on the river. Even so, their rough estimates exceeded the 500-year magnitude flood estimate by 155 percent.

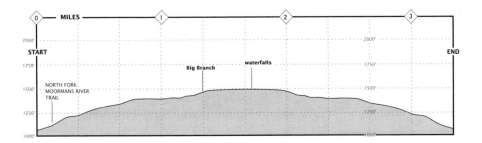

As far as recreation use of the North Fork goes, little has changed since the flood. The trail is an old fire road that follows a gently ascending route into the folds of the Blue Ridge. Streams drop off the hillsides, often in small waterfalls. Great slabs of rock attract sunbathers and shutterbugs to the picture-perfect pool at the base of Big Branch. Hikers unload packs and climb Pasture Fence Mountain to pitch a tent, legalities be damned. Veteran fly fishermen practice their timing upstream. Their protégés stand knee-high in the stream, entangled in yards of fishing line while brook and brown trout swim around them.

The flood did turn a hike that has been, for most people, a convenient excuse to skip class or work, into a showcase of geologic activity. Rock slides that crossed the trail display stones of banded gneiss with its alternating bands of light and dark streaks. Near Big Branch, the old road narrows to a footpath and crosses rock and debris flows halted by logjams. The trail here makes a short climb, then drops back to water level amid blown-down trees on the right and rubble on the left. Farther up the hillside, bare spots are just beginning to show signs of recovery. In dry

Crossing the North Fork Moormans River.

streambeds, small trees sprout up through stone rubble. Wild ginseng has returned, and naturalists have spotted the rare wildflower, white monkshood. The brook and brown trout, temporarily flushed from the basin by the flood, have returned. A fish survey two weeks before the storm counted thirteen different species in the stream, including thirty brook trout; a survey after the storm netted six fish—total.

Not all areas are so quick to recover. Before the flood, trees, ferns, and other riverside plants crowded the mouth of Big Branch. Now it is bare rock. Quieter geologic processes have begun. Over hundreds of years, soil and weathered rock will build up. Small plants first, then trees, will sink roots. Someday, the flood of 1995 will be ancient history—which makes this chance to see its bare effects today all the more special.

Miles and Directions

0.0 **START** from the Shenandoah National Park boundary. A trailboard lists park rules and regulations. Walk straight on the North Fork Trail, a dirt road. Yellow blazes are infrequent.

0.2 Pass straight by a trail sign that gives details of a 1999 forest fire in the park.

0.3 Pass through a clearing. (FYI: The streambank on the left shows signs of erosion from the 1995 flood.)

0.4 Cross the North Fork Moormans River.

0.5 Cross the river again. On the opposite bank, the stream bank may be overgrown. Climb through the vegetation and follow a footpath heading upstream. (FYI: At low water, cross the stream below the rapids. Otherwise, climb over boulders and jump the stream at a point where the water shoots between two large rocks.)

0.9 Follow the trail across a boulder field and up the right hillside, where it has been detoured to avoid a washed-out section of trail. (FYI: After this detour, the trail becomes a road.)

1.2 Descend on the trail to the stream bank and cross. On the opposite side, the trail becomes a footpath.

1.3 (FYI: Pass through an area of widespread destruction caused by the 1995 flood. Landslides moved the trees and rocks seen here, a force strong enough to snap tree trunks. On the left, uphill, a washout illustrates how wide an area these landslides affected.)

1.6 Descend to the river's edge. Turn left and climb to the falls on Big Branch, a few yards uphill. Turn back and return to the parking area on the North Fork Trail. (FYI: Take time to explore Big Branch. Once a small stream, it has been forever altered by the storm. The lower falls, especially, show signs of being blown out by massive floods of water pouring off the slope.) **Sidetrip:** North Fork Trail continues past Big Branch to reach Blackrock Gap on Skyline Drive in 3.7 miles. A section of this route upstream leaves the national park for 1.2 miles, then re-enters the park to climb steeply up a stream hollow to Skyline Drive.

3.2 Hike ends at the park boundary.

Hike Information

Local Information

Luray-Page County Chamber of Commerce, Luray, VA, (888) 743-3915, www.luraypage.com.

Charlottesville Albemarle County Convention & Visitors Bureau, (877) 386-1102, www.soveryvirginia.com.

Local Events/Attractions

Crozet Arts and Crafts Festival, May and October, Crozet, VA, (434) 823-2211.

White Hall Vineyards, White Hall, VA, (434) 823-8615, www.whitehallvineyards.com.

Monticello, Charlottesville, VA, (434) 984-9822, www.monticello.org. Thomas Jefferson's home, featuring a restored orchard, vineyard, and gardens. Open every day except Christmas.

Lodging

Inn At Sugar Hollow Farm, Charlottesville, VA, (434) 823-7086, www.sugarhollow.com. Located on VA 614 west of Charlottesville.

Quality Inn-Skyline Drive, Front Royal, VA, (540) 635-3161, www.qualityinnfrontroyal. com.

Park lodges at Skyland (Mile 41.7) and Big Meadows (Mile 51) and cabins at Lewis Mountain (Mile 57.5) are seasonal. Skyland is open late March through October; Big Meadows opens in mid-May and closes in October. Call (540) 999-3500 for information.

Reserved campsites are located at Matthews Arm (Mile 22.1), Big Meadows (Mile 51), Lewis Mountain (Mile 57.5), and Loft Mountain (Mile 79.5). For campground reservations, call (540) 999-3500.

Backcountry trail huts (seven) and **cabins** (six) are operated by the PATC. For reservations, call (703) 242-0693. You must file a responsibility statement with the club before renting. Applications may be downloaded from their Web page and mailed to their Vienna headquarters.

Restaurants

Buddhist Biker Bar & Grill, Charlottesville, VA, (434) 971-9181. Casual dining in an old home near the University of Virginia campus. (See Hike 12: Bluff Trail/AT Loop.) Countless other restaurants in Charlottesville provide ample dining opportunities after a long hike.

Hike Tours

The PATC sponsors trips in the park. Call (703) 242-0693.

SNP's Education Office. Sponsors field seminars on fly-fishing, bird identification, land management, painting, butterfly identification, and environmental threats such as air pollution. Call (540) 999-3489.

Other Resources

Potomac Appalachian Trail Club (PATC), Vienna, VA, (703) 242-0693, www.patc.net.

Shenandoah National Park Association, Luray, VA, (540) 999-3582. Publishes guidebooks, maps, brochures, and CDs on the history, flora, and fauna of Shenandoah National Park. Co-sponsors events in the park, such as Wildflower Weekend and the Christmas Bird Count.

Honorable Mentions

Shenandoah National Park

Here is an index of great hikes in the Shenandoah National Park that didn't make the A-list this time around but deserve recognition. Check them out and let us know what you think. You may decide that one or more of these hikes deserves higher status in future editions or, perhaps, you may have a hike of your own that merits some attention.

30 Jeremy's Run

Begin at Elkwallow Picnic Area, milepost 24 on Skyline Drive in the park's northern district. The descent is steep and stream crossings are difficult, but the rewards of hiking along this beautiful, cascading stream far outweigh the challenges. Call (540) 999–3500. *DeLorme: Virginia Atlas & Gazetteer:* Page 74, C2.

31 Nicholson Hollow

Park at Stony Man Overlook at milepost 38.6 on Skyline Drive in the park's central district. Nicholson Hollow was once a populated area of 400 families. Old home foundations and other evidence of past lives are visible along this 5.8-mile one-way trail. Use Corbin Hollow Trail and Indian Run Trail to make an extended backcountry loop. Call (540) 999–3500. *DeLorme: Virginia Atlas & Gazetteer:* Page 74, D1/2.

32 Whiteoak Canyon

Parking for the Whiteoak Canyon Trail is at milepost 42.6 on Skyline Drive in the park's central district. The steep gorge that features waterfalls, giant boulders, and quiet pools make this one of the most popular and beautiful places in the park. There are old-growth hemlocks along the connecting Limberlost Trail. Call (540) 999–3500. *DeLorme: Virginia Atlas & Gazetteer:* Page 74, D1/2.

33 Big Run Portal-Rockytop Loop

Begin this hike at Browns Gap at milepost 83 on Skyline Drive in the park's southern district. A classic Shenandoah hike: all downhill to the park boundary, followed by a steep climb back to Skyline Drive. In total, a strenuous 14.6-mile loop. Call (540) 999–3500. *DeLorme: Virginia Atlas & Gazetteer:* Page 67, C6.

34 Riprap Hollow–Appalachian Trail Loop

The parking area for this 10-mile hike is at milepost 90 on Skyline Drive in the park's southern district. Chimney Rock and Calvary Rock are two highlights on this trip. So are the springtime mountain laurel blooms along Riprap Trail as it descends through Cold Spring Hollow. Call (540) 999–3500. *DeLorme: Virginia Atlas & Gazetteer:* Page 67, C5.

Valley & Ridge

I am now in the very midst of that great congregation of hills, comprising all the spurs, branches, knobs and peaks of the great chain which has been called, with a happy attitude, the backbone of America.

James Kirk Paulding wrote this during his Virginia travels in 1816. Any person might think as much when venturing into the Allegheny Mountains today. Bringing order to this landscape is hopeless. The hills are long, straight ridges tending in a northeast-southwest direction, divided by deep, narrow valleys, like waves and troughs of the earth's crust folded and faulted by gigantic continental collisions millions of centuries ago.

Little is consistent about the valley and ridge region. Shoulder spurs shoot off in all sorts of directions, appearing as broad buttresses for the many rocky balds and tree-covered knobs. An otherwise straight ridge will warp with S turns, alluding to the powerful, earth-shaping forces that create mountains. Streams cut deep grooves in the mountain slopes, and a trove of plants and trees soak up life from these veins of moisture, giving rise to the Appalachian cove forest, one of Earth's most diverse ecosystems. Rock slides inhibit forward progress in one direction, while in the other, a sharp-rising ridge presents a seemingly insurmountable obstacle.

The Appalachian Mountains, which include the Allegheny chain of Virginia and West Virginia, are among the oldest mountains on the planet. The Southern Appalachians as a whole are considered a biological wonderland. Virginia's valley and ridge region supports that claim with vigor. In Laurel Fork, elements of northern boreal forest inhabit the high-altitude knobs and stream valleys, while miles away, dry forests on lower ridges display the classic oak-hickory forest type. So it is that the hiker passes from dank, moist streambeds to high, exposed cliff-lines to laurel-shrouded mountain slopes in a single day.

Anyone who travels the mountains of Virginia with any regularity is bound, sooner or later, to come upon a spot so special, so utterly beautiful at that moment in time, it brings them to pause. It could be a soaring view, a mist-shrouded wilderness pond or a mountain stream, a swath of pink and white—blooming mountain laurel or a sun-dappled cove cooled by the shade of old-growth hemlock. Wherever, whenever, this spot remains an abiding image long after the hike ends. That is the gift of Virginia's mountains.

Valley & Ridge

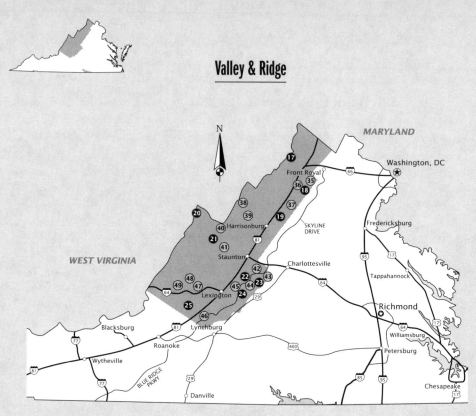

The Hikes	Honorable Mentions
Big Schloss **17.**	35. Shawl Gap–Massanutten East Trail
Stephens Trail **18.**	36. Massanutten Mountain West/Signal Knob
Fridley Gap **19.**	37. Massanutten Mountain East/Duncan Hollow
Laurel Fork Area **20.**	38. Hone Quarry
Ramsey's Draft Wilderness **21.**	39. Wild Oak National Recreation Trail
St. Mary's Wilderness **22.**	40. Shenandoah Mountain Trail/South
Three Ridges **23.**	41. North Mountain/Crawford Mountain
Mount Pleasant **24.**	42. Torry Ridge–Mill Creek Loop
Roaring Run/Hoop Hole **25.**	43. Humpback Rocks
	44. Crabtree Falls
	45. Whetstone Ridge
	46. Apple Orchard Falls–Cornelius Creek Loop Trail
	47. Rich Hole Wilderness
	48. Rough Hole Wilderness
	49. Douthat State Park

17 Big Schloss

In German, *schloss* means "castle." In Virginia, *schloss* can only refer to one geologic wonder, a towering outcrop of sandstone on Mill Mountain. Big Schloss is a popular day trip from Wolf Gap Recreation Area, a primitive camping site 2 miles south. A more strenuous trip begins far to the north, in a quiet river valley better known by hunters than hikers. The hike begins at Wilson Cove Wildlife Management Area, a 5,200-acre piece of the national forest designated for muzzleloader buck hunting only, in late November and early December. Along Pond Run, old-growth hemlocks stand out from the smaller trees growing thick along this stream. Rock slides, steep inclines, overlooks, and quiet views off Mill Mountain follow in succession.

Start: From the bridge over Waites Run on Waites Run Road (West Virginia Route 5/West Virginia Route 1).
Distance: 19.5-mile loop.
Approximate hiking time: 12 hours.
Difficulty rating: Moderate due to the length, sections of rocky and uneven trail, and steep climbs.
Trail surface: Dirt forest paths and old logging roads lead through rock formations and cove forests along Pond Run and Little Stony Creek.
Land status: National forest.
Nearest town: Wardensville, WV.

Other trail users: Mountain bikers, cross-country skiers, and hunters (in season).
Canine compatibility: Dogs permitted.
Trail contacts: Lee Ranger District, Edinburg, VA, (540) 984-4101, www.southernregion.fs. fed.us/gwj/lee.
Schedule: Open year-round. Hunting is permitted in national forests. Wilson Cove Wildlife Management Area hosts a special muzzle-loading season in December. Deer season lasts from November to early January.
Fees/permits: No fees or permits required.
Maps: USGS maps: Wardensville, WV; Woodstock, VA; Wolf Gap, VA.

Finding the trailhead: From Strasburg: Follow Virginia Route 55 (also called Wardensville Pike) west for 20 miles, crossing into West Virginia en route. In Wardensville, bear left at the Virginia Route 55/Virginia Route 259 junction. In 0.5 mile, turn left onto Carpenters Avenue, at the 7-Eleven store. In 0.8 mile, turn right onto Waites Run Road (WV 5/WV 1). Pass a community park on the left. Enter George Washington National Forest in 1.3 miles. In 5.3 miles, reach a concrete bridge spanning Waites Run. Across the bridge a sign indicates the boundary of Wilson Cove Wildlife Management Area (WMA). There are pull-offs for cars on either side of the stream and campsites for late-day arrivals. *DeLorme: Virginia Atlas & Gazetteer:* Page 73, A6.

The Hike

The Native American phrase for Appalachia translates roughly as "endless mountain." That seems an apt description standing atop one of Mill Mountains many outcrops. The view west is of one mountain rippling onto another and another, each one dissected by a narrow, wooded valley. Trees drape the entire landscape—a rare scene in these otherwise well-developed hills.

Big Schloss.

Mill Mountain attracts hikers just for these kinds of panoramas. The trail is well marked and the views easy to find. It's hard to imagine that this same trip, if undertaken 300 years ago, would be considered folly. On the whole, early settlers avoided steep uphill routes across mountains. Huge oaks and chestnut trees made passage difficult; a frustrating undergrowth of laurel, creeper, and shrubs reduced their pace to a crawl. Instead, settlers stuck to roads through the valleys, routes first blazed by Native Americans. The most famous, the Great Warriors Path, became the Great Wagon Road as settlers replaced indigenous populations. So numerous were the Scotch-Irish, German, and English migrants moving south on the Great Wagon Road from Pennsylvania, it has been said travelers numbered in the tens of thousands up to the Revolutionary War.

Before settlers, Iroquois Indians had used the north-south route for hundreds of years. Virginia Governor Alexander Spotswood and his companion explorers found the route when they reached the shores of the Shenandoah River. Marked by hatchet notches in trees, the Great Warriors Path aided Iroquois travel from Canada into southern regions for war and trade. It was on one such trip that a band of Iroquois stayed south and settled in villages on the Neuse and Pamlico Rivers in northeastern North Carolina, which is where European traders and explorers encountered these "mild" and "gentle" people. Their name, from the Iroquoian word for "hemp gatherers," was Tuscarora.

Whatever the English's first impression, relations between the Tuscaroras and settlers turned ugly. Broken treaties and a rash of kidnappings of Indian children contributed to a Tuscarora-led massacre in 1711, at New Bern in North Carolina. (English settlers had built New Bern on the site of a Native American town, Chattoka.) The killings were unusually brutal. Women were pinned to the floor and staked through, children killed, and homes burned. A two-year war ensued. By 1713, the Tuscaroras were defeated. Chieftains sent word north along the Great Warrior Path to the League of Five Nations, in upstate New York, asking for help. In 1714, the Tuscaroras began migrating up the Appalachians into Virginia, Maryland, Pennsylvania, and, finally, New York. A Virginian settler in the 1750s and 1760s might see groups of these Indians, their worldly possessions piled on horseback, traveling in small bands, sometimes settling in an area for years, then moving north again. Officially, the Tuscaroras were accepted into the League of Five Nations (now Six Nations) in 1722. Their migration lasted at least another half century beyond this date. Today, their tribe numbers 600 people on reservation land near Niagara Falls.

In name and spirit, the Tuscaroras remain in Virginia to this day. At Waites Run, a hiker who steps onto Tuscarora Trail enters a forest world of mountain streams and hemlock groves. The wide-trunked evergreens show black, gnarled roots, some reaching into Pond Run, soaking in the water. Along this stream, Tuscarora Trail

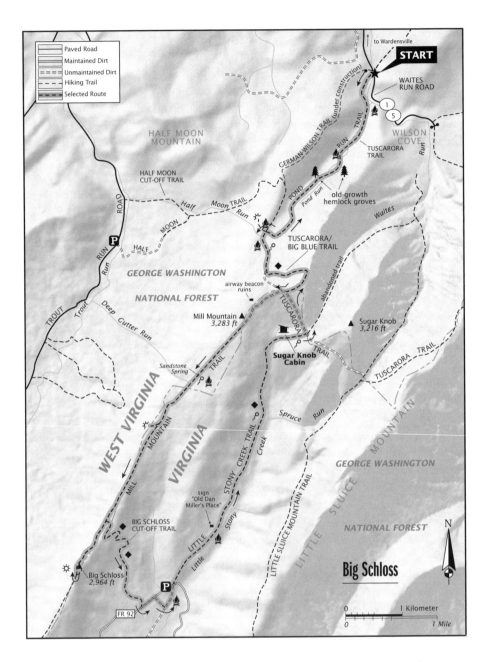

Legend:
- Paved Road
- Maintained Dirt
- Unmaintained Dirt
- Hiking Trail
- Selected Route

to Wardensville

START

WAITES RUN ROAD

1
5

WILSON COVE

HALF MOON MOUNTAIN

HALF MOON CUT-OFF TRAIL

GERMAN-WILSON TRAIL (under construction)

TUSCARORA TRAIL

POND RUN TRAIL

Pond Run

old-growth hemlock groves

Waites Run

Half Moon TRAIL

Half Moon Run

HALF MOON ROAD

P

HALF Run

HALF MOON

TUSCARORA/ BIG BLUE TRAIL

abandoned trail

GEORGE WASHINGTON

NATIONAL FOREST

airway beacon ruins

Mill Mountain ▲ 3,283 ft

TUSCARORA

Sugar Knob ▲ 3,216 ft

TROUT

Trout Run

Deep Cutter Run

Sandstone Spring

Sugar Knob Cabin

TUSCARORA TRAIL

TUSCARORA TRAIL

WEST VIRGINIA

VIRGINIA

MILL MOUNTAIN TRAIL

STONY CREEK TRAIL

Spruce Run

Stony Creek

GEORGE WASHINGTON

LITTLE SLUICE MOUNTAIN TRAIL

LITTLE SLUICE MOUNTAIN

sign "Old Dan Miller's Place"

BIG SCHLOSS CUT-OFF TRAIL

LITTLE Stony

Little Stony

NATIONAL FOREST

N

Big Schloss 2,964 ft

P

Big Schloss

FR 92

0   1 Kilometer

0   1 Mile

shares the path with Pond Run Trail. In a gap between Half Moon and Mill Mountains, Tuscarora Trail branches east. Uphill from a good spring at the headwaters of Half Moon Run, the blue-blazed route plunges left into heavy woods. The grade steepens. Boulders and small rocks make walking difficult. The fractured gray rock underfoot shows a quartz-pebble conglomerate. In these stones, the Tuscarora name crops up again as Tuscarora sandstone, a type found at the core of mountains from Virginia to Pennsylvania. (Admittedly, the term *sandstone* gives reason to pause. This is, after all, one of the most erosion-resistant rocks in the Appalachians, a fact at odds with the idea of sand, which is easily eroded. The key here is metamorphism—a change in which a rock, subjected to intense, volcanolike heat and pressure, changes and becomes a new rock. So the chief ingredient of sandstone is recrystallized sand—sand subjected to so much heat and pressure it turned to quartzite, which is one of the most resistant rocks around.)

The hiker and Tuscarora Trail part on Mill Mountain, where the latter turns east and heads for the Shenandoah National Park while the Mill Mountain Trail follows the ridgeline south. From Waites Run, the trail has climbed 1,500 feet; the next 4 miles undulate more gently on a slope leading south to Big Schloss. It's a dry hike. Except for water at Sandstone Spring, there are no reliable sources on the ridge. There are, however, views. Short branch trails end at rough-textured rocks that will skin knees and elbows if you scramble up for a view. Finally, there is Big Schloss (German for "castle") visible above tree line, accessible by boardwalks over crevices and steep rock faces. Free-fall views surround the high point on this rock formation—there's nothing but blue sky east-west-north-south and straight up.

From the high-and-dry altitude of Mill Mountain, Big Schloss Cut-off Trail descends through a sea of mountain laurel (peak blooms in June) to reach Little Stony Creek. Where the trail on Mill Mountain is bedded with sand and stone flints, the route up Stony Creek Trail is muddy, lined with ferns, and full of chirping birds. There are red-eyed vireos, Acadian fly catchers, and oven birds rustling about the brush. Scarlet tanager roost on treetops, then swoop in a flash of red to feed on insects in the brush. Also present are warblers, although hardly in numbers they once were. This songbird's decline in the Southern Appalachians is an alarm for naturalists. The decline rate varies by species, but as a whole, nearly three-quarters of the fifty warbler species known to inhabit the southern forests are in decline. For an explanation, look no further than the burned and clear-cut forest along Little Stoney Creek below Forest Road 92. Habitat loss and fragmentation, whether caused by logging, development, or natural events, has impacted warblers to a degree that has made it an issue of study by the Forest Service.

Past Sugar Knob Cabin, Stony Creek Trail intersects the Tuscarora Trail and the return to Waites Run begins. Just when it feels the hike won't end, reach the gap between Half Moon and Mill Mountains. The route downhill along Pond Run leads to the trailhead, but consider shedding the pack here for one final viewpoint. Follow white blazes out of the campground to a rock outcrop on the edge of the mountain. The view from here is endless. The Indians had an apt description for this kind of view: Appalachian.

Miles and Directions

0.0 **START** from a signboard for Pond Run Trail. (Note: The Pond Run Trail is also known as the Tuscarora Trail.) Standing on the concrete bridge spanning Waites Run, looking upstream, the signboard is on the right stream bank. From it, a blue-blazed dirt footpath climbs over a small hill and drops back to water and follows Waites Run upstream.

0.4 Veer right to follow the trail up Pond Run. Prior to this, there are campsites under hemlocks on your left. (Note: Green paint slashes on trees alongside the trail designate the wildlife management area, not the trail.)

0.5 Make the first of eight stream crossings on Pond Run as you walk up a cove past fine specimens of old-growth hemlock.

1.4 After crossing Pond Run once again, the trail passes a thick-trunked hemlock and climbs a rocky route up the right hillside. (FYI: Berry bushes crop up in the understory, signaling passage from the moist environment of the stream to drier slope environs.)

2.2 A glade of waist-high ferns heralds the approaching gap in Great North Mountain between Mill Mountain and Half Moon Mountain.

2.4 Reach a grassy junction. Turn left and immediately pass a campsite on the right. (An unmarked footpath, marked with white "i" blazes, descends from this campsite to a rock outcrop with a beautiful view of unspoiled forest land.) (Note: One-tenth of a mile past the campsite is a spring, the last reliable water source for 3 miles.)

2.7 Bear left onto a narrow, rocky, blue-blazed footpath. Avoid the old road that climbs the hill to the right. A sign states this road is closed for re-seeding. The footpath is a newly constructed leg of the Tuscarora Trail and covers some rugged ground as it bends around Mill Mountain to a bluff overlooking Wilson Cove and Paddy Mountain, before cutting southeast to meet Mill Mountain Trail.

3.9 Tuscarora Trail empties into a grassy clearing. Walk straight through the clearing and onto Mill Mountain Trail, a dirt road overgrown with grass. (A right turn leads along a now-abandoned section of Tuscarora/Big Blue. A left turn is the return trail from Sugar Knob Shelter.)

4.3 A trail branches off to the right to a now-destroyed air beacon site and a metal shed. Past this junction, the trail threads a set of concrete posts and reverts to a singletrack woods path. (FYI: The trail to the old air beacon is crowded with huckleberry, which bloom in early June.)

5.4 After a steep, rocky decline, reach Sandstone Spring, shaded by hemlocks. (FYI: This is a good water source and campsite.)

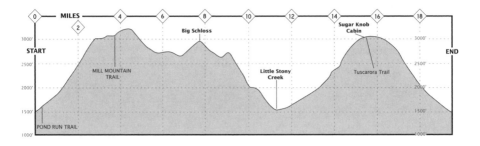

Scenic view off the west side of Mill Mountain.

6.0 An unmarked trail to the right reaches an overlook west to Long Mountain. From here, you also get a nice view south along the spine of Great North Mountain, a range once called Devil's Backbone.

6.7 Reach the Big Schloss Cut-off Trail branching left off Mill Mountain Trail. From here, the Big Schloss rock formation is 1.2 miles straight ahead on Mill Mountain Trail. Continue straight.

7.9 Reach Big Schloss. Views span 360 degrees east across the Great Valley and west into West Virginia. To continue this loop hike, return to Mill Mountain Trail and the Big Schloss Cut-off.

9.1 Back at the junction of Mill Mountain Trail and Big Schloss Cut-off Trail, descend the east slope of Mill Mountain on the Cut-off Trail on steep switchbacks amid slicks of mountain laurel.

10.8 Pass a signboard inviting hikers to join the Stonewall Brigade, a trail maintenance group. The trail drops to Forest Road 92. Turn left and follow the gravel road downhill.

11.1 An unmarked logging road drops off the right side of FR 92. This marks a bushwhack to Little Stony Creek that takes you through landscape scarred by clear-cutting and fire. After descending on the logging road and passing through a clearing, find any one of a number of animal paths through the entanglement of vines and briars. Past this thick undergrowth is a dirt logging road. At this point, Little Stony Creek is audible, but obscured by a fringe of woods. Turn left and follow the logging road. There are several large blowdowns that force detours into the brush, but this logging road remains the main trail to FR 92.

11.5 Pass a dirt road leading to campsites on Little Stony Creek. Two more roads leading to Little Stony and good campsites follow in quick succession.

11.7 Reach FR 92. Cross the gravel road and re-enter the woods. Little Stony Creek Trail is a narrow yellow-blazed path that follows the stream, crosses several times, then climbs with alternating steep pitches and level stretches.

15.2 Reach Sugar Knob Cabin, a PATC-sponsored hut. There is a spring in the vicinity and several fire rings. (FYI: The PATC cabin is locked and for use through reservations only. Call (703) 242-0693.)

15.3 Turn left onto the Tuscarora/Big Blue Trail, a wide road overgrown with grass. (FYI: As you climb, look off to the sides for knee-high ant mounds.)

15.9 Turn right at the junction with Mill Mountain Trail. This spot completes the Mill Mountain/Little Stony Creek loop.

17.1 Turn right onto Pond Run Trail and head down the shaded mountain stream valley. (FYI: Take time as you descend to notice how different the trees and terrain seem. You climbed this trail at the start of the hike, but it seems a different trail altogether as you descend.)

19.5 Hike ends at Waites Run Road.

Hike Information

Local Information

Shenandoah Valley Travel Association, New Market, VA, (877) VISIT SV, www.svta.org.

Local Attractions

Route 11 Chips, Middletown, VA, (800) 294-SPUD, www.rt11.com. Virginia's own. Follow your nose up U.S. Highway 11 from Strasburg to the small town of Middletown, where this potato chip maker makes and sells snackables.

North Mountain Vineyard & Winery, Maurentown, VA, (540) 436-9463, www.north mountainvineyard.com. Secluded winery with a friendly touch. Produces Chardonnay, Riesling, Chambourcin, Claret, Vidal Blanc, and spiced apple wines.

Lodging

Hotel Strasburg, Strasburg, VA, (540) 465-9191, (800) 348-8327, www.hotel strasburg.com. Pets allowed.

Restaurants

Kac-Ka-Pon Restaurant, Wardensville, WV, (304) 874-3232.

Organizations

Potomac Appalachian Trail Club (PATC), Vienna, VA, (703) 242-0693, www.patc.net.

Other Resources

The Tuscarora Trail: A Guide to the South Half in West Virginia and Virginia, 1997, PATC. A bare-bones guide to the lower twelve sections of the Tuscarora Trail.

18 Stephens Trail

Camp Roosevelt opened in 1933 as America's first Civilian Conservation Corps camp. Living in tents and earning $30 a week, unemployed men built the roads, campgrounds, picnic shelters, and fire towers we still use today. Their handiwork included a limestone block tower and shelter on Kennedy Peak. Its squat, low-rising design often surprises hikers expecting a tall lookout, but it's still high enough to give commanding views off the 2,600-foot Kennedy Peak. Eastward lies Page Valley and, to the west, Shenandoah Valley, both outlined with patchwork farms, towns, and forests.

Start: From the Camp Roosevelt Recreation Area.
Distance: 8.5-mile loop.
Approximate hiking time: 5 hours.
Difficulty rating: Easy, with a few climbs and most of the trail following old logging roads.
Trail surface: Dirt footpaths and dirt forest roads lead to ridgetops, forest coves, and the craggy Kennedy Peak with views of the Blue Ridge and Allegheny Mountains.
Land status: National forest.
Nearest town: Luray, VA.
Other trail users: Mountain bikers, equestrians, cross-country skiers, and hunters (in season).

Canine compatibility: Dogs permitted.
Trail contacts: Lee Ranger District, Edinburg, VA, (540) 984-4101, www.southernregion.fs. fed.us/gwj/lee.
Schedule: Open year-round. Camp Roosevelt is open from the first Tuesday in May to the third Monday in October. Hunting is permitted in national forests, and the busiest season is November to early January.
Fees/permits: No fees or permits required. Camp Roosevelt: $10 per night.
Maps: USGS maps: Hamburg, VA; Luray, VA; Rileyville, VA; Edinburg, VA.

Finding the trailhead: From Luray: Exit the U.S. Highway 211 Bypass at U.S. Highway 340 and drive south on US 340 for 0.2 mile. Turn right onto Virginia Route 675, which immediately crosses Hawksbill Creek and passes through a neighborhood of small homes. In 1.7 miles, VA 675 forks left (Virginia Route 654 continues straight). Cross the South Fork Shenandoah River at 3.3 miles, turn left and follow VA 675 as it climbs Massanutten Mountain. At 8.1 miles from US 340, turn right into Camp Roosevelt Recreation Area. Parking is on the right; camping is up the access road bearing left. *DeLorme: Virginia Atlas & Gazetteer:* Page 73, C7; Page 74, B1.

The Hike

Spotted wintergreen's tolerance of poor soil makes this exotic-looking plant stand out amid the otherwise drab mountain slope leading to Kennedy Peak. From the flower's telltale green-and-white leaves rises a single, top-heavy stem crowned by five white petals that arc backwards. To see the green pluglike pistil and pale yellow stamens, gently lift the flower and peek beneath.

View from Kennedy Peak east toward the Blue Ridge.

Dry forest conditions breed more than curious-looking wildflowers. They breed forest fires, the threat of which prompted Jack Stephens to walk from his home in Fort Valley to Kennedy Peak on a regular basis. Stephens's route up Kennedy Peak varied little. From Fort Valley, he climbed on switchbacks to a small saddleback between what is now called Stephens Pass. Turning right, he walked atop the narrow Massanutten Ridge, then made his way up the steep, rocky hill to the fire tower.

Stephens's route is now engraved into the slope of Massanutten Mountain by a generation of hikers and horseback riders. Blueberries and scrub oak crowd the forest understory, a monotone landscape highlighted in places by very colorful spotted wintergreen. Grouse and turkeys and deer inhabit this woodland, too. In the saddlebacks between small knobs, grass grows waist-high. Trees are spaced and signs of old orchards and stone walls are visible.

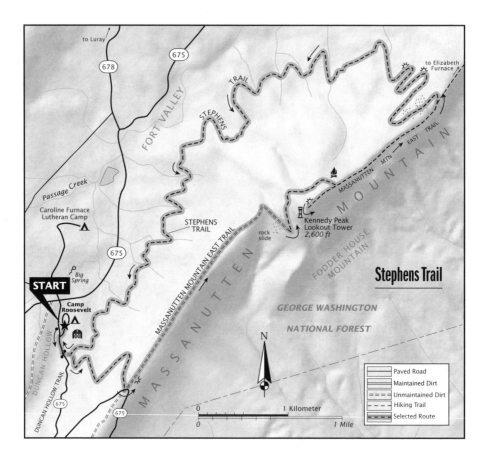

The advantages of a tower on Kennedy Peak are clear from the moment you ascend. Massanutten Mountain stretches 55 miles from Front Royal to Harrison-burg, and along its entire length there are few if any steep or dramatic interruptions. Kennedy Peak is the exception, sticking up 200 feet from the main trunk just before the ridge descends to a small gap. The knob, barren of trees, affords unblocked views in all directions. If you could peer back in time from here as well, you would wit-ness a time when local wardens received $5.00 a year to monitor fire activity in a newly created national forest. The period was World War I, and two forest units existed in northern Virginia, the Massanutten and Potomac Districts. To build pride and win over suspicious locals, the forest supervisor fostered a rivalry between them. For three years—1913–1916—wardens from each side met for a tug-of-war at the Shenandoah County Fair. The winner took home bragging rights and a wooden Forest Service shield. The rivalry ended in 1917 when the two districts merged. (For the record, Massanutten District won the tug-of-war twice, Potomac once. Both regions fall within the present-day Lee Ranger District.)

Where Stephens Trail retraces the footsteps of one man, a different route to Kennedy Peak, on the Massanutten East Trail out of Camp Roosevelt, follows the steps of hundreds of men. The first Civilian Conservation Corps camp opened at Camp Roosevelt in 1933, and for nearly a decade following, unemployed men and World War I veterans spread across what was then Shenandoah National Forest (the name was later changed to George Washington National Forest to avoid confusion with Shenandoah National Park). Nicknamed Roosevelt's Tree Army, these men planted trees to replace the acres clear-cut for charcoal and timber. To build the Kennedy Peak fire tower, they carried limestone blocks quarried from the mountains.

FYI Stephens Trail is named for the local Fort Valley resident who manned the Kennedy Lookout tower in the 1950s and 1960s.

Limestone proved a valuable commodity for others, too: early American blast furnaces required limestone to make pig iron. Along Stephens Trail, hikers can see clearly the red cakelike rocks, some the size of bricks, that iron-ore producers craved. These stones are hematite-laden; the red color ensured prospectors that the rocks would produce good quality iron. They were carted off to local blast furnaces, where molten pig iron flowed out of the bottom of the furnace into molds for pots and kettles and tools.

During the Civil War, blast furnaces shifted production. Out of mountain iron works such as Elizabeth Furnace and Catherine Furnace came the bullets, cannons, and guns that supplied Confederate troops. General Stonewall Jackson stated, "If the Valley is lost, Virginia is lost," and embarked on the Valley Campaign of 1862 to ensure that wouldn't happen. Battles at Kernstown, McDowell, Cross Keys, and Front Royal kept the Valley in Confederate hands until 1864, when Northern general Philip Sheridan began sweeping through the Shenandoah Valley, burning homes, looting supplies, and slaughtering livestock.

The best view from Kennedy Peak lies west, across the northern Shenandoah Valley. This is the valley traveled by Quakers and Scots-Irish from Pennsylvania and Maryland in the early 1700s. With their arrival, two Virginias evolved. In coastal regions, a few wealthy landowners controlled land and an economy based on tobacco and slave labor. Mountain Virginia reflected the religious fervor of German and Scots-Irish immigrants. Wheat fared better here than tobacco, due in part to limestone-rich soil. Nicknames for these two Virginians developed: Easterners were *Tuckahoes,* a term derived from the arum root that grows around marshes; western Virginians were *Cohees,* slang derived from "Quothe he," a reflection of the settlers' strong religious backgrounds.

From the Cohees' valley towns, Massanutten Mountain appears as a single, continuous ridge. At its northern reach, the bedrock divides into two ridges separated by a bowl-like depression called Fort Valley. In the 1700s, English colonists built a fort here for trading and protection against the French and Native Americans. The boast "Washington Slept Here" rings true in Fort Valley and neighboring towns such as Winchester and Front Royal. These mountains and valley were a proving ground for the young George Washington, who first visited as a surveyor for Lord Fairfax, and then as an officer in the Virginia militia.

The views off Kennedy Peak show that a century of human progress has erased physical signs of the destruction of the past. The whole of Massanutten Mountain appears separate from the valley that unfolds at its feet. In reality, it is just the opposite. You cannot remove the mountain from the valley. Nor would it seem right to do so.

Miles and Directions

0.0   **START** at the entrance of Camp Roosevelt. Turn left and walk up VA 675 to a white forest gate on the left in 0.1 mile. (FYI: On the right side of the road is a trailhead for Duncan Hollow Trail. It leads south to New Market Gap.)

0.1   Turn left onto orange-blazed Massanutten East Trail. It climbs uphill past the white forest gate.

0.2   Enter a clearing, turn right, and climb on the Massanutten East Trail. The trail passes under a set of power lines several times and narrows from a dirt road into a footpath. (FYI: There is a locked equipment shed in the clearing. The trail that leads straight past the shed is Stephens Trail.)

0.8   The trail reaches VA 675. Turn left and walk 50 yards up the left side of the road, re-entering the woods on a forest road. (FYI: There is an impressive view over Fort Valley on the side of VA 675.)

1.9   Massanutten East Trail branches right from the dirt road to circumvent a knob. In 0.2 mile, the trail repeats this pattern. (FYI: There are nice views here, across Fort Valley to Massanutten Mountain's west ridge.)

2.2   Pass a campsite on the right side of the trail. Kennedy Peak is visible at this point.

2.4   The trail switchbacks northwest amid a rock slide.

2.6   Where the trail bends right around the side of Kennedy Peak, there are good views west over Fort Valley. (FYI: At shoulder height on your right side, thick slabs of sedimentized rock stick out of the hillside at a 45-degree angle. A lone mountain laurel grows from between two slabs.)

3.2   Reach the spur trail to Kennedy Peak. Turn right and make the short, 0.2-mile uphill trek to a stone shelter/lookout tower constructed by the Civilian Conservation Corps stationed

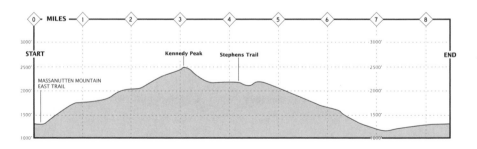

Section of Massanutten East Trail leading to Kennedy Peak.

at Camp Roosevelt in the 1930s. Return to the Massanutten East Trail and hike north atop the ridge.

4.0 Where the trail drops briefly off the right side of a knob, look for exposed sections of rock that show the layered sandstone rock formations. (FYI: This is Massanutten sandstone, light gray and highly resistant rock found only in the Massanutten Range.)

4.2 Stephens Trail branches left while Massanutten East Trail continues a northward route to Elizabeth Furnace. Turn left onto Stephens Trail and make a beeline through open hard-wood forest. Where the downslope pitch steepens, the trail switches back to descend along the northwest flank of Massanutten Mountain. (FYI: Watch for red flinty rocks underfoot, indicative of the iron-ore deposits found in the mountain bedrock.)

5.3 (FYI: As you wrap around a shoulder ridge and begin a lateral descent on the wavy course of Stephens Trail, there are good views over Fort Valley west. For 2 miles, the trail will alternate between moist coves and exposed hillsides as it crosses the many unnamed tributaries of Passage Creek, which flows through Fort Valley, a basin formed by the east and west ridges of Massanutten Mountain.)

8.3 Enter a clearing and hike straight past a junction with the Massanutten East Trail. The brown equipment shed is on your right.

8.4 Reach VA 675. Turn right and walk downhill to Camp Roosevelt.

8.5 Hike ends at Camp Roosevelt.

Hike Information

Local Information

Luray-Page County Chamber of Commerce, Luray, VA, (540) 743-3915, (888) 743-3915, www.luraypage.com.

Shenandoah County Travel Council, Woodstock, VA, (540) 459-6220.

Shenandoah Valley Visitor Center, New Market Gap, VA, (877) 847-4878, www.svta.org.

Local Events/Attractions

Heritage Days, Mount Jackson, VA, (540) 459-6220. A quaint Main Street affair with a can't-miss feature: homemade baked goods from the Mennonite Church women.

CCC Reunion, second Sunday in September, Camp Roosevelt, VA, (540) 984-4101. Annual gathering of folks interested in the history of the Civilian Conservation Corps.

Luray Caverns, Luray, VA, (540) 743-6551, www.luraycaverns.com. One of several commercial caves in the Shenandoah Valley. Guided tours available.

Lodging

The Widow Kips, Mount Jackson, VA, (540) 477-2400, www.widowkips.com. Pets welcome in their guest cottages. Best B&B breakfast around.

Restaurants

The Spring House, Woodstock, VA, (540) 459-4755. Casual eatery with great food.

Organizations

Potomac Appalachian Trail Club (PATC), Vienna, VA, (703) 242-0693, www.patc.net.

19 Fridley Gap

Some days, you can hike for miles and feel like you never left the parking lot. Other times, it can feel like you walked through four different worlds in a single afternoon. Thankfully, you'll find Fridley Gap fits the latter experience. Squeezed together accordionlike, the long, parallel ridges of First, Second, Third, and Fourth Mountains concentrate an awful lot of up-and-downs into a day of hiking, and, consequently, a number of different habitats. At the lower elevations, stream valleys attract deer to the water's edge. Skinny rays of sunlight filter down to the forest floor through hemlock. A half mile away stands another world: the dry, barren ridgetops. With no tree cover, views stretch for miles. Two different worlds, one hike.

Start: From the gate across Forest Road 65.
Distance: 9.4-mile loop.
Approximate hiking time: 5 hours.
Difficulty rating: Moderate, with steep climbs up Third and Fourth Mountains.
Trail surface: Dirt paths, old logging roads, and gravel forest roads wind through a hemlock grove along Fridley Run and rock outcrops along Fourth Mountain, and lead to a waterfall and swimming hole on Mountain Run.
Land status: National forest.
Nearest town: Shenandoah, VA.

Other trail users: Equestrians, mountain bikers, cross-country skiers, and hunters (in season).
Canine compatibility: Dogs permitted.
Trail contacts: Lee Ranger District, Edinburg, VA, (540) 984–4101, www.southernregion. fs.fed.us/gwj/lee.
Schedule: Open year-round. Hunting is permitted in national forests, and deer season is the busiest from November to early January.
Fees/permits: No fees or permits required.
Maps: USGS maps: Elkton West, VA; Tenth Legion, VA.

Finding the trailhead: From Shenandoah: Follow Virginia Route 602 south across the South Fork Shenandoah River. At 3.8 miles, turn right onto Virginia Route 636 (Runkles Gap Road). In 2.2 miles, enter the George Washington National Forest. In 0.1 mile past the forest boundary, VA 636 ends, although the gravel road straight ahead continues as gated FR 65 (Cub Run Road). Gated Forest Road 65A turns right uphill. There is a parking lot for five cars at this intersection. *DeLorme: Virginia Atlas & Gazetteer:* Page 67, A6.

The Hike

Oak trees have always fascinated people. Pagan worshipers likened the tree's physical traits—tall, sturdy, and long-lived—with the most powerful gods. Zeus, the Greek god of thunder and lightning, considered the oak sacred. This, in turn, may have informed the old English saying: "Beware the oak; it draws the stroke," a reference to just how often oaks get struck by lightning.

Reverence for the oak seems justifiable given its usefulness. Ancient people treated it like a department superstore, a complete package, able to provide all the

Swimming hole on Mountain Run.

stuff for living. Acorns not only made food (acorn cakes), but also attracted the deer, bear, and small game that became food. Homes and furniture were built of oak boards. Oak logs provided fuel for heating and cooking. And while it's true that Europeans looked down their noses at the North America white oak sent to them, the wood proved durable enough to construct the first ships for the U.S. Navy.

Oaks, in their natural setting, define the forest type between southern New England and Georgia. Their presence sets the tone for how large or widespread other trees grow. Additionally, more than 200 known species live off the oak, from the squirrels that survive on its acorns to the mushrooms growing on its trunk. Elevation and soil conditions matter little; there's a type of oak for every location. In the mountains, white oaks grow in stream valleys and on moist hillsides. Chinquapin and bear oak are found as thickets in the young second- or third-generation forests. Red oaks mix with the whites, the beeches, and the maples at low elevations, but emerge in pure stands at higher elevations. Chestnut oaks, so named for the leaf's resemblance to that of the much-diminished American chestnut, take root on rocky hillsides and dry ridges.

Changes in elevation and moisture occur quickly over short distances in the Massanutten Mountain chain. This 55-mile-long grouping of ridges and knobs rises from the floor of the Shenandoah Valley in the shape of a needle, with forks of the Shenandoah River flowing along either flank. At its southern end—the point of the needle—stand the highest points, Lairds Knob (3,282 feet) and Massanutten Peak (2,922 feet). Here also stands Third Mountain, as well as its neighbors First, Second, and Fourth Mountains, all of them long, parallel ridges squeezed together like the folds of an accordion. For every wrinkle in this mountain landscape, there's an oak tree to tell hikers about the soil conditions, climate, and annual rainfall. Leaf litter along the Massanutten South Trail shows telltale signs of white oak. Along this same trail, a mile past Boone Run, red oaks replace white as the dominant tree along the descending ridge of Fourth Mountain. (Hikers should be able to distinguish between the two most abundant oaks—red and white. The leaf of a white oak has rounded tips between the deep lobes; a red oak leaf has pointed or bristly tips.)

Oak trees aside, little about the terrain on the southern portion of Massanutten Mountain is consistent. Boone Run and Fridley Run illustrate how a small geographic area can hold such contrasting habitats within close proximity. The streams flow off in opposite directions: Boone Run south to the South Fork Shenandoah River, Fridley Run north to Mountain Run. Third Mountain separates these two streams, and the Massanutten South Trail follows alongside both.

As you climb to a gap in Third Mountain and pass the headwaters of Boone Run, the forest canopy disappears, and the ground is a flinty stone or sand. This is in sharp contrast to the sun-dappled pleasures of Fridley Run, which runs at the base of Third Mountain's northwest slope. Along Fridley Run, hemlocks loom over the

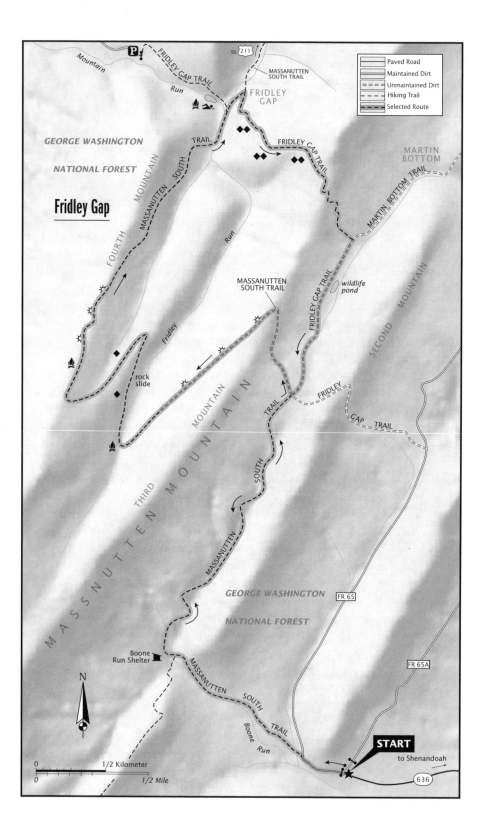

Fridley Gap

GEORGE WASHINGTON

NATIONAL FOREST

to 211

MASSANUTTEN
SOUTH TRAIL

FRIDLEY
GAP

P

FRIDLEY GAP TRAIL

Mountain

Run

FOURTH MASSANUTTEN SOUTH MOUNTAIN TRAIL

FRIDLEY GAP TRAIL

MARTIN
BOTTOM

MARTIN BOTTOM TRAIL

Run

Fridley

MASSANUTTEN
SOUTH TRAIL

FRIDLEY GAP TRAIL

wildlife
pond

SECOND MOUNTAIN

rock
slide

MOUNTAIN

MASSANUTTEN SOUTH TRAIL

FRIDLEY GAP TRAIL

THIRD MOUNTAIN

SOUTH

TRAIL

MASSANUTTEN

GEORGE WASHINGTON

NATIONAL FOREST

FR 65

MASSANUTTEN MOUNTAIN

Boone
Run Shelter

MASSANUTTEN SOUTH TRAIL

FR 65A

N

START

to Shenandoah

Boone Run

636

	Paved Road
	Maintained Dirt
	Unmaintained Dirt
	Hiking Trail
	Selected Route

0   1/2 Kilometer
0   1/2 Mile

stream bank. Green moss blankets wet rocks. The river flows for a short distance, then spills over a ledge and collects in a pool, repeating this pattern again and again as it moves downhill. It is a scene as lush and beautiful and sheltered as the top of Third Mountain is dry, exposed, and nondescript.

The red oaks don't look healthy on Fourth Mountain. There are signs of gypsy moth infestation, a blight to which oaks are particularly vulnerable. Damage from the gypsy moth is not limited to eating the leaves off the tree; acorn production declines in their wake. Animals migrate in search of a more reliable food source. A thinning of the forest canopy lets light reach the forest floor. Fast-growing trees and shrubs replace oaks. A pattern of forest succession begins. It will take hundreds of years before the climax forest returns, too long for one human to witness. We can take simple comfort in knowing how it ends, though. The oaks will return.

Miles and Directions

0.0 **START** at a gate across FR 65 at the end of gravel VA 636. Walk past this gate up the left side of the road. Boone Run flows in the gully on the left.

0.2 Descend left off the FR 65 road embankment, following orange blazes of the Massanutten South Trail. The trail immediately crosses a stream. The trail is as wide as an old road, narrows into a footpath, then widens again. Watch for orange blazes. (FYI: Faint traces of old roads branch into the woods.)

0.7 Hillsides close in and Massanutten South Trail narrows to become a footpath. (FYI: Boone Run cuts through some impressive exposed rock that shows the uplifting that created the series of First, Second, and Third Mountains.)

1.0 Hike past a blue-blazed trail on the left. In a few feet, a white-blazed trail goes left to a shelter in 0.1 mile. (FYI: The blue-blazed trail leads to Kaylor Knob.)

1.9 The trail steepens. Boone Run, once a bubbling stream, is a dry, sandy groove in the hillside.

2.2 Follow the Massanutten South Trail as it enters a clearing and turns left at a four-corners trail junction. (FYI: The trail straight ahead is Fridley Gap Trail, which is the return leg of this loop hike.)

3.1 Massanutten South Trail, as it descends Third Mountain, narrows and enters a dark hemlock cove on Fridley Run. (FYI: There is a campsite here with signs of hunter use.)

3.5 The trail wraps around Fourth Mountain and steepens.

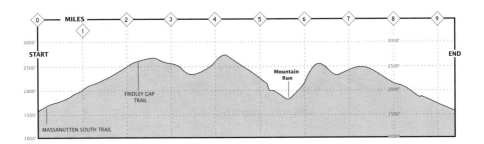

4.0 Begin a descent off Fourth Mountain.

4.2 Pass a campsite on the left. (FYI: There is a rock outcrop and views behind the campsite. The next half mile brings more excellent views on similarly marked trails on the left.)

5.4 Massanutten South Trail crosses Fridley Run just above the stream's junction with Mountain Run. There is a waterfall and deep swimming hole near here. (FYI: This spot gets heavy use from day-trippers, with Forest Road 722 just a half mile downstream.)

5.5 Turn left and hike uphill. In a few feet, turn right onto purple-blazed Fridley Gap Trail. (FYI: At the junction with Fridley Gap Trail, the Massanutten South Trail goes straight, eventually reaching the national forest visitor center at New Market Gap.)

6.3 After a very steep climb, cross the wooded crest of Third Mountain.

6.6 Exit the woods onto a dirt road. Turn right and follow Fridley Gap Trail uphill. (FYI: The road left is the Martin Bottom Trail)

7.2 Enter a clearing and walk straight through a four-corners intersection. This is the Massanutten South Trail. (FYI: Fridley Gap Trail turns left at this junction downhill on an old forest road to FR 65A.) Follow Massanutten South Trail past the pine tree for a return to FR 65 along Boone Run.

8.4 Pass the Boone Run Shelter access trail on the right.

9.2 Exit the woods onto FR 65 and turn right to the parking lot.

9.4 Hike ends at the gate across FR 65.

Crossing Boone Run along the Massanutten South Trail.

Hike Information

Local Information

Harrisonburg-Rockingham Convention & Visitors Bureau, Harrisonburg, VA, (540) 434-2319, www.hrcvb.org.

Shenandoah Valley Visitor Center, New Market Gap, VA, (877) 847-4878, www.svta.org.

Lodging

Edinburg Inn Bed & Breakfast, Edinburg, VA, (540) 984-8286.

The Village Inn, Harrisonburg, VA, (540) 434-7355. Pets welcome.

20 Laurel Fork Area

Laurel Fork once ranked as a top site in Virginia for wilderness protection, but strong opposition from inholders—families who own private property inside national forest boundaries—beat this proposal back. The desire to keep this place forever wild is understandable. There's a whiff of spruce in the air. Songbirds trill and peep in the bushes. Pine needles pile thick on the forest floor. Streams wriggle around and over the deadfall and boulders strewn in their path by storms and hurricanes. Native trout swim the Laurel Fork. It has been a long seventy years since loggers cleared the red spruce and fir trees. Nature has reclaimed Laurel Fork fully, and for this, we're all better off.

Start: From the Locust Spring Picnic Area.
Distance: 11.2-mile loop.
Approximate hiking time: 6 hours.
Difficulty rating: Moderate due to numerous stream crossings and steep trails up Middle Mountain that merge with streambeds. Because of its elevation, Laurel Fork receives heavy snowfall in winter.
Trail surface: Dirt footpaths and old forest roads wind through high-altitude red spruce forests and stream coves.
Land status: National forest.

Nearest town: Monterey, VA.
Other trail users: Mountain bikers, equestrians, and hunters (in season).
Canine compatibility: Dogs permitted.
Trail contacts: Warm Springs Ranger District, Hot Springs, VA, (540) 839-2521.
Schedule: Open year-round. Hunting is permitted in national forests, and deer season runs from November through early January.
Fees/permits: No fees or permits required.
Maps: USGS maps: Thornwood, VA; Snowy Mountain, VA.

Finding the trailhead: From Monterey: Drive west on U.S. Highway 250. In 22 miles, turn right onto Virginia Route 28 and drive north for 6.7 miles. Turn right onto Forest Road 60/Forest Road 106, following signs for Locust Spring Picnic Area. In 0.3 mile bear left onto FR 60. At a second intersection in 0.3 mile, bear right and uphill, following signs for Locust Spring Picnic Area. The picnic area is on the right on Forest Road 142 in 0.4 mile. *DeLorme: Virginia Atlas & Gazetteer:* Page 64 (inset), A1.

The Hike

Laurel Fork is a classic mountain stream, appreciation of which requires little effort. A big boulder helps. Sit on the rock and stare. In early morning hours a haze wraps around overhanging branches. Spray tossed up by the water sparkles. And just like that, an entire day watching birds flit from branch to branch seems a reasonable proposition.

It would, however, preclude exploration of the 10,000 acres in Laurel Fork Special Management Area. The steep west slope of Middle Mountain beckons. Up

Rhododendron blooms across a stream in Laurel Fork.

Christian Run or Cold Spring Run, the narrow footpaths are overrun with rhododendron. Trails and creeks intermingle without regard. The moss is spongy. There's a dank smell of moist, decomposing leaves. When the trails widen, the earth buckles and ripples where railroad ties were once embedded. Laurel Fork was privately

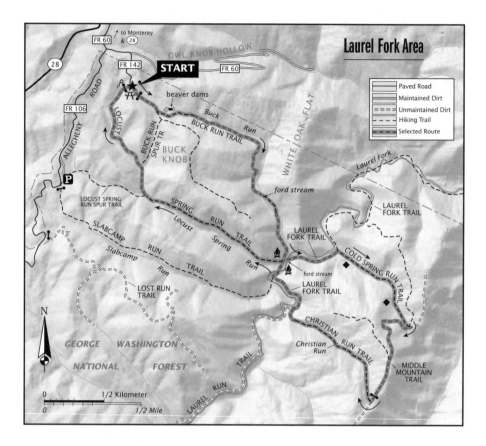

Laurel Fork Area

to Monterey & 28

FR 60
28
FR 142
START
FR 60
OWL KNOB HOLLOW

FR 106
ALLEGHENY ROAD
LOCUST
beaver dams

Buck Run
BUCK RUN TRAIL

BUCK RUN SPUR TR
BUCK KNOB

WHITE OAK FLAT

Laurel Fork

	Paved Road
	Maintained Dirt
	Unmaintained Dirt
	Hiking Trail
	Selected Route

P
LOCUST SPRING RUN SPUR TRAIL

SPRING
Locust
RUN TRAIL
Spring
Run

ford stream

LAUREL FORK TRAIL

LAUREL FORK TRAIL

SLABCAMP
RUN
TRAIL
Slabcamp Run

LAUREL FORK TRAIL
ford stream
LAUREL FORK TRAIL

COLD SPRING RUN TRAIL

LOST RUN TRAIL

N

CHRISTIAN RUN TRAIL

Christian Run

GEORGE WASHINGTON
NATIONAL FOREST

LAUREL RUN TRAIL

MIDDLE MOUNTAIN TRAIL

0   1/2 Kilometer
0   1/2 Mile

owned until 1922. Railroads chugged up and down the mountain slopes carrying workers in and logs out. Today's trail network follows these grades, and rusted cast-iron remains of old railroad engine parts lie near the junction of Bearwallow Trail and Laurel Fork Trail.

Loggers were after the red spruce that gives Laurel Fork a unique aura. Much of it went to pulp mills. The highest quality boards, craftsmen used in musical instruments; they preferred spruce to other woods because of its consistent growth patterns. Consider that a felled tree exhibits growth rings of varying size. Thick rings indicate the salad years, when sunlight and water were plentiful. Narrow rings reflect leaner times. Spruce somehow avoids these highs and lows; its growth rings are almost always the same size and compact, two qualities favorable for musical instruments. (Another interesting aside: the older the instrument, the better it sounds—but that's only if it's played, not left under glass to age. Wood becomes elastic with vibration, so an old wood instrument can sound as poor as one made of "green" wood if left untouched.)

For a hiker whose exposure to needle-leaf trees extends from jack pine to hemlock, a spruce forest can seem like an altered state. Technically, Laurel Fork is an

"Appalachian extension of a northern boreal forest." Non-technically-speaking, it's cold, snows like crazy in winter, and harbors animals normally found farther north. If you're lucky, a snowshoe hare might hop across the trail. The distribution map for this animal shows a shaded area over all of Canada and parts of Minnesota, Wisconsin, and New York. The map also shows fingerlike extensions reaching down the chain of Appalachian Mountains as far south as the Great Smoky Mountains in Tennessee. This sums up nicely the whole boreal forest effect. Glaciers never reached as far south as Virginia (as indicated by the dearth of natural lakes). But even if the ice never made it, the northern species of trees and animals suited for that environment did.

Buck Run Trail is a good introduction to the habitat. From Locust Spring Picnic Area the trail leads first past beaver dams. In the backwaters of all the major drainages—Buck Run, Slabcamp Run, and Bearwallow Run—you'll find sizable beaver populations. Their handiwork is not confined to dams. Springtime finds logs felled across trails; the gnawed pointed trunk gives away the culprit. The shallow ponds created by the dams are thick with salamanders and frogs and the shrill of spring peepers.

One of the northern trees you'll see along with the red spruce is the Fraser fir. In 1784, the tree's namesake, John Fraser, a Scotsman, sailed into Charleston hoping to follow in the footsteps of his contemporaries, William Bartram and Andre Michaux, botanists who made names for themselves studying the flora and fauna of the Southern Appalachians. Fraser was an amateur, primarily concerned with making a fortune (why he chose botany as a career is a mystery). He roamed the Southern Appalachians collecting specimens for the highest bidder. His short list at times included the king of England, Catherine the Great of Russia, and her successor, Czar Paul. For a brief period, Fraser and Michaux traveled together, but their competing interest (Michaux was sending samples to Louis XVI of France) soon caused them to part company. Michaux let Fraser travel ahead, and, as a result, Fraser had the good fortune of being the first to discover the tree that now bears his name.

Nature is an exact science, down to the arrangement of needles on a red spruce branch. Clusters of needles minimize heat loss and keep the tree branch warm through the winter. The interlocking branches weave a canopy that blocks out sun and lends everything below a gloomy aspect. Thick piles of fallen needles mat the forest floor. Moist green sphagnum moss covers roots and rocks. Besides moss, little else grows under a mature spruce-fir forest canopy. It's a vicious little circle, whereby needles and moss give the soil a high acid content, and the acid soil in turn slows decomposition. The moss, especially, thrives by coating dead logs and whatever else will host it.

The red spruce that dominate in Laurel Fork are well suited for life here. The soil is thin, a product of years of logging and erosion. The tree spreads wide, shallow roots into this soil. Porcupines like to nibble on the sweet bark of these trees, while red squirrels seem adept at extracting seeds from cones. Berry shrubs sprout and survive to feed a host of birds and small rodents through the lean winter months. Bearberry and prickly gooseberry mingle with the more readily identified high- and low-bush blueberries.

When West Virginia seceded from Virginia after the outbreak of the Civil War, it took with it some of the roughest natural terrain on the East Coast. Virginia's valleys and ridges seem downright pastoral when compared to the jumble of peaks, cliffs, and ridges that form the Allegheny Mountains in West Virginia. Virginia can at least take some comfort in having kept this corner of Highland County and the Laurel Fork watershed.

Miles and Directions

0.0 **START** at the Locust Spring Picnic Area. Walk up a dirt road at the east end of the picnic area. Almost immediately, look for a gated forest road on the right, marked with blue blazes and a hiker sign. This is the Buck Run trailhead. Turn right, pass by the gate, and follow the road, which is overgrown with grass.

0.4 Turn left off the grass road. Pass through a stand of red spruce. The ground is flat and the trail is now a dirt singletrack. There are several beaver dams in this area (FYI: Buck Run Spur Trail is straight ahead on the grass road.)

1.3 The trail descends off the side of Buck Knob and switchbacks five times as it drops to Buck Run.

1.6 A rock cairn marks the crossing of Buck Run on a bridge constructed of three skinny logs. Cross and walk downstream following the left bank. In 0.1 mile, re-cross Buck Run to the right stream bank. (FYI: From now until the junction with Laurel Fork Trail, note how the slopes on either stream bank host starkly different plants: The left slope is covered with rhododendron, while the right supports more hardwoods, and sparse at that. Many exposed rock formations on this leg make it a geologist's delight, amateur or otherwise.)

3.0 Buck Run Trail ends at a junction with the Laurel Fork Trail. Turn left onto Laurel Fork Trail and cross the stream. After crossing, turn left and hike downstream. (FYI: From the end of Buck Run Trail, Laurel Fork Trail also leads straight upstream and intersects Locust Spring Run Trail, Slabcamp Run Trail, and Christian Run Trail.) (Note: In the river floodplain, yellow sundrops may be in bloom. Pink ladyslippers and the white bell-shaped flowers of Solomon seal grow near the edge of the forest. Red elderberry displays its fruit in August.)

3.7 Turn right and ascend on blue-blazed Cold Spring Run Trail. The trail joins the stream for a short stretch, then widens to show signs of an old railroad bed.

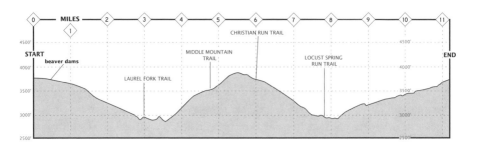

Downed log across Laurel Creek.

4.7 The ground levels on both sides of the trail as it enters a grassy meadow. (FYI: The fields on Meadow Mountain were cleared for grazing when the mountain was privately owned. Today, The Stamp, an in-holding farther south on the mountain, remains the last piece of private property in the special management area.)

4.9 Turn right onto Middle Mountain Trail, following blue blazes.

6.0 Pass a hunters' camp on the left and by a Forest Service gate. A large field opens up on your left. Turn right and walk through a meadow. Blue arrows on trees on the right fringe of the field will guide you to where the Christian Run Trail enters the woods.

6.7 The trail narrows and runs close to Christian Run. It crosses three times.

7.0 Christian Run Trail junctions with Laurel Fork Trail. Turn right and walk along the right stream bank.

7.4 Where Slabcamp Run Trail branches left and crosses Laurel Run, continue straight on Laurel Fork Trail. There are several good campsites on this stretch of trail, including one, just prior to crossing Laurel Fork, that overlooks a swimming hole.

7.6 Cross Laurel Fork and hike along the left stream bank.

7.8 Turn left onto Locust Spring Run Trail. The next mile and a half brings numerous stream crossings. In places, the stream and trail merge for some messy hiking.

9.9 Bear right and away from a left-branching trail, which is Locust Spring Run Spur Trail. It leads to FR 106.

11.2 Hike ends at the Locust Spring Picnic Area.

Hike Information

Local Information

Bath County Chamber of Commerce, (800) 628–8092, www.bathcountyva.org.
Highland County Chamber of Commerce, Monterey, VA, (540) 468–2550, www.highland county.org.

Local Events/Attractions

Durbin Days, July, Durbin, WV.

21 Ramsey's Draft Wilderness

Welcome to a wilderness smorgasbord where ten Appalachian knobs surround a rugged valley etched by Ramsey's Draft. The highest knob, Hardscrabble Knob, reaches an impressive 4,282 feet. Ramsey's Draft Trail is the main route up the center of the wilderness area. All told, there are some 30 miles of trails that make multiple loops possible. Far into the interior of Ramsey's Draft stand lonely sentinels, virgin hemlocks that escaped logging thanks to the area's remoteness. Along with the rugged terrain comes solitude and the freedom to bushwhack and camp wherever you like. Be aware: Spring is a dangerous time to hike up the Draft because of high water and eroded trail conditions.

Start: From the parking area at Mountain House Picnic Area on U.S. Highway 250.
Distance: 16.2-mile loop.
Approximate hiking time: 10 hours.
Difficulty rating: Difficult due to unmaintained trails, tree and storm debris, and steep climbs. High water on Ramsey's Draft may pose a danger in spring.
Trail surface: Dirt footpaths along high ridges and through rugged valleys, with many stream crossings.
Land status: National forest and wilderness area.
Nearest city: Staunton, VA.
Other trail users: Equestrians, anglers, and hunters (in season).

Canine compatibility: Dogs permitted.
Trail contacts: Deerfield Ranger District, Staunton, VA, (540) 885–8028.
Schedule: Group size in the wilderness areas of George Washington and Jefferson National Forests is limited to ten people. The Virginia Department of Forestry prohibits campfires before 4:00 P.M. from February 15 to April 30 in all forest areas. For more information, visit www.southernregion.fs.fed.us/gwj.
Fees/permits: No fees or permits required.
Maps: USGS maps: West Augusta, VA.
USFS maps: Ramsey's Draft Wilderness. Available at the Deerfield Ranger District for $4.00.

Finding the trailhead: From Staunton: Take US 250 west. From the village of Churchville, it's 15.4 miles to the Mountain House Picnic Area and the trailhead. Turn right into the picnic area and drive past the bathroom. After crossing a concrete spillway, look on the right for parking for up to eight vehicles. *DeLorme: Virginia Atlas & Gazetteer:* Page 66, C2.

The Hike

Mountain House. The name conjures up images of nineteenth-century travelers pulling up to a remote tavern as dusk falls. The Mountain House at the base of Shenandoah Mountain was just that kind of stopover for westbound travelers on the Staunton-Parkersburg Turnpike. Here, they ate a meal and took a rest while the stage driver arranged for a fresh team of horses. A steep climb over Shenandoah Mountain and more mountains stretching west to the Ohio Valley awaited these travelers.

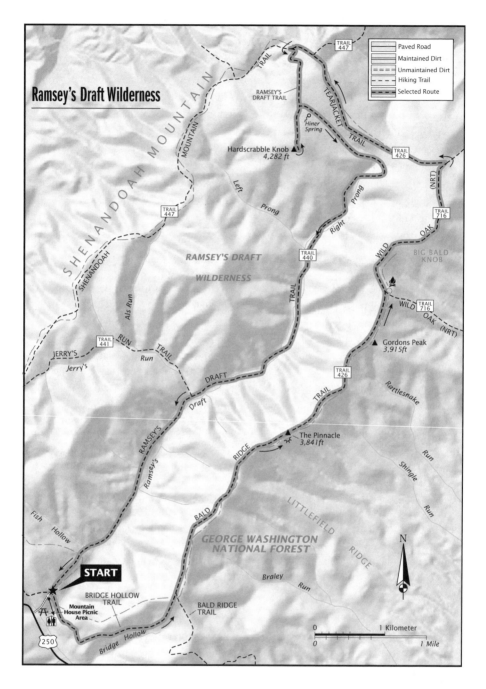

Ramsey's Draft Wilderness

The wildness of this route didn't deter travelers 200 years ago any more than today's visitors of Ramsey's Draft Wilderness. The 6,500-acre federal wilderness fills a trough carved by Ramsey's Draft, a beautiful, scenic mountain stream. Shenandoah

Mountain forms a high boundary on the west while Bald Ridge runs along the eastern edge. Like a horseshoe, they arc to meet Tearjacket Knob. From this secluded nook, the headwaters of Ramsey's Draft's right prong bubbles from Hiner Spring. Old-growth hemlocks shade the stream, which twists and drops in small cascades between mossy rocks and logs.

Federal law prohibits mechanical tools or transport in Ramsey's Draft. The trace of an old road that leads upstream from Mountain House predates the wilderness designation, which came in 1984. Hard as it is to imagine, as you straddle the umpteenth log or pick your way on rocks across the fast-moving stream, cars once traveled the road, built by the Civilian Conservation Corps in 1930s. That ended in 1969, when Hurricane Camille blew out the stream crossings. A flood in 1985 wiped out more sections of road. Finally, Hurricane Fran in 1996 blew through, leaving downed trees, washouts, and eroded hillsides in its wake.

The natural disasters have accented the wilderness's already rugged character. The Draft saw little in the way of mining, which is otherwise typical in Virginia's national forests. Small-time prospectors worked the stream and hillsides, but difficult access and marginal yields made full-scale mining operations impractical. Loggers succeeded them, but they found the area too rugged for systematic clear-cutting. This ensured the survival of what are now old-growth Eastern hemlocks clustered at Hiner Spring. The state record for the Eastern hemlock is here, a behemoth measuring 120 feet tall, 14 feet and 2 inches in circumference, and 52.2-inches in diameter. Its size makes the affliction of the microscopic hemlock woolly adelgid all the more tragic. The bug coats the underside of hemlock needles with tiny white sacs, eventually resulting in defoliation. Silvaculturalists are investigating natural predators to combat the bug. Failing a solution, the days are numbered for Eastern hemlock in Ramsey's Draft Wilderness.

The hike to reach the old-growth trees is a cauldron of tricky stream crossings, boulder hopping, and scampering across downed trees. It requires care, especially in spring, not only for personal safety, but also to ensure you don't lose the trail. Footbridges and trails up the Draft are at the mercy of storms. Downed trees, sheared away by spring's high water, litter the banks. Bear in mind that this is intentional neglect, fostered by the spirit of the 1964 Wilderness Act. The intent is to allow nature to shape the landscape, instead of human beings. Ramsey's Draft was one of the eleven areas included in the 1984 Virginia Wilderness Act, and in many a hiker's opinion, is one of the most wild.

If Ramsey's Draft runs too high for safe passage, alternate routes to the headwaters lead up the steep sides of both Shenandoah Mountain and Bald Ridge. On Shenandoah Mountain, south of an intersection with Road Hollow Trail, earthen mounds, called breastworks, date from the Civil War. Confederate and Union forces considered Shenandoah Mountain a strategic position largely for the turnpike, which permitted movement of troops and supplies in and out of the western territories.

One of the earliest battles of the Civil War was over control of this road, which had been completed just twenty years prior to the war. The Battle of Rich Mountain (West Virginia) was a draw, and opposing forces holed up for the winter of 1862 within miles of each other, in present-day West Virginia. A harsh winter drove them east as spring came to the mountains. In May, North and South clashed at the Battle of McDowell, in Highland County in the western foothills of Shenandoah Mountain. The breastworks atop Shenandoah Mountain were held alternately by Confederate and Union troops. The Forest Service has identified, but not excavated, Civil War–era camps in the Draft, in the hollows at the base of the mountain.

Camping is still a treat in these hollows, especially Jerry's Run, a small, dark, and moist hollow running up the side of Shenandoah Mountain. Jerry's Run Trail plays tag with the small stream that feeds the Draft, touching it, then darting away into cover of woods. In small coves, dogwood trees bloom Virginia's state flower in spring. Cool temperatures under the evergreens are a reminder that, while this is Virginia, the weather in the Draft is unpredictable. Befitting this unpredictable spot, our first-ever winter hiking experience came on a trip to Ramsey's Draft. A storm dropped 5 inches of snow in an afternoon. Ramsey's Draft's location, in a weather *pocket,* makes such sudden storms a regular occurrence.

The majesty of the old-growth hemlocks at Hiner Spring, and their uncertain status, has created something of a "hikers-rush" on Ramsey's Draft. Mountain House, already a popular picnic site, complete with a freshwater pump and bathrooms, is a launching point for a long, 6-mile hike to Hiner Spring. No one keeps track, but an educated guess—based on how many times it took us to reach the spring—says more than half of the people who begin this hike never make it to Hiner Spring. Difficult and eroded trail conditions slow progress to a point where hikers must turn around to make it out by sunset. As it has for centuries, the rugged nature of Ramsey's Draft keeps human tampering to a minimum.

Miles and Directions

0.0 **START** at Mountain House Picnic Area off US 250. Walk up the dirt road and, in a few feet, turn right to descend to the stream bank of Ramsey's Draft.

0.1 Cross Ramsey's Draft. On the opposite bank, enter the woods on the Bridge Hollow Trail. Although unblazed, the trail is clearly defined as a wide footpath.

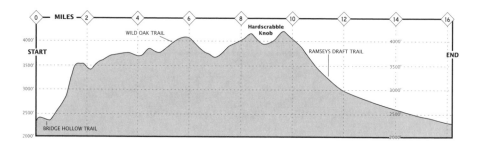

1.0 Wrap around a shoulder ridge of the Peak and ascend up Bridge Hollow.

2.0 Ascend on a short, steep stretch of trail to a T intersection on top of the wooded summit of the Peak. At the intersection, turn left onto Bald Ridge Trail.

2.5 Pass to the left of a small, tree-covered knob. Bald Ridge Trail dips into saddlebacks and then climbs past three more knobs en route to the Pinnacle. Views are limited.

3.9 Reach the Pinnacle (3,841 feet). (FYI: For a view east, drop your pack and climb through the forest to a rocky vista atop the Pinnacle. Views extend east across the valley cut by the Calfpasture River.)

4.7 Cross over Gordons Peak (3,915 feet). (FYI: There are no views from this mountain.)

5.5 After a long descent, enter a clearing. There is a wildlife pond on the right and small primitive campsites. Follow Bald Ridge Trail through the clearing, past the Wild Oak National Recreation Trail (NRT) on the right. (FYI: On the USGS topographic map, West Augusta quadrant, the Wild Oak NRT is labeled as Dividing Ridge Trail. For the next 1.6 miles, the Wild Oak NRT and Bald Ridge Trail follow the same trail route.)

6.3 Cross Big Bald Knob. Through the trees on the right side of the trail are nice views east down Stillhouse Hollow onto the North River.

7.1 After a long descent, reach an intersection of Tearjacket Trail and Wild Oak NRT. Turn left onto Tearjacket Trail. (FYI: Wild Oak NRT turns right and descends on the spine of Spring-house Ridge to Camp Todd, a national recreation area with picnic facilities.)

8.8 Tearjacket Trail ends at a junction with the Shenandoah Mountain Trail, a yellow-blazed trail. Turn left and follow Shenandoah Mountain Trail.

9.0 Enter a clearing and turn left onto Ramsey's Draft Trail.

9.6 Turn right and ascend a trail to Hardscrabble Knob (4,282 feet), the highest mountain in the wilderness. Views are limited in summertime due to tall trees. Turn and descend back to Ramsey's Draft Trail.

9.9 Turn right on Ramsey's Draft Trail.

10.3 Pass a spring on the right. This is the source of the Right Prong Ramsey's Draft, which the trail follows for the next 1.8 miles. There is a campsite in this area. (FYI: In 200 yards past this spring and campsite, an old road branches left. This is an abandoned section of Tearjacket Trail.)

10.4 (FYI: Ramsey's Draft Trail turns into a rough, unmarked trail. Frequently, the route is washed out. Large trees may hinder progress. For all its difficulty, however, this is a scenic stretch of trail. Small waterfalls ripple over mossy rocks. The stream is not so wide as to make crossings difficult. Large hemlocks provide shade and lend the area a deep-forest atmosphere. Because of the steep mountains that enclose the valley, there's little chance of getting lost as you bushwhack around the blowdowns and washouts.)

12.1 Ramsey's Draft Trail joins an old forest road. Continue hiking downstream. (Note: This spot is located just below where Left Prong Ramsey's Draft meets Right Prong to form Ramsey's Draft.)

14.0 Pass a junction with Jerry's Run Trail on the right. Continue hiking downstream. (FYI: Jerry's Run Trail climbs through a dark, hemlock-lined hollow to a junction with the Shenandoah Mountain Trail.)

16.2 Hike ends at the parking area at Mountain House Picnic Area.

Hike Information

Local Information

Staunton/Augusta County Travel Information Center, Staunton, VA, (540) 332-3972, www.augustachamber.org.

Local Events/Attractions

Museum of American Frontier Culture, Staunton, VA, (540) 332-7850, www. frontiermuseum.org.

The Highland Maple Festival, March, Monterey, VA, (540) 468-2550. Celebrates the county's status as Virginia's only producer of maple syrup.

22 St. Mary's Wilderness

There are two types of Virginia hikers: Those who have visited St. Mary's Wilderness and those who soon will; more people visit this 10,000-acre plot of protected wild land on the western slope of the Blue Ridge than any other Virginia wilderness. Easy access to the premier attraction, St. Mary's Falls, ensures this won't change any time soon. And a beauty this waterfall is—a wide, 15-foot drop into a deep, narrow gorge replete with massive river boulders and mountain laurel. Beauty of a subtler nature lies deeper into the wilderness. Take the time to explore a bit farther.

Start: From the gravel parking lot opposite Fork Mountain Overlook, milepost 23 on the Blue Ridge Parkway.

Distance: 10.6-mile loop.

Approximate hiking time: 7 hours.

Difficulty rating: Moderate due to the hike length and the steep grades along Mine Bank Creek.

Trail surface: Dirt roads and footpaths traverse steep mountain slopes, upland meadows, pond, and waterfalls.

Land status: National forest and wilderness area.

Nearest town: Steeles Tavern, VA.

Other trail users: Cross-country skiers and hunters (in season).

Canine compatibility: Dogs permitted.

Trail contacts: Glenwood-Pedlar Ranger District, Natural Bridge Station, VA, (540) 291-2188.

Schedule: Open year-round.

Fees/permits: No fees or permits required.

Maps: USGS maps: Vesuvius, VA; Big Levels, VA.

Finding the trailhead: From Steeles Tavern: Drive east on Virginia Route 56. In the town of Vesuvius, the road turns left, crosses railroad tracks, and continues east. After a long stretch of winding road and switchbacks, VA 56 junctions with the Blue Ridge Parkway 5.6 miles from Steeles Tavern. Proceed north on the Blue Ridge Parkway for 3.8 miles. At the Fork Mountain Overlook (milepost 23), turn left into a gravel parking lot. There is room for eight to ten cars. *DeLorme: Virginia Atlas & Gazetteer:* Page 54, A2.

The Hike

People visit St. Mary's Wilderness for one overriding reason: waterfalls. The largest, on St. Mary's River, impresses not so much with height as with width and power. Farther upstream, smaller cascades await in the mountain gullies that feed St. Mary's River. In these sheltered coves, rock and water interact in more subtle ways, as on Mine Bank Branch, where the stream glistens and shines as it tumbles down stepfalls. It's a small reminder why the path less-traveled can sometimes be the most rewarding.

The hunt for waterfalls leads farther up into the wilderness. Small streams run off Mine Bank Mountain, Bald Knob, Big Levels, and Cellar Mountain. On them, cascades of varying shapes and sizes spill water en route to St. Mary's River. There

Waterfall on Mine Bank Branch.

are 20-foot drops into small pools on Sugartree Branch. On Mine Branch, water rolls down like a slinky down the streambed. Small as they appear, each stream contributes volumes of water to St. Mary's River, which changes from a meandering stream near its headwaters into the frothing, churning powerhouse at St. Mary's Falls.

In late spring, the rash of mountain laurel blossoms along Mine Bank Branch serves as a timely reminder that waterfalls aren't the only attraction here. For a few days, the landscape looks as if a late-season snowstorm hit. The dusting of pink and white fills folds and faults where the stream cuts steeply through bedrock, as if Tinkerbell had brushed hills with a pixie dust. This is the Appalachian wake-up call that marks the end of spring blooms; mountain laurel is the last to flower, after the redbuds, apple blossoms, and dogwood have shown their stuff.

The sheer volume of mountain laurel makes one consider how this tree reproduces. Stamen on the flower act like a spring. When triggered by bees, the podlike fruit opens, the anther is released, and oblong pollen beads shake out. Leave the laurel's honey to the bees, though; if ingested, it'll cause cramps and chills—even vomiting in extreme cases.

Not to be outdone by the rush of pink and white laurel, June-blooming rhododendron adds its color a month later. Along the fire road that links Green Pond to the Bald Mountain Trail, pink blossoms are abundant. Lore has it that rhododendron hid the moonshiner's still. Growth is so dense, so high, and seemingly impenetrable, it's quite possible to pass within a yard or so of someone—or something—and never know it. The tree's spindly hardwood trunk is unyielding. Not surprisingly, rhododendron and laurel wood have never amounted to much commercially, outside of use in making briar pipes, a tobacco pipe shaped from the root burls, or knots, of heath plants. Manufacturers favored the *burl*—the hard, dense knots found on roots of these trees—for shaping the bowl of the pipes because it burned slowly.

In late July, mountain laurel and rhododendron flowers give way to the blueberry—the *uber*-berry of its class. Trapped inside these little blue bombers are enough cancer-fighting antioxidants to rank the small blueberry Number One among fruits and vegetables in this category. Health benefits don't stop there, either. Anthocyanin, a chemical that gives berries their blue color, is said to ease eyestrain and improve circulation. Other studies suggest blueberries may even slow the aging process, reason enough to toss another handful into your mouth.

Health is an appropriate subject to consider in light of the threats that face St. Mary's Wilderness. Here, direct human activity has only the slightest impact. Even scars from mining activity as recently as the 1950s fade as grass and trees overgrow the old railroad grades and mine camps. More insidious is acid rain, which has raised pH levels in St. Mary's River to a point where native trout are suffering—to say nothing of such small aquatic life-forms as salamanders and frogs. The issue put the Forest Service in a quandary: Wilderness areas, by their very definition, are exempt from the tinkering of forest rangers and land managers. This area is intended to return to nature in whatever form that takes. There is an exception to this rule,

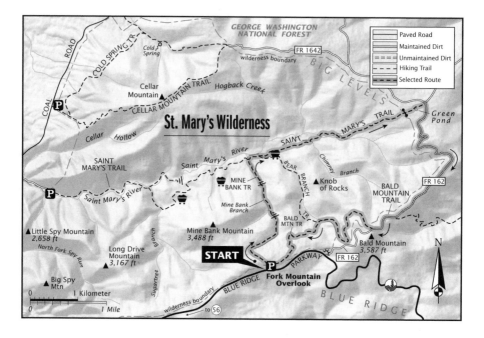

however. In cases of fire, insect infestation, or disease, the Forest Service can intervene, as it has since done in St. Mary's. If one considers acid precipitation a disease, then the possibility of liming the river (lime is a natural base that counterbalances the acid) is justified. Barring this, recovery hinges on the long-term reduction of pollutants as required by the Clean Air Act.

Miles and Directions

0.0 **START** from a trail sign for the Mine Bank Trail on the wooded side of the gravel parking lot. A few feet after starting the hike, turn left and follow the orange blazes of Mine Bank Trail. The Bald Mountain Trail that turns right at this junction is the return portion of this hike.

0.3 The trail switches back several times as it drops down the side of Mine Bank Mountain. The trail surface is loose pebbles. (FYI: In fall, the views soar across the river valley below to Cellar Mountain.)

0.5 After a steep descent, reach the headwaters of Mine Bank Branch. The trail bears left and descends with the stream to the right. (FYI: Mountain laurel and rhododendron are plentiful here. A few hemlocks grow alongside the streambed.)

1.0 Cross the stream to the right bank. As you cross, the stream drops 20 feet or so on a series of steps cut into the bedrock. The trail descends steeply with the stream on the left.

1.3 Cross back to the left stream bank. The trail continues to descend past rock outcrops on the left hillside. (FYI: Take time to cut through the woods on the right for wonderful photo-ops of the stream's many small waterfalls.)

2.1 Mine Bank Branch takes the first of two steep plunges off the mountain slope. The trail, which has descended at a moderate rate, steepens at each waterfall.

2.6 The trail and stream part ways, with Mine Bank Trail arcing left through the oak-hardwood forest. (Note: In spring, this is a muddy stretch of trail.)

3.0 Turn right onto blue-blazed St. Mary's Trail. Follow St. Mary's River upstream. **Sidetrip:** St. Mary's Trail to the left leads 2.3 miles to the St. Mary's Falls Trail. The trail passes first through an old mine operation and, farther downstream, rugged Sugar Hollow. St. Mary's Falls Trail is a 0.5-mile hike to the 15-foot St. Mary's Falls. This detour adds 5.6 miles and several hours to this loop hike.

3.2 Cross Bear Branch as it enters from the right. Follow St. Mary's Trail upstream. **Option:** To shorten your trip, you can turn right onto the unmarked Bear Branch Trail as it follows Bear Branch for a return to the Bald Mountain Trail. This bushwhack requires you to follow the Bear Branch stream bank for about a mile, after which an old road leads another mile to Bald Mountain Trail.

3.3 (FYI: Signs of old iron-ore mining operations are visible off the trail. Dirt mounds cover rusted buckets, and an inspection of the tall grassy areas reveal twisted pieces of metal and concrete footings.) The trail passes through some shallow mining pits and re-enters the woods.

4.0 After crossing a much diminished St. Mary's River several times, the trail begins climbing on an old road. Several times, it dips into the woods for switchbacks to aid the steep ascent.

5.1 Enter Big Levels, a mountain plateau. Continue straight on St. Mary's Trail.

5.6 Reach Green Pond. Pass to the left of the pond. The trail leaves the wilderness area for 0.3 mile.

5.9 Turn right onto Forest Road 162. This wide dirt and gravel road with no markings climbs Bald Knob on switchbacks.

7.1 FR 162 levels as it crosses Flint Mountain.

7.4 (FYI: Views open on the left side of the trail. Torry Ridge is visible to the north. To the east, Three Ridges looms beyond the Blue Ridge Parkway.) The trail arcs southwest and climbs at a more gradual pace.

8.8 Turn right onto the yellow-blazed Bald Mountain Trail. Look for a wilderness boundary sign on the right as a guide mark. (FYI: The trail drops down the slope through a young hardwood forest. Where it crosses small hillside drainages, hemlocks are present.)

9.3 Continue straight past an unmarked road that descends downhill on the right. This is the upper end of the Bear Branch bushwhack.

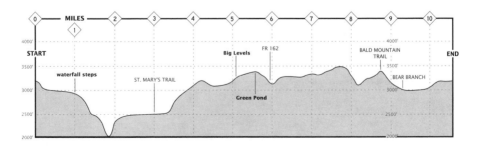

Ladder Falls on Mine Bank Creek.

9.6 Cross a small stream on a three-log bridge amid heavy growth of hemlock, mountain laurel, and rhododendron.

9.8 The trail arcs left and the climb, which has been gradual the last half mile, steepens.

10.2 Cross several earthen embankments intended to block vehicle traffic on the trail, which is now an old roadway. There are campsites in this area.

10.5 Turn right onto a narrow footpath and walk several hundred yards to a junction with Mine Bank Trail.

10.6 Turn left onto Mine Bank Trail. Hike ends at the gravel parking lot.

Hike Information

Local Information

Staunton/Augusta County Travel Information Center, Staunton, VA, (540) 332-3972, www.augustachamber.org.

Local Events/Attractions

Wintergreen Performing Arts Summer Music Festival, July, Wintergreen, VA, (434) 325-8292. Chamber and symphony music.

The Cyrus McCormick Farm & Workshop, Steeles Tavern, VA, (540) 377-2255, www.vaes.vt.edu/index.html. Site where McCormick invented the first mechanical reaper. Blacksmith shop, gristmill, and museum. Admission is free.

23 Three Ridges

The term *wilderness* conjures visions of craggy peaks and untamed woodland far from the beaten track. Virginia's newest designated wilderness area, Three Ridges and The Priest region, isn't quite that. And that's not necessarily a bad thing. The Appalachian Trail (AT) traverses both peaks and the two AT shelters on either side of Three Ridges suits an overnight hike perfectly. The link between them, the Mau-Har Trail, follows Campbell Creek past a 40-foot waterfall and numerous smaller cascades. The treacherous terrain, soaring views, and sheer elevation gain makes this one of the most strenuous and dramatic hikes in Virginia.

Start: From the swinging bridge over the Tye River, 0.1 mile downhill from Virginia Route 56.
Distance: 13.8-mile loop.
Approximate hiking time: 10 hours.
Difficulty rating: Difficult due to the steep climb up Three Ridges via Chimney Rock, and rocky, eroded trail conditions along Campbell Creek.
Trail surface: Dirt footpaths and old dirt forest roads run through steep mountain ridges, high-elevation rock outcrops, stream gorges, and sloping hardwood forests.

Land status: National forest and wilderness area.
Nearest town: Lovingston, VA.
Other trail users: Hunters (in season).
Canine compatibility: Dogs not permitted.
Trail contacts: Glenwood-Pedlar Ranger District, Natural Bridge Station, VA, (540) 291-2188.
Schedule: Open year-round.
Fees/permits: No fees or permits required.
Maps: USGS maps: Massies Mill, VA; Horseshoe Mountain, VA; Sherando; Big Levels, VA.

Finding the trailhead: From Lovingston: Drive south on combined U.S. Highway 29/VA 56. In 4.6 miles, follow VA 56 west as it branches right, off US 29. In 4.9 miles, VA 56 merges with VA 151. Turn right and follow the combined VA 56/VA 151 north. In 2.7 miles, follow VA 56 west as it branches left off VA 151. Drive 6 miles on VA 56 as it crosses back and forth over the Tye River. Pass through the small communities of Massie Mill and Tyro. In 6 miles from the split from VA 151, turn left into a dirt parking area. *DeLorme: Virginia Atlas & Gazetteer:* Page 54, B4.

The Hike

The region surrounding the mountains of Three Ridges and The Priest packs gorgeous scenery and rugged terrain into a small area. Situated in Virginia's Blue Ridge Mountains and spread over 10 square miles, the two peaks boast an elevation gain of 3,000 feet and rank among the hardest climbs in Virginia. Approaching Three Ridges from the Tye River, the mountain soars 2,973 feet in 6 miles to an elevation of 3,970 feet. The Priest, visible from Three Ridges's southern cliffs and rock outcrops, offers an almost identical elevation gain. Standing at Harpers Creek and staring up the seemingly vertical ascent up Three Ridges leaves you with a feeling not often encountered in Virginia—that is, a feeling of being completely dwarfed by the land.

The author (front) and friends climbing Three Ridges along the AT.

Hikes that start with this kind of bang are prone to ending with a whimper. The return along Campbell Creek on the Mau-Har Trail happily defies this notion. The trail downhill from Maupin Field Shelter is a narrow footpath etched into the steep-sided stream banks traversing loose rocks. Footing in some areas is as dangerous as the ascent of Three Ridges is difficult.

In 2000, President Clinton signed a bill designating 11,000 acres in The Priest and Three Ridges area as Virginia's seventeenth wilderness area. The Forest Service and Appalachian Trail Conference (ATC) have, since 1993, treated the area as wilderness in anticipation of this move. (Which includes, by the way, volunteers maintaining the Appalachian Trail (AT) by nonmechanical means. The ATC has held workshops on Three Ridges on the proper use of crosscut saws to fell trees 3 feet in diameter.) When the wilderness designation went to Washington, D.C., in 2000, Nelson County residents and wilderness advocacy groups cited development pressures as a reason for protection. The land itself is too rugged for timber management, but it protects headwaters of three rivers: the Tye, Piney, and Rockfish Rivers. Two other streams, Campbell and Harpers Creeks, source from the slopes of Three Ridges itself. (Lest anyone think designating wilderness is a regular occurrence, the Three Ridges-The Priest Wilderness was the first for Virginia in thirteen years.)

FYI The odd-sounding name Mau-Har is derived from the features it links: Maupin Field Shelter and Harpers Creek.

Another view of why Three Ridges deserved wilderness protection comes on Chimney Rock, a well-placed rest and overlook on the AT along the south tip of the mountain. From this elevation of 3,204 feet, the rugged aspect of Virginia's Blue Ridge fills the horizon. Absent are, long, parallel ridgelines that define Virginia's mountains to the west. Here, it appears a force punched the earth's crust from below, randomly pushing up steep-sided mountains etched with deep V-shaped gorges down their slopes. It's as clear a picture a hiker will receive of Virginia's dual mountain systems. The Blue Ridge Mountains originated in prehistoric volcanic activity. The Allegheny Mountains to the west, by contrast, evolved into long ridges and valleys during extensive folding and faulting of layered rock.

The ruggedness of Three Ridges has given rise to an unusual variation on old-growth trees. You won't find the enormous trunks and towering heights normally associated with centuries-old stands of oaks, hemlocks, and other ancient hardwoods here. Instead, it's small oaks—called Virginia orchard oaks—that qualify as old growth. They occupy the highest portions of Three Ridges, a factor that shaped both their appearance and their preservation. Why were they spared? They were simply too difficult to get to and remove.

Designation of Three Ridges as a wilderness completes a triumvirate of specially protected lands in the central Blue Ridge of Virginia that includes St. Mary's Wilderness and the special management area at Mount Pleasant. Special protection doesn't

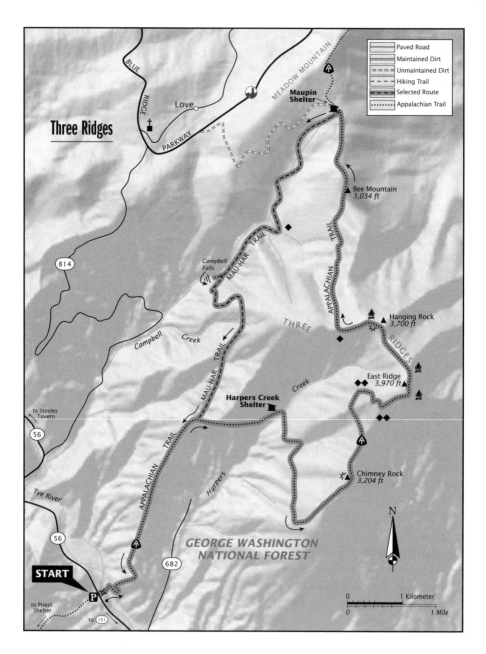

Three Ridges

	Paved Road
	Maintained Dirt
	Unmaintained Dirt
	Hiking Trail
	Selected Route
	Appalachian Trail

Love

Maupin Shelter

MEADOW MOUNTAIN

BLUE RIDGE PARKWAY

Bee Mountain
3,034 ft

814

MAU-HAR TRAIL

APPALACHIAN TRAIL

Campbell Falls

Hanging Rock
3,700 ft

THREE RIDGES

Campbell Creek

Creek

East Ridge
3,970 ft

to Steeles Tavern

56

MAU-HAR TRAIL

Harpers Creek Shelter

APPALACHIAN TRAIL

Harpers

Chimney Rock
3,204 ft

Tye River

56

N

GEORGE WASHINGTON
NATIONAL FOREST

682

START

P

to Priest Shelter

to 151

0	1 Kilometer
0	1 Mile

necessarily mean solitude, however. The 20-foot waterfall on Campbell Creek, 3 miles from VA 56 on the Mau-Har Trail will likely ensure Three Ridges remains a popular destination for day-trippers. St. Mary's remains the most heavily used of all Virginia's wilderness areas—reports of hikers carrying coolers up to the falls on St. Mary's River persist. Thankfully, the ascent from Harpers Creek Shelter to the highest point on Three Ridges is so severe, a backpack is all the weight that can be safely transported. And that's the way it should be.

Miles and Directions

0.0 **START** at a parking area on the south side of VA 56. Cross the highway and descend 0.1 mile to a hand-built cable suspension bridge (reconstructed in 1992 by AT club members). Walk across the bridge and follow the white-blazed AT as it climbs on switchbacks through a forest of mixed hardwoods.

0.3 The AT levels out atop a small knob. It eases across the knob and in 0.1 mile begins another steep climb through an oak forest. During the climbs, the slope downhill to the right segues into a field and apple orchard.

1.7 Turn right and follow the AT at a junction of the AT and Mau-Har Trail. The next mile is a descent to Harpers Creek.

2.5 Cross Harpers Creek and hike upstream with the brook on your left. In one-tenth of a mile, turn right as the AT switches back and begins a steep ascent. (FYI: At this turn, a faded dirt road leads straight to the Harpers Creek Shelter in about 400 yards. The shelter sleeps six and there is room to pitch tents around it.)

4.4 Pass Chimney Rock off the left side of the AT (FYI: This overlook, along with Hanging Rock on the north side of Three Ridges, offers the best views off Three Ridges. The term "chimney" refers to the rock formation of solid, uniform blocks of granite beneath your feet.)

5.8 Begin a traverse of the highest point on Three Ridges. The landscape is flat. The grassy forest floor and widely spaced maple and oak trees give this summit approach the appearance of a wooded meadow.

6.1 Turn left at a double white blaze and follow the AT over the top of Three Ridges. (FYI: There are some well-used campsites in this area. Farther up, off the right side of the trail, are more secluded spots with access to small rock outcrops with views north to the Blue Ridge Parkway.)

6.8 The dirt AT turns to open rock face as the trail crosses Hanging Rock. Views to the south take in The Priest and the Harpers Creek stream valley. The view makes this one of the most coveted tenting spots on this stretch of trail.

8.4 Cross Bee Mountain. After this 3,034-foot knob, the AT continues its descent on a narrow, rocky footpath. In 0.3 mile, it widens and turns grassy.

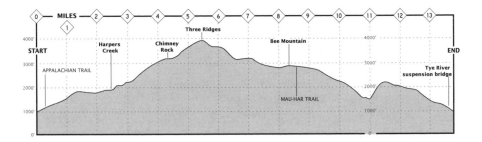

The author standing on Chimney Rock on the AT with the Harpers Creek Valley in the background.

8.8 Reach Maupin Field Shelter and turn left onto a wide road. Cross the headwaters of Campbell Creek at the shelter and, in 300 yards, turn right and descend on the blue-blazed Mau-Har Trail along Campbell Creek.

9.3 Cross Campbell Creek twice in the next 0.3 mile. (Note: Use caution on this narrow section of trail; portions are eroded.)

10.0 The trail climbs into and out of a gorge where a stream, tumbling off Three Ridges's steep slope, empties into Campbell Creek.

10.5 Mau-Har Trail bears left and uphill, departing the stream valley for a return to the AT. (FYI: There is a swimming hole here.) Downstream 0.1 mile is Campbell Falls, a 40-foot waterfall.

12.1 Turn right onto the AT for a return to VA 56 and the Tye River.

13.7 Cross the Tye River on the suspended bridge.

13.8 Hike ends at parking lot on VA 56. (FYI: Author recommendation: Ditch the pack, return to stream, and soak yourself in the icy cool of the Tye River. You deserve it!)

Hike Information

Local Information

Nelson County Department of Tourism, Lovingston, VA, (800) 282-8223, www.nelsoncounty.com.

Local Events/Attractions

Waltons Mountain Museum, Schuyler, VA, (434) 831-2000. The school attended by Earl Hammer Jr., creator of *The Waltons* television series. Preserves sets from this classic '70s show. Open first Sunday in March until first Sunday in November.

Spring Wildflower Symposium, Wintergreen, VA, May, (434) 325-7451.

Lodging

Wintergreen Resort, Wintergreen, VA, (800) 266-2444, www.wintergreenresort.com. Lodging in ridgetop condos, Nature Foundation, Wilderness School, and 30 miles of its own hiking trails.

The Acorn Inn, Nellysford, VA, (434) 361-9357, www.acorninn.com.

Organizations

Tidewater Appalachian Trail Club, Norfolk, VA, www.tidewateratc.com.

24 Mount Pleasant

Mount Pleasant must rank as one of Virginia's most aptly named peaks. Few hikes, if any, offer so much for so little work. For the price of a small elevation gain, hikers can climb two of the Blue Ridge's highest peaks on a loop trail that is, for lack of a better phrase, quite pleasant. Steep, rocky climbs along the final miles to Mount Pleasant will appease the gung ho hiker. Otherwise, it's easy hiking on wide paths and old roads through thick masses of rhododendron and mountain laurel, forests of oak, hickory, and beech, and small pockets of high-grass open forest.

Start: From a parking area at the intersection of Forest Road 8 and Forest Road 51, 0.3 mile past a forest gate at Hog Camp Gap.
Distance: 4.8-mile loop.
Approximate hiking time: 4 hours.
Difficulty rating: Moderate due to a long uphill approach along the Henry Lanum Loop Trail and a single, steep climb on Mount Pleasant Spur Trail.
Trail surface: Dirt roads and forest footpaths lead through open rock formations, fields, open peaks, mountain meadows, remnant chestnut forests, steep cliffs, and along streams.

Land status: National forest special management area.
Nearest town: Buena Vista, VA.
Other trail users: Hunters (in season).
Canine compatibility: Dogs permitted.
Trail contacts: Glenwood-Pedlar Ranger District, Natural Bridge Station, VA, (540) 291-2188.
Schedule: Open year-round.
Fees/permits: No fees or permits required.
Maps: USGS maps: Montebello, VA; Forks of Buffalo, VA.

Finding the trailhead: From Buena Vista: Drive east on U.S. Highway 60 for 8.8 miles to the town of Oronoco. Turn left onto Virginia Route 634 at a small general store. In 1.6 miles, turn right onto Virginia Route 755, which turns into dirt Forest Road 48 in 1.4 miles. Continue on FR 48 across the Appalachian Trail (AT) in 1.3 miles. There is a seasonal forest gate and parking area 0.1 mile past the AT. If the gate is closed, park here. By foot or vehicle, pass the forest gate and proceed 0.3 mile to an intersection with FR 51. Turn right onto FR 51 and enter a parking area. *DeLorme: Virginia Atlas & Gazetteer:* Page 54, B2.

The Hike

The wind—you notice it first and it never really goes away. Long gusts wrap around Mount Pleasant's highest point, a 4,090-foot exposed rock face with views in all directions. It chaffs cheeks and hands as you stare out to the low-lying Piedmont rolling east from the mountain. Falcons or some other raptor too far off to distinguish with certainty circle on the upward-spiraling currents. A blurry rush fills your ears, and soon after it chills your bones.

View from the top of Mount Pleasant.

You descend off the peak, but the wind isn't done yet. In an under-grown forest gap below the Mount Pleasant summit, streaks of air rustle a thin forest canopy. Sunlight leaks through a patchwork of young oak and poplar, playing crazy angles with pole-size tree trunks. As the day lengthens, the wind picks up strength. Streaks of light and shadows interlace across the woodland. Grass bristles in the breeze. Here, a circle of light stretches halfway up a tree trunk. There, the setting sun alights on branch tips of an oak. In the darkness that drops suddenly, the wind remains, wrapping around you as it races through the trees.

Wind generates some of the Virginia mountain's most severe storms. As systems of high and low pressure move eastward across the mountains, the haphazard arrangement of steep-sided mountains and deep valleys creates small tempests. Under proper conditions, a storm pocket will wreak sizable damage. Far more common, however, are isolated windthrows (aka *downbursts* or *microbursts*), where a sudden, fierce storm has torn down, snapped, or uprooted a few acres of trees. These are the seemingly out-of-place gaps in an otherwise solid forest that appear suddenly as you approach Mount Pleasant from the southwest. These gaps lack the clear, defined lines of a meadow. A rash of subcanopy vegetation, plants such as Virginia creeper or poison ivy, blur the line between forest and open space. Grasses that normally perish in the shadows of a forest canopy lend the subforest a pastoral look. To a

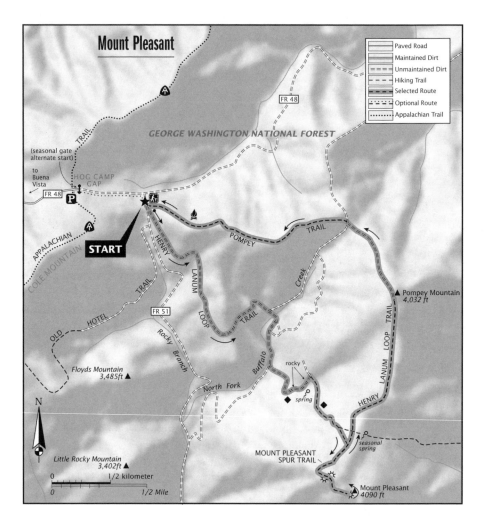

Mount Pleasant

	Paved Road
	Maintained Dirt
	Unmaintained Dirt
	Hiking Trail
	Selected Route
	Optional Route
	Appalachian Trail

GEORGE WASHINGTON NATIONAL FOREST

FR 48

(seasonal gate alternate start)

to Buena Vista

HOG CAMP GAP

FR 48

APPALACHIAN

COLE MOUNTAIN

START

HENRY

LANUM LOOP

TRAIL

POMPEY TRAIL

Creek

TRAIL

OLD HOTEL

FR 51

Rocky Branch

LANUM LOOP TRAIL

Pompey Mountain 4,032 ft

Floyds Mountain 3,485ft ▲

North Fork

Buffalo

rocky

spring

HENRY

N

Little Rocky Mountain 3,402ft ▲

MOUNT PLEASANT SPUR TRAIL

seasonal spring

0   1/2 kilometer
0   1/2 Mile

Mount Pleasant 4090 ft

bone-weary hiker, they appear as a perfectly peaceful spot to camp. Closer inspection, however, shows mounded soil where trees came uprooted, indicating a violent episode sometime in the past.

Disturbances, whether natural or man-made, have long been a part of the Mount Pleasant landscape. Meadows atop Cole Mountain, in the southern portion of the 7,580-acre Mount Pleasant Special Management Area, date from a time when private landowners grazed livestock (indicated by place names such as Cow Camp Gap and Hog Camp Gap). Maintaining the open fields through prescribed burns and timber management kept Mount Pleasant from being named a federal wilderness. Instead, in 1994, it was designated a special management area, a status that allows forest rangers to keep the fields open and clear. Although much smaller, the fields inevitably invite comparisons to the high-country meadows of Mount Rogers National Recreation Area.

The southern slope of Cole Mountain drops into the North Fork Buffalo River, and from this stream rises Chestnut Ridge, a long ascending buttress that leads to Mount Pleasant's peak. Unfortunately, the ridge's name only reminds us of when the American chestnut tree blanketed the Appalachian forest. Here's a reminder that ecological disturbances come in many forms, not just wind. Consider as you descend along the trail that a forest canopy once rose 100 feet and higher overhead, that tree trunks measured 10 feet in diameter. "No greater catastrophe has ever befallen a tree in our time," Roger Tory Peterson wrote of the chestnut blight. That may well be an understatement. Imported from Asia, the blight—a fungus that appears as a black canker on the tree trunk—spread virulently down the Appalachian chain, destroying, in a span of twenty years, an estimated 3.5 million trees. (Look for signs of chestnut blight beyond Pompey Mountain as you hike the Henry Lanum Loop Trail away from Mount Pleasant.) It also deprived today's hiker the opportunity to see this once strong tree grow past head-height—the size at which, today, the blight destroys chestnut trees. This is a humbling status for a tree once considered North America's most productive.

Hope, however, is not lost. Biologists believe they now have an American chestnut that is 95 percent resistant to the blight. Here in Virginia, the American Chestnut Cooperator's Foundation is experimenting with grafting techniques in the Warm Springs Ranger District of the George Washington National Forest. This technique takes young American chestnuts with no signs of blight and grafts resistant chestnut stems onto them. The hope is that the tree will produce nuts with blight-resistant genetics. In the Lesane State Forest, located in Virginia's mountain region, three American chestnuts were grafted in a similar manner in 1980. Cankers appeared, but botanists injected them with a hypovirulence—essentially a virus that attacked the blight that was attacking the tree. Presently, the three trees survive, while around them untreated specimens die off. A reason, perhaps, to hope.

Miles and Directions

0.0 START from a trailboard in the parking area on FR 51. Walk straight past the trailboard and follow the blue-blazed Henry Lanum Loop Trail as it descends gently on a dirt road. (FYI: The Pompey Trail, which is the return leg of this loop hike, departs from this parking area. It climbs left from the trailboard on a dirt road.)

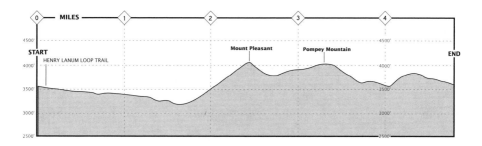

0.8 Cross two seasonal streams. The trail slowly arcs right and continues to descend.

1.5 Turn left at a double blaze and climb. The trail, a bit rockier, crosses a stream. A mature hardwood forest covers the slopes, replacing the fields and gaps at lower elevations.

1.7 Turn right at another junction with an unmarked forest road. The trail is now a footpath and crosses several seasonal drainages. (Note: Do not count on water from these sources during summer or fall.)

1.9 A relentless climb marks the approach to Mount Pleasant. The trail switches back several times. Large boulders along the trail make for convenient rest points.

2.3 Turn right onto the Mount Pleasant Spur Trail and begin a final ascent of Mount Pleasant.

2.6 Reach the open rock face of Mount Pleasant's 4,090-foot summit. To return to the Henry Lanum Loop Trail, turn and descend 0.3 mile on the Mount Pleasant Spur Trail. (FYI: Before doing so, however, take time to soak in the views that encircle the mountain. Far eastward rolls the Piedmont. To the north is Pompey Mountain. Chestnut Ridge approaches the mountain from the south. Through the valley south of the mountain runs the Buffalo River.)

2.9 Intersect the Henry Lanum Loop Trail and hike straight ahead. As you descend off the mountain, continue straight ahead. (FYI: A sign points to a spring right of the trail. It is a steep drop to the water source, which turns out to be hardly reliable.)

3.0 The blue-blazed trail crosses a saddle between Mount Pleasant and Pompey Mountain. Several gaps in the forest open up as you walk through a grassy landscape.

3.2 The trail passes just to the left of Pompey Mountain. (FYI: Although only a few feet shorter than Mount Pleasant, Pompey Mountain is wooded with no views.) After passing the summit, the trail drops hard down the north slope.

3.6 Turn left onto a narrow footpath that wends its way through a spare forest notable for the waist-high grass. The trail climbs and re-enters forest land, where rhododendron form a brief tunnel. There are campsites off either side of the trail along this section.

4.1 Cross a small knob and begin a descent to the parking area.

4.8 Hike ends at the parking area on FR 51.

Hike Information

Local Information
Lexington Visitor Center, Lexington, VA, (877) 453-9822, www.lexingtonvirginia.com.

Local Events/Attractions
Food & Wine Festival at the Theater at Lime Kiln, first weekend in September, (540) 463-5375, www.theateratlimekiln.com.

25 Roaring Run/Hoop Hole

In an inconspicuous corner of Botetourt County, seven peaks converge to form a backcountry nook where bears just may outnumber human visitors. The region's namesake, Roaring Run, pulses through a break in Rich Patch Mountain with force enough to have powered a blast iron furnace for half a century. Ruins of that furnace mark the beginning of a loop hike that takes you along the high, dry top of Pine Mountain, then down to headwaters of three small streams. Between ridgetop and riverbed spreads a forest that is as secluded as it is satisfying.

Start: From the signboard next to the bathrooms at Roaring Run Furnace National Recreation Area.

Distance: 10-mile loop.

Approximate hiking time: 5 hours.

Difficulty rating: Moderate due to long climbs and length. The bushwhack up Pine Mountain requires skills in across-country hiking, including the ability to use a compass.

Trail surface: Dirt footpaths and old dirt roads lead along dry ridges, through extended fields of heath, boulder fields, and stream headwaters.

Land status: National forest.

Nearest town: Clifton Forge, VA.

Other trail users: Hikers only.

Canine compatibility: Dogs permitted.

Trail contacts: New Castle Ranger District, New Castle, VA, (540) 864-5195.

Schedule: Open year-round.

Fees/permits: No fees or permits required.

Maps: USGS maps: Strom, VA.

Finding the trailhead: From Clifton Forge: Drive west on I-64 to the Low Moor exit. Drive south on Virginia Route 696 and, in 0.1 mile, turn left onto Virginia Route 616. Drive 5.7 miles, then turn left onto Virginia Route 621 at Rich Patch Union Church. In 3.3 miles, turn right into the Roaring Run National Recreation Area. *DeLorme: Virginia Atlas & Gazetteer:* Page 52, C3.

The Hike

In 1804, William Clark, a man whose name would become synonymous with exploration, left the small town of Fincastle in Botetourt County, Virginia, for the unknown of the American frontier. He and friend Meriwether Lewis would lead the Corps of Discovery through the void of middle America to the Pacific Ocean, and back. Three years later, Clark returned to Fincastle a national hero. He settled and married the daughter of wealthy landowner George Hancock. Clark's journals from the Corps of Discovery expedition were stored and edited in Fincastle, in Hancock's home. In 1810, President Thomas Jefferson appointed him governor of the Missouri Territory, thus ending his Virginia residency. Clark departed for St. Louis and left behind a legend proudly guarded by Fincastlians, who are known to claim their town as the real point-of-embarkation for the Lewis and Clark expedition.

Fincastle, a town of roughly 300 souls, is as fitting a beginning for Clark's journey as any spot. For a brief period before the Revolutionary War, this town sat on

Roaring Run iron-ore furnace.

the edge of the great unknown. The boundaries of Botetourt County, of which Fincastle was the county seat, stretched as far as the Mississippi and contained parts of seven present-day states. Standing atop Pine Mountain on a clear fall or winter day, you get a small sense of that vast landholding, where views stretch into West Virginia and the imagination, if prodded, farther. And as is the case for all good explorations, getting to this secluded vista on Pine Mountain is as much a reason for going as the payoff.

The journey begins at Roaring Run Furnace, a national recreation area south of Clifton Forge in Botetourt County. The Iron Ore Trail climbs from the ruins of a blast furnace on old dirt roads and abandoned railroad grades. In a saddle between Shoemaker Knob and Iron Ore Knob, the trail turns and skirts the slope of Pine Mountain as a footpath. If a hiker sticks to the blazed trails, the route eventually leads to a forested saddle of the Pine Mountain ridge. But there's an alternate route up Pine Mountain, a short, steep path—more a detour than a true bushwhack. Look for this route as you climb Hoop Hole Trail, less than half a mile uphill from the T intersection with Iron Ore Trail. In a world of well-blazed, clearly defined paths, this side trail is a gift. Marked by infrequent plastic squares the size of a quarter, following it still requires hunt-and-peck skills. These are times a hiker falls back on basic skills: orientating, identifying telltale plants, determining whether they are typical of a certain elevation or slope, and wondering who, or more precisely what, has walked here before you. (Lewis and Clark would be *so* proud.)

FYI Pig iron is another term for cast iron produced in a blast furnace. Molten iron was poured into shallow holes fed by a trench. The arrangement reminded someone of newborn pigs suckling, with the trench the "sow" and the holes the "pigs."

The last question is answered atop Pine Mountain. Amid the outcrops of sandstone, logs show signs of being clawed and shredded by black bears looking for larva and insects. By-products of their munching, scat piles, lay in clumps here and there. With a range up to 15 miles, a number of bears have made the Pine Mountain/Rich Patch Mountain slopes home turf.

From Pine Mountain's first knob, a sight line carries southwest along the 3,000-foot-high ridge to a point where Pine Mountain buttresses against Rich Patch Mountain. Patches of stunted vegetation grow in thin shale soil on the upper slopes of the ridge. Berry bushes thrive here, where the larger, moisture-loving witch hazel will not. Wild grasses propagate in gaps of forest created by fire. Among the berry bushes, poverty oat grass grows in gray-green mats. Another grass, yellow sedge, is found on more gently graded slopes. Both grasses are present in early stages of forest recovery and may be indicators of a recent fire. The shoots need only a thin soil cover and seem adaptable to the acidic, nutrient-deficient soil typical of dry, fire-ravaged areas.

So thick is the undergrowth at points, Hoop Hole Trail can become difficult to follow. At these times, it pays to watch for the red stone flakes that litter the trail; this color indicates the mineral hematite. Hematite is a principal iron-ore mineral and its presence, embedded in sandstone deposits formed 400 million years ago, helped catapult this region into a leading producer of iron ore during the second half of the nineteenth century.

Roaring Run Furnace, where this described loop begins, operated as a blast furnace for only thirty years. That's a short time in a region famous for iron production. The furnace's obscurity may explain, in a backhanded way, how it survived

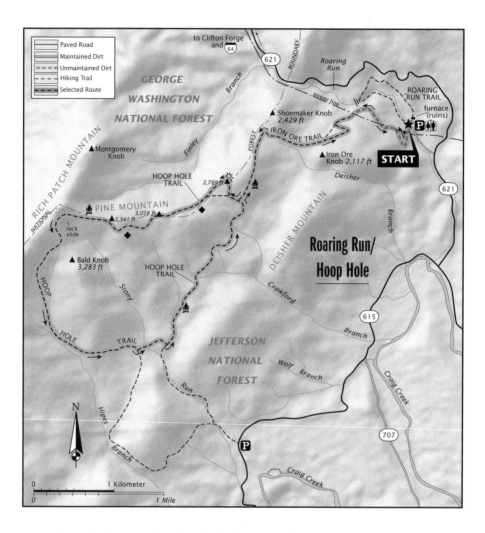

intact through the years. During the Civil War, Tredegar Iron Works leased Roaring Run as an insurance policy against losing its larger furnaces located in the Great Valley. Union forces eventually destroyed three of Tredegar's mines in an effort to disrupt the Confederate's supply of bullets, cannons, and gun parts. Tredegar, especially, held significance. From its Virginia furnaces, it produced the cannons at Fort Sumter, South Carolina, site of the first battle between North and South. And even Grace Furnace, an iron-ore furnace 5 miles west of Roaring Run, fell to Union forces. It all points to a conclusion that Roaring Run survived because it wasn't producing iron ore. Tredegar's records show it blasted the furnace once, in 1865, just before the war ended. This inactivity made it an impractical target for Union forces.

Evidence of mining activity around Roaring Run Furnace is visible in the large depressions cut from the mountainside. In other spots, talus (rock piles) lay beneath gouged out chunks of hillside. For some unknown reason, the minerals around Roaring Run were never exploited to the extent they were elsewhere in Virginia. By 1870, Virginia iron furnaces were switching to a more efficient, coke-based fuel source. Charcoal-burning furnaces such as Roaring Run faded into obscurity. Given that a furnace consumed on average 750 bushels of charcoal in a single day—the equivalent of an acre of woodland—the furnace's inactivity once again held an unintended benefit. This time, it saved a beautiful corner of the forest from mining and logging—a benefit hikers can certainly appreciate.

Miles and Directions

0.0 **START** from a trailboard next to the bathrooms at Roaring Run Furnace. Follow the wide, orange-blazed Iron Ore Trail under hemlocks and table mountain pines.

0.2 At a fork in the trail, bear left and climb on the Iron Ore Trail. Soon, the falls on Roaring Run are audible downhill on the right.

0.4 Pass under power lines.

0.7 At a T junction, turn left and follow the orange-blazed Iron Ore Trail, which is still a dirt road. (FYI: Avoid the road that leads straight from this intersection. It is marked with yellow blazes.)

0.8 Pass a road that splits right and uphill away from Iron Ore Trail. In another 20 yards, Iron Ore Trail forks right onto a narrow trail leading uphill; bear right at this fork and follow the Iron-Ore Trail uphill. It breaks from the woods to pass under power lines, then re-enters the woods.

1.0 Switchback up the northeast slope of Iron Ore Mountain. Iron Ore Trail climbs steadily to a gap between Iron-Ore (2,117 feet) and Shoemaker Knob (2,429 feet). (FYI: Iron Ore Trail is wide and well-graded in sections where it follows old roads or railroad that date from a time in the nineteenth century when the blast furnace at Roaring Run was in operation.)

1.7 At a double blaze, turn left and cross the dry creek bed of Deisher Branch.

2.0 Pass a campsite nicely situated in a large, flat clearing on the left side of Iron Ore Trail.

2.3 At a T intersection, turn right onto yellow-blazed Hoop Hole Trail. (FYI: A left onto Hoop Hole leads along the lower elevations of Pine Mountain. It is the return leg of this loop hike.)

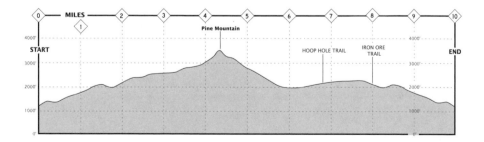

2.5 Turn right on an overgrown path that leads sharply uphill. The route is marked with plastic yellow diamonds, about the size of a quarter, nailed into trees. Be alert: The trail is overgrown and hard to follow. Markers are small and infrequent. (FYI: This route is a steep, 0.3-mile ascent of Pine Mountain's first knob [2,789 feet]. In fall and winter, this peak provides the best views off the mountain into West Virginia.) **Option:** The climb up Pine Mountain's first knob, while blazed, is difficult. A hiker can avoid it by continuing straight on the Hoop Hole Trail. A half mile from this junction, Hoop Hole Trail enters a clearing in a saddle between Pine Mountain's first and second knob. In this clearing, the route from Pine Mountain's first knob rejoins Hoop Hole Trail.

2.8 At the top of Pine Mountain's first knob, turn left onto an overgrown trail marked with faint yellow paint slashes. The trail descends. (FYI: This route description applies to hikers who followed the detour to Pine Mountain's first knob. Otherwise, see route cue 3.0.)

3.0 Rejoin the Hoop Hole Trail in a saddle between Pine Mountain's first and second knobs. Hike straight on the Hoop Hole Trail along the top of the ridge as it climbs toward Pine Mountain's second knob.

3.5 Shale rock outcrops on the right mark the approach of Pine Mountain's second knob (3,038 feet). (FYI: This stretch of trail is enveloped in waist-high berry bushes and mountain laurel.)

3.8 Climb out of the gap between Pine Mountain's second and third knobs. Hoop Hole Trail stays left of the ridgetop.

4.1 Climb on Hoop Hole Trail to the spine of Pine Mountain. In a few hundred yards, reach a campsite. From this spot, Hoop Hole Trail drops gradually off the left side of Pine Mountain. (FYI: Another unmarked trail leads from this campsite up the spine of Pine Mountain and tops out on Rich Patch Mountain.)

4.4 A mass of boulders marks the rocky joint of the Pine Mountain ridge and Rich Patch Mountain. Follow Hoop Hole Trail as it turns left and threads a gap between Rich Patch Mountain and Bald Knob.

5.7 Cross the headwaters of Hipes Branch.

6.4 Turn left at a T junction and follow Hoop Hole Trail. (A right turn at this T junction leads to parking on Virginia Route 615.)

6.7 At a fork in the trail, bear left onto the yellow-blazed Hoop Hole Trail. (Bearing right at this fork leads to parking on VA 615.)

8.0 Turn right onto Iron Ore Trail.

9.1 After descending along a section of trail with steep banks and a troughlike appearance, Iron Ore Trail bears right. Look straight into the woods for an ill-defined footpath marked with faint yellow-painted blazes. It descends to a power line cut in one-tenth of a mile. Follow the power line easement downhill to a T junction with a dirt road. Turn left onto this dirt road and, in 0.1 mile, turn left onto the Iron Ore Trail.

10.0 Hike ends at the trailboard near the bathrooms at Roaring Run Furnace.

Hike Information

Local Information

Botetourt Chamber of Commerce, Fincastle, VA, (540) 473-8280.

Local Events/Attractions

Allegheny Highlands Arts & Crafts Center, Clifton Forge, VA, (540) 862-4447.

Lodging

Milton Hall Bed & Breakfast Inn, Covington, VA, (540) 965-0196. Children and pets welcome.

Longdale Bed & Breakfast, Clifton Forge, VA, (540) 862-0892. Historic B&B with cabin for travelers with pets.

Restaurants

Clifton Forge Inn, Clifton Forge, VA, (540) 862-7506.

Club Car Shop & Deli, Clifton Forge, VA, (540) 862-0777.

Honorable Mentions

Valley and Ridge

Compiled here is an index of great hikes in the valley and ridge region that didn't make the A-list this time around but deserve recognition. Check them out and let us know what you think. You may decide that one or more of these hikes deserves higher status in future editions or, perhaps, you may have a hike of your own that merits some attention.

35 Shawl Gap-Massanutten East Trail

Start at Elizabeth Furnace on Virginia Route 678. This 12.4-mile loop uses the Botts Trail and Sherman Gap Trail, with a return along Massanutten East Trail. Elizabeth Furnace, an antebellum iron-ore blast furnace, is the start and end point, with camping facilities available. Call (540) 984–4101. *DeLorme: Virginia Atlas & Gazetteer:* Page 74, A2.

36 Massanutten Mountain West/Signal Knob

From Strasburg, drive east on Virginia Route 55 and then south on Virginia Route 678 to the Signal Knob Trail parking area on the right. This 17-mile hike climbs Signal Knob, then swings south down the western ridge of Massanutten and provides great views overlooking the Shenandoah Valley. Hike it as an out-and-back, or a point-to-point with a shuttle on Virginia Route 653 east of the village of Toms Brook. Call (540) 984–4101. *DeLorme: Virginia Atlas & Gazetteer:* Page 74, A2.

37 Massanutten Mountain East/Duncan Hollow

Begin at Camp Roosevelt on Virginia Route 675. (See "Finding the trailhead:" directions for Hike 18: Stephens Trail.) Duncan Hollow is a lesser-used portion of the Massanutten East Trail with great loop options using Peach Orchard Gap and Scothorn Gap. Call (540) 984–4101. *DeLorme: Virginia Atlas & Gazetteer:* Page 73, C7.

38 Hone Quarry

From Harrisonburg, head west on Virginia Route 42, then west on Virginia Route 257. Follow signs for Hone Quarry Recreation Area, an abandoned mine turned backcountry playground; there are a variety of hike options. Hone Quarry Ridge Trail gives the hiker glimpses of the scars created by mining, while Wolf Ridge Trail leads past the quarry to Reddish Knob. Call (540) 828–2591. *DeLorme: Virginia Atlas & Gazetteer:* Page 66, A2.

39 Wild Oak National Recreation Trail

This 25.4-mile loop trail begins near the North River Gorge area north of Churchville, off Forest Road 95, 1 mile north of Stokesville. There are views off Little Bald Knob and difficult terrain past Camp Todd, a full-service national forest recreation area with a lake, campsite, and picnic area. The Wild Oak Loop intersects with trails leading into Ramsey's Draft Wilderness. Call (540) 828–2591. *DeLorme: Virginia Atlas & Gazetteer:* Page 66, B2.

40 Shenandoah Mountain Trail/South

A 22-mile end-to-end hike that begins at the Confederate breastworks on Virginia Route 250, 17 miles west of Churchville. The southern end is on Virginia Route 627 (Scotchtown Draft Road), off Virginia Route 629. This difficult, high-ridge hike along the spine of Shenandoah Mountain is best done as a two-day trip. Call (540) 885–8028. *DeLorme: Virginia Atlas & Gazetteer:* Page 65, B7.

41 North Mountain/Crawford Mountain

From Staunton, take Virginia Route 254 west to Virginia Route 42. South of Buffalo Gap, turn right onto Virginia Route 688; the trailhead is on the left side of VA 688. This hike combines two mountain paths for an end-to-end trek along Great North Mountain, the western barrier of Shenandoah Valley. Highlights include Elliott Knob (4,463 feet) and low-lying saddlebacks (1,600 feet at Dunlap Hunter access road). Call (540) 885–8028. *DeLorme: Virginia Atlas & Gazetteer:* Page 66, C1.

42 Torry Ridge–Mill Creek Loop

A long trek that departs from White Oak Campground at Sherando Lake. Reach the lake via the Blue Ridge Parkway, milepost 16. This Blue Ridge hike has it all: mountains and streams, blueberries, rhododendron, and the convenience of a base camp with showers and flush toilets. Call (540) 291–2188. *DeLorme: Virginia Atlas & Gazetteer:* Page 54, A3.

43 Humpback Rocks

A challenging day hike off the Blue Ridge Parkway (BRP) 6 miles south of Rockfish Gap and I-64. Trailhead located at BRP milepost 6. Humpback Rocks is a 3,080-foot outcrop of greenstone with wide views west to the Shenandoah Valley. The hike to the rocks is 1 mile on the Appalachian Trail. Humpback Mountain and more views await another mile down the trail. Call (540) 291–2188. *DeLorme: Virginia Atlas & Gazetteer:* Page 55, A5.

44 Crabtree Falls

Trailhead is 17 miles northeast of Buena Vista on Virginia Route 56. This 3-mile trail runs along a creek that has five major cascades, overlooks, and ends at a parking lot on Virginia Route 828. The cumulative 1,200-foot drop in elevation along Crabtree Creek makes this one of the highest waterfalls east of the Mississippi. The Forest Service has built steps and installed railings along the trail to aid with hiking over treacherous terrain. Call (540) 291–2188. *DeLorme: Virginia Atlas & Gazetteer:* Page 54, B3.

45 Whetstone Ridge

An end-to-end hike with the northern trailhead on the Blue Ridge Parkway, milepost 29, and southern access on Virginia Route 603, northeast of Buena Vista. This is the longest trail in the Glenwood-Pedlar Ranger District of the George Washington–Jefferson National Forest. Notable for views of Three Ridges, The Priest, and Adams Peak. Call (540) 291–2188. *DeLorme: Virginia Atlas & Gazetteer:* Page 54, B2.

46 Apple Orchard Falls–Cornelius Creek Loop Trail

Begin at Sunset Field Overlook near milepost 78 on the Blue Ridge Parkway for this 7.5-mile loop. Two-hundred-foot waterfalls and old-growth forest are the highlights of this special management area. Call (540) 291–2188. *DeLorme: Virginia Atlas & Gazetteer:* Page 53, D6.

47 Rich Hole Wilderness

Located 12 miles west of Lexington off I-64. There are only 8 miles of marked trails in this wilderness, but its small size makes it ideal for exploring. Past mining and iron-ore activity, as well as a fire tower, created a network of easy-to-follow trails. Call (540) 962–2214. *DeLorme: Virginia Atlas & Gazetteer:* Page 53, B5.

48 Rough Hole Wilderness

Situated 17 miles northeast of Covington off Virginia Route 42. There's only one marked route in this 9,300-acre wilderness, the 4-mile Crane Trail. Bushwhacking is a tough task amid steep terrain. Wintertime is the best season to scale the summit of Griffith Knob. Call (540) 839–2521. *DeLorme: Virginia Atlas & Gazetteer:* Page 53, A5.

49 Douthat State Park

Located 5 miles north of Clifton Forge on Virginia Route 629. A 4,493-acre state park on Wilson Creek between Brushy Mountain and Middle Mountain. There are more than 36 miles of trails that weave their way through the park and surrounding George Washington National Forest. Beards Gap Trail leads to Mountain Top Trail with views of the 50-acre Douthat Lake and surrounding hillsides. Lake, picnicking, fishing, and fee camping. Call (540) 862–8100. *DeLorme: Virginia Atlas & Gazetteer:* Page 52, A4.

Southwest Highlands

outhwest Highlands covers two distinct geological regions of the state: a southwest portion of the Valley and Ridge province, and the Appalachian Plateau of
far southwest Virginia. This is the land of timber, iron ore, and coal—and more
recently, natural gas production. The rugged terrain, coupled with its distance
from metropolitan centers on the East Coast, gives the area a remoteness that adds
to its allure as a destination.

Rivers shape and define this region as much as the mountains. The New River,
the oldest flowing body of water on the North American continent, flows northwest out of the North Carolina hills. Moving in the opposite direction is the
Roanoke River. Farther south, the Clinch and Powell Rivers flow along deep
troughs between tall mountain ridges, their supply feeding the Tennessee River.
Most spectacular of all is Russell Fork, viewed from atop the 1,000-foot cliff walls
where it passes over the Virginia-Kentucky border.

The forces that wrought southwest Virginia's mountains are inseparable from
those elsewhere in the state: volcanic activity along the Blue Ridge, sedimentary
rock in the valley and ridge region, then periods of heat, pressure, folding, and faulting. Amid this, one area stands apart. Pine Mountain, along the Virginia-Kentucky
border, is a stellar example of thrust plate movement, where one piece of the earth's
crust ramped up onto another. North from Pound Gap, the edge of the mountain
drops steeply into Kentucky, while to the east, the terrain rolls downhill.

For generations, southwest Virginia remained an isolated region, both from the
state and the country as a whole. Even after timber and coal barons brought riches
in the form of logging and mining, pockets of poverty persisted. The booms in economic and cultural life were grand times. Big Stone Gap lured vacationers from
New York City and royalty from abroad. When busts hit, they hit hard. Throughout
the twentieth century, quality of life hinged on the price of coal. Since the 1970s,
demand and price for Virginia coal has declined. That has forced leaders to find other
economic stimuli, chief among them is outdoor recreation. Given the natural beauty
of the region, this is a happy development for hikers and mountain bike riders alike.

Southwest Highlands

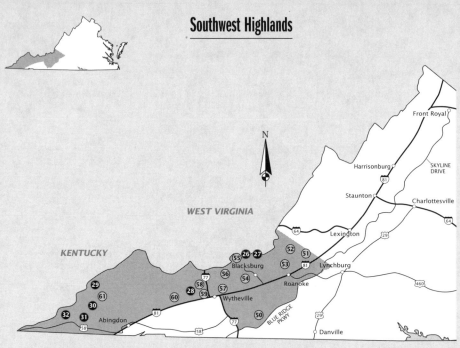

The Hikes	**Honorable Mentions**
Huckleberry Loop **26.**	50. Rock Castle Gorge
Mountain Lake Wilderness **27.**	51. Patterson Mountain
Crawfish/Channel Rock **28.**	52. Bald Mountain
Pine Mountain Trail **29.**	53. North Mountain–AT Loop
Chief Benge Scout Trail **30.**	54. Poverty Creek
Devils Fork Loop **31.**	55. The Rice Fields
Stone Mountain Trail **32.**	56. Ribble Trail–AT Loop
	57. Tract Fork Trail
	58. Trail Boss–AT Loop
	59. Seven Sisters Trail
	60. Hungry Mother State Park
	61. Guest River Gorge Trail

26 Huckleberry Loop

Two of Virginia's long trails, the Appalachian Trail and the Allegheny Trail, pass through Peters Mountain Wilderness, a patch of forestland on the steep ridge that constitutes the Virginia–West Virginia border. But neither well-traveled trail quite captures what it means for a forest to turn wild as well as the Huckleberry Loop. The trail down Dismal Creek on the eastern slope of Peters Mountain is as rough as they come, overrun with rhododendron, blocked by blowdowns, and often lost altogether in the streambed. There are car-size boulders en route, and rotted logs litter the creek bed. This trail sums up everything a wilderness should be: beautiful, difficult, and, in the end, extremely satisfying.

Start: From the dirt road off Virginia Route 722/Glen Alton Drive.
Distance: 8-mile loop.
Approximate hiking time: 4 hours.
Difficulty rating: Moderate due to easy hiking on clearly marked, well-graded trails, with one very difficult stretch down Dismal Creek.
Trail surface: Dirt woods paths and dirt roads through hardwood forest slopes, fields, a river valley, and streambed.
Land status: National forest.

Nearest town: Pembroke, VA.
Other trail users: Hunters (in season).
Canine compatibility: Dogs permitted.
Trail contacts: New River Valley Ranger District, Blacksburg, VA, (540) 552-4641.
Schedule: Open year-round. Hunting is permitted in national forests, and November through January is the busiest season.
Fees/permits: No fees or permits required.
Maps: USGS maps: Interior, VA.

Finding the trailhead: From Pembroke: Drive north on U.S. Highway 460 for 2 miles and turn right onto Virginia Route 635. After 5.6 miles, follow VA 635 as it turns left and crosses Stony Creek. Drive another 8.1 miles and turn left onto VA 722/Glen Alton Drive. Immediately cross Stony Creek and, in 0.1 mile, turn left onto a bumpy dirt road. Follow the road past a red forest gate as it bears right and uphill. In less than 0.1 mile, park at a second forest gate that blocks further vehicle traffic on the dirt road. *DeLorme: Virginia Atlas & Gazetteer:* Page 41, A5.

The Hike

Dismal Branch runs a noisy route for 3 miles down the slope of Peters Mountain. In a gully between Pine Swamp Ridge and Huckleberry Ridge, a series of obstacles force stream and hiker to detour. A blown-down tree too big to either crawl over or under sends the hiker through rhododendron so dense it requires pushing back thickets with both arms. At this point, Dismal Creek disappears underground beneath a rock slide. Five paces downhill, this unsinkable stream spurts from beneath the rocks and runs around a huge boulder. The stream disappears beneath rocks once

Milkweed and butterflies in the meadows of Kelly Flats.

more, then returns to the surface to spill off a small rock cleft into a pool. So calm is this pool, so calm is the water, it's almost as if the stream is making a statement: "See, that wasn't so hard, was it?"

Huckleberry Loop, an 8-mile trail through Peters Mountain Wilderness and pastoral Kelly Flats, cannot be judged by one difficult stretch of trail. But it's a fact: Memories of Dismal Creek will stay with a hiker long after sweet-smelling hemlocks along Dixon Creek and the quiet solitude of the North Fork fade. The reason is simple. Dismal Creek captures the essence of wilderness in Virginia, a place where plants and land are free to take whatever shape nature deems appropriate.

Virginia's forestland is, by and large, comprised of second- and third-generation trees. Axes, crosscut saws, plows, shovels, dynamite, fire, even the hands of the herb and mushroom collector—all have reshaped the land, plants, and trees. Clear-cutting of Virginia forests reached a peak between 1890 and 1920, when nearly every usable tree was cut and shipped to the sawmill. There's a rusted railroad car wheel lying in the brush alongside the North Fork, evidence of this area's logging past. The wide,

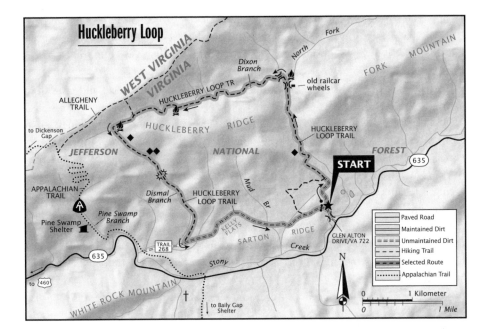

flat terrain along the stream was the grade on which railroad cars ran, loaded with wood. Few areas escaped the clear-cutting. Where old-growth timber stands, it's as much thanks to chance as any intent to preserve the trees.

Despite all this, forests are adaptable. Left unchecked, climax species will return on land clear-cut for lumber. On Peters Mountain, oak and hickory will someday stand tall. (Efforts are ongoing, but it's debatable whether chestnut, once a dominant tree of the Southern Appalachians, will ever return. A blight, *cryphonectria parasitica,* attacks the chestnut in its infancy. The tree, which once towered 100 feet high, may grow head-height before succumbing.) At lower elevations, nature has a head start on forty acres near Dixon Branch. Here you'll find a stand of old-growth Eastern hemlocks, a climax tree that normally requires generations to reach its peak growth. It took hundreds of years to reach the breadth of those that stand along Dixon Branch—a staggering thought, given the timber industry's penchant to shear mountaintops of all usable lumber.

Forest recovery begins in the forest understory, where competition for sunlight and water is stiff among the many small trees and shrubs. Hardly the stars of any forest, spicebush, witch hazel, black haw, and maple leaf viburnum fill an important niche. Fox, grouse, and pheasant eat the fruit, bark, and leaves of these trees. White-tailed deer will tug on clusters of blackish-blue berries on the black haw, or nibble the bark off a mountain maple sapling. Huckleberry Ridge and neighboring Peters Mountain are home to a population of black bear, and the blueberry and huckleberry patches that cover higher slopes are a primary food source for this animal.

Heath-type shrubs, especially, are dynamos. A huckleberry (a bit darker in the bark than the blueberry and peppered with telltale yellow resin spots on the leaves) has ten seeds per berry. Its cousin, the blueberry, has more than one hundred seeds in each blue ball.

A half mile into this loop, where the trail turns off a gravel road and rises on a gentle shoulder of Locust Knob, shrubby plants gobble up the dry, leafy forest real estate. It stands in stark contrast to the shaded, moist terrain along Dixon Branch and, especially, Dismal Branch, both of which lie ahead. On these dry slopes, mountain laurel and rhododendron are conspicuously absent. You'll see young chestnut oak and maple trees, flowering dogwood with its characteristic white blossom in springtime, and sassafras, a curious tree with three distinctly different leaves. Along Dixon and Dismal Branches, by comparison, the moist ground supports a habitat marked by slicks of rhododendron, mosses, and ferns. Taller still are the hemlock, tulip poplar, sweet buckeye, and, most beautiful in spring, mountain silverbell. As different as these two environments appear, both are less than one hundred years recovered from logging.

Sassafras is one clue to a forest's ongoing recovery, and the small tree is plentiful in this area. Sassafras's three leaves are distinct: one oblong, one shaped like a mitten, the other lobed in the center. During spring and summer, a hiker is likely to brush past one without a second notice. In fall, however, the tree's brilliant red foliage catches your attention; sassafras is one of the more showy autumn plants in southern forests. Safrole, a clear oil extracted from the bark, has long been used to flavor root beer, teas, and stews. (Recently, safrole has been shown to cause cancer in laboratory experiments. The FDA bans use of the oil in foodstuffs.) I can't help but pass along, however, that boiling the leaves and twigs for tea produces an intense buzz. I now know that it's sassafras roots—not twigs and leaves—that have for years flavored teas and root beer. But when you've forgotten your edible plant book and you're feeling adventurous, strange things happen.

Miles and Directions

0.0 **START** at the red Forest Service gate on VA 722. The Huckleberry Loop Trail follows VA 722 for 0.4 mile and is blazed with single yellow triangles nailed on trees on the left side of the road.

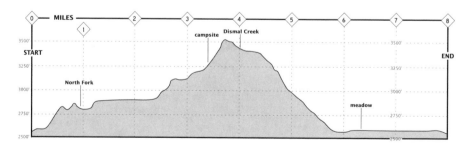

Crossing the North Fork.

0.4 Turn right off the gravel road onto a well-blazed narrow woods path through chestnut oak and maple. A small yellow and brown sign with a hiker symbol marks this turnoff.

0.9 Thick stands of rhododendron line the descent to the North Fork, where you'll turn left and hike upstream, climb a short hill, then drop to the river's edge to cross.

1.1 Cross the North Fork and hike up the right side of the stream on a flat, narrow woods path. (FYI: Small hemlocks and rhododendron separate the trail and stream. Up the slope to the right of the trail is a young hardwood forest. This trail used to be called *Flat Peter*—a hybrid of Kelly *Flats* and *Peters* Mountain—and some brochures and books still refer to it by that name. Mayapple grows along the path, and rotting logs and trees host a variety of coral and trumpet mushrooms.)

1.9 Pass by an unblazed trail that branches right off Huckleberry Loop Trail. In a few yards, pass rusted pieces of a railcar in the underbrush on the right side of the trail.

2.0 Pass over the North Fork on a wooden footbridge. There is a nice streamside campsite on the opposite bank. Bear left out of the campsite, follow Dixon Branch upstream a few feet and cross it on three moss-coated logs. The trail now follows Dixon Branch up the north side of Huckleberry Ridge to a saddle between the ridge and Peters Mountain. (FYI: The route is lined with hemlocks and rhododendron. Numerous stream crossings make for a wet hike during the spring.)

3.4 Reach a campsite on Dixon Branch just before your seventh stream crossing. On the other side, trail conditions deteriorate steadily. Logs block the trail and stretches of the path are very rocky. The next half mile brings four more stream crossings.

4.0 (FYI: As the trail approaches the headwaters of Dismal Branch, it passes through a fern glade and a tall canopy forest dominated by tulip poplar.) After a stretch of trail overgrown with mountain laurel and berry bushes, you'll reach Dismal Branch and turn southeast to travel downstream past a nice campsite with a fire ring.

4.7 A massive blowdown forces you off the trail and into the creek bed. Here, the stream runs through narrow channels formed by car-size boulders, then under a rock slide. It's audible, but you can't see it. The next half mile brings numerous stream crossings. At points, the trail and stream run the same course.

5.9 Exit Peters Mountain Wilderness. The trail, which has slowly changed from torturous, rocky streambed to wide, grassy road, turns left to return through the fields of Kelly Flats, a series of old fields flanked by Huckleberry and Sarton Ridges.

6.3 Enter a clearing bordered by plantations of white pines and wide-open fields of grass, milkweed, and other weeds. The trail follows a rutted road along the upper edges of the meadow.

8.0 Reach a forest gate, pass through, and turn left onto a gravel road. The parking area is a few short feet uphill.

Hike Information

Local Information

Giles County Chamber of Commerce, Pearisburg, VA, (540) 921-5000, www.personal.picusnet.com/gcc/.

Local Events/Attractions

Festival in the Park, June, Pearisburg, VA, (540) 921-2955. Barbecue by the Lions Club and homemade arts and crafts.

Glen Alton, Giles County, VA. Glen Alton is a 304-acre farm purchased by the national forest in 1999. Besides farm buildings, there are ponds, canals, dams, and orchards. Call the USFS at (540) 552-4641 in Blacksburg for more information.

Lodging

Nesselrod on the New, Radford, VA, (540) 731-4970, www.nesselrod.com. A B&B on the cliffs overlooking the New River.

White Rocks National Recreation Area, Giles County, VA, (540) 552-4641. There are forty-nine campsites and flush toilets, and there's a $4.00 site fee. Open April 1 through December 1.

Claytor Lake State Park, Montgomery County, VA, (540) 643-2500, (800) 933-7275 for reservations only. Cabins and camping ($18 to camp).

27 Mountain Lake Wilderness

Hear a name like Mountain Lake Wilderness and thoughts of Caribbean-blue lakes and tall peaks might pop into mind. In fact, Virginia's only true mountain lake sits outside this, the largest of all Virginia wilderness areas. And most of your climbing is done in the car getting here. Which is just fine, really, because this saves your breath for exploring upland bogs on Lone Pine Peak, slabs of Tuscarora sandstone on Salt Pond Mountain, and a red spruce glade on Potts Mountain. Trails through Mountain Lake Wilderness are well marked and maintained (the Appalachian Trail is the most-traveled route).

Start: From the parking lot for the War Spur-Chestnut Loop on the right side of Virginia Route 613.
Distance: 10.2-mile loop.
Approximate hiking time: 6 hours.
Difficulty rating: Moderate due to distance, steep climbs, and poor trail markings on Potts Mountain.
Trail surface: Narrow dirt woodland paths lead through fern glades, mountaintop swamps, and steep rock outcrops.

Land status: National forest wilderness.
Nearest town: Blacksburg, VA.
Other trail users: Hikers only.
Canine compatibility: Dogs permitted.
Trail contacts: New River Valley Ranger District, Blacksburg, VA, (540) 552-4641.
Schedule: Open year-round. Hunting is permitted on national forest property, and November through January is the busiest season.
Fees/permits: No fees or permits required.
Maps: USGS maps: Waiteville, VA; Interior, VA.

Finding the trailhead: From Blacksburg: Drive north on U.S. Highway 460 for 10 miles and turn right onto Virginia Route 700. In 6.8 miles, pass through Mountain Lake Resort. Here, VA 700 changes to VA 613 and wraps around the west side of Mountain Lake. The road turns to gravel 0.7 mile past the hotel. After another 0.8 mile the road forks; bear left. The parking area for the War Spur-Chestnut Loop is 3.4 miles past the resort. **Option:** If using a shuttle, drive a second car 2.1 miles up VA 613 to a parking area for Wind Rock and the Appalachian Trail (AT). *DeLorme: Virginia Atlas & Gazetteer:* Page 41, A5.

The Hike

Admit it. Hiking is an obsession. The gear, the trail, the miles—all of it has consumed your life. The new grill in the backyard stands idle while you sprint from work on Friday to meet that mountaintop on Saturday. The lawn needs mowing, but you've got no time for such frivolity. On the trail, your mantra is *Farther, Faster.*

Suddenly, after a long, sweaty day in pursuit of the almighty loop, you encounter the unusual. Maybe it's a great view. Maybe it's a morning mist rising off a wildlife pond, or a stream's song as it cuts through crowded woodland. Whatever form it takes, these are as unexpected and pleasant as a breeze on a hot day. They stir something

Hikers have many trail choices in Mountain Lake Wilderness.

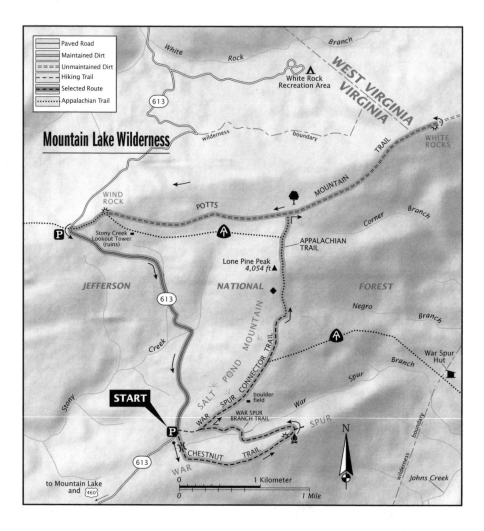

Mountain Lake Wilderness

Legend:
- Paved Road
- Maintained Dirt
- Unmaintained Dirt
- Hiking Trail
- Selected Route
- Appalachian Trail

White Rock Recreation Area

WEST VIRGINIA / VIRGINIA

613

WIND ROCK

POTTS

MOUNTAIN

TRAIL

WHITE ROCKS

Stony Creek Lookout Tower (ruins)

APPALACHIAN TRAIL

Lone Pine Peak 4,054 ft

Corner Branch

JEFFERSON

NATIONAL

FOREST

Negro Branch

613

War Spur Hut

Creek

SALT POND MOUNTAIN

CONNECTOR TRAIL

Spur

START

WAR SPUR

boulder field

War

SPUR

WAR SPUR BRANCH TRAIL

Stony

P

CHESTNUT

TRAIL

N

613

WAR

to Mountain Lake and 460

0   1 Kilometer

0   1 Mile

Johns Creek

deep within. The mellow *you,* the one who tugs at your conscience, says, *Hey, hold up. Stay here a while.*

Because the experience is both unusual and infrequent, coming across an upland bog ranks as that type of special moment. The observant hiker finds upland bogs in small depressions on a flat mountaintop or in broad gaps. They often form the head-waters of streams—even when the stream doesn't appear to be in the immediate area. Steeped in water year-round, an upland bog hosts plants that wouldn't survive 10 feet away in dry, gray-brown soil of the deciduous forest. Animals converge on it as if it were a desert oasis, both to eat and sometimes to be eaten.

Salt Pond Mountain in Mountain Lake Wilderness holds the right ingredients for an upland bog. The highest point is a flat pan of forest stretching a half mile in a northwest direction. The forest is mostly skinny hardwoods—oak, beech, poplar. As

War Spur Connector Trail approaches a downhill stretch that will end at the Appalachian Trail (AT), trees on the left give way to a grassy patch. It looks at first glance like a nice campsite. One step into the clearing, the ground turns soft and wet. Perhaps, you think as you pull a foot from the mire, this is why there are no fire rings. Walking the perimeter of the bog, you see Indian pipe stem and Virginia chain fern. Unseen to the eye, the fern spreads long, thin rhizomes beneath the soil. New ferns grow off this rhizome while roots sink deep into the bog, with its layered leaf rot. Bogs hold water like a sponge, ensuring lush conditions even in drought.

After you've climbed to the summit of Lone Pine Peak, you'll notice another upland opening on the right side of the AT on Lone Pine Peak. Here, the ground is drier. Laurel and winterberry add a shrubby, dense appearance to the forest understory encircling the bog. Camouflaged and positioned carefully, you might see a deer pick its way through mountain maple and scrub oak, nibbling on the grass or ferns covering the wet, spongy earth. In August or September, the red or gray fox might approach a mountain winterberry for a mouthful of red fruit. Long-stalked holly, similar in appearance to the winterberry, grows exclusively in the moist conditions of upland bogs. The chief difference between these two deciduous shrubs is the flowers: Long-stalked holly's flowers are a yellow-green color; the flower of a mountain winterberry has white petals.

Sit next to either bog for a spell and the sound of busy birds calling and singing fills your ears. If it's early spring, it's a male songbird who has arrived early from southern environs to prepare a nest. You might hear black and white wrens, a solitary vireo, and robins. You might see a tufted titmouse flit from thin branch to ground for a quick forage among the leaf litter. But whether you can tell the song of an Eastern wood-pewee (*pee-ah-wee*) from a white-breasted nuthatch's call (a rapid *wer-wer-wer*) isn't really the point. Purse your lips and make up your own song, then see what kind of bird comes to investigate.

The best of Mountain Lake Wilderness's bogs comes last. In the Southern Appalachians, where you find red spruce, you'll find Fraser fir (like a married couple, they're always together, thus giving rise to the nicknames: *he-balsam* for spruce and *she-balsam* for fir). Not so on Potts Mountain, a long, high ridge that forms the state border of Virginia and West Virginia. Potts Mountain lost its oak, chestnut, and red spruce in the first decade of the twentieth century—all, that is, except for small patches now protected by federal wilderness. A red spruce bog grows in the headwaters of Stony Creek on Potts Mountain's south-facing slope; there are strong ecological ties between this spot and the highland wilderness of Mount Rogers. Despite a difference in elevation of about 1,000 feet, both Little Wilson Creek Wilderness at Mount Rogers National Recreation Area (NRA) and Mountain Lake Wilderness Areas protect old-growth red spruce. It's worth pondering, as you sit next to this rarest of upland bogs, why the red spruce, the most common of the native spruce trees in the East and a mainstay of northern forests, is relegated to isolated spots here in Virginia. No matter what answer you arrive at, their rarity makes listening to that inner voice—the one that tells you to *Stay here a while*—a lot easier.

Miles and Directions

0.0   **START** at the parking area on VA 613. Enter the woods and immediately turn right onto Chestnut Trail.

1.0   Reach a junction with War Spur Branch Trail, which enters on the left. Continue straight on Chestnut Trail to an overlook in 1.2 mile.

1.2   Chestnut Trail ends at an overlook. Return to the War Spur Branch Trail.

1.4   Turn right onto the War Spur Branch Trail.

1.8   Reach War Spur Branch. In this dark stream valley, turn left and follow the trail as it leads upstream beneath old-growth hemlocks. **Sidetrip:** Experienced hikers can bushwhack War Spur Branch downstream for 1.6 miles to the Appalachian Trail (AT). Where War Spur Branch intersects with the AT, turn left onto the AT. In 75 yards, pass the War Spur Shelter on the right. The AT climbs steeply and, in 1 mile from the War Spur Shelter, intersects War Spur Connector Trail on the left. The first part of this sidetrip is a difficult bushwhack with many stream crossings. War Spur Branch is overgrown with mountain laurel and rhododendron, which hinders passage.

2.2   Reach a T junction of War Spur Branch and War Spur Connector Trails. Turn right onto the War Spur Connector Trail. **Option:** A left turn leads 0.2 mile to the parking area on VA 613.

2.5   (FYI: Scrub oak, Allegheny chinquapin, and witch hazel open onto a grassy, fern-ringed upland bog on the left side of the trail. A few feet past this on the right, a boulder field is visible through the trees. Large slabs of Tuscarora sandstone lay scattered over three or four acres. There are no tall cliffs or rock ledges—just disrupted, disjointed chunks of rock.)

2.9   Turn left onto the AT and begin a short, steep ascent of Lone Pine Peak. You'll climb 335 feet in less than a half mile to reach the wooded 4,054-foot summit.

3.7   Another upland bog opens up on the right side of the AT.

4.0   Double white blazes mark a hard left turn onto the AT. Instead of following the AT left, continue straight into the woods on a faint, unblazed path. In one-tenth of a mile, emerge from the woods onto Potts Mountain Trail, a wide, grassy forest road. A tall oak

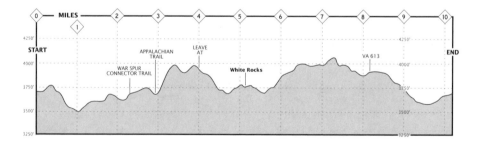

tree in the middle of the road marks this spot. Turn right onto Potts Mountain Trail and walk along the gently sloping ridgeline. (FYI: There are several campsites within the next mile.)

5.2   Reach White Rocks, an exposed rock formation on Potts Mountain with overlooks onto Little Mountain and beyond to Stony Run. To the east you will see Johns Creek Mountain and the War Spur drainage. Turn and retrace your steps along Potts Mountain Trail.

6.3   Pass the tall oak that marks the spur trail to the AT; continue straight on Potts Mountain Trail. You may see faint white blazes on trees, leftovers from days when the AT followed Potts Mountain Trail.

7.1   Enter a large, sloping field overgrown with tall grass. The trail climbs from the bottom of the field to a clearing in the grass in the middle of the field. The trail then arcs gently right and re-enters woods at the top of the field. (FYI: Stay alert: There are no blazes or trail markers through this field. Several roads branch off from the clearing in the middle of the field.)

7.3   Potts Mountain Trail passes through another clearing. Concrete pilings off the left side of the trail are all that remain of the Stony Creek lookout tower.

7.7   Potts Mountain Trail junctions with the AT, which enters from the left side. Off the right side of Potts Mountain Trail is Wind Rock, another overlook across to Fork Mountain and the West Virginia state line.

8.1   The AT ends at a gravel parking lot on VA 613. If you're shuttling, the hike ends here. If not, turn left and hike 2.1 miles on gravel VA 613 to the hike starting point.

10.2   Hike ends at the gravel parking area for the War Spur-Chestnut Loop.

Views to a ridge of Salt Pond Mountain from the War Spur overlook.

Hike Information

Local Information

Giles County Chamber of Commerce, Pearisburg, VA, (540) 921-5000.

Montgomery County Chamber of Commerce, Blacksburg, VA, (540) 382-4010, www.montgomerycc.org.

Local Events/Attractions

Oktoberfest, September and October, Mountain Lake Hotel, Mountain Lake, VA, (540) 626-7121, www.mountainlakehotel.com.

Pembroke Heritage Days, September or October, Pembroke, VA, (540) 626-7772, bswms@swva.net.

Radford Highlanders Festival, October, Radford, VA, (540) 731-9235.

Summer Art Festival Concerts, Fridays in June and July, Blacksburg, VA, (540) 231-5921. Local artists featured in outdoor concerts.

Museum of Natural History, Blacksburg, VA, (540) 231-3001. Limited summer hours.

Lodging

Mountain Lake Hotel, Pembroke, VA, (540) 626-7121, www.mountainlakehotel.com.

The Dogwood Lodge at Radford, Radford, VA, (540) 639-9338.

White Rocks National Recreation Area, Giles County, VA, (540) 552-4641. There are forty-nine campsites and flush toilets, and there's a $4.00 site fee. Open April 1 through December 1.

Claytor Lake State Park, Montgomery County, VA, (540) 643-2500, (800) 933-7275 for reservations only. Has cabins and camping ($18 to camp).

Restaurants

Portabellas, Blacksburg, VA, (540) 552-7111.

28 Crawfish/Channel Rock

Originating in the flat bottomland and old fields of Crawfish Valley, the Crawfish–Channel Rock Trail ascends Brushy Mountain on steep, narrow footpaths to run northeast parallel to Walker Mountain. En route, you'll cross the Tennessee Valley Divide, where Reed Creek and Bear Creek vividly illustrate the effects of the divide. Flowing off opposite sides of the divide, each enters separate, ever-expanding stream networks that eventually reach the Ohio River, albeit 100 miles distant from one another. Deer and raccoon forage along the stream edges; turkey and ruffed grouse hunt for acorns on the slopes of Brushy and Walker Mountains. Beaver leave the most lasting impression: a two-stage dam you'll traverse on Bear Creek.

Start: From the parking area at the dead end of Forest Road 727-2 (Strawberry Road). As you enter the parking area, the trailhead is on a dirt road on the right.
Distance: 11.2-mile loop.
Approximate hiking time: 6 hours.
Difficulty rating: Moderate due to several steep climbs up Brushy Mountain.
Trail surface: Dirt forest road and singletrack woods paths wind through stream valleys and old fields, along dry ridgetops, and up steep climbs.

Land status: National forest.
Nearest town: Rural Retreat, VA.
Other trail users: Mountain bikers, equestrians, and hunters (in season).
Canine compatibility: Dogs permitted.
Trail contacts: New River Valley Ranger District, Wytheville, VA, (540) 228-5551.
Schedule: Open year-round. Hunting is allowed in national forests, and the busiest season is November through early January.
Fees/permits: No fees or permits required.
Maps: USGS maps: Rural Retreat, VA.

Finding the trailhead: From Rural Retreat: Drive north on Virginia Route 90 for 0.8 mile to Staley Crossroads, where the road becomes Virginia Route 680. (If traveling on I-81, take exit 60 (Rural Retreat) and turn left on VA 680, 1.3 miles north of Rural Retreat). Take VA 680 for 2.7 miles, turn left onto Virginia Route 625, and follow it 4.2 miles to a fork in the road. Bear left onto FR 727-2, which is signed as Strawberry Road. Drive 1.9 miles and reach a large, circular turnaround area and parking for the trail, which begins at a rusty red Forest Service gate on the right. *DeLorme: Virginia Atlas & Gazetteer: Page 23, A6.*

The Hike

Traveling with surveyors into Cherokee Indian territory, eighteenth-century botanist William Bartram recorded a memorable scene while encamped northwest of Big Lick, Georgia: In a mountain stream, below a set of minor rapids, gold darters swarmed around small mounds made of rock and mud below the water surface. Periodically, crayfish rushed forth from the towers, "at which time a brilliant fight presented; the little gold-fish instantly fled from every side, darting through the transparent waters like streams of lightning," Bartram wrote.

Beaver dam on Bear Creek.

Crayfish, crawdads, freshwater lobsters, mud bugs—call them what you will, they're a fascinating part of a forest stream's ecology. The battle with "gold-fish" described by Bartram in his *Travels,* published in 1791, is a reminder of the surprisingly vicious underworld they inhabit. In a mountain stream, small fish regularly prey on one another. Around rock ledges near a creek's headwaters, chubs cannibalize their young. Trout circle in riffling water searching for lunch. A crayfish, sensing danger, flicks up a cloud of silt and scuttles backwards under a rock. When a predator approaches, schooling fish draw into a tight pack and flee upon sensing a chemical alarm emitted by one of their own. Tadpoles, too, scatter with a telltale odor. The alarmer, in doing so, cannot escape and sacrifices itself.

There's no guarantee that Reed Creek, a stocked trout stream running down Crawfish Valley between the steep slopes of Brushy and Walker Mountains, will yield the same battle royal Bartram observed. You'll see plenty of crawfish and their mud-and-rock mounds in the stream. It's these that make Reed Creek and Bear Creek—the two streams that define the lower elevations of this loop hike—great theater. By midsummer, the water level has dropped from spring highs, leaving isolated pools. Here, a myriad of life-forms—darters and shiners, crayfish, salamanders, and water bugs—play out their busy, and in some cases, very short lives.

Along stretches of these creeks, especially through Channel Rock Hollow, larger hemlock trees draw nourishment from the stream water. This evergreen splits and crumbles rocks with a tenacious root grip, contributing over time to a buildup of sediment in the small pools where the stream rests between cascades. Tennessee dace, a tiny fish with markings from olive to scarlet red, inhabit pools like this in Bear Creek. The dace is threatened; the only other community is on the Lick Creek in Bland County.

Easier to spot are the darts that return to the same pool in which they were born to lay eggs. Once it establishes residency, a fish will rarely venture from the area during spawning. One theory on the how and why of their return links the fish and the shoreline trees in a symbiotic relationship. Tree roots release organic molecules into the water and the fish may use the chemical as a homing signal.

STAY OUT OF THE STREAM! Virginia ranks eighth in the nation for the amount of freshwater fish considered endangered or threatened. Trail conditions along Reed and Bear Creeks, and up Channel Rock Hollow, can only make the situation worse. At several points in the lower portion of Channel Rock Hollow, the stream and trail merge as one, endangering aquatic life. Bridge construction and trail relocations that would divert trails away from the water are pending.

Rising from the stream, the bottomlands in Crawfish Valley exhibit various stages of old-field succession. For 2 miles from the trailhead, fields drop gently left of the dirt road trail, reaching a fringe of trees that camouflage the stream. Ragweed grew tall the first year after the fields were abandoned. When it decomposes, this weed (the bane of hay fever sufferers) poisons the soil. Each subsequent year, the plant grows smaller and smaller until the stunted bunches of stalks, visible here, are all that remains. Queen Anne's lace with its telltale red spot—in folklore, a drop of Queen Anne's blood—sways on tall stalks. The flower is a member of the parsley family, with a tuberlike root resembling the carrot—it's also known as the wild carrot. Dig up the root in the autumn and it's the best carrot you've ever eaten. Beware, however. The plant looks similar to the water hemlock, an extremely poisonous (tough to find) plant.

Along Bear Creek, the process of old-field succession is more advanced. This stream runs off the southwest side of the Tennessee Valley Divide. Skinny hardwoods and thickets of rhododendron grow alongside the stream. Poplar and its varieties, big tooth aspen and quaking aspen, are encroaching, step by step, on the old fields

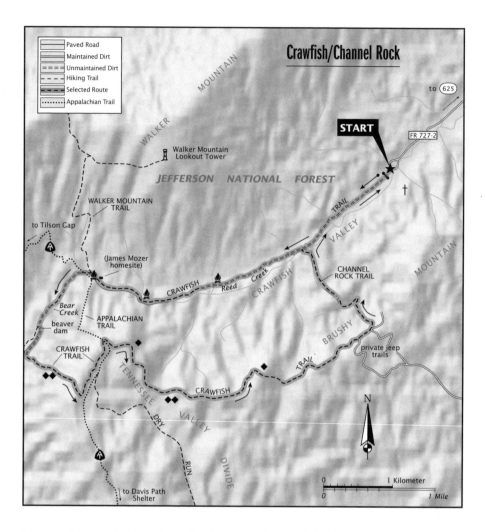

beyond the riverbanks. These hardwoods, disdained by lumber companies that wanted the harder chestnut and oaks, are pioneer species in the woody stage of old-field succession. Their tough seedlings can bear the exposure to sun and other elements that climax trees such as oak, hickory, or hemlock cannot. They reach top potential growth in fifty to sixty years, in the process creating the forest canopy that allows climax tree species to grow.

Overgrown fields are just one indicator along this hike that the land here was farmed. If you missed the more subtle clues—fruit trees, overgrown fields, barbwire, cut stone blocks—of past homesteaders, the board tacked onto an oak tree in a clearing near the trail's junction with the Appalachian Trail (AT) gives it away. The board reads MOZER'S PLACE, marking the homesite of James Mozer, who farmed the upper reaches of Crawfish Valley at the turn of the last century. Lower in the valley, Simon

Foglesong farmed 1,000 acres on Reed Creek in 1790; the family cemetery is on the south side of the stream on national forest land, as are the remnants of the home-site. Between these sites, plots of sorghum, a wild grain, dot the roadside. These are not indicators of someone following in the pioneer's footsteps. Rather, they're wildlife plots planted by the state Department of Conservation & Recreation for turkey and small songbirds.

From the valley floor, Brushy Mountain and its foothills frame Crawfish Valley on the east, and Walker Mountain rises to the west. The Wilderness Society calls this region one of the largest roadless areas in the Jefferson National Forest (referring to active forest roads, not the roads-turned-trails that comprise large parts of this loop). This and the presence of the Tennessee dace in lower Bear Creek make it a candidate for wilderness designation. The sense of isolation so often associated with a wilderness area creeps up on you on the steep climb up Brushy Mountain. Berry bushes crowd the narrow trail, scratching at your pant legs. Allegheny chinquapin and chestnut oak grow in the forest understory. Views in all directions are blocked by the dense understory of these thin trees. Your footsteps may flush a turkey. These popular game birds awaken the hiker who camps on Brushy Mountain. Before sunrise, the birds call out to one another, a signal to head downslope to the river. And so, too, you rise, pack up your belongings, and head down the final stretch of trail off Brushy Mountain.

Miles and Directions

0.0 **START** at a brown forest gate across the dirt road leading from the parking lot. Crawfish Trail begins at the forest gate and follows the dirt road as it runs along the base of Walker Mountain amid black-eyed Susans, asters, blackberries, and grasses. Wide fields open up left of the trail, and beyond the fields flows Reed Creek.

1.0 Come to a junction of Crawfish Trail and Channel Rock Trail; continue straight. (FYI: Channel Rock Trail branches left off the road through a field and crosses Reed Creek. This is the return leg of this loop hike.)

1.5 Pass a good campsite amid pines and tulip poplar.

1.8 Pass through a grassy clearing. Crawfish Trail is now a dirt path. (FYI: Blackberries are abundant in midsummer. Pass another campsite on the right within two-tenths of a mile.)

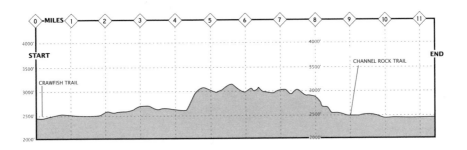

2.6 Pass through a clearing dominated by a single large oak. (FYI: A board nailed to the tree identifies this as the one-time homesite of James Mozer, a settler who farmed this valley in the early 1900s. Pieces of a home foundation lie in the overgrown grass.)

2.8 Turn left onto the Crawfish Trail at a T junction with Walker Mountain Trail (Walker Mountain Trail continues straight). This junction is marked by orange arrows tacked onto a tree. A few feet after turning, cross Reed Creek and enter a clearing with a fire ring. From the clearing, turn right and enter the woods under a tunnel of rhododendron. (FYI: A signboard marks where the white-blazed AT exits the clearing.)

3.5 The trail passes several fields overgrown with grass. Past the second clearing, turn left and follow Crawfish Trail as it descends downhill into woods. (Note: Be alert. This is an unmarked turn in the trail. If you hike more than 0.1 mile without seeing an orange blaze, turn around and search for the turn, which will now be on the right.)

3.8 Crawfish Trail and Bear Creek finally run alongside one another amid tall hemlocks. Just as quickly as they join, however, they separate. Follow Crawfish Trail as it climbs a grassy road to a clearing. In this clearing, turn left and follow a grassy road downhill. (Note: In this clearing, avoid a grassy road that continues uphill. It is marked with yellow blazes.)

4.2 Reach a beaver dam across Bear Creek. This is a two-stage dam. (Note: At high water, you will have to hike downstream and cross at a shallow bend in the stream. Return to a large maple tree on the trail. From this tree, walk up the grass road for 100 yards, turn right, and follow the faintly defined road. The trail is obscured by waist-high grass. Bear Creek flows in a deep gully on your right.)

4.5 Turn left and follow Crawfish Trail as it climbs steeply up Brushy Mountain as a narrow dirt footpath.

5.9 Cross the AT and head downhill. (FYI: The next mile brings more steep climbs along the spine of Brushy Mountain amid a ridge forest of chestnut oak, maple, scrub pines, and berry bushes.)

7.8 Crawfish Trail steeply drops off the right side of the ridge, descending along the forest boundary marked by red paint slashes. The trail winds up and down the foothills of Brushy Mountain, straddling the forest boundary the entire way.

9.0 The trail converts to a grassy road as it descends into a clearing. Several old roads merge here. Avoid roads that are yellow blazed and posted private property. Instead, turn left onto Channel Rock Trail and follow plastic orange blazes downhill past rhododendron.

9.7 Reach the first of several points on the trail where Channel Rock Branch merges with the trail. (FYI: The stream's name is clear—the water has eroded a channel through the schist bedrock. Portions of the trail are very wet.)

10.2 Cross Reed Creek and rejoin Crawfish Trail. Turn right to return to the parking area.

11.2 Hike ends at the forest gate across Crawfish Trail. Walk past the gate to enter the parking area.

Hike Information

Local Information
Wythe Convention & Visitors Bureau, Wytheville, VA, (877) 347-8307, http://visit.wytheville.com.

Local Events/Attractions
Chautauqua Festival, June, Wytheville, VA, (276) 223-3355. Nine-day arts festival.

The Settlers Museum of Southwest Virginia, Atkins, VA, (276) 686-4401. Dedicated to the mountain pioneers of southwest Virginia.

Lodging
Virginia House Inn, Marion, VA, (276) 783-5112. Pets allowed. Dogs will love the big lawn.

Hungry Mother State Park, Smyth County, VA, (276) 781-7400, (800) 933-7275 (for reservations only). Cabins and camping ($18 tent site).

Restaurants
Log House Restaurant, Wytheville, VA, (276) 228-4139. Lunch and dinner inside a 1776 log cabin.

Scrooge's Restaurant, Wytheville, VA, (276) 228-6622.

Organizations
Appalachian Trail Conference, Harpers Ferry, WV, (304) 535-6331, www.appalachiantrail.org.

29 Pine Mountain Trail

Pine Mountain Trail traces a razor's edge along the Virginia–Kentucky border. You're walking a geological fault line known as an overthrust plate—a chunk of the earth's crust that buckled, broke, and ramped up over another chunk hundreds of millions of years ago. The resulting terrain slopes gently east to Virginia, while to the west, sheer drops of 500 feet or more fall away into Kentucky. The stunning views from Buzzard Rock, Eagle's Nest, and Birch Knob combined with the rugged terrain make this one of Virginia's most dramatic and scenic trails. The length of the trail and its remoteness make it one of the most challenging as well.

Start: From the parking lot at Heart of Appalachia visitors kiosk at U.S. Highway 23 and Virginia Route 667.
Distance: 30.8-mile point-to-point.
Approximate hiking time: 2–3 days.
Difficulty rating: Strenuous due to length and rugged terrain.
Trail surface: Dirt footpaths and dirt roads lead to upland bogs, high escarpments, upland forest, and spectacular vistas off exposed rock faces.
Land status: National forest.
Nearest city: Pound, VA.
Other trail users: Mountain bikers, equestrians, and hunters (in season).

Canine compatibility: Dogs permitted.
Trail contacts: Clinch Ranger District, Wise, VA, (276) 328-2931.
Pine Mountain Trail Conference, P.O. Box 784, Whitesburg, KY, 41858, (606) 633-2362, www.pinemountaintrail.com.
Schedule: Open year-round. Hunting is allowed on national forest property. Deer-hunting season in Wise and Dickenson Counties runs October through January. The national forest limits hiking groups to ten people.
Fees/permits: No fees or permits required.
Maps: USGS maps: Jenkins West, VA; Jenkins East, VA; Clintwood, VA; Hellier, VA; Elkhorn City, VA.

Finding the trailhead: Start Point
From Pound: Drive north on US 23 for 4 miles. Just before passing through Pound Gap into Kentucky, look for a parking lot and Heart of Appalachia information kiosk on the left at VA 667. *DeLorme: Virginia Atlas & Gazetteer:* Page 36, C2.
Shuttle Point
From Pound: Drive north on US 23 for 11.8 miles to a junction with Kentucky Route 197 in Shelby Gap, Kentucky. Bear right onto KY 197 and drive 16.5 miles to Elkhorn City and Kentucky Route 80. Turn right onto KY 80 and in 0.4 mile, turn right into a gravel parking area for the Elkhorn City Police Station. *DeLorme: Virginia Atlas & Gazetteer:* Page 37, B5.

The Hike

A short hike past Pine Mountain Trail's south trailhead lies some of the best this hike has to offer. Ravens Nest, with its smooth rock surface and soaring views east and

A long way to go. . . . The view from an escarpment on Pine Mountain north of Pound Gap Trailhead.

west—to Virginia and Kentucky—is the first in a succession of high overlooks that culminate at Birch Knob (3,449 feet), 14.4 miles into the hike. The 30 miles between Pound Gap and Breaks Interstate Park feature long views east and west off open rock faces, followed by long, torturous stretches through woodland. At trail's end, the feeling isn't so much that you completed Pine Mountain, but you survived.

The difficulty only heightens the rewards. Long the domain of horseback riders and ATVs (ATVs are now prohibited), Pine Mountain Trail enjoys a wider fame today thanks to enthusiastic hikers in Virginia and Kentucky. A group is working to make this trail the northern leg of a 120-mile-long trail through the Cumberland Mountains. Volunteers have rebuilt and reblazed sections of trail. When finished, the entire Pine Mountain Trail will run from Breaks Interstate Park to Cumberland Gap Historical Park. It should rank with other long trails, like the Bartram in North Carolina, Allegheny in West Virginia, and Tuscarora in Virginia, in offering some of the best long-distance trekking in the East.

Pine Mountain's story is the story of people who moved to southwest Virginia seeking isolation—from people, politics, and/or culture. Most settlers worked hard in the logging and mining industry. They were fiercely independent, to the point of suspecting any kind of authority. Some turned outlaw, others ran moonshine. Doc Taylor, aka "Red Fox," a notorious local outlaw, hid amid the caves and hollows of Pine Mountain. He was later hanged in Big Stone Gap for murder. In the gaps of Pine Mountain, settlers eked out a living—barely. Their cows grazed on rocky slopes. Cornfields cheapened already thin soil. Crop rotation simply meant clearing a few more acres and planting anew. Wherever they set roots, settlers guarded their holdings closely, often to protect their stills. Moonshine was the real cash crop of the region.

Knowing a bit of this history made meeting Henry Mullins special. Dusk had settled on our second day of hiking when Mullins stepped from the shadow of Birch Knob and introduced himself. He and his girlfriend, Penny, had driven up to Birch Knob to catch the sunset. (Newly improved Forest Road 616 permits vehicle access to Pine Mountain's ridgetop from the Virginia side.) Together, the four of us climbed Birch Knob's final rocky upthrust (there are two approaches, one using a rope ladder, the other a scramble between huge boulders). Sitting atop the second-highest bump in the long Pine Mountain ridge, Henry pulled out a beverage and lit a cigarette. I figured this was as good a time as any to ask if he knew the Henry Mullins killed on Pine Mountain.

The Henry Mullins I had read about lived at Dutton Bottom Farm, one gap northwest of Birch Knob. Today a rusted metal bed frame marks the spot. As the story goes, deputized Virginians came upon Mullins's cabin while hunting for stills in the mountains. They had, earlier that day, found a still and partook in some of the spoils. Drunk and ornery, they found a bottle of moonshine on Mullins's front porch—which was located on the Virginia side of the Virginia-Kentucky border—and confronted him. Mullins protested his innocence. A scuffle broke out and a deputy shot and killed Mullins. Local authorities decided jurisdiction lay with Kentucky, and the deputies were tried and convicted, although they served minimal time.

Atop Birch Knob, the setting sun slipped behind the Kentucky mountains. The modern-day Henry Mullins confessed never having heard the story. His name, it turns out, is a pretty common name in the area. We climbed down off the peak and parted ways in the dark, Mary and I to our tent, Henry and Penny to civilization in a Ford Bronco.

Pine Mountain's past rests easy with the outlaws and homesteaders. Its future is in good hands, too. If the 120-mile Pine Mountain Trail can match the splendor of this inaugural leg, every backpacker, nature lover, and rock hound should count himself lucky. Distance alone makes this one of the most physically demanding hikes in Virginia. Scenery varies from upland bogs in the vicinity of The Doubles to wind-shaped rock formations between Blowing Rock Gap and Skegg Knob. Long stretches of trail pass through forestland, emerge for a length on sun-baked rock faces, then re-enter the woods.

At its core, Pine Mountain is a geologic phenomenon called the Cumberland Overthrust Block. The mountain range formed when a piece of the earth's crust buckled and broke. The southeast chunk of rock (the Virginia piece) moved between 6 and 11 miles west and slid up and over the northwest rock (the Kentucky piece) at an angle of 30 to 40 degrees. The highest bits of rock on Pine Mountain are sandstone normally found 2,000 feet underground. And here's a kicker: It's thought that the Pine Mountain we see today is half its original size.

Miles and Directions

0.0   START from parking lot at VA 667 and US 23. Walk north on US 23 for about 100 yards and turn right onto Apostolic Drive (you should begin seeing yellow blazes). Walk 0.3 mile

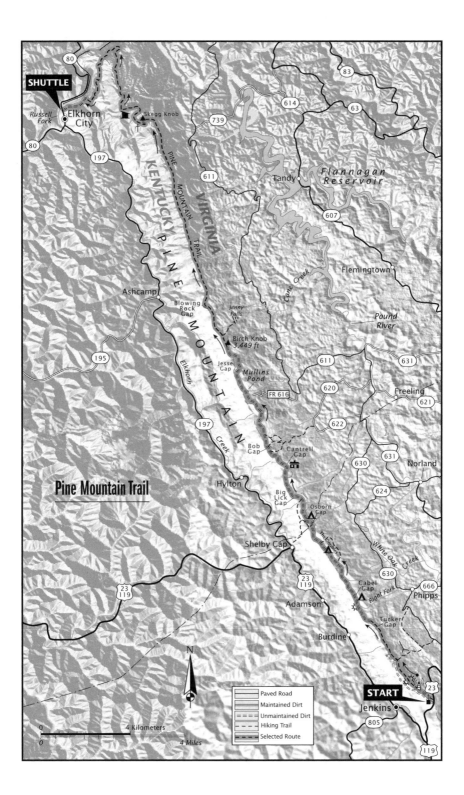

Pine Mountain Trail

SHUTTLE

START

Russell Fork

Elkhorn City

Skegg Knob

80

197

80

739

614

83

63

611

Tandy

Flannagan Reservoir

607

KENTUCKY

VIRGINIA

PINE MOUNTAIN TRAIL

Flemingtown

Ashcamp

Blowing Rock Gap

Jenny Falls

Birch Knob 3,449 ft

Pound River

Cane Creek

195

PINE MOUNTAIN

Jesse Gap

Mullins Pond

611

631

Elkhorn Creek

FR 616

620

Freeling

621

622

197

Bob Gap

Cantrell Gap

630

631

Norland

Hylton

Big Lick Gap

624

Osborn Gap

Shelby Gap

630

Cabel Gap

Right Fork

White Oak Creek

666

Phipps

23 119

23 119

Adamson

Tucker Gap

Burdine

N

START

805

119

Jenkins

23

Paved Road
Maintained Dirt
Unmaintained Dirt
Hiking Trail
Selected Route

0   4 Kilometers

0   4 Miles

uphill to a church parking lot on the left. Walk 0.6 mile uphill on a four-wheel-drive road to a set of radio towers.

2.1 Cross an exposed rock face. Ravens Nest is a short scramble up to the lip of the ridge. (FYI: A type of erosion called spherodial weathering created these formations, which are said to resemble a raven in flight. Views from this point include High Knob to the southeast and strip mines.)

2.5 Step off the left side of the trail on an unmarked, but well-worn dirt trail. (FYI: This overlook permits a long view of Pine Mountain's undulating course—and a glimpse of what the next 20-plus miles hold in store.)

2.7 Come to a four-way intersection in Austin Gap. The left spur leads onto private property and a locked forest road gate. To the right, a blue-blazed trail leads to Indian caves. Continue straight on Pine Mountain Trail.

3.7 Drop off the ridgeline into Tucker Gap. Turn left onto a dirt road and hike downhill.

3.9 Reach a T junction with several forest roads and turn right. (Note: Avoid any areas blazed red, which indicates private property.) (FYI: The next 5 miles, Pine Mountain Trail follows dirt forest roads)

5.0 A view opens on the left side of the road overlooking a quarry. (FYI: This is called Cooling Place for the breeze that blows through the gap.)

6.2 The trail turns right and traverses The Doubles. (FYI: In the depression between these small knobs lay upland bogs.)

7.7 Descend on a dirt forest road into Osborn Gap and a confusing web of dirt forest roads. Continue straight through the first intersection, and then past a second dirt road that enters from the right. The third junction is a fork in the road. Turn right and climb uphill on the dirt road. In 0.1 mile, switchback and follow the road around a small knob.

8.3 (FYI: A root cellar and old home foundation are visible off the left side of the trail as you hike between Big Lick and Cantrell Gaps.)

9.6 A wood log cabin with a sheet-metal roof marks Cantrell Gap. After the shed, the trail turns left and dips. A spring comes out from under a tree on your right.

11.9 Descend on a wide footpath to FR 616. Turn left and follow the road downhill. It passes Mullins Pond on the right. From the pond, follow FR 616 as it begins a long uphill climb.

13.7 (FYI: Pass by stone monument and plaque marking a 1965 airplane crash into the side of Pine Mountain that killed three men.)

14.4 Reach Birch Knob. Turn left off FR 616 and enter the woods on a footpath. **Sidetrip:** From the point where Pine Mountain Trail enters the woods, hike up FR 616 to a small vehicle

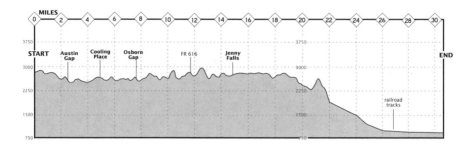

pull-off. Follow the road right and downhill a few feet. Look for a rope ladder to ascend the rock face to reach the rock summit of Birch Knob. For a lengthier, but easier, approach to the peak, turn left on a marked trail that leads left from the vehicle pull-off area. Enter the woods, descend to the base of a cliff, and follow the cliff wall. In 200 yards, turn right and climb up a long notch in the rocks. When you reach the top, turn right. There's a new viewing platform at the top.

14.7   **Sidetrip:** The side trail branches right and leads downhill to Jenny Falls, a small trickle of water that falls 100 feet or more off a horseshoe-shaped rock cliff. (Note: The descent to Jenny Falls is long and steep in some sections. Give yourself an hour or more to make this sidetrip.)

20.2   Pass Flag Rock with views west into Kentucky. (Note: The trail here crosses private property on a right-of-way. A flag is embedded in marble rock inscribed with the landowner's name.)

22.2   After walking along a cliff with views left into a quarry, the trail turns sharply left and drops to descend along the base of the cliff. At the bottom, follow a dirt road around a pond. At the second intersecting road, turn left. Climb the dirt road away from the pond.

22.7   Turn right and leave the dirt road, following yellow blazes. The trail enters the woods as a footpath.

23.4   Pass a fenced-in cemetery on the left.

25.0   Pass a spur trail on the left that leads 100 yards to Indian Council rock shelter. (FYI: The shelter is a rock overhang at the head of a small canyon.)

29.3   Turn right and follow Big Island Branch downhill. There are new gas well installations on the left side of the trail. In 0.2 mile, turn left and follow a dirt road alongside Russell Fork.

30.8   The hike ends at the Elkhorn City Police Station.

Hike Information

Local Information
Heart of Appalachia, Big Stone Gap, VA, (888) 798-2386, www.heartofappalachia.com.

Local Events/Attractions
Ralph Stanley Bluegrass Festival, May, Coeburn, VA, (276) 395-6318.
Virginia Highlands Festival, August, Abingdon, VA, (800) 435-3440. Southwest Virginia's premier event.
Carter Fold Music Gathering and A. P. Carter Museum, Saturday nights year-round, Hiltons, VA, (276) 386-9480.

Lodging
Breaks Interstate Park, (276) 865-4413, www.breakspark.com.
Gateway to the Breaks Motel, Breaks, VA, (276) 531-8481.

Restaurants
Rhododendron Restaurant, Breaks Interstate Park, VA, (276) 865-4413.

30 Chief Benge Scout Trail

Mountain Fork and Little Stony Creek thread the mountains of Wise and Scott Counties in wild and unpredictable fashion. Sticking with them faithfully is the 15-mile Chief Benge Scout Trail, a trek that links the cool waters of High Knob Lake with 30-foot falls, rapids, and small pools on the Little Stony. The trail follows old railroad grades at river level but makes several steep climbs up the ridges that make southwest Virginia such a rugged, wonderful place to hike. There is real variety of plants along this trail, from big-leaf magnolia to the huckleberries on the dry ridges. Bring a fishing pole and test stream waters or the wide Bark Camp Lake. With reliable water sources and only a few steep climbs, this hike is a highlight of any southwest trip.

Start: From the parking lot for High Knob Lake in High Knob National Recreation Area (NRA).
Distance: 15.3-mile point-to-point.
Approximate hiking time: 8 hours.
Difficulty rating: Moderate due to the length and a number of unaided stream crossings.
Trail surface: A combination of dirt footpaths, grassy forest roads, and gravel forest roads lead along streamsides and fern glades, through hardwood forests to two lakes and a craggy river gorge with three tall waterfalls.
Land status: National forest.
Nearest town: Norton, VA.
Other trail users: Hikers only.
Canine compatibility: Dogs permitted.

Trail contacts: Clinch Ranger District, Wise, VA, (276) 328-2931.
Schedule: Open year-round. Hunting is permitted on national forestland. Deer-hunting season in Wise and Scott Counties runs October through January. The national forest limits hiking groups to ten people.
Fees/permits: High Knob Recreation Area: $3.00 day-use per vehicle, $10.00 per site. Bark Camp Lake Recreation Area: $3.00 day-use per vehicle; $12.00 for tent site.
Maps: USGS maps: Wise, VA; Fort Blackmore, VA; Coeburn, VA; Dungannon, VA; Norton, VA; East Stone Gap, VA.

Finding the trailhead: Start Point
From Norton: Take Virginia Route 619 south for 4.5 miles. Turn left onto Forest Road 238. In 0.6 mile, turn right and enter High Knob NRA. Drive 0.4 mile and turn right, following signs for High Knob Lake. Continue another mile, to where the road dead-ends at a parking area for the lake. *DeLorme: Virginia Atlas & Gazetteer:* Page 20, A3.

Shuttle Point
From Norton: Drive 9 miles east on U.S. Highway 58 to a junction with Virginia Route 72. Turn right onto VA 72. In 0.4 mile, bear right at the fork, continuing south on VA 72. The entrance to Hanging Rock Picnic Area is another 8.6 miles south. Turn right into the picnic area and drive 0.2 mile to a parking area for Little Stony National Recreation Trail. *DeLorme: Virginia Atlas & Gazetteer:* Page 20, A3.

The falls at Little Stony.

The Hike

Mountain Fork creek swallows the sunlight with each step along the Chief Benge Scout Trail, as hills on either side steepen and the valley narrows. Thick patches of laurel, small trees, and an earthy smell fill the valley. Downed trees force water into narrow channels that spill over small rock ledges. Rushing water is always audible, even when the stream itself is obscured by vine and shrub entanglements. Soon trail and stream meet, cross, meet again, and cross again—before the wide, flat trail narrows and climbs the left hillside.

At this point, where mountain laurel gives way to oak and maple, we part ways with Mountain Fork—and the spirit who's been stalking silently behind since High Knob Lake. The ghost of Chief Bob Benge won't be following us up Bark Camp Branch; instead, he'll steer right along Big Stony Creek. Painted in warrior colors and traveling by night, he'll head south to the Livingston Farm on the North Fork Holston. He'll return this way, with prisoners and booty, evading militia by traveling obscure mountain passes. Eleven miles north of here, in a gap overlooking the city of Norton, he'll die as he did in 1794, of a bullet to the head.

Chief Benge entered southwest Virginia in April 1777 leading a band of Cherokee and Shawnee, marking the start of an eighteen-year reign of terror. A man who had, in his youth, lived with his Native American mother and English stepfather at Dorton's Fort on the Copper River, would kill between forty to fifty settlers as retribution for their encroachment on Native American land. Hunting parties fell prey to his ambushes. Farmers looked up from work to find him standing over them. Women peered from their homes, saw nothing…looked again…and saw Benge. Like a ghost, he materialized, murdered, plundered, and moved on.

What caused a man with an English father, trader John Benge, and Cherokee mother, Elizabeth Watts Dorton, to strike out so?

Benge came of age in the 1770s, a tense time in the colonies. City folk on the Eastern seaboard were ruffled by such concepts as taxation without representation. In southwest Virginia, a more tangible threat occupied settlers. Local Native American tribes were lashing out against settlers' land gains down the Clinch, Powell, and Holston Valleys. When the American Revolution broke out in 1776, British-instigated Cherokee and Shawnee war parties returned to southwest Virginia for revenge. Virginia's Holston Militia retaliated by burning Cherokee towns in Tennessee. Bob Benge, who had run away from Dorton's Fort as a teenager to live out his days as a Cherokee, lost his home twice in these raids. Neighbors from his childhood years helped pillage his village.

With his red head and fair complexion, Benge could pass as a settler. He spoke flawless English and knew the mountains of the Clinch, Holston, and Powell Valleys like few others. His discovery of a pass between Stone and Powell Mountains enabled him to move in and out of the region undetected.

The morning of April 6, 1794, found Benge at the home of Elizabeth Livingston near Mendota on the North Fork Holston River. Elizabeth Livingston's daughter described the scene:

One bright morning…after the sun had risen and the men had gone to the clearings and the women were busy at their wheels and looms, all joyous and jovial amid the fragrance of wild flowers and the music of songbirds, and not dreaming of coming danger, Benge and his painted warriors stealthily approached and surrounded the cabins.

In short order, Benge's band killed a woman and three children, burned the house, and carried off eight prisoners.

Runners carried the alarm northeast to Castlewood (then Castle's Wood) and northwest to Yoakum's Station near present-day Dryden. Militias moved to predetermined mountain passes Benge might use. A small group started out after Benge and tracked him down the North Fork Holston River to Hilton, across Clinch Mountain at Hamilton Gap, and north to the Clinch River. Yet as hours slipped past, the Cherokee's trail grew faint.

At the Clinch River just south of present-day Dungannon, Benge's raiding party made a fateful misstep—literally. Author Lawrence Fleenor recounts in his book *Benge!* how a wet moccasin print on a dry stone tipped pursuers to his route. Benge moved downstream to the confluence of Big Stony Creek near Fort Blackmore, turned upstream, and followed Big Stony up Powell Mountain, his pursuers closing ground.

In late afternoon, the sun slips behind Powell Mountain, shrouding one entire side of the Mountain Fork stream valley in dusk. The opposite bank remains bathed in warm light, although the hiker still feels vulnerable to ever-encroaching shadows. At this point, Chief Benge Scout Trail climbs up the left hill, first gradually, then at a steeper grade. Mountain Fork is 200 feet below you. Sunlight baths a large fern glade on the valley floor. It's tempting to imagine Benge walking here on April 7, 1794. He would have kept one prisoner, Susannah Livingston, out in front. The remaining prisoners would be behind him. In single file, the party would pass out of the light into the shadows of the stream valley, picking their way upstream to High Knob and spending the night at Camp Rock.

Benge did spend his last night alive at Camp Rock, but best evidence shows he followed a more direct route up Powell Mountain, one roughly approximated by VA 619. He was headed for a gap in the mountains overlooking a town called Prince's Flats (present-day Norton). At this pass, now called Benge's Gap, the party turned west and entered Hoot Owl Hollow.

Benge's pursuers set an ambush in Little Stony Gap, a deep mountain pass flanked by steep ridges and a valley floor covered with large rocks. Militia men watched as Benge hustled his prisoners up the trail. One man took aim, but noise in lifting his rifle alerted Benge to danger. The Cherokee ran and, as he fled, stepped in a hole. The bullet intended to hit him square in the back lodged in his head.

Benge's death is a watershed event in southwest Virginia; raids on settlers ceased with his passing. The Cherokee, already pushed far beyond their homelands, never threatened the region again in any material way.

The Chief Benge's Scout Trail touches only briefly on its namesake. Still, the warrior lingers with you on a 15-mile trek to the falls at Little Stony. The trail is a fitting tribute to a Native American whose hidden paths along dark mountain stream valleys enabled him to make a statement, however destructive, against the expansion of white settlers into Cherokee land.

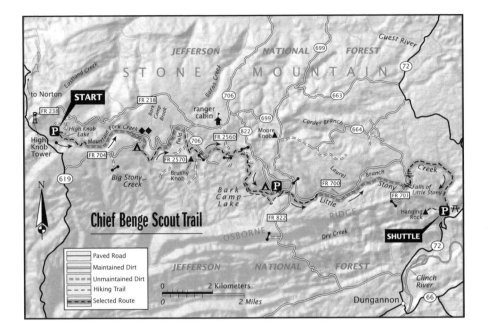

Chief Benge Scout Trail

Paved Road
Maintained Dirt
Unmaintained Dirt
Hiking Trail
Selected Route

0   2 Kilometers
0   2 Miles

Miles and Directions

0.0 **START** at the High Knob Lake parking area. Walk two-tenths of a mile downhill, turn left in front of a shower house, and cross a small bridge spanning Mountain Fork Creek (on USGS topo quadrant Wise, this stream is labeled Stony Creek. It has been renamed). (FYI: There is a water spigot near the shower house. Stock up on water here. The trail follows streams almost its entire route, but this is the only treated water source for 9.5 miles.)

0.5 Cross a concrete dam at the top of High Knob Lake and turn right on Chief Benge Trail, a wide, flat dirt trail along the left bank of Mountain Fork Creek. Through this ever-deepening stream valley, you'll hop the rough-and-tumble creek five times in the next 2 miles.

1.9 Pass a nice campground amid hemlocks on the right side of the trail.

2.4 Cross Forest Road 704 and drop down the opposite bank. (FYI: The trail keeps its wide, flat course while Mountain Fork Creek runs through some wild stretches, obscured by rhododendron, other times nearly dammed by tree debris.)

3.5 Climb out of the stream valley up the left slope and wrap around a small hill. (FYI: Mountain Fork takes a much longer route around the base of this hill.) The climb, at first gradual, steepens considerably as a drainage forms downslope on the right.

4.2 Cross Bark Camp Branch and climb out of this stream gully to a large field within a half mile.

4.6 Pass by a natural gas well and enter a young hardwood forest. The trail, ascending on a gentle slope, is wide, grassy, and dry.

5.2 Turn left onto a gravel road (Forest Road 2570). Within 20 paces, turn right and hike along a wide grassy road.

5.8 The trail reverts to a singletrack woods path as it descends off a small hill, crossing by the headwaters of Little Stony Creek.

6.1 Cross Virginia Route 706 and descend on another grassy woods road. Between here and Little Stony Creek, two trails branch right off this road. Stay left each time.

6.9 Cross Little Stony Creek and hike along the left stream bank. After a short distance, the trail climbs the hill on your left to meet a forest road.

7.3 Cross a gravel road (Forest Road 2560) and re-enter woods directly opposite on a narrow woods path. (FYI: Ferns line the trail and there are several large specimens of bigleaf magnolias.) From here, the trail drops back to Little Stony Creek and you'll follow the right stream bank for a short distance, then hop it to follow the left streamside.

8.4 Reach the Lakeshore Loop Trail encircling Bark Camp Lake. Signs show the Chief Benge Trail turns right and traces the backside of the lake. Turn left for a nice respite at Bark Camp Lake Recreation Area.

9.5 After wrapping in and out of the lake's marshy fingers, enter the picnic area. (FYI: There are bathrooms, a water spigot, and picnic tables.) Reconnect with the Chief Benge Trail by following the Lakeshore Loop Trail to a dam on the lower end of Bark Camp Lake. Cross the concrete portion of the dam, then immediately turn left and follow the right stream bank of Little Stony Creek. This is a difficult stretch of trail, obscured by tall shrubs and poorly marked. Cues for the turnoff include several rusted metal posts and a rotted stump slashed with double yellow blazes found on the earthen embankment just after the concrete portion of the dam.

9.7 Reach Forest Road 822, a gravel road. Turn right and walk along the road for less than one-tenth of a mile. A sign on the left side reads FALLS OF LITTLE STONY, 4.9 MILES. Turn left and drop back into woods. The river is on your left side. Seven stream crossings follow in quick succession.

10.4 (FYI: After the ninth stream crossing, look for a nice campsite on the right side of the trail.) Ahead, the trail skips across Little Stony eight more times.

12.2 Look right immediately after crossing Little Stony Creek. (FYI: There is a campsite under hemlocks on a small bluff at a bend in the river. Large stream boulders are ideal for lounging.)

12.5 Reach Forest Road 701. Follow the gravel road right, enter a vehicle turnaround, and look for the trailhead for Little Stony National Recreation Trail at a signboard at the back of the parking lot.

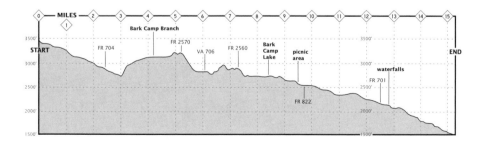

12.7 Cross over the top of a spectacular 25-foot waterfall. Two other falls (10 feet and 30 feet) follow in quick succession. After this, the trail drops to stream level and passes through hemlock and cove forests.

15.3 Reach Hanging Rock Picnic Area and the southern terminus of the Chief Benge and Little Stony Trails.

Hike Information

Local Information

Wise County Chamber of Commerce, Norton, VA, (276) 679–0961, www.wisecountychamber.org.

Heart of Appalachia, Big Stone Gap, VA, (888) 798–2386, www.heartofappalachia.com.

Local Events/Attractions

Mountain Treasures Festival, July, Dungannon, VA, (276) 467–2306.

Carter Family Fold, Hiltons, VA, (276) 386–9480.

Country Cabin, Norton, VA, (276) 679–3541. Live bluegrass by local performers.

Mountain People's Music Fair, June, Wise, VA, (276) 679–4858.

Lodging

Natural Tunnel State Park, Duffield, VA, (276) 940–2674. $14 for tent site.

Days Inn, Norton, VA, (276) 679–5340.

Restaurants

Shannon's Restaurant, Norton, VA, (276) 679–5617. Hamburgers, seafood, and all kinds of American food.

Fish Tales, Norton, VA, (276) 679–1651. Seafood and barbecue.

Other Resources

Benge!, by Lawrence J. Fleenor. Biography of Chief Benge. Call (276) 523-1600 for ordering information.

31 Devils Fork Loop

Devils Fork is a luxuriant streamscape of rocks, cliffs, and small cascades that grow in size and frequency as you hike. It all comes together at the Devils Bathtub, where a long waterfall trips step by step over shale bedrock and crashes in a swirl of currents into a bowl-like pool—the bathtub. Framed by tall hemlocks and rhododendron, this scenery is as lush and abundant as the landscape a few hundred feet upslope is simple and unadorned.

Start: From the forest gate at the end of Forest Road 2631.
Distance: 7.3-mile loop.
Approximate hiking time: 4 hours.
Difficulty rating: Moderate due to the unaided stream crossings and one steep climb.
Trail surface: Dirt footpaths and dirt roads through hardwood forest slopes and hemlock groves along streams.
Land status: National forest.
Nearest town: Norton, VA.
Other trail users: Hikers only.

Canine compatibility: Dogs permitted.
Trail contacts: Clinch Ranger District, Wise, VA, (276) 328-2931.
Schedule: Open year-round. Hunting is allowed on national forestland. Deer hunting season in Scott County runs October through January. The national forest limits hiking groups to ten people.
Fees/permits: (See Hike 30: Chief Benge Scout Trail.)
Maps: USGS maps: East Stone Gap, VA; Fort Blackmore, VA.

Finding the trailhead: From Dungannon: Drive 0.3 mile north on Virginia Route 72. Turn left onto Virginia Route 653. It is 8.9 miles west to Virginia Route 619. Turn right onto VA 619, and in 1.1 miles, bear left as VA 619 forks. In 0.4 mile, bear left onto FR 2631. Continue straight on the fire road past two pull-offs. Just before a forest gate, pull off left into a turnaround and parking area. *DeLorme: Virginia Atlas & Gazetteer:* Page 20, B3.

The Hike

The trip up Devils Run hollow is 3 miles of tricky hiking. At each stream crossing, shrubs and ferns hide where the trail might climb the opposite bank. The deeper into the hollow, the more damp and shaded the scenery. The rocky, uneven trail creeps up in elevation until stream banks become small cliffs, and the river froths 20 feet below your feet.

This ruggedness makes it hard to fathom how a railroad once ran along this stream. It's been seventy years or more since private landowners carted oak, beech, chestnut, and poplar trees off the mountain slopes around Devils Fork. These were old-growth trees, described by one nineteenth-century traveler as "walls and buttresses, square structures like the titanic ruins of castles." As had been the case

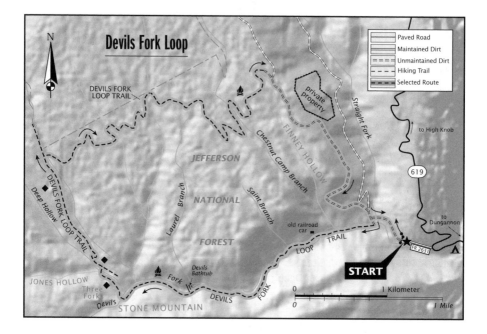

Devils Fork Loop

Legend:
- Paved Road
- Maintained Dirt
- Unmaintained Dirt
- Hiking Trail
- Selected Route

DEVILS FORK LOOP TRAIL

JEFFERSON

NATIONAL

FOREST

Laurel Branch

Saint Branch

Chestnut Camp Branch

FINNEY HOLLOW

Straight Fork

Private property

old railroad car

LOOP TRAIL

START

to High Knob

619

to Dungannon

FR 2631

DEVILS FORK LOOP TRAIL

Deep Hollow

JONES HOLLOW

Three Forks

Devils Fork

Devils Bathtub

DEVILS FORK

STONE MOUNTAIN

0   1 Kilometer

0   1 Mile

throughout much of southwest Virginia, companies from New York and Philadelphia owned the timber. A sawmill could produce 12,000 board feet from just three of these trees. (A small home uses about 6,000 board feet of timber—which means three of these trees could supply the lumber needed for two homes.) At the other end of the scale, Singer Manufacturing Company bought and removed all black walnut of a certain size in neighboring Wise County for their sewing machine cabinets and base plates.

Halfway between Straight Branch and Devils Bathtub, a rusted coal car lies half-buried in trailside brambles. Uphill from this, speculators dug a mining prospect in search of coal. These were "punch mines," small dents dug out of hills in hopes of finding a vein. Coal's era has passed, while natural gas production is rising. The return leg of Devils Fork Loop crosses a dirt road high on Stone Mountain. Embedded in the dirt road path are signs of modern prospecting. Exploratory drilling for natural gas produces long pieces of smooth, round stones—as large as a silver dollar and broken into 2- or 3-inch pieces.

When coal miners worked this area, they did so exclusively on the north bank of Devils Fork. The stream follows a geologic fault between sandstone on the north stream bank, which holds coal deposits, and limestone on the south bank. On its north stream bank, acid soil supports the hemlock and rhododendron that lend the hollow its lush setting. There are few, if any, of these type plants on the south stream bank, where the soil is less hospitable.

The hemlocks along Devils Fork are second- and third-growth. Rhododendron, which seems to grow hand in hand with hemlock, fills the gaps in the forest floor. A spring hike here, while certain to net you wet feet, also leaves a lasting impression of both these evergreens. As you climb, the hemlock and rhododendron decrease in number until, on well-drained mountain slopes, white oak and hickory trees form the forest canopy. Off the slope run five streams and numerous seasonal runoffs, all of which feed Devils Fork. A century ago, when chestnut trees grew tall and wide, loggers would range throughout this forest, cutting rings around the trunk at certain intervals. Using tools called spuds, they ripped bark from the tree in sheets, piled it high onto wagons, and hauled it to tanneries. Before railroads and on-site sawmills, the trees were too difficult to remove. More often than not, they were left to rot.

At times, the route across Stone Mountain's slope pitches sharply downhill and right. This pitch is what, in part, led Appalachian Power in the mid-1970s to propose flooding Devils Fork and creating a reservoir out of the stream valley. Using a pipeline, the company could have generated electricity by directing the flow of water between the proposed reservoir and Big Cherry Reservoir on Long Mountain. Opposition from local residents was swift, and Appalachian Power abandoned the plan. The idea of protecting Devils Fork persisted, however. When the national forest proposed a road up the side of Little Mountain, a local trail club rose to the cause. Roadwork progressed to the point where a survey crew cut a first pass through the forest, but then the project was dropped. Sensing an opportunity, the trail club made use of the crew's work. Today, the road that would have opened the Devils Fork watershed up for timber harvest and natural gas production is one section of this loop.

Miles and Directions

0.0 **START** at a forest gate at the end of FR 2631. Walk around the gate and climb a small knoll on a wide forest road. It drops to Straight Fork in 0.3 mile.

0.3 Cross Straight Fork. Turn left and follow the Devils Fork Loop Trail, a well-worn, grassy trail. (FYI: A yellow-blazed dirt road arcs right and uphill from this clearing. It is the return leg of the loop.)

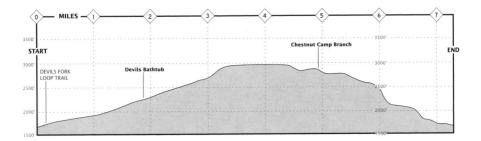

0.4 Cross Devils Fork and follow the trail that arcs right and follows the stream's left shoulder. (Avoid the road that continues alongside Straight Fork.) There are ten stream crossings in the next 2 miles.

1.7 (FYI: A V-shaped cut in the shale streambed funnels a small waterfall into a pool below. As it falls, water ripples over 50- or 60-inch-high or smaller shelves. This is the beginning of the Devils Bathtub formations.)

2.3 The trail takes a sharp right turn and heads northwest out of the Devils Fork gorge. Deep Hollow forms below on the right. This steep, narrow section drops into Deep Hollow and crosses the stream after a short distance.

2.8 Switchback over a shoulder ridge separating Deep and Corder Hollows. The footpath will climb, then drop off this ridge into Corder Hollow.

3.6 Cross a streambed (dry in late summer) and begin a traverse of Little Mountain's undulating slope. A number of streams run down this hill to Devils Fork.

4.8 Cross over an unmarked forest road leading downhill to the right. (FYI: If you have time, examine this roadbed closely. There are narrow, cylinder-shaped stones compacted into the dirt, possibly remnants of core samples taken during exploratory drilling.) Also in this clearing, uphill on the left, is a small, primitive campsite.

5.3 The trail widens into a grassy doubletrack path.

5.5 Turn right (downhill) onto the Devils Fork Loop Trail.

5.8 Bear right on Straight Fork as the trail merges with another grassy road. Uphill is private property.

7.0 Enter a clearing alongside Straight Fork. Cross the stream and hike up a small knoll.

7.3 The hike ends at the forest gate.

Hike Information

Local Information
Heart of Appalachia, Big Stone Gap, VA, (888) 798-2386, www.heartofappalachia.com.

Local Events/Attractions
Homeplace Mountain Farm & Mansion, Weber City, VA, (276) 386–6300, www.scarlet.org/homeplace. Captures the spirit of a mountain farmstead with interpreters churning butter, making apple cider, crafts, and, of course, enjoying old-time music. Open April through December.

Lodging
(See Hike 30: Chief Benge Scout Trail.)

Organizations
Devils Fork Trail Club, Dungannon, VA, (276) 479-2176.

32 Stone Mountain Trail

The 14.2-mile Stone Mountain Trail begins with the long climb from Cave Springs. The tall cliffs and boulders that crop out from the mountain slope make for a dramatic introduction to the ridge, and soon give way to whopping views off Stone Mountain's ridgetop. From the last of these overlooks, High Butte, it's possible to see the bumpy profile of Kentucky's Black Mountains to the west, while eastward run Virginia's narrow ridges and valleys. The final leg of the Stone Mountain Trail down Roaring Run is tailor-made for people who save the best for last. The stream cascades through small gorges beneath hemlock and rhododendron.

Start: From the Cave Springs Recreation Area.
Distance: 14.2-mile point-to-point.
Approximate hiking time: 7 hours.
Difficulty rating: Moderate to difficult with steep climbs up Stone Mountain.
Trail surface: Dirt footpaths and dirt forest roads lead to exposed cliff lines, stream gorges, old-growth hemlocks, and expansive views.
Land status: National forest.
Nearest town: Big Stone Gap, VA.
Other trail users: Hunters (in season).

Canine compatibility: Dogs permitted.
Trail contacts: Clinch Ranger District, Wise, VA, (276) 328-2931.
Schedule: Open year-round. Hunting is permitted on national forestland. Deer-hunting season in Wise and Lee Counties runs October through January. The national forest limits hiking groups to ten people.
Fees/permits: No fees or permits required. Cave Springs Campground: $12 per night.
Maps: USGS maps: Keokee, VA; Big Stone Gap, VA; Appalachia, VA.

Finding the trailhead: Start Point
From Big Stone Gap: Turn left onto Alternate U.S. Highway 58 and drive 3.9 miles west to Virginia Route 621. Turn right onto VA 621 and drive 6.8 miles to Cave Springs Recreation Area on the right. Turn right into the recreation area and follow signs for picnic parking in 0.4 mile. *DeLorme: Virginia Atlas & Gazetteer:* Page 19, B7.

Shuttle Point
From Big Stone Gap: Head north on U.S. Highway 23, 1.4 miles from its intersection with US 58. Reach a trailhead on the left side of the highway, with room for three cars to park. (If there's no room, head back to Big Stone Gap. There's overflow parking downtown at a park-and-ride lot next to the Chrysler-Jeep dealership on US 23. The trailhead is 0.9 mile north on US 23. *DeLorme: Virginia Atlas & Gazetteer:* Page 20, A1.

The Hike

A view off High Butte spans the Powell Valley and reaches into folds and contours on Wallen Ridge. These shady nooks are the "dark hollows" made famous in stories such as John Fox Jr.'s *Trail of the Lonesome Pine.* Fox's heroine, a mountain girl named June Tolliver, left a closely guarded mountain home and close-knit family for schooling in Big Stone Gap. In the hills, her family grappled with changes

Hiking Stone Mountain Trail near Cave Springs.

brought by discovery of coal and the clash of mountain culture with the law and order of civil society.

Hiking Stone Mountain Trail, it's difficult to separate characters, real and imagined, from the natural wonders. The model for Fox's June Tolliver, a woman named Elizabeth Morris, hailed from Keokee. At Olinger Gap, the Olinger Gap Trail descends to Lake Keokee, a remote, man-made lake stocked with bass and muskie. Fox based other characters on colorful real-life personalities such as "Devil John" Wright, a desperado, and "Red Fox," a preacher, herb doctor, and moonshiner. Both were publicly hanged in 1893 for killing three members of the Mullins family in an ambush on Pine Mountain.

Recent history takes the form of carved stone steps alongside Roaring Branch. Local masons, out of work and destitute from the boom-bust cycle of the coal industry, carved the steps while working for the Civilian Conservation Corps (CCC). (In the 1960s, the Forest Service completed similar stonework at Cave Springs Recreation Area, where this hike begins.) The beauty of the moss-covered steps and shady hemlocks makes the Roaring Run stretch of Stone Mountain Trail a "rangers' choice" (national forest district rangers compete for maintenance duty on this section of the trail!).

Roaring Run gurgles and tumbles into the Powell River, which flows to nearby Big Stone Gap. The Gap was built by Eastern industrialists who made—and lost—fortunes on coal. Stone Mountain, centrally located in a region known for coal production, never yielded the deposits that made nearby Dickenson, Wise, and Buchanan Counties famous. Stone Mountain did, however, supply lumber by the railroad-car full. Chestnut and oak came off the dry ridgetops. From the slopes, lumbermen took oak, poplar, ash, and beech. Out of the coves came thick-trunked hemlocks. Today, every species has returned in quantity, if not size, among the present-day forests of Stone Mountain—except the chestnut tree, which suffered a debilitating blight in the early twentieth century.

The mountain itself originated from a cycle of oceanic, sedimentary, and mountain-building events, repeated several times. Walking the high, exposed cliff lines to High Butte, it defies rational thought to imagine that, hundreds of millions of years ago, this land appeared as shoals and beaches of the prehistoric Iapitus Ocean. Two and a half miles up the Stone Mountain Trail, an up close inspection of massive rock cliffs shows a pebbly conglomerate. The rocks are the size of loose change—dimes, nickels, and quarters—melded together in a stuccolike consistency. Streaks of colors indicate the layering that built this rock over millions of years. Here and there, red streaks mark hematite, an iron oxide.

This rock outcrop punctuates a steep climb out of Cave Springs. Along twenty-five switchbacks, the trail traces Stone Mountain's contours, running from moist drainages to dry, exposed slopes. As it climbs, the trail takes an increasingly narrow, precipitous route. Green spleenwort fern adds color to the orange and brown carpet of leaves in moist areas. In fall, acorns litter the trail. Large, isolated boulders appear

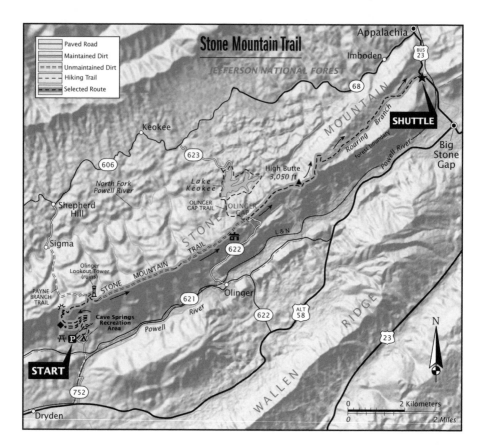

Stone Mountain Trail

amid the trees; these blocks of rock were split from formations higher upslope by a process of freezing and thawing that expanded cracks until large chunks fell away and tumbled downhill.

Departing from the old Olinger fire tower (only four concrete corner post bases remain, resting in the overgrowth off the left side of the trail), the wide, undulating road serves as nice relief from the first 4 miles of the hike—though you still have a steep climb in and out of Low Gap. Past Low Gap, the trail follows a cliff line with overlooks onto the Powell River Valley. The Powell River, along with the Clinch, runs a southwest course between Stone Mountain and Wallen Ridge. The river is home to the odd-looking species known as the paddlefish. Scaleless, with a large head and a body measuring up to 64 inches, the paddlefish is currently threatened nationwide, a result of overfishing by the caviar industry. In Virginia, the fish suffers from high levels of sediment in the Powell River, a problem that has placed a number of fish, mussels, snails, and mollusks that inhabit the river on the threatened and endangered list.

The Powell name extends beyond the river to one of the region's prominent landforms, Powell Mountain. In Virginia, a unique mountain culture thrived here and radiated into surrounding hills, including Stone Mountain. The Melungeon, a mixed-race group of mountain inhabitants, were once thought to be part Portuguese and part Cherokee. Today, tracing their race and ethnicity is a cottage industry. Melungeon gatherings celebrate the heritage of a people long discriminated against because of their dark complexion. Genetic and language analysis explore links between the Melungeons and Mediterranean, Middle Eastern, and Central Asian immigrants. These were not, however, your Ellis Island–variety newcomers. A theory currently in vogue traces their arrival to Sir Francis Drake, an English privateer who deposited several hundred Turkish and Moorish sailors onto Roanoke Island, on the coast of North Carolina, in 1586. When Drake returned to resupply, there were no signs of the sailors. Survivors, it's assumed, mixed with the Native American population. How their ancestors reached the hidden coves and folds of Appalachia makes for dandy daydreaming as you stare off the high outcrops of Stone Mountain.

Miles and Directions

0.0 **START** at the picnic parking area for Cave Springs Recreation Area. Walk to the back of the parking lot and climb five stone steps adjacent to a pond. Follow a narrow dirt trail next to a stream. For 0.3 mile, the trail passes over three small streams and past stone walls built by the Forest Service.

0.3 (FYI: Cave Springs's namesake, a cave and water source springing from beneath the side of a hill, is off the right side of the trail.)

0.5 Reach Cave Springs Overlook, a round, elevated earthen dais with, unfortunately, poor summertime views of Powell Valley. From here, the Stone Mountain Trail climbs via twenty-five switchbacks through a hardwood forest. (FYI: A trail departing the overlook downhill left returns to the picnic area parking lot.)

2.5 Pass by the first of several imposing rock outcrops and tall cliffs. (FYI: Red streaks in this rock indicate the presence of iron ore. Close inspection reveals the rock's composite of dime- and quarter-size pebbles melded together.)

2.9 Pass alongside the largest of the rock overhangs. (FYI: Sandy ground underfoot is a good place to look for animal tracks.)

3.3 The trail turns left, and the forest understory grows denser with rhododendron, sassafras, and mountain maple. The trail will achieve the top of Stone Mountain in 0.1 mile and bear right to follow the ridgeline in a north-northeast direction.

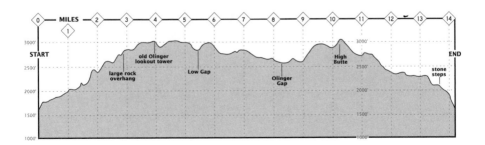

4.0 The trail arcs left around a small knob and, after 0.1 mile, pops over an earthen embankment onto a wide dirt forest road. Follow the road right and uphill. At the top, in woods off the left side of the trail, are remnants of the old Olinger lookout tower.

5.6 Pass through Low Gap and climb along steep cliff lines off the right side of the trail.

6.0 (FYI: Excellent views open up from a cliff on the right side of the trail.)

7.7 A road exits the right side of the trail. It leads to a decrepit log cabin with sheet metal roof a hundred feet or so downslope. (FYI: There's a campsite near the trail.)

8.2 Trail enters Olinger Gap. Three trails exit from this point, with yellow-blazed Stone Mountain heading uphill. A left turn on blue-blazed Olinger Gap Trail descends to Lake Keokee in 1 mile. A right onto a dirt road takes you a half mile to parking at the end of Virginia Route 622.

10.1 After a series of small dips and ever-steeper climbs, the trail opens onto High Butte (3,050 feet), the highest point on the hike, with views east across Powell Valley and west to the Black Mountain range.

10.6 (FYI: Stone Mountain trail enters a young, mixed hardwood forest of chestnut oak and maple, leaving behind the exposed ridgetop vegetation of berries, shrubs, and scrub oak. The 4-mile descent to US 23 passes through three distinct Appalachian forests types: the heaths, oaks, and hickories on the ridge, mixed hardwoods of tulip poplars, maples and buckeyes midway down the slope, and finally eastern hemlock and mountain laurel in the moist soil along Roaring Branch.)

13.4 The trail, which has arched away from Roaring Branch, descends on a small shoulder ridge to cross the stream near a nice campsite on the right side of the trail. A set of stone steps built by the CCC begins in 0.2 mile that last until the trailhead on US 23.

14.2 Descend the last few moss-covered stone steps to US 23.

Hike Information

Local Information

Town of Big Stone Gap, VA, (276) 523-0115, www.bigstonegap.org.
(See also Hike 30: Chief Benge Scout Trail.)

Local Events/Attractions

Coal/Railroad Days, first weekend in August, Appalachia, VA, (276) 565-0055.

Trail of the Lonesome Pine Outdoor Drama, late June–August, Big Stone Gap, VA, (800) 362-0149. Virginia's official state outdoor theater is a retelling of John Fox Jr.'s novel about mountain folk.

Southwest Virginia Museum, Big Stone Gap, VA, (276) 523-1322. Majestic stone home that ably chronicles the boom and bust of Big Stone Gap.

June Tolliver House, Big Stone Gap, VA, (276) 523-4707.

Lodging

Country Inn & RV Park, Big Stone Gap, VA, (276) 523-0374. The campgrounds are for RVs only.

Other Resources

My Melungeon Heritage, by Mattie Ruth Johnson, Overmountain Press.

Honorable Mentions

Southwest Highlands

Compiled here is an index of great hikes in the Southwest Highlands region that didn't make the A-list this time around but deserve recognition. Check them out and let us know what you think. You may decide that one or more of these hikes deserves higher status in future editions or, perhaps, you may have a hike of your own that merits some attention.

50 Rock Castle Gorge

A premier hike in Virginia's southern Blue Ridge region. Begin at a campsite at milepost 167 on the Blue Ridge Parkway (hikers must register at the visitor center, milepost 169, before embarking on an overnight trek). Starting in a pasture, this hike quickly plunges off the precipitous side of Rocky Knob. There are developed campsites along Rock Castle Creek. The return is a longer walk that caps out along the Parkway, allowing final views down into the lush cove below. *DeLorme: Virginia Atlas & Gazetteer:* Page 25, B6.

51 Patterson Mountain

From Fincastle on Virginia Route 220, take Virginia Route 606 west and turn right on Virginia Route 612, which leads to Forest Road 184 and the trailhead. The 6.5-mile Patterson Mountain Trail connects with three other trails for extended backcountry trip options. Great views off Patterson Mountain. Call (540) 864–5195. *DeLorme: Virginia Atlas & Gazetteer:* Page 52, D3.

52 Bald Mountain

A remote hike situated northwest of New Castle on Virginia Route 617. The Pines Recreation Area serves as a base camp for exploring the streams that lead up Bald and Potts Mountains. Recent clearing activity on the ridges has opened up views into West Virginia. Call (540) 864–5195. *DeLorme: Virginia Atlas & Gazetteer:* Page 52, D2.

53 North Mountain-AT Loop

A long hike northwest of Roanoke. Take exit 140 off I–81 and follow Virginia Route 311 to trailhead parking opposite the intersection of VA 311 and Virginia Route 624. Volunteers have recently cleared the North Mountain leg of this difficult 28.7-mile loop. An added bonus is the proximity of Dragons Tooth, one of

Virginia's most impressive short hikes. Call (540) 864–5195. *DeLorme: Virginia Atlas & Gazetteer:* Page 42, B1.

54 Poverty Creek

From Blacksburg, take Virginia Route 460 west and turn left onto Virginia Route 621, following signs for Pandapas Pond Day-use Area. This trail links Pandapas Pond with a host of backcountry trails. The area is multiuse, so hikers should be prepared to share the trail with equestrians and mountain bikers. Call (540) 552–4641. *DeLorme: Virginia Atlas & Gazetteer:* Page 41, B6.

55 The Rice Fields

From Blacksburg, take Virginia Route 460 west to Virginia Route 641; make a right onto VA 641 and follow to a parking lot (within a half mile of where the Appalachian Trail (AT) crosses the road). The Rice Fields are open meadows on top of Peters Mountain accessed via the AT. For 10 miles along this stretch, the AT follows the Virginia–West Virginia border. Where it intersects the Allegheny Trail, the AT descends back into Virginia. This is an out-and-back hike with no loop possibilities. Call (540) 552–4641. *DeLorme: Virginia Atlas & Gazetteer:* Page 40, B3. (Also see page 325.)

56 Ribble Trail–AT Loop

From I–81, drive north on Virginia Route 100, east on Virginia Route 42, right onto Virginia Route 606, and right again onto Virginia Route 201. Start at a red gate past Walnut Flats campground. This is a multiuse trail that ascends Flat Top Mountain, used by hikers and horseback riders alike. Hikers can link with the Appalachian Trail from Ribble Trail to complete a 10-mile loop. Call (540) 552–4641. *DeLorme: Virginia Atlas & Gazetteer:* Page 40, C3.

57 Tract Fork Trail

A point-to-point hike located between Wytheville and Pulaski. To reach the southern trailhead, take Virginia Route 603 north to Virginia Route 600, and then head east on VA 600 to the top of Little Walker Mountain. The other end of this easy 4-mile hike along Tract Fork Creek is on Tract Mountain, at the end of Forest Road 692, which is an extension of Virginia Route 641. Call (540) 228–5551. *DeLorme: Virginia Atlas & Gazetteer:* Page 24, A1; page 40, D2.

58 Trail Boss–AT Loop

Located near Bland, in the vicinity of Wytheville. From Bland, take Virginia Route 42 west to Virginia Route 615 north. There is a parking lot on the left side of VA

615. This 2.1-mile trail combines with the AT for a 5.1-mile loop, which features a boulder-strewn stream and ridge hiking. Call (540) 228–5551. *DeLorme: Virginia Atlas & Gazetteer:* Page 39, C7. (Also see page 325.)

59 Seven Sisters Trail

A short day hike out of Stony Fork Campground north of Wytheville. Reach the campsite via U.S. Highway 52, then make a left onto Virginia Route 717. The trail ascends Little Walker Mountain from the campground and follows the ridge for 2.5 miles before ending at a parking area on VA 717. There are giant old-growth white pines near Stony Fork. Call (540) 228–5551. *DeLorme: Virginia Atlas & Gazetteer:* Page 39, D7.

60 Hungry Mother State Park

A gem of a park located 3 miles north of Marion on Virginia Route 16. There are 12 miles of trails in this 2,180-acre state park. Highlights include inspired views from the Lake Trail of early morning mist rising off Hungry Mother Lake against a backdrop of brilliant fall foliage. Molly's Pioneer Trail and Molly's Knob Trail lead 2.2 miles to a 3,270-foot peak with views of Mount Rogers. Call (540) 783–3422. *DeLorme: Virginia Atlas & Gazetteer:* Page 23, A5.

61 Guest River Gorge Trail

A 6-mile point-to-point on a former railroad grade along the Guest River west of St. Paul. Starting at the northern end, this pleasant walk is a gradual and scenic descent into the gorge. The railway hauled the coal and saltpeter mined in the gorge, leaving behind sheer cliffs. The area harbors several threatened and endangered animals and plants. Call (540) 328–2931. *DeLorme: Virginia Atlas & Gazetteer:* Page 20, A4.

Mount Rogers National Recreation Area

I n Virginia, the Blue Ridge escarpment culminates in a large concentration of peaks and ridges near the North Carolina border. Here, Mount Rogers pokes a tree-shrouded summit above neighboring mountains to lay claim as the state's highest point. Competition is stiff, with only a 200-foot difference between it and nearby Whitetop Mountain. Striking about both—other than their size—is how little these peaks and the rural landscape around them resemble the more dramatic and sharply etched mountains in the northern Blue Ridge. The difference reflects forces that have shaped each. Folding and faulting characterized late-era mountain-building activity to the north. Here in southwest Virginia, the Blue Ridge's sweeping mountain slopes and rounded stream valleys resulted from hundreds of millions of years of erosion.

Little about Mount Rogers's high country resembles Virginia's other mountain regions. The spruce-fir forest at the highest elevations contains plants and animals typical of northern boreal forests, a result of the last ice age, which pushed plants and animals southward in its path. Mount Rogers's volcanic bedrock contains rhyolite, a mineral found nowhere else in Virginia. Even views seem otherworldly. Looking west from a wide meadow between Cabin Ridge and Mount Rogers appears more Big Sky Montana than southern Appalachian.

In the high-mountain meadows that slope away from Mount Rogers, horses graze in knee-high grass. A hiker's approaching footsteps may stir a foal that lies hidden in the overgrowth on Wilburn Ridge. Hawthorn trees and large, house-size boulders scattered randomly across the fields above Scales break up the smooth lines of these meadows. The fields here are entirely man-made, created after clear-cut logging and since maintained, first by grazing and now through periodic burning done by the Forest Service.

Mount Rogers
National Recreation Area

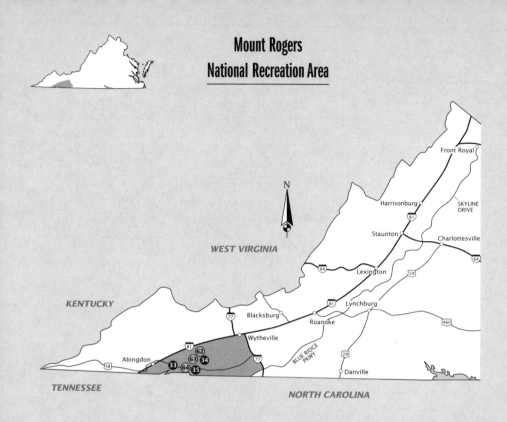

The Hikes

Feathercamp Ridge **33.**

Little Wilson Creek Wilderness **34.**

Mount Rogers Summit **35.**

Honorable Mentions

62. Four Trails Circuit

63. Rowland Creek Falls Circuit

64. Whitetop Laurel Circuit

Given the popularity of climbing Mount Rogers, visitors would do well to disperse their activity over as wide an area as possible. In a recreation area of 117,000 acres, it's easy to find other attractions, be it the laurel-choked streams on Iron Mountain or the rugged backcountry in Little Dry Run Wilderness, in the often-overlooked eastern section of Mount Rogers National Recreation Area.

33 Feathercamp Ridge

If Mount Rogers's summit is the heart, Iron Mountain is the backbone of southwest Virginia's mountain playground. Its breadth, 80 miles from the Tennessee-Virginia state line to the New River, makes it one of Virginia's longest ridges. The natural resources it holds made it a target of mineral and timber industries in earlier times. Now it simply offers miles of uninterrupted hiking and access to remote, less-visited parts of Mount Rogers National Recreation Area. On Feathercamp Branch, the scenery rivals any along Virginia's many mountain streams. As it ducks under thick rhododendron, it gathers speed between the steep shoulders of Iron Mountain and drops into shallow pools deep enough to wade.

Start: From the Appalachian Trail (AT) at U.S. Highway 58.

Distance: 8.1-mile loop.

Approximate hiking time: 5 hours.

Difficulty rating: Moderate due to well-graded trails, good signage, gentle ascents, and only a few steep sections of trail.

Trail surface: Dirt woodland paths and old roads lead to dry ridges, cove forests, and streams.

Land status: National recreation area.

Nearest town: Damascus, VA.

Other trail users: Equestrians.

Canine compatibility: Dogs permitted.

Trail contacts: Mount Rogers National Recreation Area, Marion, VA, (276) 783-5196, (800) 628-7202, www.southernregion.fs.fed.us/gwj. The visitor center is 10 miles north of Troutdale on Virginia Route 16.

Schedule: Open year-round. Hunting permitted, with the busiest season between November and January. Forest rangers conduct prescribed burns of 100 to 500 acres outside the wilderness in fall and spring.

Fees/permits: No permits required. Camping: $5.00-$15.00 tent site (backcountry camping is free); $2.00 shower for nonregistered campers; $2.00-$3.00 day-use parking at some areas.

Maps: USGS maps: Konnarock, VA. Mount Rogers High Country & Wilderness. Available at the Mount Rogers Visitor Center for $4.00.

Appalachian Trail Map 1: Mount Rogers National Recreation Area. Available from Appalachian Trail Conference, Harpers Ferry, WV.

Finding the trailhead: From Damascus: Drive east on US 58 for 3.5 miles. Look for a pull-off on the right side of the road; it has a picnic table and parking for three vehicles. *DeLorme: Virginia Atlas & Gazetteer:* Page 22, D2.

The Hike

As mountain ridges go, Iron Mountain is classic—undulating and, as you huff up and over your umpteenth knob, seemingly never-ending. Small peaks punctuate the long ridgeline. Hikers know a day spent "up on the ridge" is both an exhilarating and exasperating experience. The latter emotion results, unfortunately, from sheer

Crossing Feathercamp Branch at its lower reaches.

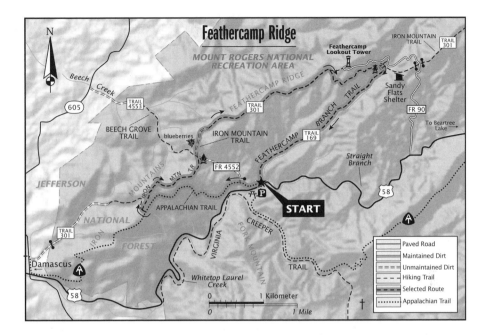

monotony. Woods-covered ridges lack the glamour of a peak, or the drama, say, of a canyon. After the sixth knob (Was it the *sixth* or was that last one the sixth?), they start to resemble a popular television rabbit: They keep going and going and going. . . .

Iron Mountain Trail would suffer this unkind judgment, if not for some key redeeming features. Among them, in my humble opinion, are blackberry thickets near Clark Mountain. One hundred yards of trailside thickets hold blackberries so juicy and plump, a mere touch stains the fingers with dark juice. No one should ever become so busy walking that she ignores the fruits of her labor.

Iron Mountain's other treasure lies in the many coves formed by ridge spurs that intersect it from all directions. Streams, torturous in their route, cut down these narrow, lush valleys. In the shade of tall trees, layers of leaf rot make a fertile bed for an array of mushrooms. The scaly vase chanterelle is an eye-catcher. Orange or yellow in color, its shape looks suspiciously like a waffle cone. Unlike waffle cones, however, tasting this mushroom is not recommended. It's not poisonous, but has a bitter taste and may cause indigestion. Other mushrooms pop up unexpectedly as you hike: slickners (poisonous), American Caesar's (edible, but not choice), and yellow and violet corals, as well as milky mushrooms.

The abundance of mushrooms on the Iron Mountain section of the Appalachian Trail makes the plant worth a closer look. Technically, mushrooms are plants. Unlike green plants, however, they do not contain chlorophyll; their food source is organic material. Where a mushroom grows not only helps identify the type, but also the food source. The thick, pink beefsteak polypore grows on dead trees and extracts food from the rotting wood. The largest and most-studied mushroom type, the mycorrhizal, has a symbiotic relationship with their host plant. Out of sight, beneath the earth, a mycorrhizal mushroom coats root stems of plants with threadlike strands; this helps the host plant grow. In exchange, the mushroom receives food. Of course, most people identify a mushroom by its cap—technically the fruit of a mushroom. And while tracking edible wild mushrooms is a booming hobby (remember, never eat a wild mushroom unless *absolutely* sure it is edible), their plentiful shapes and colors on Iron Mountain approach the beauty of wildflowers in spring.

The wildflowers on Feathercamp Branch emerge in April. The white blossom of mayapple hides away beneath umbrella-shaped leaves on a single, delicate stem (only plants with two leaves produce a flower). Appearances notwithstanding, this small wildflower is cousin to barberry, a thorny bush favored by professional landscapers—the link between them is berries. Anyone familiar with the orange and yellow barberry fruit will see a resemblance in the mayapple, which bears a single, red fruit three months after the flower blossoms. Herbalists use crushed barberry root for treating pink eye, diarrhea, and giardiasis (which hikers know as the infection contracted from drinking untreated stream or spring water). The unripe mayapple fruit isn't poisonous, but it will give you a stomachache.

Feathercamp Branch is a beauty of a stream, decked out in rhododendron, mountain laurel, and shrubby trees. After a rainstorm, shrubs and thickets fairly burst with chirps and peeps of warblers and songbirds. The stream sings as well, running a gentle grade between two steep ridges. An impenetrable thicket of rhododendron camouflages the stream near its headwaters. Farther downstream, you can sit on boulders and watch buds fall from rhododendron and float past. If they were seaworthy, they'd eventually reach the Gulf of Mexico via Laurel Creek, the New River, the Kanawha River, the Ohio River, and, finally, the great Mississippi. Across Iron Mountain, Rush Creek flows off in the opposite direction of Feathercamp Branch; it empties into the South Fork Holston River. It, too, will reach the Gulf of Mexico someday, but because the ridge of Iron Mountain marks the Tennessee Divide, these two streams follow very different routes. That's the effect of the Divide: Streams that begin a mere 2,500 feet apart empty into the Ohio River more than 100 miles distant from one another.

The Ohio and Mississippi Rivers and the Gulf of Mexico are distant thoughts as you nestle into your sleeping bag on Feathercamp Ridge. Leaves rustle, twigs crack, tree branches sway. If you're straining your ears, trying to attach size and shape to the noises (Feathercamp Ridge is home to deer, turkeys, a host of other animals, and a good number of bears as well), take comfort that you're not alone. Somewhere above you, in the trees, a great horned owl swivels its head. The owl's eyes are encased in bone. To compensate for little eye movement, they turn their heads on *very* flexible necks, with a rotation range of 270 degrees in some species. The great horned owl is among the largest of owls, and streamsides such as Feathercamp Branch make ideal hunting ground for live prey. But before you ever hear it swoop for a mouse or frog, you'll hear its signature call: three to eight *hoots,* the second and third rapid and doubled. Superstition labels owls as harbingers of ghosts and omens of death—in part due to their silent flight and stalking nature. It's also true, however, that when salted and eaten, the owl was thought to cure gout. I prefer to think of them as sentinels, sitting stock-still on a branch. If I'm feeling spooked, I mimic their call. There's a good chance the owl will respond.

Miles and Directions

0.0 **START** from a pull-off on US 58 at the confluence of Laurel Creek and Straight Branch. Cross US 58, enter the woods, and hike upstream following white AT blazes. (FYI: The Forest Service built a large earthen mound where the trail enters woods to block off-road vehicles.)

0.1 Blue-blazed Feathercamp Branch Trail continues straight. Turn left and follow the AT for a 2-mile climb to Iron Mountain Trail through rich hardwood forests.

0.6 The AT intersects with a dirt road (Forest Road 4552). Cross the road and continue straight along the AT. **Option:** A right turn on FR 4552 will take you up to the top of Iron Mountain, making for a shorter hike. The trail is nicely constructed to dip in and out of Iron Mountain's folds. You'll pass under white oak, chestnut oak, hickory, and dogwood. The ground is covered with several types of mosses and numerous mushrooms.

2.0 Turn right onto an unnamed blue-blazed trail that connects the AT and Iron Mountain Trail. In a tenth of a mile, turn right onto yellow-blazed Iron Mountain Trail. (FYI: Iron Mountain Trail skirts a knob to the right, passing by the wavy fronds of black snakeroot.)

3.1 Enter a clearing where the trail becomes a wide, grassy road. There are blueberry thickets on your left. Follow the road straight. Ahead on the right you'll find a fire ring that sees frequent use.

3.4 Iron Mountain Trail re-enters woods, climbing amid bear oak, poplar, and table mountain pine to skirt right of another knob. (FYI: There are lots of mountain laurel here and a large dogwood tree.)

5.0 Arrive at a fork in the trail; bear right and continue on Iron Mountain Trail up a small knob. **Sidetrip:** If you bear left at the fork, you can take Feathercamp Ridge Trail 0.2 mile to Forest Road 90 and Feathercamp Lookout Tower.

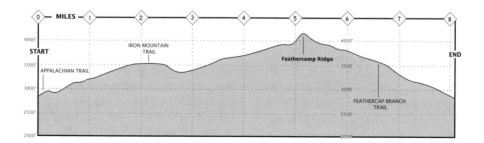

5.9 Take a hard right and follow Iron Mountain Trail downhill through a grove of hemlock. Within a tenth of a mile, it drops you onto blue-blazed Feathercamp Branch Trail, which begins as a doubletrack dirt road. Turn right to return to US 58. **Sidetrip:** Sandy Flats Shelter is three-tenths of a mile up Iron Mountain Trail.

6.0 Pass through a clearing with a fire ring. As you re-enter the woods, Feathercamp Branch Trail reverts to a singletrack woods path.

7.0 (FYI: The stream on your left, Feathercamp Branch, has gained enough strength at this point to create nice toe-dipping pools at the bottom of small cascades.)

7.6 Cross a feeder stream that enters Feathercamp Branch from the right. This marks the start of a series of stream crossings between here and the AT.

8.0 Feathercamp Branch Trail merges with the AT trail. Follow the white-blazed AT trail straight.

8.1 Hike ends at US 58.

Hike Information

Local Information

Town of Damascus Tourism, (276) 475–3542, www.damascus.org.
Grayson County Tourism, Independence, VA, (276) 773–3711, www.graysoncountyva.com.
Abingdon Convention & Visitors Bureau, Abingdon, VA, (800) 435–3440, www.abingdon.com/tourism.

Local Events/Attractions

Blue Ridge Backroads at the Rex Theater, Galax, VA, (276) 236–0668. Live radio music show every Friday from Galax's downtown theater. Programs air on 98.1 WBRC-FM.
Galax Old Time Fiddlers Convention, second week in August, Galax, VA, (276) 238–8130. Attracts national and international recording acts. Grayson Highlands State Park and the town of Fries also host bluegrass, old-time, and country music festivals every year.
Grayson County Fiddlers Convention, last full weekend in June, Elk Creek, VA, (276) 655–4740.
Naturalist Rally, second weekend in May, Mount Rogers, VA, (276) 579–7092.
Whitetop Mountain Ramp Festival, third Sunday in May, Whitetop, VA, (276) 773–3711. Ramps are a term for wild leeks, and this festival features an eating contest that can bring you to tears—from laughter or from the onion itself.

Grayson Highlands Fall Festival, last full weekend of September, Grayson Highlands State Park, Mouth of Wilson, VA, (276) 579–7092. Just one of many fall festivals in the area. Independence, Fries, Baywood, and Marion all hold fall festivals through September and October.
Appalachian Trail Days, third week in May, Damascus, VA, (276) 475–3542. Annual gathering of AT thru–hikers in the town dubbed "friendliest town on the AT."
Grandfather Mountain Country Store, Damascus, VA, (423) 739–2557. Hams, jellies, syrups, and jerky—it's all authentic handmade or homemade mountain food. A nice collection of mountain crafts, T-shirts, and books as well.

Lodging

The Enchanted Lodge, White Top, VA, (276) 466–4044, www.enchantedlodge.com. Log lodge surrounded by mountain views and seventeen acres with hiking trails. Spa treatments available.
More than half a dozen **Damascus** residents have turned their homes into bed-and-breakfasts to accommodate the many hikers and bikers who frequent the small town. Call (276) 475–3542, or visit www.damascus.org.
Abingdon has numerous bed-and-breakfasts, motels, and the famed **Camberley's Martha**

Washington Inn, (800) 555-8000, www.marthawashingtoninn.com.
For other lodging in Abingdon, contact the Convention & Visitors Bureau, (800) 435-3440, www.abingdon.com/visitors/lodging/htm.
North of the Mount Rogers area, the town of **Marion** has several motels. Call Smyth County Chamber of Commerce, (276) 783-3161, or visit www.Smythchamber.org.
Grayson Highlands State Park has camping on the southern boundary of the Mount Rogers area, (800) 933-PARK.

Restaurants

Side Track Computer Café, Damascus, VA, (276) 475-6106. A favorite hangout for hikers.
Damascus Old Mill, (276) 475-3745, www.damascusoldmill.com. A recently renovated 1912 mill turned restaurant and sports bar with outdoor seating on the banks of Laurel Creek.

Cowboys, Damascus, VA, (276) 475-5444. This deli, located inside a service station, has great Southern breakfasts.
In the Country, Damascus, VA, (276) 475-5319. Bakery, eatery, and ice cream shop.

Organizations

Appalachian Trail Conference, Harpers Ferry, WV, (304) 535-6331, www.appalachiantrail.org.
Virginia's Southwest Blue Ridge Highlands, Inc., Abingdon, VA, (800) 446-9670, www.virginiablueridge.org. A regional tourism agency with information on festivals and attractions throughout southwest Virginia.

Other Resources

Appalachian Trail Guide to Southwest Virginia, Appalachian Trail Conference, Harpers Ferry, WV.

34 Little Wilson Creek Wilderness

Most hikers enter Little Wilson Creek Wilderness on trails out of Grayson Highlands State Park. Scales, an area named for the livestock scales once located here, makes a great alternate starting point. You not only avoid crowds but get a high-country fix that much faster. Scales sits smack-dab in the midst of Mount Rogers' crest zone, flanked by Stone Mountain and Wilburn Ridge. Huckleberry bushes bloom profusely (there are reports of folks carrying three gallons or more out of thickets along Scales Trail). On Stone Mountain, wild horses graze. As you approach them, young foals bolt from cover of tall grass and dart behind their mothers. In the words of a passerby, "It's as wild as it gets up here."

Start: From the corralled campground at Scales.
Distance: 7.6-mile loop.
Approximate hiking time: 5 hours.
Difficulty rating: Moderate due to some long climbs and several muddy, eroded sections of trail.
Trail surface: A combination of dirt footpaths, old dirt wagon roads, and railroad grades lead through high-altitude meadows, mountain balds, and mixed hardwood forests.
Land status: National recreation area.
Nearest town: Troutdale, VA.
Other trail users: Equestrians.

Canine compatibility: Dogs permitted.
Trail contacts: Mount Rogers National Recreation Area, Marion, VA, (276) 783-5196, (800) 628-7202, The visitor center is 10 miles north of Troutdale on Virginia Route 16. Grayson Highlands State Park, (276) 579-7092, www.dcr.state.va.us/parks/graysonh.htm.
Schedule: (See Hike 33: Feathercamp Ridge.)
Fees/permits: (See Hike 33: Feathercamp Ridge.)
Maps: USGS maps: Trout Dale, VA. (See also Hike 33: Feathercamp Ridge.)

Finding the trailhead: From Troutdale: (Four-wheel-drive with high clearance required). Take Virginia Route 603 west from its intersection with VA 16. In 2.8 miles, turn left onto Forest Road 613, a dirt road. (Look for a sign on the right-hand side of the road.) Road conditions are rocky, rutted, and sometimes wet. Once on FR 613, you'll pass a fork at 0.7 mile. Turn left. Turn left at the second fork at 2 miles. At 2.8 miles, turn right at the fork. In 3.8 miles, pass through a metal gate (the gate may be closed, but not locked.) In 0.2 mile past the gate, enter the campground at Scales. *DeLorme: Virginia Atlas & Gazetteer:* Page 23, C5.
Option (for two-wheel-drive or low-clearance vehicles)
From Troutdale: Drive south on VA 16. In 7 miles, turn right onto U.S. Highway 58. It is another 7.6 miles on US 58 to the Grayson Highlands State Park entrance road, Virginia Route 362. Turn right onto VA 362, and, in 3.1 miles, turn right onto the Grayson Highlands State Park campground access road. It dead-ends at the campground in 1.3 miles. Wilson Creek trailhead is clearly marked near the ranger station. Follow it downhill and, in 1.8 miles, turn right onto Scales Trail, which is an old road. Reach the Scales area in 1.3 miles (for a total 3.1 trip from the state park campground). *DeLorme: Virginia Atlas & Gazetteer:* Page 23, C5.

View from a high-country meadow back to Wilburn Ridge.

The Hike

They stare at you from a black-and-white photograph, fourteen men in dirty over-alls wearing brimmed hats, saws and poles gripped firmly in hand. Remember them as you soak in the high-country meadows around Scales, a swale in Pine Mountain tucked between Wilburn Ridge and Stone Mountain. If not for loggers like them, this landscape wouldn't exist.

Transformation of Scales, once a weigh-in site for livestock, took a mere twenty years. Starting around 1900, lumber companies and private landowners stripped virgin spruce and fir, chestnut, maple, and oak from the hillsides. What's developed since is a product of man and nature. Erosion carried away fertile soil and exposed portions of volcanic bedrock. Livestock grazing and periodic fires set by the Forest Service keep the forest at bay. From this, Virginia's most striking landscape evolved: miles of meadow awash in green, orange, red, and purple cresting against a horizon filled with Virginia's highest peaks, fading into the haze of North Carolina's Blue Ridge.

First Peak Trail climbs through just this type of landscape en route to Little Wilson Creek Wilderness, a 3,900-acre tract protecting three peaks and five creek watersheds, including the dual headwaters of Little Wilson Creek. As you pass just under the summit of Third Peak, isolated clumps of hawthorn, buckeye, and beech grow increasingly thick and dense. This is how all of the Mount Rogers's crest zone—land 4,000 feet or more above sea level—would look if left to nature. Huckleberry grows in ever-larger thickets. Scrubby witch hazel (the divining rod of choice for modern-day dowsers), flame azaleas, and mountain laurel grow head-high. Small American chestnut intersperse with beech and chinquapin oak.

A blight has stunted the chestnut from growing even big enough to produce its burrlike fruit. Only one hundred years ago, it grew so large, residents of Troutdale, a boomtown at the foot of Pine Mountain, cut 12x12x2-inch-thick pieces for stepping stones across their muddy roads. C. P. Greer, a Troutdale resident, logged trees so big in this wilderness that, with his daughter perched on his shoulders, the base of a felled tree dwarfed them both. Greer is the man responsible for the faint trace of railroad grades visible on Hightree Rock Trail, one of the wilderness's less-traveled footpaths. He built a small-grade railroad on his own land to carry logs to his mill on Fox Creek, where he processed it for furniture and building

KEEP AN EYE OUT FOR... Hawthorn, identifiable by its thorny branches, is a common tree sprouting from the thin soil of Mount Rogers high country. But what kind of hawthorn, exactly, are you seeing? There are at least 165 species. Of them, thirty are native to the eastern region of the United States. Around Mount Rogers, you can narrow the search to cockspur, fanleaf, dotted, red plum, and fleshy hawthorns, all of which grow at elevations of 5,000 feet or higher.

material. (Ever the entrepreneur, Greer later converted the mill into a dynamo, or power plant, and supplied Troutdale's first electricity.) It was in the vicinity of Hightree Rock that Greer felled his largest trees.

A mile and a half past where it splits from First Peak Trail, the Kabel Trail takes on the appearance of an old railroad grade: wide and flat with high banks. What might have been a rail spur angles left and peters out in thick woods. Rocks buttress the underside of the trail here, the masonry work visible by looking downslope off the left side. Locomotives crossed grades like this daily during the boom years on Pine Mountain, traveling from Fairwood, a company town on FR 613. Before a fire destroyed it in 1911, Fairwood served as base of operations for the U.S. Spruce Lumber Company's Pine Mountain operations. Life there and in nearby Troutdale hummed along with the lumber business. Two furniture manufacturers employed any able-bodied man not working in timber. Farmers traveled the dirt roads between their homes and town, carrying livestock and produce to a rail depot at Troutdale. On their return trip, they were loaded with chairs from the factory for their wives and children to cane. Passenger trains ran twice a day from Troutdale south to Sugar Grove and Marion. For a time, Troutdale families rode the rails to Fairwood every Fourth of July for an annual baseball game, since the Spruce Lumber Company had built the finest baseball diamond in the valley.

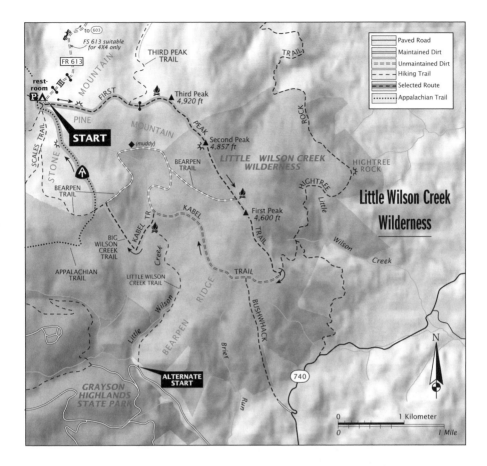

It was for Spruce Lumber Company that engineer Kent Steffey worked on the fateful September day he took a Shay Locomotive No. 9 up Pine Mountain. After uncoupling a boxcar and reversing the engine, he started downhill. The train gathered speed and Steffey blew two sharp whistles, signaling for brakes. Nothing happened. The train careened on. Steffey's repeated whistle blows pealed across the mountain. The conductor and fireman jumped, but Steffey stayed aboard. Workers later found his body under the smoking wreckage of the 65-ton Shay. All that's left today is his tombstone in Rural Retreat, Virginia, and a ballad, "The Wreck of Ole Number Nine."

Still on the rails the bell / Began its pondering clang / And out upon the mountain air / the mourning whistle rang / "Farewell, farewell," it seemed to say / And the wheels like death did sing / It struck the curve with an awful shock / And from the rails she sprang.

They stare at you, men in dirty overalls and brimmed hats sitting atop Steffey's wrecked Shay No. 9. Say what you will about habitats destroyed, species lost, trees gone forever. But don't forget their faces.

Miles and Directions

0.0 **START** from the trailboard at Scales, an enclosed campground on Pine Mountain. Past the trailboard, exit the corral via a pass-thru in the fence. Turn left, keep the fence to your left, and round the next corner of the corral. Bear right and uphill at a signboard for First Peak Trail. (FYI: Avoid the Appalachian Trail (AT), which also ascends through these fields. The AT is clearly marked with white blazes.)

0.8 Pass a junction with Third Peak Trail; continue straight.

1.0 Pass a campsite on the left side of the trail. (FYI: This is an ideal spot for anyone looking for a sheltered evening under red spruce and hardwoods.)

1.1 Pass to the right of 4,920-foot Third Peak.

1.8 (FYI: Near the top of Second Peak, look out for several footpaths, unblazed, that branch left and disappear into the low forest cover. These trails lead a few hundred feet to a rock outcrop with views.) Continue straight on First Peak Trail.

2.3 Enter a clearing. A fire ring marks this as an established backwoods campsite and there are signs of heavy use. Pass straight through the clearing on the First Peak Trail. (FYI: Bearpen Trail departs this clearing to the right. It descends to Little Wilson Creek before climbing to a junction with Big Wilson Creek Trail.)

3.0 Reach a T junction and turn right onto Kabel Trail. (FYI: Hightree Rock Trail leads left from this T junction to an overlook in 2 miles.)

4.8 After passing over some wet ground, climb on Kabel Trail as the route widens from a footpath into a dirt road.

4.9 Turn sharply left and downhill, still on the Kabel Trail.

5.2 Cross a fork of Little Wilson Creek. There's a prime camping spot on the left in a grassy meadow before you cross.

5.5 Kabel Trail ends at Big Wilson Creek Trail. Turn right onto Big Wilson Creek Trail.

6.2 Leave the Little Wilson Creek Wilderness. Just beyond the wilderness sign, Big Wilson Creek Trail intersects Bearpen Trail at a T junction. Turn left onto Bearpen Trail. (Note: A right turn onto Bearpen leads back to First Peak Trail. Hiking on this trail is not advisable in wet weather because of eroded and muddy trail conditions.)

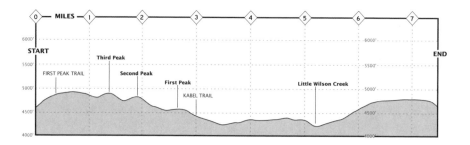

6.4 At a four-way intersection, turn right onto the AT and climb. The trail crosses a barbed-wire fence on a step-up, and enters high-country meadows. (FYI: The grass is waist-high in spots, tall enough to hide young foals resting on the ground. This stretch of the AT is one of the best to see the wild horses of Mount Rogers high country, in part because it is less traveled than trails near the Mount Rogers summit.)

7.6 Hike ends at Scales. (Note: If your hike began in Grayson Highlands State Park, it's another 3.1 miles on the Scales Trail and Wilson Creek Trail to the campground and parking area.)

Hike Information

Local Information

Town of Damascus Tourism, (276) 475-3542, www.damascus.org.

Grayson County Tourism, Independence, VA, (276) 773-3711, www.graysoncountyva.com.

Abingdon Convention & Visitors Bureau, Abingdon, VA, (800) 435-3440, www.abingdon.com/tourism.

Local Events/Attractions

Blue Ridge Backroads at the Rex Theater, Galax, VA, (276) 236-0668. Live radio music show every Friday from Galax's downtown theater. Programs air on 98.1 WBRC-FM.

Galax Old Time Fiddlers Convention, second week in August, Galax, VA, (276) 238-8130. Attracts national and international recording acts. Grayson Highlands State Park and the town of Fries also host bluegrass, old-time, and country music festivals every year.

Grayson County Fiddlers Convention, last full weekend in June, Elk Creek, VA, (276) 655-4740.

Naturalist Rally, second weekend in May, Mount Rogers, VA, (276) 579-7092.

Whitetop Mountain Ramp Festival, third Sunday in May, Whitetop, VA, (276) 773-3711. Ramps are a term for wild leeks, and this festival features an eating contest that can bring you to tears—from laughter or from the onion itself.

Grayson Highlands Fall Festival, last full weekend of September, Grayson Highlands State Park, Mouth of Wilson, VA, (276) 579-7092. Just one of many fall festivals in the area. Independence, Fries, Baywood, and Marion all hold fall festivals through September and October.

Appalachian Trail Days, third week in May, Damascus, VA, (276) 475-3542. Annual gathering of AT thru-hikers in the town dubbed "friendliest town on the AT."

Grandfather Mountain Country Store, Damascus, VA, (423) 739-2557. Hams, jellies, syrups, and jerky—it's all authentic handmade or homemade mountain food. A nice collection of mountain crafts, T-shirts, and books as well.

Lodging

Fox Hill Inn, Troutdale, VA, (276) 677-3313, (800) 874-3313, www.bbonline.com/va/foxhill.

Sugar Grove Bed & Breakfast, Sugar Grove, VA, (276) 677-3351. Offers hiker discount and shuttles. Ask for "Peggy." Restaurant and lodging. Each room has a kitchen, sitting area, bed, and bath.

The Enchanted Lodge, White Top, VA, (276) 466-4044, www.enchantedlodge.com. Log lodge surrounded by mountain views and seventeen acres with hiking trails. Spa treatments available.

More than half a dozen **Damascus** residents have turned their homes into bed-and-breakfasts to accommodate the many hikers and bikers who frequent the small town. Call (276) 475-3542, or visit www.damascus.org.

Abingdon has numerous bed-and-breakfasts, motels, and the famed **Camberley's Martha Washington Inn,** (800) 555-8000, www.marthawashingtoninn.com.

For other lodging in Abingdon, contact the Convention & Visitors Bureau, (800) 435-3440, www.abingdon.com/visitors/lodging/htm.

North of the Mount Rogers area, the town of **Marion** has several motels. Call Smyth County Chamber of Commerce, (276) 783-3161, or visit www.Smythchamber.org.

Grayson Highlands State Park has camping on the southern boundary of the Mount Rogers area, (800) 933-PARK.

Restaurants

Ona's Country Kitchen, Mouth of Wilson, VA, (276) 579-4440. Restaurant is inside John Conklin's Trading Post.

The Troutdale Trading Post, Troutdale, VA, (276) 677-3010. Good food, decent prices.

Side Track Computer Café, Damascus, VA, (276) 475-6106. A favorite hangout for hikers.

Damascus Old Mill, (276) 475-3745, www.damascusoldmill.com. A recently renovated 1912 mill turned restaurant and sports bar with outdoor seating on the banks of Laurel Creek.

Cowboys, Damascus, VA, (276) 475-5444. This deli, located inside a service station, has great Southern breakfasts.

In the Country, Damascus, VA, (276) 475-5319. Bakery, eatery, and ice cream shop.

Organizations

Appalachian Trail Conference, Harpers Ferry, WV, (304) 535-6331, www.appalachiantrail.org.

Virginia's Southwest Blue Ridge Highlands, Inc., Abingdon, VA, (800) 446-9670, www.virginiablueridge.org. A regional tourism agency with information on festivals and attractions throughout southwest Virginia.

Other Resources

The Virginia Creeper: Remembering the Virginia-Carolina Railway, by Doug McGuinn, Bamboo Books.

The Switchback Scenic Route: A history of the Marion and Rye Valley Railway, by Gary P. Price, Mallicote Printing Inc.

35 Mount Rogers Summit

Dispense with the suspense right off: This 5,729-foot monolith of volcanic rock—third loftiest mountain in the Southern Appalachians—is not hard to climb. Yes, you must hike 7 miles to reach it from Grindstone Campground, and, yes, the elevation change hovers around 2,000 feet. This, however, only ranks somewhere between climbing Flat Top Mountain at Peaks of Otter and Three Ridges near Lexington, both mountains 4,000 feet or smaller. In other words, there are tougher climbs out there. But what Mount Rogers lacks in mountaineering daring-do, it easily compensates for in sheer presence, the diversity of its plant and animal life, the breathtaking views across high-country meadows, and, of course, its wild ponies. And to those eager for bragging rights, it affords the modest claim: "I climbed the highest mountain in Virginia."

Start: From the Mount Rogers Trailhead, 0.1 mile past the ranger station in Grindstone Campground off Virginia Route 603.
Distance: 13.3-mile loop.
Approximate hiking time: 7 hours.
Difficulty rating: Moderate due to the overall length, the long climb up Mount Rogers, a steep descent down the Cliffside Trail, and wet trail conditions on Lewis Fork Trail.
Trail surface: Dirt footpaths and forest roads lead to Virginia's highest peak, grassy highlands, cove forests, and wooded slopes.
Land status: Federal wilderness and national recreation area.

Nearest town: Troutdale, VA.
Other trail users: Equestrians.
Canine compatibility: Dogs permitted.
Trail contacts: Mount Rogers National Recreation Area, Marion, VA, (276) 783-5196, www.southernregion.fs.fed.us/gwj. The visitor center is 10 miles north of Troutdale on Virginia Route 16.
Schedule: (See Hike 33: Feathercamp Ridge.)
Fees/permits: (See Hike 33: Feathercamp Ridge.)
Maps: USGS maps: Whitetop, VA. (See also Hike 33: Feathercamp Ridge.)

Finding the trailhead: From Troutdale: Take VA 603 west from its intersection with VA 16. The entrance to Grindstone Campground is 6.2 miles west on VA 603; turn left into the campground. Alternate parking for Mount Rogers Trail is on VA 603, 0.2 mile before Grindstone, on the left side of the road. *DeLorme: Virginia Atlas & Gazetteer:* Page 23, D5.

The Hike

You reach a point climbing Mount Rogers's north slope where nature gets a little giddy. A relatively tame, wooded mountainside slips into a jumble of cliff and rock outcrops. In a short span of trail, large boulders appear. Down a steep grade on the right is a cliff and, at the base of the cliff, a shallow cave formed by the overhanging rocks. A birch tree grafts on exposed roots of another birch. A cleaved rock exposes the entire root system of a hemlock growing out its top side. The trail becomes more

A mossy, moist stand of forest near the Mount Rogers summit.

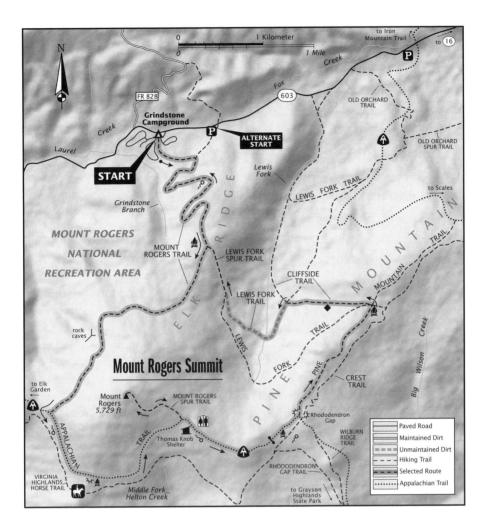

streambed than dirt footpath. On rainy days, runoff will trickle underfoot. All that's missing, really, is a big sign: WELCOME TO 5,000 FEET. ENJOY YOUR STAY.

That's a magic number, 5,000. In the whole Blue Ridge chain, from southern Pennsylvania to north Georgia, only seven peaks exceed that threshold. Two of them stand in Virginia. One, Whitetop Mountain, has a road leading to the top. It's tempting to say the same about Mount Rogers, judging by the number of people who climb it every year. In truth, Mount Rogers, namesake for the 117,000-acre national recreation area, harbor for remnant boreal forests and threatened species, is in a class all its own.

Mount Rogers hasn't always enjoyed fame. For two centuries after colonial settlement in Virginia, it was just another obstacle to westward travel. During his 1728 survey of the "dividing line" between Virginia and North Carolina, Colonel William

Byrd never reached the peak, thwarted as he was by the Blue Ridge Mountains, which he described from afar as "ranges of blue clouds." Byrd's group turned for home, frustrated by slow progress through "troublesome thickets and underwood," and the Southern Appalachians remained the "back of the beyond," as Horace Kephart described them, until a series of scientific explorations in the early 1800s. Not that the mountains remained unsettled. Pioneers were followed by mining and logging, but the region as a whole remained a place where people in neighboring hollows could pass a lifetime meeting only once or twice.

FYI Mount Rogers's namesake, William Barton Rogers, left Virginia to found the Massachusetts Institute of Technology (MIT) in Boston, but he never left the Old Dominion's earth sciences behind. His dying words were "bituminous coal." A fleeting "Rosebud" to the commonwealth he helped map? Actually, Rogers collapsed dead in midsentence during a speech to the MIT graduating class of 1882.

As it happens, the honor for mapping Mount Rogers goes to William Barton Rogers, Virginia's first state geologist. Rogers climbed the mountain during his geologic survey of Virginia in 1836, a mission ordered by the state legislature. These first decades of the 1800s were a busy time for scientists. States up and down the East Coast were interested in exploiting their mineral, plant, and animal resources. Rogers's brother, Henry Darwin Rogers, had conducted a geologic survey for Pennsylvania. Based on information gathered, the Rogers brothers published their famous theory on the Appalachian Mountains, a theory that generated some controversy for its assumption that the earth was at least several million years old. It's a notion few question today, but in the 1800s, the scientists who believed in creationism—that God created the world in a single moment—condemned Rogers's work. As it turns out, the criticism proved merely a warm up for Charles Darwin's *The Origin of Species,* published in 1859, and the work of biologist Asa Grey, who wrote of similarities between plants found in East Asia and North America.

Rogers didn't need to span continents in search of similar flora among regions far-removed from one another. Atop Mount Rogers, the fir-spruce forest indicates a mixing of temperate and cold-weather plants. At its highest points grow northern hardwoods, red spruce, and mountain wood sorrel wildflower. There are northern flying squirrels and birds such as the chestnut-sided warbler (its call: a slow *please, please, pleased to meet you*) and Swainson's thrush (its call: a *whit* and a *heep*). These species, normally associated with northern forests, arrived with the last ice age in North America, when encroaching ice and cold weather pushed habitats south into Virginia. Eventually, the ice receded and so did the flora and fauna—except on high peaks such as Mount Rogers. Naturalists like to describe this peak as a Southern sentinel for plants and animals more common to America's northeast. The summit also supports stands of Fraser fir, an evergreen that grows no farther north than the crest zone of Mount Rogers. Mount Rogers, then, stands as a link in a north-south chain of ecosystems, those typically found on cool, moist mountaintops such as Mount Mitchell in North Carolina and the 6,000-foot-plus peaks of the Great Smoky Mountains. It's a stepping stone, especially for such birds as the magnolia warbler (its call: *weetee weetee weeteo*), which has extended its range out of New York and Pennsylvania and into North Carolina and Tennessee.

Mount Rogers is a threatened ecosystem. Many people worry about air pollution, which weakens a tree's resistance to disease. Survival of Mount Rogers's spruce-fir trees is fiercely debated, given the almost total obliteration of Fraser fir on Mount Mitchell, 75 miles to the south. The firs on Mount Rogers show resistance to the balsam woolly adelgid, a microscopic pest that coats the crowns of fir trees, leading to defoliation and eventually death. Nonetheless, eerie parallels exist between the trees on Mount Rogers and the hemlocks in Ramsey's Draft Wilderness and Shenandoah National Park, where the hemlock woolly adelgid is defoliating Eastern hemlock at such a rate that park rangers predict virgin stands will disappear within twenty years. Mount Rogers's foresters say reports of the fir tree's demise in Virginia are greatly exaggerated, but it's difficult, when staring at the bleached spikes of dead conifers scattered across the summit, not to wonder.

It's worth looking back over your shoulder as you hike up the Appalachian Trail (AT) toward Wilburn Ridge, savoring another view of a special mountain. Colonel Byrd, the surveyor who never made it this far west, couldn't help but do so. His reaction rings true today.

We could not forbear now and then facing about to survey them (the mountains), as if unwilling to part with a prospect which at the same time . . . was very wild and very agreeable.

Miles and Directions

0.0 **START** at the Grindstone Campground. Walk uphill from the ranger station. In less than 0.1 mile, turn left and enter the woods at a sign for the Mount Rogers Trail. (FYI: There is a fee to park at Grindstone.)

0.4 Reach a T junction and turn right to continue climbing the Mount Rogers Trail. (FYI: The trail left leads downhill to a parking area for the Mount Rogers Trail on VA 603.)

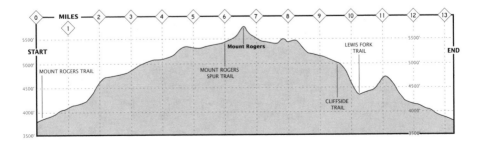

A high-country meadow in the vicinity of Cabin Ridge and Brier Ridge.

0.8 Climb a gentle grade to a switchback right, the first of four on this slope of Mount Rogers.

2.1 Pass the Lewis Fork Spur Trail on the left in a clearing of ferns, grasses, and nettles; continue straight on the Mount Rogers Trail. (FYI: The Lewis Fork Spur Trail leads 0.3 mile to Lewis Fork Trail. It is the return leg of this loop hike.)

2.7 The landscape roughens a bit. The ground becomes rocky. Mount Rogers Trail passes through several wet sections, which indicate water sources (no water sources are visible from the trail).

2.9 The trail winds through a large rock formation with sections of exposed rock showing the volcanic bedrock of the Mount Rogers formation.

3.5 (FYI: Pass through a patch of stinging nettles. Here, two distinct wildflowers, the red Indian paintbrush and orange-yellow Turks cap lily, may be spotted in July. Beyond this patch, you'll catch your first up close view of the straight, smooth-trunked red spruce.)

4.0 Nice views off the right side of the trail into the Laurel Creek Valley and Iron Mountain rising beyond.

4.2 Turn left onto the Appalachian Trail (AT).

4.7 Two switchbacks in quick succession take you out of dark, sheltered pine forest to a stretch of exposed trail. (FYI: The woods at this point have changed to a red spruce/Fraser fir-dominated forest. The air is fresh with scent of evergreens.)

4.9 The trail enters a grove of evergreens. Look downhill to your right for unblazed footpaths that lead to a few campsites. (FYI: If you follow these side trails past the campsites, the tree cover breaks onto a wide-open and beautiful view of Mount Rogers's famous high-country meadows. The Virginia Highlands Horse Trail runs through this meadow, descending west to Elk Garden.)

5.4 Pass a campsite on the right. There is a flowing stream nearby. The AT crosses several more reliable water sources for the next half mile. (Note: All water should be treated before being consumed.)

6.0 Turn left onto the Mount Rogers Spur Trail.

6.5 Reach a flat area atop Mount Rogers. A boulder on the left contains the USGS marker. This is the summit of Mount Rogers, Virginia's highest mountain. Turn and descend back to the AT.

7.0 At a T junction, turn left onto the AT. (FYI: The trail passes through meadow vegetation of huckleberry, fireweed, and hawthorn trees.)

7.2 Thomas Knob Shelter sits on the right side of the trail. There's a covered outhouse on the left as you approach, and a reliable water source just past the shelter.

8.2 A huge rock formation on the left marks the spot where Wilburn Ridge butts up against Pine Mountain. The AT makes a hard right turn at the base of this rock formation. Avoid the right turn, and continue straight on the blue-blazed Pine Mountain Trail. This trail winds through head-high thickets of rhododendron as it descends. (FYI: After it makes a hard right turn, the AT crosses the Highlands Horse Trail and climbs Wilburn Ridge to Grayson Highlands State Park.)

9.4 At a T intersection, turn left onto Lewis Fork Trail. There is a campsite on Pine Mountain Trail just before this junction. (FYI: Lewis Fork Trail is multiuse and may show signs of heavy use by horses.)

9.5 At a fork in the trail, veer right onto Cliffside Trail. (FYI: This is a hiker-only path that descends over rough terrain to rejoin the Lewis Fork Trail.)

10.1 Turn left onto Lewis Fork Trail. (Note: The trail is heavily used by horses and is often muddy.)

10.9 At a switchback left in the Lewis Fork Trail, continue straight on a grassy road. In 100 yards, turn left and climb the Lewis Fork Spur Trail, a dirt footpath.

11.2 Turn right onto Mount Rogers Trail and begin a descent to Grindstone Campground.

13.3 Hike ends at Grindstone Campground. Mount Rogers Trail exits the woods onto the campground access road. The ranger station is less than 0.1 mile to the right.

Hike Information

Local Information

Town of Damascus Tourism, (276) 475-3542, www.damascus.org.

Grayson County Tourism, Independence, VA, (276) 773-3711, www.graysoncountyva.com.

Abingdon Convention & Visitors Bureau, Abingdon, VA, (800) 435-3440, www.abingdon.com/tourism.

Local Events/Attractions

Blue Ridge Backroads at the Rex Theater, Galax, VA, (276) 236-0668. Live radio music show every Friday from Galax's downtown theater. Programs air on 98.1 WBRC-FM.

Galax Old Time Fiddlers Convention, second week in August, Galax, VA, (276) 238-8130. Attracts national and international recording acts. Grayson Highlands State Park and the town of Fries also host bluegrass, old-time, and country music festivals every year.

Grayson County Fiddlers Convention, last full weekend in June, Elk Creek, VA, (276) 655-4740.

Naturalist Rally, second weekend in May, Mount Rogers, VA, (276) 579-7092.

Whitetop Mountain Ramp Festival, third Sunday in May, Whitetop, VA, (276) 773-3711.

Ramps are a term for wild leeks, and this festival features an eating contest that can bring you to tears—from laughter or from the onion itself.

Grayson Highlands Fall Festival, last full weekend of September, Grayson Highlands State Park, Mouth of Wilson, VA, (276) 579-7092. Just one of many fall festivals in the area. Independence, Fries, Baywood, and Marion all hold fall festivals through September and October.

Appalachian Trail Days, third week in May, Damascus, VA, (276) 475-3542. Annual gathering of AT thru-hikers in the town dubbed "friendliest town on the AT."

Grandfather Mountain Country Store, Damascus, VA, (423) 739-2557. Hams, jellies, syrups, and jerky—it's all authentic handmade or homemade mountain food. A nice collection of mountain crafts, T-shirts, and books as well.

Lodging

The Enchanted Lodge, White Top, VA, (276) 466-4044, www.enchantedlodge.com. Log lodge surrounded by mountain views and seventeen acres with hiking trails. Spa treatments available.

More than half a dozen **Damascus** residents have turned their homes into bed-and-breakfasts to accommodate the many hikers and bikers who frequent the small town. Call (276) 475-3542, or visit www.damascus.org.

Abingdon has numerous bed-and-breakfasts, motels, and the famed **Camberley's Martha Washington Inn,** (800) 555-8000, www.marthawashingtoninn.com.

For other lodging in Abingdon, contact the Convention & Visitors Bureau, (800)

435-3440, www.abingdon.com/visitors/lodging/htm.

North of the Mount Rogers area, the town of **Marion** has several motels. Call Smyth County Chamber of Commerce, (276) 783-3161, or visit www.Smythchamber.org.

Grayson Highlands State Park has camping on the southern boundary of the Mount Rogers area, (800) 933-PARK.

Restaurants

Side Track Computer Café, Damascus, VA, (276) 475-6106. A favorite hangout for hikers.

Damascus Old Mill, (276) 475-3745, www.damascusoldmill.com. A recently renovated 1912 mill turned restaurant and sports bar with outdoor seating on the banks of Laurel Creek.

Cowboys, Damascus, VA, (276) 475-5444. This deli, located inside a service station, has great Southern breakfasts.

In the Country, Damascus, VA, (276) 475-5319. Bakery, eatery, and ice cream shop.

Organizations

Appalachian Trail Conference, Harpers Ferry, WV, (304) 535-6331, www.appalachian trail.org.

Virginia's Southwest Blue Ridge Highlands, Inc., Abingdon, VA, (800) 446-9670, www.virginiablueridge.org. A regional tourism agency with information on festivals and attractions throughout southwest Virginia.

Other Resources

The Dying of the Trees, by Charles E. Little, Penguin Books, New York, NY.

Appalachian Trail Guide to Southwest Virginia, Appalachian Trail Conference, Harpers Ferry, WV.

Honorable Mentions

Mount Rogers

Compiled here are great hikes in the Mount Rogers region that didn't make the A-list this time around but deserve recognition. Check them out and let us know what you think. You may decide that one or more of these hikes deserves higher status in future editions or, perhaps, you may have a hike of your own that merits some attention.

62 Four Trails Circuit

Located near Hurricane Campground. Head south of Sugar Grove on Virginia Route 601, turn right onto Virginia Route 650, and then left onto Forest Road 84 to Hurricane Campground. This moderately difficult 9.6-mile loop uses a portion of the Appalachian Trail (AT) and three other trails. Terrain varies from the dry ridgetop of Iron Mountain to cool waterfalls on Comers Creek. Call (800) 628–7202. *DeLorme: Virginia Atlas & Gazetteer:* Page 23, C5.

63 Rowland Creek Falls Circuit

Located west of Sugar Grove. From Virginia Route 16, turn right onto Virginia Route 601, which after 3.5 miles turns into Virginia Route 670 in Teas. Continue on VA 670 for 4.4 miles and then fork left onto Virginia Route 656 (if you pass the Butler Fish Culture Station on the right, you've missed this left turn. Go back 1 mile and look for the turnoff). Stay on VA 656 for 1.7 miles, then turn left onto Virginia Route 668, which turns into dirt Forest Road 643. Park at the first trailhead on the right-hand side. After following Jerry's Creek Trail to Iron Mountain, hikers can return via Rowland Creek or head west and explore Skulls Gap for a total hike of 11.8 miles. Rowland's Creek Falls is a highlight of this trip. Call (800) 628–7202. *DeLorme: Virginia Atlas & Gazetteer:* Page 22, B4.

64 Whitetop Laurel Circuit

From Damascus, take U.S. Highway 58 east and turn right onto Virginia Route 728 to Creek Junction parking lot. This 11.5-mile loop uses portions of the Appalachian Trail (AT) and the Virginia Creeper Trail, and includes a number of crossings over the cascading Whitetop Laurel Creek. Call (800) 628–7202. *DeLorme: Virginia Atlas & Gazetteer:* Page 22, C3. (Also see page 324.)

The Great Escape
The Appalachian Trail
through Virginia

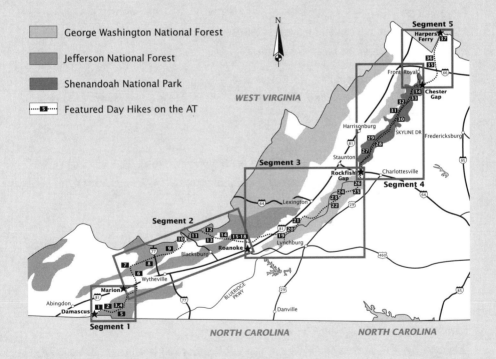

George Washington National Forest

Jefferson National Forest

Shenandoah National Park

····5···· Featured Day Hikes on the AT

TRAVELING GREEN: PUBLIC TRANSPORTATION TO THE AT IN VIRGINIA

The leave no trace ethic goes beyond the trailhead. Choosing not to drive farther reduces the footprint you leave on the environment. Taking a bus or train also eliminates the hassle of shuttling two cars at opposite ends of the trail. Remember that these services are infrequent, so it's best to call ahead and plan carefully. The Appalachian Trail Conference (ATC) also publishes names of drivers who will shuttle thru-hikers and section-hikers to major transportation centers. For more information contact the ATC at (304) 535-6331 or www.appalachiantrail.org.

The major transit carriers that access towns all close to Virginia's AT are Greyhound Bus Lines, (800) 229-9424 or www.greyhound.com, and AMTRAK, (800) 872-7245 or www.amtrak.com. Often you may want to use a combination of the two. AMTRAK can get you to Lynchburg, Staunton, Charlottesville, Culpepper, and Harpers Ferry—all of which provide access, whether by bus or by shuttle, to the AT.

The following towns are accessible by bus or by train and lie within a reasonable walking distance of the AT. This is not a complete list, but it is the most practical.

Abingdon (accesses Segment 1)
Greyhound services Abingdon. It's a 16-mile hike via the Virginia Creeper Trail to accesss the AT in Damascus. Or, you can seek out one of the several private shuttle services in town, which will take you directly to the Damascus trailhead.

Roanoke (accesses Segment 2)
Greyhound services Roanoke. It's 7 miles to the AT trailhead at the U.S. Highway 220 crossing. Local taxi services will take you there.

Buena Vista (accesses Segment 3)
Greyhound has limited services to Buena Vista (no ticketing available). It's 5 miles up Virginia Route 607 (east) to the Blue Ridge Parkway (south) to access the AT trailhead. Local taxi services will take you there.

Roseland (accesses Segment 3)
JAUNT commuter van services Roseland from Charlottesville weekdays, during commuting times only. Call (434) 296-3184 or visit www.commuterinformation.com for rates and schedules. Once in Roseland, it's a 5-mile walk up Virginia Route 56 to the AT trailhead at the Tye River swinging bridge.

Waynesboro (accesses Segment 4)
Greyhound services Waynesboro. It's 4 miles up U.S. Highway 250 (east) to the AT trailhead at Rockfish Gap. Local taxi services will take you there.

Harpers Ferry (accesses Segment 5)
AMTRAK services Harpers Ferry, with connections to Washington, Pittsburgh, and Chicago. From Washington, D.C., hikers can take the more frequent (and cheaper) MARC commuter rail, (866) RIDE–MTA or www.mtamaryland.com. From the train station in Harpers Ferry, take a left onto Potomac Street and head down to Shenandoah Street, where you'll find the AT.

The Appalachian Trail through Virginia

It takes a northbound thru-hiker about six weeks to reach Virginia on the Appalachian Trail. Once here, there are another six weeks of difficult and rewarding trail ahead before the hiker exits Virginia at Harpers Ferry. The Old Dominion holds nearly a quarter of the AT's 2,173 miles—more miles than any other state along the trail. A half-million day hikers hit Virginia's portion of the AT each year. Most follow the south-north direction we've chosen to feature. Since hiking the entire length of the trail is a luxury most of us cannot afford, we've included a list of suggested day hikes or short overnight trips that capture Virginia's greatest natural highlights. And so, whether you choose one long trip, or small bite sizes, plan on a showcase of some of the East's most beautiful mountain scenery.

Start: Damascus, VA.
End: Harpers Ferry, WV.
Distance: 549.1 miles.
Approximate hiking time: 40 days.
Difficulty rating: Difficult.
Trail surface: The trail climbs Virginia's highest mountain range; crosses the Great Valley and a succession of steep, narrow ridges and valleys; rejoins the Blue Ridge crest; crosses several steep, outlying mountains; parallels Skyline Drive through Shenandoah National Park; and, from Stony Man, descends through the northern Blue Ridge to the Potomac River.
Land status: National scenic trail.
Other trail users: Hikers only.
Canine compatibility: Dogs permitted (must be on a leash in Mount Rogers National Recreation Area and in Shenandoah National Park).

GREAT RESOURCES FOR HIKING THE AT

- Appalachian Trail Guides - available for purchase from the ATC at (800) AT-STORE or at www.atctrailstore.org.
- Appalachian Trail Thru-hikers' Companion - available for $3.50 from the ATC at (800) AT-STORE.
- *Story Line: Exploring the Literature of the Appalachian Trail,* by Ian Marshall, University Press of Virginia.
- MAPTECH Appalachian Trail set - An exhaustive resource, with digital coverage of the entire AT, featuring complete versions of official AT guides. Visit www.maptech.com for more information.
- *A Walk in the Woods,* by Bill Bryson, Broadway Books.
- *A Walk for Sunshine,* by Jeff Alt, Dreams Shared Publications.

Segment 1 Damascus to Marion

As an introduction to Virginia, it's hard to top Mount Rogers National Recreation Area. The Appalachian Trail passes near the tallest mountains in the state. Close to the summit of Mount Rogers, wild ponies graze in the high-country meadows. There are steep climbs up Iron Mountain, past small waterfalls and tunnels of rhododendron. The hike seems over too soon. Longer lasting are memories of wide-open sky, jagged rock outcrops, and a refreshing dip below the falls on Comers Creek.

Start: From the Damascus Town Hall.
Distance: 63.8-mile point-to-point.
Difficulty rating: Difficult.
Trail surface: Using dirt footpaths and abandoned dirt roads, hike along rocky peaks, cliffs, and steep ridges, through deep valley hollows, and across high-altitude meadows.
Nearest towns: Damascus, VA (south access); Marion, VA (north access).
Canine compatibility: Dogs permitted (must be on a leash in the Mount Rogers National Recreation Area).

Trail contacts: Appalachian Trail Conference, Harpers Ferry, WV, (304) 535-6331, www.appalachiantrail.org.
Piedmont Appalachian Trail Hikers, www.path-at.org.
Mount Rogers Appalachian Trail Club, Abingdon, VA, www.geocities.com/Yosemite/Geyser/2539.
Maps: ATC map #1: Mount Rogers National Recreation Area.

Finding the trailhead: To the Damascus Trailhead
In Damascus, locate the Damascus Town Hall, 208 West Laurel Avenue, between Smith Street and Reynolds Avenue. You can use on-street parking or park at Mount Rogers Outfitters, 110 West Laurel Avenue—there's a $2.00 per-day fee and a shower available. Begin walking east on Laurel Avenue (U.S. Highway 58). *DeLorme: Virginia Atlas & Gazetteer:* Page 22, C2.
To Marion Trailhead (See Segment 2: Marion to Roanoke.)

The Hike

A few miles north of the Tennessee-Virginia border, the Appalachian Trail (AT) wraps around Holston Mountain, part of the Iron Mountain range, and descends into Damascus. The small town, first visible from an overlook high atop the ridge, bills itself as the "friendliest town on the AT." Its downtown strip, Laurel Avenue, doubles as the trail route. Shopkeepers and restaurants welcome AT hikers as friends. The hospitality really shows itself each May during the Appalachian Trail Days festival, when hundreds of hikers converge on Damascus and swap stories about the 2,173-mile trail.

Surrounding Damascus is scenery unlike any you've seen in Virginia. In Mount Rogers National Recreation Area (NRA), herds of wild ponies roam expansive mountain meadows. A strong spruce-fir scent lingers around the tree-capped Mount

View of Mount Rogers high-country meadow from the Appalachian Trail.

Rogers (5,729 feet), Virginia's tallest peak. Colorful mushrooms and large patches of wild berries brighten the slope and crest of Iron Mountain. Rhododendron's pink and purple blooms seem ever-present in June. Turks cap lily, orange and delicate, is one of an array of wildflowers seen spring through fall.

The route north from Damascus begins with a 1,000-foot ascent of Feathercamp Ridge. The next 14 miles of AT bring two more steep climbs up Straight Mountain and Lost Mountain. Between each ridge, rhododendrons choke stream valleys cut by Straight Branch and Whitetop Laurel Creek. As the AT climbs and descends each ridge, flashes of yellow and red amid the drab-colored leaf rot signal mushroom colonies. Chanterelle, waxy caps, and a host of other types grow along the trail. Occasionally, a view of the rooftop of Virginia, as the high country is nicknamed, breaks out through the heavy oak forest atop the ridges.

From Elk Garden, the AT begins an ascent past Virginia's three tallest mountains—Mount Rogers, Whitetop, and Pine. All three peaks exceed 5,000 feet, and the AT slips past without actually crossing any of them. Whitetop Mountain (5,520 feet) has a road leading to its top. When the Virginia Creeper Railroad operated one hundred years ago, the Whitetop station had the distinction of being the highest railroad depot east of the Rockies. Past Whitetop, the AT enters Lewis Fork Wilderness, which surrounds and covers Mount Rogers. Elevation is above 5,000 feet, and the forested summit of Mount Rogers appears a mere bulge in the high ridge. A spur trail leads a half mile from the AT up to Rogers's summit area. It's a cool, moist

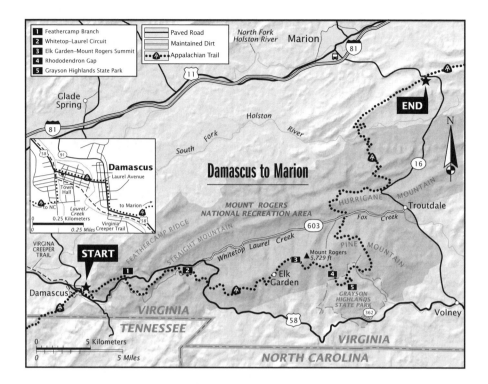

woodland that covers Mount Rogers, with dangling bunches of moss and rotted logs everywhere. Many of the trees, plants, and animals at the summit are vestiges of a northern forest environment that developed here during the last glacial period in North America some 10,000 years ago.

Pine Mountain, the third in Mount Rogers NRA's triumvirate of 5,000-foot peaks, is a series of rocky promontories rising sharply from the sweeping meadows. This gray-purplish rock is rhyolite, formed 800 million years ago when the Blue Ridge was volcanically active. The trail passes several jagged piles of rock on Wilburn Ridge, then disappears into tunnels of rhododendron. When the AT

AT SHELTERS/HUTS (mileage on the AT north from Damascus to Virginia Route 16)

Mile 9.4 – Saunders Shelter

Mile 15.8 – Lost Mountain Shelter

Mile 28.0 – Thomas Knob Shelter

Mile 33.1 – Wise Shelter

Mile 39.0 – Old Orchard Shelter

Mile 50.7 – Raccoon Branch Shelter

Mile 53.2 – Trimpi Shelter

Mile 63.7 – Partnership Shelter

re-enters meadows, stunted hawthorn trees offer shade and a rest spot for watching wild horses graze. Meadow grass grows knee-high. Wildflowers wash the fields with orange and red. The meadows are burned regularly by the Forest Service in order to hold back total reforestation, creating conditions ideal for fireweed. Were it not for the fires, a new forest of hardwoods would reclaim the meadows.

A descent from Scales (an old cattle-weighing station dating back one hundred years) to Fox Creek signals the end of the Mount Rogers high country. From Fox Creek, the AT climbs again to the crest of Iron Mountain (4,200 feet). Yellow blossoms of the Indian cucumber root put on a spring show along streams. Absent its blooms, which appear in May and June, the cucumber root is identified by a distinct double-decker whorl of leaves. The tuber is edible, but should only be collected if they're found in abundance. As it crosses Iron Mountain Trail (which used to be the AT until it was relocated), the AT follows sections of old logging roads. There's little in the way of forest canopy, but the constant exposure to sunlight makes the blackberries that grow along the trail especially plump and juicy, much like the huckleberries that grow off the trail in the high-country meadows.

The route north from Iron Mountain might seem anticlimactic when compared with the high country; that is, until the AT crosses Comers Creek. As it runs down Hurricane Mountain, the stream forms a 10-foot waterfall. There's a small swimming hole here that is popular with hikers. It's a nice spot to tarry, dip your feet in cool water, and contemplate the remaining 483 miles of Virginia's AT.

Boulders on Stone Mountain.

Rock outcrop at the head of Pine Mountain Trail on Mount Rogers.

Miles and Directions

0.0   **START** at Damascus Town Hall and head east on Laurel Avenue, following US 58/Virginia Route 91 out of town.

1.0   Turn left off US 58 and enter the woods. Look for the white blazes on the left, or westbound side, of US 58.

3.5   Turn right and descend. (FYI: Blue-blazed connector trail leads to yellow-blazed Iron Mountain Trail.)

5.6   Cross US 58. Immediately descend to Straight Branch and cross. After crossing, turn right and follow Straight Branch downstream.

9.4   **Shelter** 🛈 Pass a side trail that leads left 300 yards to Saunders Shelter.

11.7   Pass a T junction with Bear Tree Gap–Shaw Gap Trail on the left; continue straight on the AT.

14.0   Cross the Luther Hassinger Memorial Bridge over Green Cove and Whitetop Laurel Creeks. (FYI: The bridge is named in honor of a lumberman who clear-cut the woodland around Damascus in the early 1900s.)

15.8   **Shelter** 🛈 Pass Lost Mountain Shelter on the right.

20.6   Reach Buzzard Rock with views of Iron Mountain to the north, and Grandfather Mountain (North Carolina) to the south. Follow the AT as it descends off Buzzard Rock and skirts an open area below the summit of Whitetop Mountain.

21.3   Cross Whitetop Road and enter the woods on the opposite side. (FYI: Whitetop Road leads left uphill to the top of Whitetop Mountain [5,520 feet].)

24.4   Enter Lewis Fork Wilderness Area; continue climbing on the AT.

27.6   Turn right at a T junction with the Mount Rogers Spur Trail. A few feet past this junction, exit Lewis Fork Wilderness. (FYI: The Mount Rogers Spur Trail leads 0.5 mile to the tree-shrouded summit of Mount Rogers [5,729 feet]).

28.0   **Shelter** 🛈 Pass the Thomas Knob Shelter on the right.

29.8   Cross through the open fields. Wilburn Ridge rises to points of exposed rock to the right.

30.4   Enter Grayson Highlands State Park by passing over a wooden fence.

33.1   **Shelter** 🛈 Pass Wise Shelter on the right. In 0.1 mile, exit Grayson Highlands State Park and re-enter Mount Rogers NRA.

35.6   Cross Stone Mountain. (FYI: Wild horses graze in the open meadows that cover this mountain.)

35.1   Descend to Scales, a corralled campground open to four-wheel-drive vehicle traffic via Virginia Route 613. Walk around the campsite and follow the AT as it climbs Pine Mountain.

39.0   **Shelter** 🛈 Pass the Old Orchard Shelter.

40.7   Cross Virginia Route 603. On the opposite side, cross Fox Creek.

47.1   At a T junction with a blue-blazed trail, turn right and climb. (Campground: The blue-blazed trail leads 0.5 mile to Hurricane Campground.)

48.0   Cross Comers Creek at the base of a 10-foot waterfall.

50.7   **Shelter** 🛈 Pass a blue-blazed trail that branches right to the Raccoon Branch Shelter.

51.3 Continue straight past a blue-blazed trail that branches right to a view off High Point (4,040 feet).

53.2 At a fork in the trail, bear left on the AT. **Shelter** ➤ A blue-blazed trail leads right to Trimpi Shelter in 0.1 mile.

55.9 Cross the South Fork Holston River on a 12-foot-long footbridge.

63.7 **Shelter** ➤ Pass the Partnership Shelter.

63.8 Hike ends at VA 16 in front of the Mount Rogers Visitor Center.

Hike Information

Local Information

Damascus Web site: www.damascus.org.
Abingdon Convention & Visitors Bureau, Abingdon, VA, (800) 435-3440, www.abingdon.com/tourism.

Local Events/Attractions

Appalachian Trail Days, May, Damascus, VA, www.traildays.org.

Lodging

The Place, 200 East Laurel Avenue, Damascus, VA, (276) 475–5572. Run by the Damascus United Methodist Church, the hostel accommodates roughly thirty-five hikers with tent space in the yard. Has hot showers but no heat. Open seasonally, usually April 1 to November 1. Donations appreciated.

Segment 2 Marion to Roanoke

The Appalachian Trail through southwest Virginia forsakes the Blue Ridge for the valley and ridge region, but loses none of the beauty or steep climbs. Open cliffs on Tinker Mountain and overlooks from McAfee Knob and Dragons Tooth are popular day hikes. More remote are Wind Rocks in Mountain Lake Wilderness, or a perch on Angels Rest, near Pearisburg, with views of the New River. It's been sixty-plus years since volunteers moved the AT off the Blue Ridge, in hopes of saving the trail's remote character. It's safe to say they succeeded.

Start: From the Mount Rogers Visitor Center.
Distance: 190.3-mile point-to-point.
Difficulty rating: Difficult.
Trail surface: Using dirt footpaths and abandoned dirt roads, hike along steep ridge crests, through deep valley hollows and bogs, and across high-altitude meadows.
Nearest towns: Marion, VA (south access); Roanoke, VA (north access).
Canine compatibility: Dogs permitted.
Trail contacts: Appalachian Trail Conference, Harpers Ferry, WV, (304) 535-6331, www.appalachiantrail.org.

Roanoke ATC, c/o Bob Peckman, (540) 366-7780.
Outdoor Club at Virginia Tech, filebox.vt.edu/org/outing/.
Piedmont Appalachian Trail Hikers, www.path-at.org.
Mount Rogers National Recreation Area Headquarters, Marion, VA, (276) 783-5196, www.southernregion.fs.fed.us/gwj.
Maps: ATC map #2: Wythe Ranger District; ATC map #3: Blacksburg Ranger District.

Finding the trailhead: To Marion Trailhead
From Marion, proceed south on Virginia Route 16 to the Mount Rogers Visitor Center (6 miles from VA 16's junction with I-81). Turn right into the visitor center parking lot and park. Follow a sidewalk to the front of the visitor center, walk to VA 16, and cross the highway. The Appalachian Trail (AT) enters the woods on the northbound side of VA 16. *DeLorme: Virginia Atlas & Gazetteer:* Page 23, B5.
To Roanoke Trailhead (See Segment 3: Roanoke to Rockfish Gap.)

The Hike

From the point where it leaves the Great Valley, north of the Mount Rogers National Recreation Area, the AT crosses seven mountain ridges. Little Brushy Mountain is the first. Beyond it stand Big Walker, Lynn Camp, and Garden Mountain. Each ridge rises sharply, then drops into stream valleys. Crawfish Valley, at the base of Big Walker, is secluded and overgrown. Across Big Walker, Rich Valley is wide and busy, with the North Fork Holston River and Virginia Route 42 running along its bottomland.

The AT passing through Mount Rogers National Recreation Area.

Burkes Garden breaks the valley and ridge pattern in scenic fashion. Garden Mountain forms the southern boundary of this bowl-shaped valley, and the AT follows its crest for 5 miles. At Chestnut Knob and again at Davis Field Campsite, views west drop 900 feet into the valley, which formed millions of years ago when a basement rock of limestone eroded and washed away. The resulting claylike soil makes for prime farmland. Local lore says James Burke, the first white man to settle in the Garden, tossed a few potato peels on the ground during his first visit here in the mid-1700s. The next season, Burke returned and found potato plants. True or not, a small community of farmers continues a tradition of farming that dates back centuries. They've also managed to keep the commercial world at bay, with prohibitions on billboards and neon signs.

Northwest of Burkes Garden, the AT crosses three more ridges. On the last, Pearis Mountain, an overlook called Angels Rest provides beautiful views across the New River to the slope of Peters Mountain. The AT crosses the New on a highway bridge and follows Stillhouse Branch up the steep side of Peters Mountain. On the ridgetop, the West Virginia border and AT crisscross for 12 miles through grass fields and a portion of the Peters Mountain Wilderness.

Like Catawba Mountain to the north, which derives its name from the Catawba rhododendron, Peters Mountain shares its name with a plant. Peters Mountain mallow grows only in Giles County, Virginia. The single known community of this purple-blossoming herb is protected on land owned by The Nature Conservancy. The AT is partly to blame for its earlier decline. In the late 1960s, a section of the trail ran along the mountain's sandstone outcrops, a favored habitat of the mallow. Heavy foot traffic took its toll. Virginia and the federal government now list the plant as endangered. What communities exist are fenced in and tended carefully. Trail relocation remedied encroachment by AT hikers.

The descent off Peters Mountain marks a turn in the AT. Its direction is now once again northeast, a course that will eventually intersect with the Blue Ridge Mountains, beyond Roanoke. For the intervening 74 miles, the AT crosses eight more ridges, each with a corresponding stream valley. The first, Potts Mountain, caps out at a rocky point called Wind Rocks in Mountain Lake Wilderness. The 10,753-acre federal wilderness, like Burkes Garden, is a welcome respite to the valley-and-ridge routine. Gently graded trail leads across two flat-topped mountains, Salt Pond and Lone Pine, and their upland bogs. The descent off Salt Pond steepens and ends at Johns Creek. In quick succession, the AT then crosses Johns Creek, Sinking Creek, Brush, and Cove Mountains. Cove Mountain makes a U shape around the headwaters of Trout Creek and rises to the pointed, skin-your-knee-rough rock on Dragons Tooth.

The wide valley east of Dragons Tooth is part of the Great Valley system that runs down the Appalachian chain from southern New Jersey into Tennessee. Views of Roanoke, the largest city in southwest Virginia, signal the approaching end of this leg of the AT.

Before leaving the valley and ridge region, the AT crosses Tinker Cliffs. Blocks of sandstone in Devils Kitchen and the overhangs at Snack Bar Rock and Rock Haven make striking formations. Tinker Cliffs itself is reminiscent of another high-mountain ridge, Pine Mountain, on the Virginia-Kentucky border. Like Pine Mountain, the edge of Tinker and Catawba Mountains were, millions of years ago, a leading edge of a thrust fault—essentially a piece of the earth's crust that slid up and over another piece of the earth. The resulting topography is steep and often sheer to the west, while more graded and sloping eastward.

The subdivisions and farms visible on the last 6.5 miles of the AT signal the descent into the Great Valley. From a final rock outcrop, Hay Rock, the view reaches west across the heavily populated valley to the Blue Ridge, and another leg of the AT.

Miles and Directions

0.0 **START** at the Mount Rogers Visitor Center. Cross VA 16 and enter the woods on the opposite side of the visitor center, following white blazes.

4.1 Cross Forest Road 86 and re-enter woods on the opposite side. (FYI: A spring is located 100 yards on FR 86 to the right.)

7.0 **Shelter** ▰ Pass Chatfield Shelter.

11.5 Trail empties onto U.S. Highway 11. Turn right and hike east along the highway. Turn left onto Virginia Route 638 and cross under I-81. Follow the AT as it enters a field on the right side of VA 638 after passing under I-81.

14.2 **Shelter** ▰ Come to Davis Path Shelter. Turn right at the shelter and climb on the AT.

17.8 Descend off Brushy Mountain into a clearing and campsite in Crawfish Valley. (FYI: See Hike 28 for a detailed description of the Crawfish/Channel Rock loop hike.)

25.4 **Shelter** ▰ Come to Knot Maul Branch Shelter. Turn right at the shelter. After crossing several streams, climb Lynn Camp Mountain.

29.8 Begin ascent of Chestnut Mountain. The AT here traces a border of Beartown Wilderness. (FYI: See the Great Day Hikes along the Appalachian Trail section for a brief description of this hike.) **Shelter** ▰ At the summit of Chestnut Mountain, pass the Chestnut Knob Shelter.

36.7 Follow the ridgetop of Garden Mountain as it traces a rim of Burkes Garden. (FYI: The summit of Garden Mountain (4,052 feet) offers more views of Burkes Garden.)

41.4 Pass a blue-blazed trail that branches left 0.5 mile to Davis Farm Campsite; continue straight on the AT.

44.4 **Shelter** ▰ Pass Jenkins Shelter on the left.

48.9 Cross Virginia Route 615; enter the woods on the opposite side and climb. (FYI: The Trail Boss Trail begins 100 yards to the left on VA 615. See the Great Day Hikes along the Appalachian Trail section for a brief description of a loop hike using Trail Boss and the AT.)

55.9 Turn left onto paved U.S. Highway 21/52 and follow the road downhill. In 0.2 mile, follow Virginia Route 612 straight as US 21/52 makes a hard left switchback. Cross I-77 on a road bridge. At a fork on the opposite side of the bridge, bear right onto a gravel road.

56.7 Turn right off the gravel road and enter woods on white-blazed AT.

58.2 **Shelter** 🏕 Pass a trail on the right that leads 0.3 mile to Helveys Mill Shelter.

68.0 **Shelter** 🏕 Pass Jenny Knob Shelter on the right.

69.2 Turn left onto paved Virginia Route 608 and hike 0.1 mile. Cross the road and enter woods at the back of a small gravel parking lot, following white blazes.

76.9 Pass White Pine Horse Camp. (FYI: There is a hand pump for water located in the camp.)

80.0 Cross Dismal Creek; hike past blue-blazed Ribble Trail on the left; continue straight on the AT.

82.2 **Shelter** 🏕 Pass a blue-blazed trail that branches right and leads 100 yards to Wapiti Shelter. Continue straight as the AT climbs Sugar Run Mountain.

86.7 Proceed straight through a four-way intersection with the blue-blazed Ribble Trail. (FYI: The Ribble Trail leads right to Honey Spring Picnic Area.)

90.6 **Shelter** 🏕 Pass Doc's Knob Shelter.

96.4 Pass a blue-blazed trail on the left; continue straight on the AT. (FYI: The blue-blazed trail leads 100 yards to Angels Rest. See the Great Day Hikes along the Appalachian Trail section for a brief description of this hike.)

97.9 After a steep descent, cross paved Virginia Route 634. Cross a fence stile on the opposite side. Pass a blue-blazed trail that branches right. (FYI: The blue-blazed trail leads to downtown Pearisburg in 1 mile.)

98.9 Cross the New River on the Senator Shumate Bridge (U.S. Highway 460). At the opposite side, turn right and cross US 460. Follow a paved road 80 yards, then turn left onto a gravel road.

AT SHELTERS/HUTS (mileage on the AT from VA 16 north to U.S. Highway 220)

Mile 0.0 – Partnership Shelter (at Mount Rogers Visitor Center on VA 16)

Mile 7.0 – Chatfield Shelter

Mile 14.2 – Davis Path Shelter

Mile 25.4 – Knot Maul Branch Shelter

Mile 34.4 – Chestnut Knob Shelter

Mile 44.4 – Jenkins Shelter

Mile 58.2 – Helveys Mill Shelter

Mile 68 – Jenny Knob Shelter

Mile 82.2 – Wapiti Shelter

Mile 90.6 – Doc's Knob Shelter

Mile 105.7 – Rice Field Shelter (also called Star Haven Shelter)

Mile 118.0 – Pine Swamp Branch Shelter

Mile 121.9 – Bailey Gap Shelter

Mile 130.7 – War Spur Shelter

Mile 136.5 – Laurel Creek Shelter

Mile 142.9 – Sarver Hollow Shelter

Mile 148.9 – Niday Shelter

Mile 157.8 – Pickle Branch Shelter

Mile 171.7 – Boy Scout Shelter

Mile 172.7 – Catawba Mountain Shelter

Mile 174.9 – Campbell Shelter

Mile 180.9 – Lamberts Meadow Shelter

105.1 Enter the Rice Fields atop Peters Mountain. (FYI: See the Great Day Hikes along the Appalachian Trail section for a brief description of this hike.)

105.7 **Shelter** 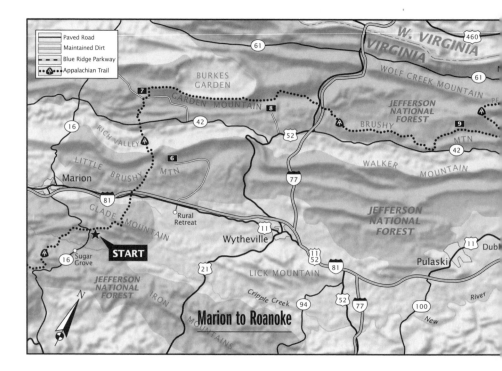 Pass Rice Field Shelter (also called Star Haven Shelter) on the left.

115.5 Reach a fork with the yellow-blazed Allegheny Trail, which enters from the left; bear right on the AT and descend Peters Mountain. (FYI: See Hike 26 for a detailed description of trails in this section of Peters Mountain.)

118.0 **Shelter** Pass Pine Swamp Branch Shelter on the right.

120.4 Cross Stony Creek, and, in 100 yards, cross paved Virginia Route 635.

121.9 **Shelter** Pass Bailey Gap Shelter on the left.

125.6 Cross gravel Virginia Route 613 and enter Mountain Lake Wilderness. In 0.3 mile, pass Wind Rock on the right. Bear right on the AT as it skirts the east slope of Potts Mountain.

128.7 Turn left at a T intersection. (Note: The War Spur Connector Trail leads right to a parking area on VA 613. See Hike 27: Mountain Lake Wilderness for a detailed description of hikes in the wilderness.)

130.7 **Shelter** Pass War Spur Shelter on the left. The trail descends and crosses Johns Creek in 0.8 mile.

134.0 Johns Creek Trail branches left off the AT; continue straight. (Note: Blue-blazed Johns Creek Trail leads 3.5 miles to Virginia Route 658.)

135.3 Pass a trail on the right that leads 100 yards to overlooks on White Rock; continue straight on the AT. In 0.3 mile, reach the summit of Kelly Knob. (FYI: See the Great Day Hikes along the Appalachian Trail section for a brief description of this hike.)

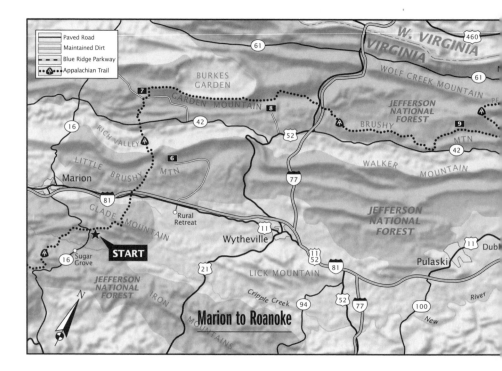

Marion to Roanoke

136.5 **Shelter** Pass Laurel Creek Shelter on the right. Descend on the AT to cross Sinking Creek.

142.9 **Shelter** After climbing Sinking Creek Mountain, pass a blue-blazed trail that leads right 0.3 mile to Sarver Hollow Shelter.

148.9 **Shelter** Pass a trail that leads 50 yards right to Niday Shelter.

150.2 Cross paved Virginia Route 621 and enter woods on the other side, following white blazes. The AT soon crosses Craig Creek and climbs Brush Mountain.

154.0 Pass a blue-blazed trail that climbs left to the Audie Murphy VFW Monument; continue straight on the AT. (FYI: See the Great Day Hikes along the Appalachian Trail section for a brief description of this hike.)

157.8 After crossing Virginia Route 620, begin ascent of Cove Mountain. **Shelter** In 1 mile, pass a blue-blazed trail that leads right for 0.5 mile to the Pickle Branch Shelter.

161.4 At a T junction, turn left and begin a difficult descent on the AT past Devils Seat and Rawies Rest. At this junction, a blue-blazed trail continues straight to Dragons Tooth in 200 yards. (FYI: See the Great Day Hikes along the Appalachian Trail section for a brief description of this hike.)

166.5 Cross Catawba Creek and begin an ascent of Catawba Mountain. At the top, the AT turns left and traces the ridge crest.

170.7 Descend steeply and cross Virginia Route 311. On the opposite side of the highway, enter the woods, following white blazes.

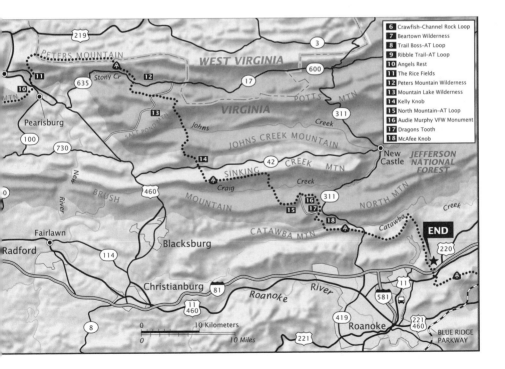

View from Mount Pleasant.

171.7 **Shelter** Pass Boy Scout Shelter.

172.7 **Shelter** Pass Catawba Mountain Shelter on the right.

174.2 After a difficult, rocky climb, reach the summit of McAfee Knob. (FYI: See the Great Day Hikes along the Appalachian Trail section for a brief description of this hike.)

174.9 **Shelter** Pass Campbell Shelter on the right.

179.8 Begin a traverse of Tinker Cliffs.

180.9 **Shelter** Pass Lamberts Meadow Shelter on the right. The next 7 miles trace the ridge of Tinker Mountain, past Julius Knob, Chimney Rocks, and Hay Rock.

190.3 Hike ends at U.S. Highway 220.

Hike Information

Local Information

Roanoke Valley Convention & Visitors Bureau, Roanoke, VA, (800) 635-5535, www. VisitRoanokeVA.com.

Montgomery County Chamber of Commerce, Blacksburg, VA, (540) 552-4503, (540) 382-4010, www.montgomerycc.org.

Segment 3 Roanoke to Rockfish Gap

The Appalachian Trail once ran the crest of the Blue Ridge from Roanoke north to Rockfish Gap, until construction of the Blue Ridge Parkway pushed sections onto outlying peaks. That's good news for hikers who like climbing. From heights of 4,000 feet atop The Priest and Cold Mountain, the trail descends to an elevation of 659 feet at the James River. The Blue Ridge, Virginia's oldest mountains, show weathered knobs of resistant bedrock at Humpback Rocks, Spy Rock, and Fullers Rocks. Views from each seem better than the last.

Start: From the shoulder of U.S. Highway 220 west of I–81.

Distance: 133.4-mile point-to-point.

Difficulty rating: Difficult.

Trail surface: Using dirt footpaths and abandoned dirt roads, hike along ridge crests, peaks, and rock outcrops; through open meadows, virgin hemlock, and the James River Gorge.

Nearest towns: Roanoke, VA (south access); Waynesboro, VA (north access).

Canine compatibility: Dogs permitted.

Trail contacts: Appalachian Trail Conference, Harpers Ferry, WV, (304) 535-6331, www.appalachiantrail.org.
Old Dominion ATC, www.odatc.org.
Tidewater ATC, www.tidewateratc.com.
Natural Bridge ATC, www.nbatc.org.
Shenandoah National Park, Luray, VA, (540) 999-3500, www.nps.gov/shen.
George Washington and Jefferson National Forests, www.southernregion.fs.fed.us/gwj.

Maps: ATC map #4: Glenwood Ranger District/Newcastle Ranger District; ATC map #5: Pedlar Ranger District.

Finding the trailhead: To Roanoke Trailhead
From Roanoke: Drive north on combined I–581/US 220 to I–81 north. Drive north on the combined routes of I–81/US 220 for 6 miles and take exit 150. Turn left at the bottom of the exit ramp onto US 220. In 0.2 mile, turn left onto Virginia Route 816 and park in the park-and-ride lot. Walk the few steps back to US 220 and turn left (north). In 0.2 mile, reach the Appalachian Trail (AT) where it crosses US 220. *DeLorme: Virginia Atlas & Gazetteer:* Page 42, B3.

To Rockfish Gap Trailhead (See Segment 4: Rockfish Gap to Chester Gap.)

The Hike

The AT route north of Roanoke begins with a steep climb up Fullhardt Knob. In Tollhouse Gap, the main trunk of the Blue Ridge is visible slightly east. It will be another 10 miles before the trail and the mountain crest intersect at the Blue Ridge Parkway, a scenic highway that runs south into the North Carolina Smokies.

Like Skyline Drive in Shenandoah National Park to the north, construction of the Blue Ridge Parkway followed a route AT volunteers blazed decades earlier. Subsequent trail relocations moved the AT off the main Blue Ridge. On the outlying

A spectacular view from the AT in Shenandoah National Park.

mountains, like The Priest and Three Ridges, the AT gains and loses 3,000 feet in elevation in a few miles. Bumpy terrain—AT thru-hikers call them PUDs *(pointless up-and-downs)*—along Cove Mountain's ten small knobs are punishing, as are the short sprints up Spy Rock and Humpback Rocks.

The newest section of AT falls within James River Face Wilderness. The James is Virginia's longest river, running 450 miles from its mountain headwaters into Hampton Roads harbor on the Chesapeake Bay. Between Buena Vista and Lynchburg, the river breaches the Blue Ridge in a deep gorge. Land south of the river falls inside Virginia's first and largest wilderness area, the James River Face. Inside the wilderness boundaries the newly constructed AT follows tall river cliffs and a scenic stream, Matts Creek. A pedestrian footbridge across the James, opened in 2000, made the relocation possible. The footbridge honors the memory of Bill Foot, a Natural Bridge ATC president who pioneered construction of the James River Foot Bridge, but passed away before seeing it completed.

On the north bank of the James River, the AT enters the Pedlar district of the George Washington/Jefferson National Forest. A series of fires dating from the 1890s, including one as recently as 1963, consumed thousands of acres of woodland in this area. The 1963 fire stopped at Little Rocky Row (reached via twenty-one switchbacks out of the gorge). It's here, from a vista on Fullers Rocks, that the last—and perhaps best—view of the James and the gorge unfolds south and west. More climbing awaits for northbound hikers to Bluff Mountain (3,372 feet) and Rice

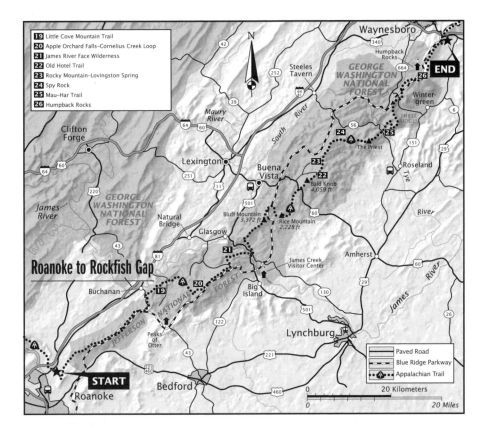

Mountain, (2,228 feet). Past Rice Mountain, the trail gains 2,000 feet to the summit of Bald Knob (4,059 feet), which is actually crowned with a healthy head of trees. After dipping into Cow Camp Gap, the AT climbs again to Cold Mountain (4,022 feet), a grassy peak once grazed by livestock. The Forest Service, swayed by the beautiful views from the peak, keeps it clear with controlled burns.

The view from Cold Mountain includes the Religious Range—a series of peaks named by Robert Rose, a large landowner in the area. There is The Priest and Little Priest, as well as the Friar and Cardinal Ridge. The Priest stands within Virginia's newest wilderness area, designated in 2000. Because of the prohibition on mechanical tools for trail maintenance in a wilderness, the board of the Natural Bridge ATC opposed this initiative. Instead, they sought a special management area designation, like that which covers Mount Pleasant. Special management areas offer similar protection as wilderness, but with relaxed rules that allow chain saws. But wilderness advocates prevailed, and, in November 2000, President Clinton announced creation of Virginia's seventeenth wilderness, The Priest–Three Ridges Wilderness Area.

Humpback Rocks (3,080 feet) is the AT's last hurrah before it descends to Rock-fish Gap and enters the Shenandoah National Park. With views in all directions, it's a perfect spot to get a glimpse of how far you've come. And what lies ahead.

Miles and Directions

0.0. **START** on the shoulder of US 220 west of I-81. Cross the highway to the northbound side and enter the woods, following white blazes.

2.6 Begin a series of switchbacks up the side of Fullhardt Knob leading to Tollhouse Gap.

5.0 **Shelter** 🏠 Pass a blue-blazed trail that leads right to Fullhardt Knob Shelter. Continue on the white-blazed AT.

8.6 Curry Creek intersects the AT on the left; continue straight on the AT.

11.2 **Shelter** 🏠 Pass a trail on the left that leads to Wilson Creek Shelter.

13.6 Cross Forest Road 186 and enter woods on the opposite side. (FYI: To the left as you cross FR 186, in 100 yards, is the Blue Ridge Parkway [milepost 97.7].)

14.4 Cross the Blue Ridge Parkway at Taylors Mountain Overlook. The AT and parkway run beside one another and cross several times for the next 6.7 miles.

18.5 **Shelter** 🏠 Pass a blue-blazed trail on the left that leads 0.2 mile downhill to Bobbletts Gap Shelter. Continue straight on the AT.

19.2 Cross the parkway at the overlook (milepost 92.5).

21.7 At Bearwallow Gap, the AT and parkway separate. Follow the AT as it branches left to follow the ridge of Cove Mountain. (FYI: The Blue Ridge Parkway continues along the main ridge of the Blue Ridge to Peaks of Otter Recreation Area in 4.9 miles. There is a restaurant, lodge, bathrooms, and campground.)

23.5 Pass Little Cove Mountain Trail, a blue-blazed trail that branches right off the AT. (FYI: See the Great Day Hikes along the Appalachian Trail section for more information on a loop hike using Little Cove Mountain Trail.)

24.9 **Shelter** 🏠 Pass Cove Mountain Shelter on the right.

28.1 Descend off Cove Mountain; cross Virginia Route 614 and, soon after, cross Jennings Creek. Past the creek, the AT climbs Fork Mountain (2,042 feet).

AT SHELTERS/HUTS (mileage on the AT from US 220 north to Rockfish Gap)

Mile 5.0 – Fullhardt Knob Shelter

Mile 11.2 – Wilson Creek Shelter

Mile 18.5 – Bobbletts Gap Shelter

Mile 24.9 – Cove Mountain Shelter

Mile 31.8 – Bryant Ridge Shelter

Mile 36.8 – Cornelius Creek Shelter

Mile 42.1 – Thunder Hill Shelter

Mile 54.5 – Matts Creek Shelter

Mile 58.4 – Johns Hollow Shelter

Mile 67.2 – Punchbowl Shelter

Mile 76.0 – Brown Mountain Creek Shelter

Mile 91.8 – Seeley-Woodworth Shelter

Mile 99.2 – The Priest Shelter

Mile 106.1 – Harpers Creek Shelter

Mile 112.3 – Maupin Field Shelter

Mile 128.4 – Paul C. Wolfe Shelter

A view from Cold Mountain.

31.8 **Shelter** Bryant Ridge Shelter. From this clearing, follow the AT right and uphill as it ascends Bryant Ridge and Floyd Mountain.

36.8 **Shelter** Pass a blue-blazed trail that leads right 0.1 mile to Cornelius Creek Shelter.

37.7 Pass a side trail that leads left to Black Rock, a rocky lookout with views of Floyd and Pine Mountains; continue straight on the AT.

38.3 Pass the blue-blazed Cornelius Creek Trail on the left; continue straight on the AT. (FYI: See the Great Day Hikes along the Appalachian Trail section for information on a loop hike along Cornelius Creek and Apple Orchard Falls.)

39.4 Pass blue-blazed Apple Orchard Falls Trail on the left; continue straight on the AT.

40.9 Cross Apple Orchard Mountain (4,222 feet), the highest point on the AT between Chestnut Knob 200 miles south and Mount Moosilauke in New Hampshire. On a clear day, there are views of Natural Bridge to the northwest.

42.1 **Shelter** ▰ Pass Thunder Hill Shelter on the left. (FYI: Except for a short section where the AT crosses the 3,683-foot peak of Thunder Ridge, the trail and Blue Ridge Parkway run beside each other for the next 5 miles.)

46.8 Enter the James River Face Wilderness at Petites Gap. (FYI: See the Great Day Hikes along the Appalachian Trail section for a brief description of trails in this wilderness area.)

48.0 Cross Highcock Knob (3,073 feet).

54.5 **Shelter** ▰ Pass Matts Creek Shelter on the left. In 0.1 mile, reach a T intersection with Matts Creek Trail on the right. Continue straight on the AT. (FYI: This leg of the AT opened in 2000. The old AT followed Matts Creek Trail to the Snowden Bridge on the James River.)

55.3 Turn right at the mouth of Matts Creek. The James River is on the left, high cliffs walls on the right; follow the AT downstream.

56.5 Turn left and cross the James River Foot Bridge. On the opposite side, cross U.S. Highway 501/Virginia Route 130. A newly constructed section of the AT climbs on Rocky Row, crossing it twice. (FYI: The new bridge across the James River is named in honor of Bill Foot, a former president of the Natural Bridge ATC, who led efforts to have it built.)

58.4 **Shelter** ▰ Pass a blue-blazed trail on the left to Johns Hollow Shelter. Continue straight on the AT as it climbs to Fullers Rocks, a lookout with views back onto the James River gorge.

65.6 Cross Bluff Mountain (3,372 feet).

67.2 Turn right at a T intersection with an old road. **Shelter** ▰ Straight ahead on the road is Punchbowl Shelter in 0.2 mile.

67.6 Cross the Blue Ridge Parkway at mile 51.7 and follow the AT as it descends the road embankment on the opposite side. The AT soon crosses a stream and climbs Rice Mountain (2,228 feet).

71.6 Enter a clearing after crossing Little Irish Creek. Beyond the clearing, turn right onto gravel Forest Road 39. For the next 2 miles, the AT skirts Pedlar Lake, a man-made reservoir that supplies water to Lynchburg, Virginia.

76.0 **Shelter** ▰ Pass Brown Mountain Creek Shelter on the right.

77.8 Cross U.S. Highway 60 and enter Long Mountain Wayside. Follow the AT as it re-enters the woods next to a dirt road on the left, or west, end of the wayside.

81.6 After climbing Bald Knob (4,059 feet), descend into Cow Camp Gap. Shelter ▰ Blue-blazed trail leads right 0.6 mile to Cow Camp Gap Shelter. Not very practical, though, given that Brown Mountain Creek Shelter (mile 76.0) is right on the AT.

82.8 Cross Cold Mountain (4,022 feet). The summit is a mountain bald with views of Mount Pleasant and the Religious Range. (FYI: See Hike 24 for a detailed description of hiking on Mount Pleasant.)

91.8 **Shelter** ▰ Pass Seeley-Woodworth Shelter on the right. In 0.3 mile, pass two unprotected springs.

92.1 Pass a blue-blazed trail (old road) on the left. It leads 2.2 miles to a campsite at Lovingston Spring. (FYI: See the Great Day Hikes along the Appalachian Trail section for a brief description of a loop hike in this area.)

94.6 Pass a campsite in a grassy gap. A trail leads right 150 feet to Spy Rock. (FYI: See the Great Day Hikes along the Appalachian Trail section for a brief description of this hike.)

99.2 Cross over The Priest (4,063 feet). **Shelter** ▮ Access to The Priest Shelter is on any of the unmarked trails that branch right off of the AT as it approaches the summit.

103.5 Cross Virginia Route 56; on the opposite side, descend to the Tye River and cross on a suspension bridge.

106.1 Turn right and cross Harpers Creek to begin a steep climb up Three Ridges. **Shelter** ▮ To reach Harpers Creek Shelter, continue straight where the AT turns right. The shelter stands about 400 yards uphill.

109.4 Cross Three Ridges. (FYI: See Hike 23 for a detailed description of a loop hike on Three Ridges.)

112.3 **Shelter** ▮ Pass a blue-blazed trail that branches left to Maupin Field Shelter.

114.6 Cross the Blue Ridge Parkway near Three Ridges Overlook. On the opposite side, enter the woods and descend the road embankment.

122.9 Cross the highest point on Humpback Mountain (3,600 feet).

124.3 Pass beneath Humpback Rocks. (FYI: See the Great Day Hikes along the Appalachian Trail section for a brief description of this hike.)

128.4 **Shelter** ▮ Pass the Paul C. Wolfe Shelter on the left.)

133.4 Hike ends at Rockfish Gap.

Hike Information

Local Information

Greater Lynchburg Convention & Visitors Bureau, Lynchburg, VA, (800) 732-5821, www.lynchburgchamber.org.

Roanoke Valley Convention & Visitors Bureau, Roanoke, VA, (800) 635-5535, www. VisitRoanokeVA.com.

Segment 4 Rockfish Gap to Chester Gap

Shenandoah National Park and the Appalachian Trail grew up together. Civilian Conservation Corps crews built Skyline Drive on right-of-ways carved by AT trail volunteers. The routes stay within a half mile of each other as they pass through mountain gaps, past old farms and orchards, and over rocky mountaintops. Recent fires, ice-storm damage, and gypsy moth infestation have decimated large areas of the forest in Shenandoah. In these areas, the AT gives hikers a view of the shrubby plants, small trees, wildflowers, and vines that mark early stages of reforestation.

Start: From the Blue Ridge Parkway south of I-64.

Distance: 107.1-mile point-to-point.

Difficulty rating: Moderate.

Trail surface: Using dirt footpaths and abandoned dirt roads, hike along ridges and outcrops; down steep wooded slopes; and through old fields, red spruce, and balsam fir at highest elevations.

Nearest towns: Waynesboro, VA (south access); Front Royal, VA (north access).

Canine compatibility: Dogs permitted (must be on a leash at all times).

Trail contacts: Appalachian Trail Conference, Harpers Ferry, WV, (304) 535–6331, www.appalachiantrail.org.
Potomac Appalachian Trail Club (PATC), Vienna, VA, (703) 242–0693, patc.net.
Shenandoah National Park, Luray, VA, (540) 999–3500, www.nps.gov/shen.

Skyland Lodge, Skyline Drive, VA, (800) 778–2851, www.visitshenandoah.com.

Schedule: Open year-round. Skyline Drive may close without advance notice due to inclement weather. Portions of this road are also closed during hunting season to discourage poachers. Call (540) 999–3500 for closures.

Fees/permits: Entrance fee: $5.00 for hikers; $10.00 per vehicle. (Honor boxes at north and south park boundaries.) Appalachian Trail (AT) hikers must register for a free backcountry permit at Tom Floyd Wayside (north district) and Rockfish Gap entrance station (south district).

Maps: PATC map #9: Shenandoah National Park, Northern District, PATC map #10: Shenandoah National Park, Central District, PATC map #11: Shenandoah National Park, South District.

Finding the trailhead: To Rockfish Gap Trailhead

From Waynesboro: At the junction of U.S. Highway 340 and I-64, take I-64 east for 5.1 miles to the Afton Mountain exit 99. At the bottom of the exit ramp turn right onto U.S. Highway 250. In 0.2 mile, turn right onto the Skyline Drive/Blue Ridge Parkway access road. Park at the Augusta County Visitor Center at Rockfish Gap, which is behind the Chevron gas station. The AT is located on the east side of the Blue Ridge Parkway. (Note: If leaving a car for multiple nights, inform the visitor center staff.) *DeLorme: Virginia Atlas & Gazetteer:* Page 67, D5.

To Chester Gap Trailhead (See Segment 5: Chester Gap to Harpers Ferry.)

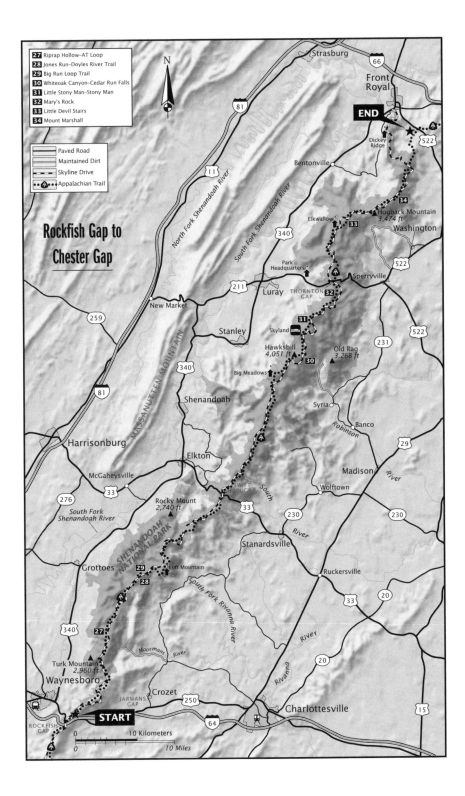

Rockfish Gap to Chester Gap

27 Riprap Hollow–AT Loop
28 Jones Run–Doyles River Trail
29 Big Run Loop Trail
30 Whiteoak Canyon–Cedar Run Falls
31 Little Stony Man–Stony Man
32 Mary's Rock
33 Little Devil Stairs
34 Mount Marshall

Paved Road
Maintained Dirt
Skyline Drive
Appalachian Trail

N

END

START

Strasburg

66

Front Royal

522

Dickey Ridge

Bentonville

81

11

North Fork Shenandoah River

South Fork Shenandoah River

340

34 Hogback Mountain
3,474 ft

Elkwallow

33

Washington

522

Park Headquarters

Sperryville

211

Luray

THORNTON GAP

32

New Market

259

MASSANUTTEN MOUNTAIN

Stanley

Skyland

31

231

522

340

Hawksbill
4,051 ft

30

Old Rag
3,268 ft

81

Big Meadows

Shenandoah

Syria

Banco

Robinson River

29

Harrisonburg

Elkton

Madison

River

McGaheysville

33

Wolftown

276

33

SWIFT RUN GAP

South River

33

230

230

South Fork Shenandoah River

Rocky Mount
2,740 ft

Stanardsville

Grottoes

SHENANDOAH NATIONAL PARK

29

Loft Mountain

Ruckersville

River

33

20

28

South Fork Rivanna River

340

27

Moormans River

Turk Mountain
2,960 ft

20

Waynesboro

Crozet

JARMANS GAP

250

Rivanna River

Charlottesville

15

ROCKFISH GAP

64

START

0   10 Kilometers

0   10 Miles

The Hike

The AT just north of Rockfish Gap passes little in the way of rock formations, gorges, and waterfalls that draw millions of visitors to Shenandoah National Park. There are, instead, acres of farmland and meadow. Cattle graze and views spill off the mountains onto farms and towns of the Shenandoah Valley.

As introductions go, this pastoral entry into Shenandoah National Park feels right. The parkland was, for hundreds of years, privately owned. Much of it was farmed. Every meadow and mountain gap, every peak, pass, and hollow holds a story or mystery about the people who lived there. At Blackrock, 20 miles north of Rockfish Gap, legend says a friend of Thomas Jefferson hid Virginia's state seal and records of the General Assembly in a cave during the Revolutionary War. The cave has never been identified (although the records and state seal survived the British raid that prompted the stash). Mystery aside, Blackrock commands attention on its own merits. This formation was once a cliff that collapsed after the soft limestone beneath it dissolved. Limestone, by its very nature, erodes faster than granite and greenstone. Where it underlies harder rock, erosion can result in the formation of talus, or large rock piles, at the base of cliffs.

North of Jarmans Gap, mountain laurel spreads roots into the cracks of exposed rock. Rhododendron grow tall and lush around stream headwaters near Moormans River Overlook. Taken together, these plants signal that more rugged, rocky terrain lies ahead. At Ivy Creek, the AT drops into a small canyon (2.7 miles north of Loft Mountain camp store). Briefly, it follows the hemlock-lined stream. The forest undergrowth is lush with mountain laurel, a plant that prefers the shade of pines and hemlocks. If it's been a mild winter, look for an extra spectacular spring laurel bloom. The many white, cup-shaped laurel flowers make this short stretch of the AT one of a kind in the park.

On the approach to Big Meadows (17.4 miles north of Swift Run Gap), a cemetery and pieces of a pasture fence are visible from the AT. Periwinkle blooms in spring. The wildflower, with small, waxy-looking leaves that spread like a ground ivy, is not a naturally occurring mountain wildflower. Its presence usually indicates that a homesite once stood in the area. Nearby, on Tanner's Ridge, residents refused to leave their homes after President Franklin D. Roosevelt dedicated the park in 1936. Old pictures show sheriff deputies carrying a woman away from her house, a vivid example of forced eviction.

Not every mountain settler resisted. Some left willingly. North of Rock Spring Hut, where the AT passes beneath the cliffs of Hawksbill Mountain (4,051 feet), a view opens north onto Ida Valley. This is where the federal government built its first resettlement community for park residents in 1937. Hawksbill is the tallest mountain in Shenandoah National Park, but the AT passes below, not over, the summit. The trail reaches its highest point in this section a few miles north on Stony Mountain. Stony is followed in quick succession by the Pinnacles and Little Stony Mountain. These peaks, short on tree-cover, offer great views from rock summits and cliffs. They are also within easy reach of Skyland Lodge, a hotel and restaurant that draws flocks of visitors.

Skyland is famous for its founder, George Freeman Pollack, who opened the resort in the 1880s. In 1924, Pollack helped sell the idea of making the Blue Ridge, from Front Royal to Rockfish Gap, America's first national park east of the Mississippi River. "A national park near our nation's capital" became the group's slogan. After twelve years, they succeeded. There is a story about local boys who climbed from the valley to watch tourists drive Skyline Drive and counted as many as six cars in a day. In 2002, Shenandoah National Park recorded 1.4 million visitors, making it the fourteenth most visited national park in the nation.

Like periwinkle, an orchard tree—apple, pear, cherry, or other fruit—signals that a homesite or farm once stood in the area. Apples were prized for making moonshine brandy in Gravel Spring Gap (14.5 miles north of Thornton Gap). Nicholson Hollow, south of Mary's Rock, was renowned for its apple brandy. Jarmans Gap, at the southern end of the park, was known for corn whiskey. Moonshine, though illegal, offered poor mountaineers extra income. If a man had the skills, nature provided the ingredients: clean, running water, fruit or corn, and yeast. Stills were hidden and well protected from suspicious strangers who wandered nearby. This included early AT trail volunteers. Stories tell of how settlers chased Potomac Appalachian Trail Club (PATC) volunteers by setting fires.

Today, the AT hiker in Shenandoah National Park is a herald of spring. Thousands of men and women begin the AT at Springer Mountain in Georgia in March. The bulk of them hit this park in May. Many have their hearts—or stomachs—set on a good meal at one of the park's three restaurants. As their thoughts wander ahead to Harpers Ferry, West Virginia—the official halfway point on the 2,173-mile trail—their feet pass over storied ground. In Shenandoah, there's a tale around every turn in the trail.

Miles and Directions

0.0 **START** on the Blue Ridge Parkway south of I-64. Walk north across a bridge spanning the interstate. (Note: For it's first 8 miles, the AT runs on a narrow strip of land owned by the Park Service. Land a few feet off either side of the trail is private property.)

5.0 Cross Bear Den Mountain (2,885 feet). In another 1.4 miles, cross Calf Mountain (2,974 feet).

7.0 **Shelter** ▶ Pass a blue-blazed trail that leads left 0.2 mile to Calf Mountain Shelter.

8.0 Pass through Jarmans Gap. The AT now traverses land in Shenandoah National Park.

13.7 Pass Wildcat Ridge Trail on the left. (FYI: See the Great Day Hikes along the Appalachian Trail section for a brief description of a loop hike using Wildcat Ridge Trail.)

20.0 (**Shelter** ▆ A trail leads right 200 yards to Blackrock Hut.) In another 0.5 mile, the AT circles around Blackrock (3,092 feet), a rock formation.

21.9 Reach a four-way intersection with Jones Run Trail; continue straight on the AT. (FYI: See the Great Day Hikes along the Appalachian Trail section for a brief description of a loop using Jones Run Trail and Doyles River Trail.)

23.6 Pass blue-blazed Big Run Loop Trail on the left; continue straight on the AT. (FYI: See the Great Day Hikes along the Appalachian Trail section for a brief description of this trail.)

27.4 Pass a trail on the left that climbs uphill to the Loft Mountain camp store, open May to October.

29.5 Cross Ivy Creek, turn right, and follow the AT downstream. The hollow is shaded in hemlock with thick undergrowth of mountain laurel.

33.2 Cross a road and continue straight on the AT. **Shelter** ▆ The road leads right 0.1 mile to Pinefield Hut.

41.4 Descend from Flattop Mountain (3,325 feet) and cross a service road. **Shelter** ▆ The road leads left to Hightop Hut in 0.1 mile; continue straight on the AT.)

44.7 Cross above U.S. Highway 33 on a bridge on Skyline Drive. Walk north until you pass an entrance road from US 33 on the left. Past this entrance road, turn right and re-enter the woods following white blazes.

53.1 A concrete post on the left signals a connector trail leading left to Lewis Mountain Campground; continue straight on the AT.

53.8 **Shelter** ▆ Pass a road on the right that leads 0.1 mile to Bearfence Hut.

56.8 Pass Laurel Prong Trail on the right. (FYI: Laurel Prong Trail leads 2.8 miles to Camp Hoover, a vacation retreat used by President Herbert Hoover.)

61.6 Pass below the cliffs of Blackrock, a tall rock formation that signals the approach of Big Meadows Campground. The AT soon passes an amphitheater and skirts around the campground.

65.3 **Shelter** ▆ Pass a trail leading left to Rock Spring Hut in 0.2 mile.

65.6 Pass the trail to Hawksbill (4,051 feet) that branches right off the AT; continue straight on the AT. The AT runs along the base of cliffs below Hawksbill's summit. (FYI: Hawksbill is the highest point in Shenandoah National Park. The highest point on the AT in Shenandoah comes 6 miles to the north, on Stony Man.)

69.9 Cross a paved entrance road to Skyland Resort and enter a parking area for the Stony

AT SHELTERS/HUTS (mileage on the AT from Rockfish Gap north to Chester Gap)

Mile 7.0 – Calf Mountain Hut

Mile 20.0 – Blackrock Hut

Mile 33.2 – Pinefield Hut

Mile 41.4 – Hightop Hut

Mile 53.8 – Bearfence Hut

Mile 65.3 – Rock Spring Hut

Mile 80.6 – Pass Mountain Hut

Mile 93.7 – Gravel Springs Shelter

Mile 104.2 – Tom Floyd Wayside (primitive site)

Man Nature Trail. Follow white-blazed AT as it climbs Stony Man. (FYI: See the Great Day Hikes along the Appalachian Trail section for a brief description of hikes in this area.)

76.2 Pass Byrds Nest #3, a day-use only shelter with a water supply; follow the AT a short distance on a dirt road, then turn left to re-enter the woods following white blazes.

77.5 Pass a trail on the left to a lookout off Mary's Rock; continue straight on the AT as it descends and crosses U.S. Highway 211 in Thornton Gap, near the Panorama Restaurant. (FYI: See the Great Day Hikes along the Appalachian Trail section for a brief description of this trail.)

80.6 **Shelter** A blue-blazed trail branches right off the AT and leads 0.2 mile to Pass Mountain Hut.

87.9 Reach a four-way intersection with Elkwallow Trail; continue straight on the AT. (Campground: Elkwallow trail leads left to Matthews Arm Campground in 1.9 miles.)

90.1 Tuscarora Trail intersects with the AT on the left; continue straight on the AT. (FYI: See Hike 17: Big Schloss for a history of the Tuscarora Trail.)

92.0 A dirt road leads right 50 yards to Skyline Drive and Little Hogback Overlook. (FYI: See the Great Day Hikes along the Appalachian Trail section for a brief description of a hike that begins at this overlook.)

93.7 The Bluff Trail intersects the AT; bear left on the AT. **Shelter** Gravel Springs Shelter is 0.2 mile to the right on Bluff Trail.

96.2 Cross the summit of Mount Marshall (3,369 feet). (FYI: See Hike 12: Bluff Trail/AT Loop for a detailed description of this trail.)

103.5 Exit Shenandoah National Park at Compton Gap. The AT follows a corridor of land owned by the National Park Service.

104.2 A path leads left off the AT to Tom Floyd Wayside; continue straight on the AT.

105.7 Enter land owned by the Smithsonian Institute's Conservation & Research Center. A few feet off the trail is private property. Camping is prohibited. In 0.2 mile, pass a blue-blazed trail leading right 0.1 mile to the Northern Virginia Trail Center; continue straight on the AT.

107.1 Hike ends at U.S. Highway 522 in Chester Gap.

Hike Information

Local Information

Front Royal Visitor Center, Front Royal, VA, (800) 338-2576, www.frontroyalchamber.com.

Luray-Page County Chamber of Commerce, Luray, VA (540) 743-3915, (888) 743-3915, www.luraypage.com.

Staunton/Augusta County Visitor Center at Rockfish Gap, Afton Mountain, VA, (540) 943-5187.

Segment 5 Chester Gap to Harpers Ferry

The Blue Ridge of northern Virginia have none of the 4,000-foot-plus heights so plentiful on the Appalachian Trail farther south. Still, the northern Virginia leg is one exhausting climb after another. On open mountain balds, views drop west onto the Great Valley. The bumpy spine of the Blue Ridge runs southward, and to the east lie the rolling meadows of Virginia's hunt country. Come fall and winter, the mountains here harbor quiet moments, interrupted occasionally by the thrashing of birds foraging among the hornbeam, dogwood, spicebush, and sassafras.

Start: From a parking lot on the southbound side of U.S. Highway 522.
Distance: 54.5 miles.
Difficulty rating: Moderate.
Trail surface: Using dirt footpaths and abandoned dirt roads, hike along low ridges, cliffs, and rock lookouts; through fields, meadows, and stream hollows.
Nearest towns: Front Royal, VA (south access); Harpers Ferry, WV (north access).
Canine compatibility: Dogs permitted.
Trail contacts: Appalachian Trail Conference,

Harpers Ferry, WV, (304) 535-6331, www.appalachiantrail.org.
Potomac Appalachian Trail Club (PATC), Vienna, VA, (703) 242-0693, patc.net.
Harpers Ferry National Historical Park, Harpers Ferry, WV, (304) 535-6298, www.nps.gov/hafe.
Schedule: Open year-round. Hunting season in G. R. Thompson Wildlife Management Area, mid-November through first week in January.
Maps: PATC Map #7 (AT–Northern VA), PATC Map #8 (AT–Northern VA).

Finding the trailhead: To Chester Gap Trailhead
From Front Royal: Drive south 3.4 miles on US 522 from its intersection with Virginia Route 55. The Appalachian Trail (AT) crosses US 522 here. There's parking for several cars on the southbound side of the highway. *DeLorme: Virginia Atlas & Gazetteer:* Page 74, A3.
To Harpers Ferry Trailhead
From Harpers Ferry, WV: Cross the Shenandoah River bridge and drive west 0.9 mile on U.S. Highway 340 to the Harpers Ferry National Historical Park Visitor Center. There's a $5.00 entrance fee. A free shuttle runs every ten to fifteen minutes into Lower Town, where the AT is located. Notify park rangers if you intend on leaving the car for multiple nights. (Alternate parking for day hikers is located at the junction of US 340 and Virginia Route 671 [in Virginia], at an unsecured roadside parking area near the Tri-State Amoco gas station. From the east end of the Shenandoah River bridge, proceed east 1.6 miles on US 340 to the parking area, on the left. On foot, backtrack 0.3 mile on US 340 to the Loudoun Heights Trail on the southbound side of the road.) *DeLorme: Virginia Atlas & Gazetteer:* Page 79, B7.

The Hike

Small as it appears on a map, Chester Gap looms big on the AT. The Blue Ridge tapers suddenly into this gap, located east of Front Royal. Northward, the range

Ted Lake Trail opens up onto the grassy shoreline of Lake Thompson.

becomes a chain of low, rounded ridges. After hundreds of miles of exposed ridges, mountain balds, and towering cliffs, this section shrinks into short, vigorous climbs. From Manassas Gap to Snickers Gap, it's either steep up, or steep down, with little in between. Thru-hikers nickname it the roller coaster for its many breath-stealing bumps.

The story of Chester Gap touches on the mystery of Virginia's first white explorer who crossed the Blue Ridge. John Lederer explored the mountains for Virginia's colonial government and, in 1670, wrote of the inspiring view from the mountains. Where exactly he stood is still debated. The AT passes a monument in Linden, Virginia, at Manassas Gap, in honor of his explorations. Some historians say he climbed the Swift Run Gap in Shenandoah National Park. Others say Mount Marshall, also in Shenandoah. Because Lederer's mission was to locate the headwaters of the Rappahannock

River, many believe Chester Gap is where he broke through the Blue Ridge in 1670. The Rappahannock starts as a small mountain stream east of Chester Gap, eventually to become a major tributary of the Chesapeake Bay.

Wherever he stood, Lederer's first impression of the mountains speaks volumes about how early explorers and settlers viewed the Blue Ridge. It was, for the English, terra incognita. Lederer, maybe feeling lightheaded from his long climb, initially described the blue haze covering the western mountain slope as some kind of great western ocean. When the haze lifted, he moved across the Great Valley and explored present-day West Virginia.

It's nostalgic, as you hike this 54-mile stretch of the AT, to imagine how volunteers in 1927 plotted the first miles of the world-famous long trail in this region. Only a few stretches of original trail remain intact north of Chester Gap. Trail relocations peaked in the 1950s, when private landowners blocked access. With Washington, D.C., only 60 miles east, and because of the many gaps that permit short hikes, the AT in this region has historically received heavy day use. Landowners' protest is now a moot point. The AT passes near homes and uses several dirt and paved roads south of Manassas Gap. But there are also long stretches through heavy forestland where the scarlet tanager's song floats down from tall treetops.

Birds make much racket in the overgrowth of spicebush, honeysuckle, and Virginia creeper along the trail. Redstarts, vireos, wood thrush, bluebirds, robins, and thrushes flit branch to branch, wavering for a second or two on a twig that can barely hold their weight. If they're lucky, the noisy forage for food ends with a prize: the grapelike fruit of Virginia creeper. Any hiker who has violently pitched forward, tripped up by a camouflaged creeper, knows this vine deserves to be pruned rather than admired. The vine grows adhesive discs on its tendrils that cement to the surfaces of trees, fence posts, and all forms of climbable surfaces. Perhaps we would all have higher regard for the creeper if Virginia's General Assembly had enshrined it as the state flower. Instead, by a one-vote margin, the vine lost to the flowering dogwood.

The climb on the AT north from Snickers Gap follows a rocky switchback ascent. After topping out, the trail drops and crosses a boulder-lined stream in Pigeon Hollow. Sounds of water bubble up from beneath the rocks. The trail will climb again, descend to another stream, and then climb once more to Crescent Rock. Beyond this folded section of Catoctin greenstone, the trail continues its roller-coaster route. Three times between Snickers Gap and Ashby Gap, the AT climbs to high points: Lookout Point, Tomblin Hill, and Buzzard Hill. Three times the trail drops, first into a valley formed by a branch of Spout Run, then into Fent Willey Hollow and Reservoir Hollow.

During the Civil War, the mountain hollows of northern Virginia sheltered a group of Confederate raiders known as Mosby's Rangers. John Singleton Mosby led the group and coordinated his soldiers' guerilla-style tactics. They sprang upon

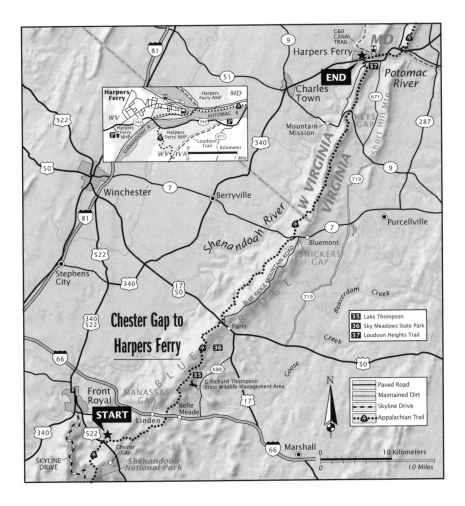

Union soldiers in the mountain passes, took clothes, weapons, and money, then led prisoners into Confederate strongholds. By the end of the war, Mosby ruled a small fiefdom in Loudoun County, from Bull Run Mountain to the crest of the Blue Ridge. Ruled isn't too strong a word, either. His rangers were not allowed to leave the boundaries of the Confederacy without permission. Any man who missed two roll calls without good reason was discharged. At war's end, Mosby received a pardon (as did most Confederate soldiers), and then supported his old battlefield enemy Ulysses S. Grant in the presidential election.

Few towns are richer in Civil War history than Harpers Ferry, West Virginia. This national historic park is the end of the AT in Virginia, at the bridge crossing on US 340. The Shenandoah River thunders below this symbolic crossing. The Blue Ridge extends into Maryland and southern Pennsylvania. In that region, the chain goes by

Walking through a sun-dappled meadow.

the name South Mountain. Not until the White Mountains of New Hampshire does the AT reach heights equal to Virginia's mountains. From Weaver Cliffs, north of Harpers Ferry, the AT hiker can look back south along the Blue Ridge. If conditions are right, you might see (or believe you see), if only for a whimsical moment, what John Lederer saw in 1670, an endless ocean of blue haze.

Miles and Directions

0.0 **START** in a parking lot on the southbound side of US 522. Cross the highway and enter the woods following the white blazes. In this area, the AT passes through land owned by the Smithsonian Institute's Conservation & Research Center. Camping is not allowed.

2.3 Leave the Conservation & Research Center property.

5.2 **Shelter** A trail branches left to the Denton Shelter.

8.1 Cross a set of railroad tracks and, in 0.1 mile, reach VA 55. Cross and follow Virginia Route 725 as it passes under I-66. (FYI: The town of Linden and the Discovery Monument in honor of John Lederer are 0.1 mile left on VA 55.)

8.5 Reach a Potomac Appalachian Trail Conference parking lot on the right. Follow the AT as it enters the woods from the back of the lot.

10.2 Enter the G. R. Thompson Wildlife Management Area, which is managed by the state. Use caution, especially during fall hunting season.

10.7 **Shelter** A blue-blazed footpath leads left to Manassas Gap Shelter. Don't confuse the shelter trail with the blue-blazed Ted Lake Trail, also in the vicinity. (FYI: See Hike 9: G. Richard Thompson Wildlife Management Area for a detailed description of these trails.)

15.1 **Shelter** Begin a descent that leads to Dicks Dome Shelter on the right side of the trail.

17.4 Enter Sky Meadow State Park. (FYI: See the Great Day Hikes along the Appalachian Trail section for a brief description of trails in the state park.)

20.5 Cross U.S. Highway 50 in Ashby Gap. As you cross, bear to the right and re-enter the woods at a PATC parking area on US 50.

24.1 **Shelter** A blue-blazed trail on the left leads to Rod Hollow Shelter. The roller-coaster ride through northern Virginia's Blue Ridge begins as the AT climbs in and out of four hollows.

31.0 Turn left at a T intersection. **Shelter** A blue-blazed trail leads straight from the junction to reach Sam Moore Shelter. Soon after turning left, you'll cross Spout Run. From here, the AT ascends to Lookout Point.

AT SHELTERS/HUTS (mileage north from Chester Gap)

Mile 5.2 – Denton Shelter

Mile 10.7 – Manassas Gap Shelter

Mile 15.1 – Dicks Dome Shelter

Mile 24.1 – Rod Hollow Shelter

Mile 31.0 – Sam Moore Shelter

Mile 45.1 – David Lesser Shelter

37.2 Reach Crescent Rock and Pulpit Rock; continue straight on the AT. (FYI: A footpath descends to the base of a cliff, where this geologic formation is visible.)

42.8 Pass a grassy field on the left, the site of an old homestead.

44.5 A trail on the left leads to Buzzard Rocks; continue straight on the AT. (FYI: Buzzard Rocks has views over the Shenandoah Valley and room for a tent.)

45.1 **Shelter** ◤ Pass the David Lesser Shelter on the right.

48.1 Cross the paved West Virginia Route 9 at Keys Gap. Re-enter the woods on the opposite side at a trail bulletin board near a gravel parking area.

52.0 At a T intersection with the Loudoun Heights Trail, turn left and descend the AT. The trail now crosses land inside Harpers Ferry National Historical Park. (FYI: See the Great Day Hikes along the Appalachian Trail section for a brief description of this area. If using the alternate trailhead described in the "Finding the trailhead:" section of this chapter, proceed straight on Loudoun Heights Trail to its intersection with US 340.)

53.6 Cross the Shenandoah River on a bridge on US 340.

54.5 The hike ends in Lower Town of Harpers Ferry National Historical Park. (FYI: The Park Service runs a shuttle every ten to fifteen minutes to the secure parking lot at the park visitor center.)

Hike Information

Local Information

Loudoun Tourism Council, Leesburg, VA, (703) 771-2617, (800) 752-6118, www.VisitLoudoun.org.

Front Royal Visitor Center, Front Royal, VA, (800) 338-2576, www.frontroyalchamber.com.

Great Day Hikes along the Appalachian Trail

Compiled here is an index of great day hikes along the Appalachian Trail (AT) in Virginia, some of which are featured hikes in this book, others are Honorable Mentions, and the rest are great sections of the AT that should be hiked at one time or another.

Segment 1 – Damascus to Marion

1 Feathercamp Branch

(See Hike 33: Feathercamp Ridge.)

Wild horses near Mount Rogers.

2 Whitetop Laurel Circuit

For nearly 6 miles, the AT follows the ridge of Straight Mountain with overlooks onto wild Whitetop Laurel Creek. At either end, it junctions with the Virginia Creeper Trail, a multiuse trail for hikers and mountain bikers. Together, the AT and Creeper Trail make a vigorous 10-mile loop. The Creeper Trail is a model for the Rails-to-Trails effort. It's total length along the former Abingdon Branch of the Virginia-Carolina Railroad measures 34 miles. The stretch used in this loop is noted for its pathway along scenic Whitetop Laurel Creek. Begin and end the loop at a parking area on Virginia Route 728, south of U.S. Highway 58 near Beartree Day Use Area. Mount Rogers NRA/JNF. Call (276) 579–7092. *DeLorme: Virginia Atlas & Gazetteer:* Page 22, C3.

3 Elk Garden-Mount Rogers Summit

(See Hike 35: Mount Rogers Summit.)

4 Rhododendron Gap

(See Hike 35: Mount Rogers Summit.)

5 Grayson Highlands State Park

There are 3 miles of the AT in this popular state park. The quickest link to the long trail is via the Highlands Horse Trail from the park ranger station at Massie Gap. From there, the AT goes north to Little Wilson Creek Wilderness and high-country meadows overlooking Scales. In the other direction, the AT ascends along Wilburn Ridge to amazing rock outcrops, deep thickets of rhododendron, and finally the Mount Rogers Spur Trail. Grayson Highlands State Park and Mount Rogers NRA/JNF. Call (276) 579–7092, (276) 783–5196. *DeLorme: Virginia Atlas & Gazetteer:* Page 23, C5.

Segment 2 – Marion to Roanoke

6 Crawfish-Channel Rock Loop

(See Hike 28: Crawfish/Channel Rock.)

7 Beartown Wilderness

It's an easy 2.4-mile hike up the AT from Forest Road 222 (an extension of Virginia Route 625) and the boundary of Beartown Wilderness. The AT skirts the south edge of this 6,375-acre federal wilderness until Chestnut Knob. From the mountain, views drop into Burkes Garden, a pocket of agricultural bliss formed when subsurface limestone eroded. Beartown Wilderness has no marked trails besides the AT, but old logging roads allow for exploring Roaring Branch and a sphagnum bog at the headwaters of Cove Branch. New River Valley Ranger District. Call (540) 228–5551, (888) 241–6669. *DeLorme: Virginia Atlas & Gazetteer:* Page 39, D5.

8 Trail Boss-AT Loop

Trail crews rerouted 2.1 miles of the AT to descend off Brushy Mountain as it approaches Virginia Route 615. The old section was renamed Trail Boss in honor of a dedicated volunteer. Combined, they make a 5.1-mile loop hike. The AT's route up Brushy Mountain is steep, with ten switchbacks, and several overlooks. This is, however, primarily a woodland hike through an oak-hickory forest. There are mountain laurel and rhododendron. In the dark hollows, look for the bloodroot wildflower, plus many mosses and ferns. New River Valley Ranger District/JNF. Call (540) 228–5551, (888) 241–6669. *DeLorme: Virginia Atlas & Gazetteer:* Page 39, C7.

9 Ribble Trail-AT Loop

(See Honorable Mention 56.)

10 Angels Rest

South of the New River from Pearisburg, the AT makes a steep, switchback-heavy trip up Pearis Mountain. In 1.5 miles, a trail leads a few hundred yards to Angels Rest. This 3,550-foot perch has views into the New River's passage through the Narrows, a rock fault between Devonian shale and Cambrian limestone. The trailhead for this 3-mile in-and-out hike is on Virginia Route 634 (Morris Avenue) in Pearisburg. A turnaround at Angels Rest makes a 3-mile day hike. New River Valley Ranger District/JNF in Blacksburg. Call (540) 552–4641. *DeLorme: Virginia Atlas & Gazetteer:* Page 40, B3.

11 The Rice Fields

From Pearisburg, the AT climbs Peters Mountain and traces the crest to a mountain meadow called the Rice Fields. The oddity of open farm meadows atop a tall ridge is matched by the beauty of views off the west slope into West Virginia. Begin the hike on Virginia Route 624 (Stillhouse Branch Road) north of U.S. Highway 460 between Pearisburg and Narrows. An AT hut 5 miles from the trailhead marks a reasonable turnaround point for this 10-mile in-and-out hike. New River Valley Ranger District/JNF. Call (540) 552–4641. *DeLorme: Virginia Atlas and Gazetteer:* Page 40, B3.

12 Peters Mountain Wilderness

(See Hike 26: Huckleberry Loop.)

13 Mountain Lake Wilderness

(See Hike 27: Mountain Lake Wilderness.)

14 Kelly Knob

A 3.3-mile trek from Sinking Creek and Virginia Route 42 to Kelly Knob ends with views off this 3,742-foot peak. The AT crosses privately owned farmland near the trailhead. Be sure to follow all posted signs regarding parking and hiking. Past Kelly Knob, the AT dips to Big Pond; a side trail here leads 100 yards to views from White Rocks. For an 8.5-mile point-to-point hike, continue hiking up the AT and descend Johns Creek Mountain Trail. Park a shuttle at the Johns Creek trailhead on Virginia Route 658 west of Twin Oaks. New River Valley Ranger District/JNF. Call (540) 552–4641. *DeLorme: Virginia Atlas & Gazetteer:* Page 41, B6.

15 North Mountain–AT Loop

(See Honorable Mention 53.)

16 Audie Murphy VFW Monument

The AT rises steeply from Virginia Route 620 to the spine of Brush Mountain. In 3.8 miles, the trail passes a monument to Audie Murphy, erected by the VFW on the site of Murphy's plane crash in 1971. Murphy was a recipient of the Congressional Medal of Honor and twenty-eight wartime medals from the United States, France, and Belgium. From the memorial, the AT continues north for another 3.8 miles to cross VA 620. New River Valley Ranger District/JNF. Call (540) 552–4641. *DeLorme: Virginia Atlas & Gazetteer:* Page 42, A1.

17 Dragons Tooth

It is a steep and rugged climb on the AT for 2.6 miles to Dragons Tooth, a craggy rock that juts 35 feet above the summit of Cove Mountain. En route, the AT traces the razor edge of Tuscarora sandstone in an area called Rawies Rest. Use the blue-blazed Dragons Tooth Trail to make a loop hike that begins and ends at Virginia Route 624. There is alternate parking and trail access on Virginia Route 311 north at the Dragons Tooth parking lot past Catawba Grocery. New Castle Ranger District/JNF. Call (540) 864–5195. *DeLorme: Virginia Atlas & Gazetteer:* Page 42, B1.

18 McAfee Knob

The AT leads 3.5 miles uphill to McAfee Knob, a 3,197-foot high point on Catawba Mountain. The southern trailhead is on Virginia Route 311, west of Salem, Virginia. For a longer day hike, continue past McAfee for another 6 miles along Tinker Mountain with its gorgeous cliff overlooks. A junction with the blue-blazed Andy Lane Trail leads 2.3 miles left to Virginia Route 600. Highlights of this trip include views of Catawba Valley, boulders in the Devils Kitchen area, and a half mile of exposed, cliff trail on Tinker Cliffs. Appalachian Trail Conference corridor, NPS: (540) 961–5551. *DeLorme: Virginia Atlas & Gazetteer:* Page 42, A/B2.

Segment 3 – Roanoke to Rockfish Gap

19 Little Cove Mountain Trail

South of Jennings Creek, the AT rides a high ridge called Cove Mountain. In total, there are ten small knobs en route, from the trailhead on Virginia Route 614 to the blue-blazed Little Cove Mountain Trail. Cove Mountain (2,720 feet) marks the highest point. A return hike on Little Cove Mountain Trail passes through the watershed of Cove Creek and Little Cove Creek. Where the Little Cove trail ends at VA 614, turn left and walk 0.7 mile up gravel VA 614 to the trailhead. This hike features a shale barren, a rare ecosystem hosting prickly pear and other fragile plants, located off the AT near VA 614. Glenwood-Pedlar Ranger District/GWNF. Call (540) 291–2188. *DeLorme: Virginia Atlas & Gazetteer:* Page 53, D5.

20 Apple Orchard Falls-Cornelius Creek Loop

The AT measures only 1.1 miles between Apple Orchard Falls National Recreation Trail and Cornelius Falls Trail. This short stint, however, makes possible a delight of a hike alongside two beautiful streams replete with waterfalls, pools, and thick stands of rhododendron and mountain laurel. There is considerable elevation loss and gain on this 7.6-mile loop—as much as 2,000 feet difference from the AT to Forest Road 59, where you pick up the Cornelius Falls Trail for a return to the AT. Begin the trip at a parking area on the Sunset Field Overlook on the Blue Ridge Parkway (milepost 78.4). Glenwood-Pedlar Ranger District/GWNF. Call (540) 291–2188. *DeLorme: Virginia Atlas & Gazetteer:* Page 53, D6.

21 James River Face Wilderness

The AT through this mountainous, 8,903-acre wilderness area was reconstructed in 2000. It now begins at the James River Foot Bridge, on the north bank of the James on U.S. Highway 501/Virginia Route 130 (the bridge is named in honor of Bill Foot, a Natural Bridge ATC volunteer who passed away in 2000). After crossing, the AT passes beneath high cliff walls in the river gorge, then climbs gradually up Matts Creek to the Matts Creek Shelter. (The old AT route has been renamed.) Several trails branch off the AT in the wilderness. Belfast Trail leads to Devil's Marbleyard, an eight-acre boulder field with rocks the size of cars. From an alternate trailhead on the Blue Ridge Parkway (milepost 71), hike the AT 1.2 miles to Highcock Knob (3,073 feet). Views from the top are limited in summer. Glenwood-Pedlar Ranger District/GWNF. Call (540) 291–2188. *DeLorme: Virginia Atlas & Gazetteer:* Page 53, D7.

22 Old Hotel Trail

(See Hike 24: Mount Pleasant.)

23 Rocky Mountain/Lovingston Spring

A 5.8-mile stretch of the AT runs from Salt Log Gap on Forest Road 63 (extension of Virginia Route 634) to the Seeley-Woodworth AT shelter. A return on Lovingston Spring Trail makes an 11.7-mile loop. Wildflowers, mosses, and ferns grow thick around the many springs on these trails. There are signs of an old apple orchard near the AT uphill from Salt Log Gap. Wolf Rocks is a scenic overlook with views of The Priest (northeast) and Rocky Mountain (west). The return trip includes a 0.8-mile sidetrip (0.4 mile each way) up Rocky Mountain, a summit with views west over the Shenandoah Valley. Glenwood-Pedlar Ranger District/GWNF. Call (540) 291–2188. *DeLorme: Virginia Atlas & Gazetteer:* Page 54, B2.

24 Spy Rock

There are two access points on the AT for this overlook, famous for its wide views of the Cardinal, The Priest, Little Priest, and the Friar. If time is short, use the 0.4 mile of the AT that links Fish Hatchery Trail (a 1.2-mile extension of Virginia Route 690 east of Montebello) with the 0.1-mile Spy Rock Trail. This makes a total loop of 3.4 miles. (Ask permission to park at the state-run fish hatchery.) For a longer trip, hike the AT for 3.2 miles between Virginia Route 826 (Crabtree Farm Road) and Spy Rock. Access to the AT is a half mile uphill from Crabtree Campground on VA 826. Glenwood-Pedlar Ranger District/GWNF. Call (540) 291–2188. *DeLorme: Virginia Atlas & Gazetteer:* Page 54, B2.

25 Mau-Har Trail

(See Hike 23: Three Ridges.)

26 Humpback Rocks

The AT departs the Humpback Rocks parking area on the Blue Ridge Parkway (milepost 6) and in 1 mile, passes a spur trail to Humpback Rocks. This 3,080 outcrop offers wide views of the Blue Ridge and Shenandoah Valley. Another mile on the AT brings the summit of Humpback Mountain (3,600 feet). A return to the parking lot makes a 4-mile hike. Blue Ridge Parkway, NPS. Call (828) 271–4779. *DeLorme: Virginia Atlas & Gazetteer:* Page 55, A4.

Segment 4 – Rockfish Gap to Chester Gap

27 Riprap Hollow-AT Loop

There is a 2.7-mile stretch of the AT between the Riprap Trail parking area (milepost 90) and Wildcat Ridge parking (milepost 92.1). To make a 10-mile loop hike, begin at the Riprap Trail parking area and descend Riprap Trail past Chimney Rock and Calvary Rock. Climb from the hollow on Wildcat Ridge Trail. Signs of a recent forest fire date from 1998 blaze that originated in the area of Calvary Rock. This a great hike for witnessing nature's regenerative powers. SNP South District. Call (540) 999–3500. *DeLorme: Virginia Atlas & Gazetteer:* Page 67, C5.

28 Jones Run-Doyles River Trail

The AT runs for 3.5 miles alongside Skyline Drive between Jones Run Trail and the Doyles River Trail. Using all three trails makes for a nice 8.2-mile hike, with small waterfalls and rock outcrops on Jones Run and the Doyles River. Begin the hike at Doyles River parking area (milepost 81.1). Descend Jones Run and ascend Jones Run Trail to Skyline Drive, then hike north on the AT. Brown Gap Road is a cut-off for a shorter 6.6-mile loop. SNP South District. Call (540) 999–3500. *DeLorme: Virginia Atlas & Gazetteer:* Page 67, C6.

29 Big Run Loop Trail

A 1.6-mile stretch of the AT links either end of Big Run Loop Trail. The hike begins at Big Run Loop Overlook (milepost 82.2), drops into the Big Run stream valley, and returns to the AT in 4.2 miles. A forest fire torched parts of the Big Run watershed. Finish the 5.8-mile loop by hiking north on the AT to the Doyles River trailhead, then uphill 200 yards to Skyline Drive. SNP South District. Call (540) 999–3500. *DeLorme: Virginia Atlas & Gazetteer:* Page 67, B6.

30 Whiteoak Canyon-Cedar Run Falls

This is an extremely popular hike that uses 3.3 miles of the AT. Popular, however, does not mean easy. At 11 miles, this loop takes the better part of the day. There are steep drop-offs and difficult climbs. Payoff comes with 40-foot cascades in Whiteoak Canyon, and the many falls and pools along Cedar Run. Use the Stony Man Nature Trail parking area (milepost 41.7) at Skyland as a starting point, and the Whiteoak-Cedar Run Link Trail to complete the loop. SNP Central District. Call (540) 999–3500. *DeLorme: Virginia Atlas & Gazetteer:* Page 74, D1.

31 Little Stony Man-Stony Man

Stony Man (3,387 feet) is a popular site thanks to Skyland, a park resort. This route uses a northern approach from the Little Stony Man parking area (milepost 39.1). The 1.2-mile hike on the AT traces tall cliffs and intersects the 0.4-mile loop trail around Stony Man's summit. Past Stoney Man, leave the AT and descend on Stony Man Horse Trail and Furnace Spring Trail. Return via the Passamaquoddy Trail. SNP Central District. Call (540) 999–3500. *DeLorme: Virginia Atlas & Gazetteer:* Page 74, D2.

32 Mary's Rock

An easy 2-mile hike on the AT leads to a 360-degree view off Mary's Rock. From the Panorama Restaurant at Thornton Gap, the AT climbs 1.9 miles on switchbacks to the overlook spur trail. Samples of rock called granodiorite from this area were carbon dated to more than one billion years, making it officially the oldest rock known in the park. Retrace the AT to the Panorama for a 4-mile hike. Parking is permitted at the restaurant. SNP Central District. Call (540) 999–3500. *DeLorme: Virginia Atlas & Gazetteer:* Page 74, C2.

33 Little Devil Stairs

Three miles of AT run between Little Hogback Overlook (milepost 19.7) and Rattlesnake Point Overlook (milepost 21.9). En route, the AT crosses Hogback Mountain (3,474 feet). Begin this hike at Little Hogback Overlook and use the Piney Branch Trail and Pole Bridge Link Trail to reach Little Devil Stairs, a 2-mile route down Keyser Run under sheer cliff walls and past picturesque waterfalls. Little Devil Stairs is a popular route, but dangerous. Use caution in icy or wet weather. Hike back up Little Devil Stairs and return to the Little Hogback Overlook on Keyser Fire Road for a 10.5-mile loop. SNP Northern District. Call (540) 999–3500. *DeLorme: Virginia Atlas & Gazetteer:* Page 74, B2.

34 Mount Marshall

(See Hike 12: Bluff Trail/AT Loop.)

Segment 5 – Chester Gap to Harpers Ferry

35 Lake Thompson

(See Hike 9: G. Richard Thompson Wildlife Management Area.)

36 Sky Meadows State Park

A 3.6-mile piece of the AT runs through this beautiful Virginia state park set hard against the eastern foothills of the Blue Ridge. Large meadows lend the area a pastoral feel, but steep climbs await hikers on North Ridge Trail. Gap Run Trail follows a woodland stream, and Piedmont Overlook Trail features nice views of the meadows that sweep off the mountainside. Sky Meadows operated as a farm in the mid-1800s. A stone farmhouse now serves as a visitor center (seasonal) and there are several outbuildings, including stables for horseback riders. Entrance to the park is on U.S. Highway 17, 1.2 miles south of U.S. Highway 50. An entrance fee varies by season, $3.00–$4.00. Call (800) 933–PARK for camping reservations. *DeLorme: Virginia Atlas & Gazetteer:* Page 75, A5.

37 Loudoun Heights Trail

A 2.4-mile stretch of the AT joins the Loudoun Heights Trail for a moderately difficult day hike. There are views over the Potomac from Split Rock, a promontory on Loudoun Heights Trail. (The view also explains why Stonewall Jackson bombarded Harpers Ferry, West Virginia, from this hill in 1862.) This hike requires some roadside trekking on busy U.S. Highway 340 and navigation through Harpers Ferry National Historical Park. There are two access points: Harpers Ferry National Historical Park ($5.00 parking fee in a secure overnight lot; $3.00 for those arriving on foot or bicycle) or a road-side pull-off on US 340 at Virginia Route 671 in Virginia (unsecured and suitable for day hikes only). Call the park at (304) 535–6298 or the ATC at (304) 535–6068. In wintertime, the ATC headquarters is closed on weekends. Outfitters at Harpers Ferry, 189 High Street, Harpers Ferry, WV, (888) 535–2087, sells maps. *DeLorme: Virginia Atlas & Gazetteer:* Page 79, B7.

The Art of Hiking

When standing nose to nose with a mountain lion, you're probably not too concerned with the issue of ethical behavior in the wild. No doubt you're just terrified. But let's be honest. How often are you nose to nose with a mountain lion? For most of us, a hike into the "wild" means loading up the SUV with expensive gear and driving to a toileted trailhead. Sure, you can mourn how civilized we've become—how GPS units have replaced natural instinct and Gore-Tex, true-grit—but the silly gadgets of civilization aside, we have plenty of reason to take pride in how we've matured. With survival now on the back burner, we've begun to reason—and it's about time—that we have a responsibility to protect, no longer just conquer, our wild places: that they, not we, are at risk. So please, do what you can. The following section will help you understand better what it means to "do what you can" while still making the most of your hiking experience. Anyone can take a hike, but hiking safely and well is an art requiring preparation and proper equipment.

Trail Etiquette

Zero impact. Always leave an area just like you found it—if not better than you found it. Avoid camping in fragile, alpine meadows and along the banks of streams and lakes. Use a camp stove versus building a wood fire. Pack up all of your trash and extra food. Bury human waste at least 100 feet from water sources under 6 to 8 inches of topsoil. Don't bathe with soap in a lake or stream—use prepackaged moistened towels to wipe off sweat and dirt, or bathe in the water without soap.

    Stay on the trail. It's true, a path anywhere leads nowhere new, but purists will just have to get over it. Paths serve an important purpose; they limit impact on natural areas. Straying from a designated trail may seem innocent but it can cause damage to sensitive areas—damage that may take years to recover, if it can recover at all. Even simple shortcuts can be destructive. So, please, stay on the trail.

    Leave no weeds. Noxious weeds tend to overtake other plants, which in turn affects animals and birds that depend on them for food. To minimize the spread of noxious weeds, hikers should regularly clean their boots, tents, packs, and hiking poles of mud and seeds. Also brush your dog to remove any weed seeds before heading off into a new area.

    Keep your dog under control. You can buy a flexi-lead that allows your dog to go exploring along the trail, while allowing you the ability to reel him in should another hiker approach or should he decide to chase a rabbit. Always obey leash laws and be sure to bury your dog's waste or pack it in resealable plastic bags.

Respect other trail users. Often you're not the only one on the trail. With the rise in popularity of multiuse trails, you'll have to learn a new kind of respect, beyond the nod and "hello" approach you may be used to. First investigate whether you're on a multiuse trail, and assume the appropriate precautions. When you encounter motorized vehicles (ATVs, motorcycles, and 4WDs), be alert. Though they should always yield to the hiker, often they're going too fast or are too lost in the buzz of their engine to react to your presence. If you hear activity ahead, step off the trail just to be safe. Note that you're not likely to hear a mountain biker coming, so be prepared and know ahead of time whether you share the trail with them. Cyclists should always yield to hikers, but that's little comfort to the hiker. Be aware. When you approach horses or pack animals on the trail, always step quietly off the trail, preferably on the downhill side, and let them pass. If you're wearing a large backpack, it's often a good idea to sit down. To some animals, a hiker wearing a large backpack might appear threatening. Many national forests allow domesticated grazing, usually for sheep and cattle. Make sure your dog doesn't harass these animals, and respect ranchers' rights while you're enjoying yours.

Getting into Shape

Unless you want to be sore—and possibly have to shorten your trip or vacation—be sure to get in shape before a big hike. If you're terribly out of shape, start a walking program early, preferably eight weeks in advance. Start with a fifteen-minute walk during your lunch hour or after work and gradually increase your walking time to an hour. You should also increase your elevation gain. Walking briskly up hills really strengthens your leg muscles and gets your heart rate up. If you work in a storied office building, take the stairs instead of the elevator. If you prefer going to a gym, walk the treadmill or use a stair machine. You can further increase your strength and endurance by walking with a loaded backpack. Stationary exercises you might consider are squats, leg lifts, sit-ups, and push-ups. Other good ways to get in shape include biking, running, aerobics, and, of course, short hikes. Stretching before and after a hike keeps muscles flexible and helps avoid injuries.

Preparedness

It's been said that failing to plan means planning to fail. So do take the necessary time to plan your trip. Whether going on a short day hike or an extended backpack trip, always prepare for the worst. Simply remembering to pack a copy of the *U.S. Army Survival Manual* is not preparedness. Although it's not a bad idea if you plan on entering truly wild places, it's merely the tourniquet answer to a problem. You need to do your best to prevent the problem from arising in the first place. In order to survive—and to stay reasonably comfortable—you need to concern yourself with the basics: water, food, and shelter. Don't go on a hike without having these bases covered. And don't go on a hike expecting to find these items in the woods.

Water. Even in frigid conditions, you need at least two quarts of water a day to function efficiently. Add heat and taxing terrain and you can bump that figure up to one gallon. That's simply a base to work from—your metabolism and your level of conditioning can raise or lower that amount. Unless you know your level, assume that you need one gallon of water a day. Now, where do you plan on getting the water?

Preferably not from natural water sources. These sources can be loaded with intestinal disturbers, such as bacteria, viruses, and fertilizers. *Giardia lamblia,* the most common of these disturbers, is a protozoan parasite that lives part of its life cycle as a cyst in water sources. The parasite spreads when mammals defecate in water sources. Once ingested, Giardia can induce cramping, diarrhea, vomiting, and fatigue within two days to two weeks after ingestion. Giardiasis is treatable with prescription drugs. If you believe you've contracted giardiasis, see a doctor immediately.

Treating water. The best and easiest solution to avoid polluted water is to carry your water with you. Yet, depending on the nature of your hike and the duration, this may not be an option—one gallon of water weighs eight-and-a-half pounds. In that case, you'll need to look into treating water. Regardless of which method you choose, you should always carry some water with you in case of an emergency. Save this reserve until you absolutely need it.

There are three methods of treating water: boiling, chemical treatment, and filtering. If you boil water, it's recommended that you do so for ten to fifteen minutes. This is often impractical because you're forced to exhaust a great deal of your fuel supply. You can opt for chemical treatment, which will kill Giardia but will not take care of other chemical pollutants. Another drawback to chemical treatments is the unpleasant taste of the water after it's treated. You can remedy this by adding powdered drink mix to the water. Filters are the preferred method for treating water. Many filters remove Giardia, organic and inorganic contaminants, and don't leave an aftertaste. Water filters are far from perfect as they can easily become clogged or leak if a gasket wears out. It's always a good idea to carry a backup supply of chemical treatment tablets in case your filter decides to quit on you.

Food. If we're talking about survival, you can go days without food, as long as you have water. But we're also talking about comfort. Try to avoid foods that are high in sugar and fat like candy bars and potato chips. These food types are harder to digest and are low in nutritional value. Instead, bring along foods that are easy to pack, nutritious, and high in energy (e.g., bagels, nutrition bars, dehydrated fruit, gorp, and jerky). If you are on an overnight trip, easy-to-fix dinners include rice mixes with dehydrated potatoes, corn, pasta with cheese sauce, and soup mixes. For a tasty breakfast, you can fix hot oatmeal with brown sugar and reconstituted milk powder topped off with banana chips. If you like a hot drink in the morning, bring along herbal tea bags or hot chocolate. If you are a coffee junkie, you can purchase coffee that is packaged like tea bags. You can prepackage all of your meals in heavy-duty resealable plastic bags to keep food from spilling in your pack. These bags can be reused to pack out trash.

Shelter. The type of shelter you choose depends less on the conditions than on your tolerance for discomfort. Shelter comes in many forms—tent, tarp, lean-to, bivy sack, cabin, cave, etc. If you're camping in the desert, a bivy sack may suffice, but if you're above the treeline and a storm is approaching, a better choice is a three- or four-season tent. Tents are the logical and most popular choice for most backpackers as they're lightweight and packable—and you can rest assured that you always have shelter from the elements. Before you leave on your trip, anticipate what the weather and terrain will be like and plan for the type of shelter that will work best for your comfort level (see Equipment later in this section).

Finding a campsite. If there are established campsites, stick to those. If not, start looking for a campsite early—around 3:30 or 4:00 P.M. Stop at the first decent site you see. Depending on the area, it could be a long time before you find another suitable location. Pitch your camp in an area that's level. Make sure the area is at least 200 feet from fragile areas like lakeshores, meadows, and stream banks. And try to avoid areas thick in underbrush, as they can harbor insects and provide cover for approaching animals.

If you are camping in stormy, rainy weather, look for a rock outcrop or a shelter in the trees to keep the wind from blowing your tent all night. Be sure that you don't camp under trees with dead limbs that might break off on top of you. Also, try to find an area that has an absorbent surface, such as sandy soil or forest duff. This, in addition to camping on a surface with a slight angle, will provide better drainage. By all means, don't dig trenches to provide drainage around your tent—remember you're practicing zero-impact camping.

If you're in bear country, steer clear of creek beds or animal paths. If you see any signs of a bear's presence (i.e., scat, footprints), relocate. You'll need to find a campsite near a tall tree where you can hang your food and other items that may attract bears such as deodorant, toothpaste, or soap. Carry a lightweight nylon rope with which to hang your food. As a rule, you should hang your food at least 20 feet from the ground and 5 feet away from the tree trunk. You can put food and other items in a waterproof stuff sack and tie one end of the rope to the stuff sack. To get the other end of the rope over the tree branch, tie a good size rock to it, and gently toss the rock over the tree branch. Pull the stuff sack up until it reaches the top of the branch and tie it off securely. Don't hang your food near your tent! If possible, hang your food at least 100 feet away from your campsite. Alternatives to hanging your food are bear-proof plastic tubes and metal bear boxes.

Lastly, think of comfort. Lie down on the ground where you intend to sleep and see if it's a good fit. For morning warmth (and a nice view to wake up to), have your tent face east.

First Aid

I know you're tough, but get 10 miles into the woods and develop a blister and you'll wish you had carried that first-aid kit. Face it, it's just plain good sense. Many companies produce lightweight, compact first-aid kits. Just make sure yours contains at least the following:

- adhesive bandages
- moleskin or duct tape
- various sterile gauze and dressings
- white surgical tape
- an Ace bandage
- an antihistamine
- aspirin
- Betadine solution
- a first-aid book
- antacid tablets

- tweezers
- scissors
- antibacterial wipes
- triple-antibiotic ointment
- plastic gloves
- sterile cotton tip applicators
- syrup of ipecac (to induce vomiting)
- thermometer
- wire splint

Here are a few tips for dealing with and hopefully preventing certain ailments.

Sunburn. Take along sunscreen or sun block, protective clothing, and a wide-brimmed hat. If you do get a sunburn, treat the area with aloe vera gel, and protect the area from further sun exposure. At higher elevations, the sun's radiation can be particularly damaging to skin. Remember that your eyes are vulnerable to this radiation as well. Sunglasses can be a good way to prevent headaches and permanent eye damage from the sun, especially in places where light-colored rock or patches of snow reflect light up in your face.

Blisters. Be prepared to take care of these hike-spoilers by carrying moleskin (a lightly padded adhesive), gauze and tape, or adhesive bandages. An effective way to apply moleskin is to cut out a circle of moleskin and remove the center—like a doughnut—and place it over the blistered area. Cutting the center out will reduce the pressure applied to the sensitive skin. Other products can help you combat blisters. Some are applied to suspicious hot spots before a blister forms to help decrease friction to that area, while others are applied to the blister after it has popped to help prevent further irritation.

Insect bites and stings. You can treat most insect bites and stings by applying hydrocortisone 1% cream topically and taking a pain medication such as ibuprofen or acetaminophen to reduce swelling. If you forgot to pack these items, a cold compress or a paste of mud and ashes can sometimes assuage the itching and discomfort. Remove any stingers by using tweezers or scraping the area with your fingernail or a knife blade. Don't pinch the area as you'll only spread the venom.

Some hikers are highly sensitive to bites and stings and may have a serious allergic reaction that can be life threatening. Symptoms of a serious allergic reaction can include wheezing, an asthmatic attack, and shock. The treatment for this severe type of reaction is epinephrine. If you know that you are sensitive to bites and stings, carry a pre-packaged kit of epinephrine, which can be obtained only by prescription from your doctor.

Ticks. Ticks can carry diseases such as Rocky Mountain spotted fever and Lyme disease. The best defense is, of course, prevention. If you know you're going to be hiking through an area littered with ticks, wear long pants and a long-sleeved shirt. You can apply a permethrin repellent to your clothing and a Deet repellent to exposed skin. At the end of your hike, do a spot check for ticks (and insects in general). If you do find a tick, coat the insect with petroleum jelly or tree sap to cut off its air supply. The tick should release its hold, but if it doesn't, grab the head of the tick firmly—with a pair of tweezers if you have them—and gently pull it away from the skin with a twisting motion. Sometimes the mouth parts linger, embedded in your skin. If this happens, try to remove them with a disinfected needle. Clean the affected area with an antibacterial cleanser and then apply triple antibiotic ointment. Monitor the area for a few days. If irritation persists or a white spot develops, see a doctor for possible infection.

Poison ivy, oak, and sumac. These skin irritants can be found most anywhere in North America and come in the form of a bush or a vine, having leaflets in groups of three, five, seven, or nine. Learn how to spot the plants. The oil they secrete can cause an allergic reaction in the form of blisters, usually about twelve hours after exposure. The itchy rash can last from ten days to several weeks. The best defense against these irritants is to wear clothing that covers the arms, legs, and torso. For summer, zip-off cargo pants come in handy. There are also nonprescription lotions you can apply to exposed skin that guard against the effects of poison ivy/oak/sumac and can be washed off with soap and water. If you think you were in contact with the plants, after hiking (or even on the trail during longer hikes) wash with soap and water. Taking a hot shower with soap after you return home from your hike will also help to remove any lingering oil from your skin. Should you contract a rash from any of these plants, use an antihistamine to reduce the itching. If the rash is localized, create a light bleach/water wash to dry up the area. If the rash has spread, either tough it out or see your doctor about getting a dose of cortisone (available both orally and by injection).

Snakebites. Snakebites are rare in North America. Unless startled or provoked, the majority of snakes will not bite. If you are wise to their habitats and keep a careful eye on the trail, you should be just fine. When stepping over logs, first step on the log, making sure you can see what's on the other side before stepping down. Though your chances of being struck are slim, it's wise to know what to do in the event you are.

If a *nonpoisonous* snake bites you, allow the wound to bleed a small amount and then cleanse the wounded area with a Betadine solution (10% povidone iodine).

Rinse the wound with clean water (preferably) or fresh urine (it might sound ugly, but it's sterile). Once the area is clean, cover it with triple antibiotic ointment and a clean bandage. Remember, most residual damage from snakebites, poisonous or otherwise, comes from infection, not the snake's venom. Keep the area as clean as possible and get medical attention immediately.

If you are bitten by a poisonous snake, remove the toxin with a suctioning device, found in a snakebite kit. If you do not have such a device, squeeze the wound—DO NOT use your mouth for suction, as the venom will enter your bloodstream through the vessels under the tongue and head straight for your heart. Then, clean the wound just as you would a nonpoisonous bite. Tie a clean band of cloth snugly around the afflicted appendage, about an inch or so above the bite (or the rim of the swelling). This is NOT a tourniquet—you want to simply slow the blood flow, not cut it off. Loosen the band if numbness ensues. Remove the band for a minute and reapply a little higher every ten minutes.

If it is your friend who's been bitten, treat him or her for shock—make the person comfortable, have him or her lie down, elevate the legs, and keep him or her warm. Avoid applying anything cold to the bite wound. Immobilize the affected area and remove any constricting items such as rings, watches, or restrictive clothing—swelling may occur. Once your friend is stable and relatively calm, hike out to get help. The victim should get treatment within twelve hours, ideally, which usually consists of a tetanus shot, antivenin, and antibiotics.

If you are alone and struck by a poisonous snake, stay calm. Hysteria will only quicken the venom's spread. Follow the procedure above, and do your best to reach help. When hiking out, don't run—you'll only increase the flow of blood throughout your system. Instead, walk calmly.

Dehydration. Have you ever hiked in hot weather and had a roaring headache and felt fatigued after only a few miles? More than likely you were dehydrated. Symptoms of dehydration include fatigue, headache, and decreased coordination and judgment. When you are hiking, your body's rate of fluid loss depends on the outside temperature, humidity, altitude, and your activity level. On average, a hiker walking in warm weather will lose four liters of fluid a day. That fluid loss is easily replaced by normal consumption of liquids and food. However, if a hiker is walking briskly in hot, dry weather and hauling a heavy pack, he or she can lose one to three liters of water an hour. It's important to always carry plenty of water and to stop often and drink fluids regularly, even if you aren't thirsty.

Heat exhaustion is the result of a loss of large amounts of electrolytes and often occurs if a hiker is dehydrated and has been under heavy exertion. Common symptoms of heat exhaustion include cramping, exhaustion, fatigue, lightheadedness, and nausea. You can treat heat exhaustion by getting out of the sun and drinking an electrolyte solution made up of one teaspoon of salt and one tablespoon of sugar dissolved in a liter of water. Drink this solution slowly over a period of one hour.

Drinking plenty of fluids (preferably an electrolyte solution/sports drink) can prevent heat exhaustion. Avoid hiking during the hottest parts of the day, and wear breathable clothing, a wide-brimmed hat, and sunglasses.

Hypothermia is one of the biggest dangers in the backcountry, especially for day hikers in the summertime. That may sound strange, but imagine starting out on a hike in midsummer when it's sunny and 80 degrees out. You're clad in nylon shorts and a cotton T-shirt. About halfway through your hike, the sky begins to cloud up, and in the next hour a light drizzle begins to fall and the wind starts to pick up. Before you know it, you are soaking wet and shivering—the perfect recipe for hypothermia. More advanced signs include decreased coordination, slurred speech, and blurred vision. When a victim's temperature falls below 92 degrees, the blood pressure and pulse plummet, possibly leading to coma and death.

To avoid hypothermia, always bring a windproof/rainproof shell, a fleece jacket, tights made of a breathable, synthetic fiber, gloves, and hat when you are hiking in the mountains. Learn to adjust your clothing layers based on the temperature. If you are climbing uphill at a moderate pace you will stay warm, but when you stop for a break you'll become cold quickly, unless you add more layers of clothing.

If a hiker is showing advanced signs of hypothermia, dress him or her in dry clothes and make sure he or she is wearing a hat and gloves. Place the person in a sleeping bag in a tent or shelter that will protect him or her from the wind and other elements. Give the person warm fluids to drink and keep him or her awake.

Frostbite. When the mercury dips below 32 degrees, your extremities begin to chill. If a persistent chill attacks a localized area, say, your hands or your toes, the circulatory system reacts by cutting off blood flow to the affected area—the idea being to protect and preserve the body's overall temperature. And so it's death by attrition for the affected area. Ice crystals start to form from the water in the cells of the neglected tissue. Deprived of heat, nourishment, and now water, the tissue literally starves. This is frostbite.

Prevention is your best defense against this situation. Most prone to frostbite are your face, hands, and feet, so protect these areas well. Wool is the material of choice because it provides ample air space for insulation and draws moisture away from the skin. Synthetic fabrics, however, have recently made great strides in the cold weather clothing market. Do your research. A pair of light silk liners under your regular gloves is a good trick for keeping warm. They afford some additional warmth, but more importantly they'll allow you to remove your mitts for tedious work without exposing the skin.

If your feet or hands start to feel cold or numb due to the elements, warm them as quickly as possible. Place cold hands under your armpits or bury them in your crotch. If your feet are cold, change your socks. If there's plenty of room in your boots, add another pair of socks. Do remember, though, that constricting your feet in tight boots can restrict blood flow and actually make your feet colder more quickly. Your socks need to have breathing room if they're going to be effective.

Dead air provides insulation. If your face is cold, place your warm hands over your face, or simply wear a head stocking.

Should your skin go numb and start to appear white and waxy, chances are you've got or are developing frostbite. Don't try to thaw the area unless you can maintain the warmth. In other words, don't stop to warm up your frostbitten feet only to head back on the trail. You'll do more damage than good. Tests have shown that hikers who walked on thawed feet did more harm, and endured more pain, than hikers who left the affected areas alone. Do your best to get out of the cold entirely and seek medical attention—which usually consists of performing a rapid rewarming in water for twenty to thirty minutes.

The overall objective in preventing both hypothermia and frostbite is to keep the body's core warm. Protect key areas where heat escapes, like the top of the head, and maintain the proper nutrition level. Foods that are high in calories aid the body in producing heat. Never smoke or drink when you're in situations where the cold is threatening. By affecting blood flow, these activities ultimately cool the body's core temperature.

Altitude sickness (AMS). High lofty peaks, clear alpine lakes, and vast mountain views beckon hikers to the high country. But those who like to venture high may become victims of altitude sickness (also known as Acute Mountain Sickness—AMS). Altitude sickness is your body's reaction to insufficient oxygen in the blood due to decreased barometric pressure. While some hikers may feel lightheaded, nauseous, and experience shortness of breath at 7,000 feet, others may not experience these symptoms until they reach 10,000 feet or higher.

Slowing your ascent to high places and giving your body a chance to acclimatize to the higher elevations can prevent altitude sickness. For example, if you live at sea level and are planning a weeklong backpacking trip to elevations between 7,000 and 12,000 feet, start by staying below 7,000 feet for one night, then move to between 7,000 and 10,000 feet for another night or two. Avoid strenuous exertion and alcohol to give your body a chance to adjust to the new altitude. It's also important to eat light food and drink plenty of nonalcoholic fluids, preferably water. Loss of appetite at altitude is common, but you must eat!

Most hikers who experience mild to moderate AMS develop a headache and/or nausea, grow lethargic, and have problems sleeping. The treatment for AMS is simple: stop heading uphill. Keep eating and drinking water and take meds for the headache. You actually need to take more breaths at altitude than at sea level, so breathe a little faster without hyperventilating. If symptoms don't improve over twenty-four to forty-eight hours, descend. Once a victim descends about 2,000 to 3,000 feet, his or her signs will usually begin to diminish.

Severe AMS comes in two forms: High Altitude Pulmonary Edema (HAPE) and High Altitude Cerebral Edema (HACE). HAPE, an accumulation of fluid in the lungs, can occur above 8,000 feet. Symptoms include rapid heart rate, shortness of breath at rest, AMS symptoms, dry cough developing into a wet cough, gurgling sounds, flu-like or bronchitis symptoms, and lack of muscle coordination. HAPE is life threatening so descend immediately, at least 2,000 to 4,000 feet. HACE usually occurs above 12,000 feet but sometimes occurs above 10,000 feet. Symptoms are similar to HAPE but also include seizures, hallucinations, paralysis, and vision disturbances. Descend immediately—HACE is also life threatening.

Hantavirus Pulmonary Syndrome (HPS). Deer mice spread the virus that causes HPS, and humans contract it from breathing it in, usually when they've disturbed an area with dust and mice feces from nests or surfaces with mice droppings or urine. Exposure to large numbers of rodents and their feces or urine presents the greatest risk. Hikers sometimes enter old buildings, and often deer mice live in these places. You may not be around long enough to be exposed, but do be aware of this disease. About half the people who develop HPS die. Symptoms are flu-like and appear about two to three weeks after exposure. After initial symptoms, a dry cough and shortness of breath follow. Breathing is difficult. If you even think you might have HPS, see a doctor immediately!

Natural Hazards

Besides tripping over a rock or tree root on the trail, there are some real hazards to be aware of while hiking. Even if where you're hiking doesn't have the plethora of poisonous snakes and plants, insects, and grizzly bears found in other parts of the United States, there are a few weather conditions and predators you may need to take into account.

Lightning. Thunderstorms build over the mountains almost every day during the summer. Lightning is generated by thunderheads and can strike without warning, even several miles away from the nearest overhead cloud. The best rule of thumb is to start leaving exposed peaks, ridges, and canyon rims by about noon. This time can vary a little depending on storm buildup. Keep an eye on cloud formation and don't underestimate how fast a storm can build. The bigger they get, the more likely a thunderstorm will happen. Lightning takes the path of least resistance, so if you're the high point, it might choose you. Ducking under a rock overhang is dangerous, as you form the shortest path between the rock and ground. If you dash below treeline, avoid standing under the only or the tallest tree. If you are caught above treeline, stay away from anything metal you might be carrying, Move down off the ridge slightly to a low, treeless point and squat until the storm passes. If you have an insulating pad, squat on it. Avoid having both your hands and feet touching the ground at once and never lay flat. If you hear a buzzing sound or feel your hair standing on end, move quickly as an electrical charge is building up.

Flash floods. On July 31, 1976, a torrential downpour unleashed by a thunderstorm dumped tons of water into the Big Thompson watershed near Estes Park. Within hours a wall of water moved down the narrow canyon, killing 139 people and causing more than $30 million in property damage. The spooky thing about flash floods, especially in western canyons, is that they can appear out of nowhere from a storm many miles away. While hiking or driving in canyons, keep an eye on the weather. Always climb to safety if danger threatens. Flash floods usually subside quickly, so be patient and don't cross a swollen stream.

Bears. Most of the United States (outside of the Pacific Northwest and parts of the Northern Rockies) does not have a grizzly bear population, although some rumors exist about sightings where there should be none. Black bears are plentiful, however. Here are some tips in case you and a bear scare each other. Most of all, avoid scaring a bear. Watch for bear tracks (five toes) and droppings (sizable with leaves, partly digested berries, seeds, and/or animal fur). Talk or sing where visibility or hearing are limited. Keep a clean camp, hang food, and don't sleep in the clothes you wore while cooking. Be especially careful in spring to avoid getting between a mother and her cubs. In late summer and fall bears are busy eating berries and acorns to fatten up for winter, so be extra careful around berry bushes and oakbrush. If you do encounter a bear, move away slowly while facing the bear, talk softly, and avoid direct eye contact. Give the bear room to escape. Since bears are very curious, it might stand upright to get a better whiff of you, and it may even charge you to try to intimidate you. Try to stay calm. If a bear does attack you, fight back with anything you have handy. Unleashed dogs have been known to come running back to their owners with a bear close behind. Keep your dog on a leash or leave it at home.

Mountain lions. Mountain lions appear to be getting more comfortable around humans as long as deer (their favorite prey) are in an area with adequate cover. Usually elusive and quiet, lions rarely attack people. If you meet a lion, give it a chance to escape. Stay calm and talk firmly to it. Back away slowly while facing the lion. If you run, you'll only encourage the curious cat to chase you. Make yourself look large by opening a jacket, if you have one, or waving your hiking poles. If the lion behaves aggressively throw stones, sticks, or whatever you can while remaining tall. If a lion does attack, fight for your life with anything you can grab.

Moose. Because moose have very few natural predators, they don't fear humans like other animals. You might find moose in sagebrush and wetter areas of willow, aspen, and pine, or in beaver habitats. Mothers with calves, as well as bulls during mating season, can be particularly aggressive. If a moose threatens you, back away slowly and talk calmly to it. Keep your pets away from moose.

Other considerations. Hunting is a popular sport in the United States, especially during rifle season in October and November. Hiking is still enjoyable in those months in many areas, so just take a few precautions. First, learn when the different hunting seasons start and end in the area in which you'll be hiking. During this time frame, be sure to wear at least a blaze orange hat, and possibly put an orange vest over your pack. Don't be surprised to see hunters in camo outfits carrying bows or muzzleloading rifles around during their season. If you would feel more comfortable without hunters around, hike in national parks and monuments or state and local parks where hunting is not allowed.

Navigation

Whether you are going on a short hike in a familiar area or planning a weeklong backpack trip, you should always be equipped with the proper navigational equipment—at the very least a detailed map and a sturdy compass.

Maps. There are many different types of maps available to help you find your way on the trail. Easiest to find are Forest Service maps and BLM (Bureau of Land Management) maps. These maps tend to cover large areas, so be sure they are detailed enough for your particular trip. You can also obtain national park maps as well as high-quality maps from private companies and trail groups. These maps can be obtained either from outdoor stores or ranger stations.

U.S. Geological Survey topographic maps are particularly popular with hikers—especially serious backcountry hikers. These maps contain the standard map symbols such as roads, lakes, and rivers, as well as contour lines that show the details of the trail terrain like ridges, valleys, passes, and mountain peaks. The 7.5-minute series (1 inch on the map equals approximately ⅖ mile on the ground) provides the closest inspection available. USGS maps are available by mail (U.S. Geological Survey, Map Distribution Branch, P.O. Box 25286, Denver, CO 80225), or at mapping.usgs.gov/esic/to_order.html.

If you want to check out the high-tech world of maps, you can purchase topographic maps on CD-ROM. These software-mapping programs let you select a route on your computer, print it out, then take it with you on the trail. Some software mapping programs let you insert symbols and labels, download waypoints from a GPS unit, and export the maps to other software programs.

The art of map reading is a skill that you can develop by first practicing in an area you are familiar with. To begin, orient the map so the map is lined up in the correct direction (i.e. north on the map is lined up with true north). Next, familiarize yourself with the map symbols and try and match them up with terrain features around you such as a high ridge, mountain peak, river, or lake. If you are practicing with a USGS map, notice the contour lines. On gentler terrain these contour lines are spaced farther apart, and on steeper terrain they are closer together. Pick a short loop trail, and stop frequently to check your position on the map. As you practice map reading, you'll learn how to anticipate a steep section on the trail or a good place to take a rest break, and so on.

Compasses. First off, the sun is not a substitute for a compass. So, what kind of compass should you have? Here are some characteristics you should look for: a rectangular base with detailed scales, a liquid-filled housing, protective housing, a sighting line on the mirror, luminous alignment and back-bearing arrows, a luminous north-seeking arrow, and a well-defined bezel ring.

You can learn compass basics by reading the detailed instructions included with your compass. If you want to fine-tune your compass skills, sign up for an orienteering class or purchase a book on compass reading. Once you've learned the basic skills of using a compass, remember to practice these skills before you head into the backcountry.

If you are a klutz at using a compass, you may be interested in checking out the technical wizardry of the GPS (Global Positioning System) device. The GPS was developed by the Pentagon and works off twenty-four NAVSTAR satellites, which were designed to guide missiles to their targets. A GPS device is a handheld unit that calculates your latitude and longitude with the easy press of a button. The Department of Defense used to scramble the satellite signals a bit to prevent civilians (and spies!) from getting extremely accurate readings, but that practice was discontinued in May 2000, and GPS units now provide nearly pinpoint accuracy (within 30 to 60 feet).

There are many different types of GPS units available and they range in price from $100 to $400. In general, all GPS units have a display screen and keypad where you input information. In addition to acting as a compass, the unit allows you to plot your route, easily retrace your path, track your traveling speed, find the mileage between waypoints, and calculate the total mileage of your route.

Before you purchase a GPS unit, keep in mind that these devices don't pick up signals indoors, in heavily wooded areas, on mountain peaks, or in deep valleys.

Pedometers. A pedometer is a small, clip-on unit with a digital display that calculates your hiking distance in miles or kilometers based on your walking stride. Some units also calculate the calories you burn and your total hiking time. Pedometers are available at most large outdoor stores and range in price from $20 to $40.

Trip Planning

Planning your hiking adventure begins with letting a friend or relative know your trip itinerary so they can call for help if you don't return at your scheduled time. Your next task is to make sure you are outfitted to experience the risks and rewards of the trail. This section highlights gear and clothing you may want to take with you to get the most out of your hike.

Day Hikes

- camera/film
- compass/GPS unit
- pedometer
- daypack
- first-aid kit
- food
- guidebook
- headlamp/flashlight with extra batteries and bulbs
- hat
- insect repellent
- knife/multipurpose tool
- map
- matches in waterproof container and fire starter
- fleece jacket
- rain gear
- space blanket
- sunglasses
- sunscreen
- swimsuit
- watch
- water
- water bottles/water hydration system

Overnight Trips

- backpack and waterproof rain cover
- backpacker's trowel
- bandanna
- bear repellent spray
- bear bell
- biodegradable soap
- pot scrubber
- collapsible water container (2–3 gallon capacity)
- clothing—extra wool socks, shirt, and shorts
- cook set/utensils
- ditty bags to store gear
- extra plastic resealable bags
- gaiters
- garbage bag
- ground cloth
- journal/pen
- nylon rope to hang food
- long underwear
- permit (if required)
- rain jacket and pants
- sandals to wear around camp and to ford streams
- sleeping bag
- waterproof stuff sack
- sleeping pad
- small bath towel
- stove and fuel
- tent
- toiletry items
- water filter
- whistle

Equipment

With the outdoor market currently flooded with products, many of which are pure gimmickry, it seems impossible to both differentiate and choose. Do I really need a tropical-fish-lined collapsible shower? (No, you don't.) The only defense against the maddening quantity of items thrust in your face is to think practically—and to do so *before* you go shopping. The worst buys are impulsive buys. Since most name brands will differ only slightly in quality, it's best to know what you're looking for in terms of function. Buy only what you need. You will, don't forget, be carrying what you've bought on your back. Here are some things to keep in mind before you go shopping.

Clothes. Clothing is your armor against Mother Nature's little surprises. Hikers should be prepared for any possibility, especially when hiking in mountainous areas. Adequate rain protection and extra layers of clothing are a good idea. In summer, a wide-brimmed hat can help keep the sun at bay. In the winter months the first layer you'll want to wear is a "wicking" layer of long underwear that keeps perspiration away from your skin. Long underwear made from synthetic fibers wicks moisture away from the skin and draws it toward the next layer of clothing, where it then evaporates. Avoid wearing long underwear made of cotton as it is slow to dry and keeps moisture next to your skin.

The second layer you'll wear is the "insulating" layer. Aside from keeping you warm, this layer needs to "breathe" so you stay dry while hiking. A fabric that provides insulation and dries quickly is fleece. It's interesting to note that this one-of-a-kind fabric is made out of recycled plastic. Purchasing a zip-up jacket made of this material is highly recommended.

The last line of layering defense is the "shell" layer. You'll need some type of waterproof, windproof, breathable jacket that will fit over all of your other layers. It should have a large hood that fits over a hat. You'll also need a good pair of rain pants made from a similar waterproof, breathable fabric. Some Gore-Tex jackets cost as much as $500, but you should know that there are more affordable fabrics out there that work just as well.

Now that you've learned the basics of layering, you can't forget to protect your hands and face. In cold, windy, or rainy weather you'll need a hat made of wool or fleece and insulated, waterproof gloves that will keep your hands warm and toasty. As mentioned earlier, buying an additional pair of light silk liners to wear under your regular gloves is a good idea.

Footwear. If you have any extra money to spend on your trip, put that money into boots or trail shoes. Poor shoes will bring a hike to a halt faster than anything else. To avoid this annoyance, buy shoes that provide support and are lightweight and flexible. A lightweight hiking boot is better than a heavy, leather mountaineering boot for most day hikes and backpacking. Trail running shoes provide a little extra cushion and are made in a high-top style that many people wear for hiking. These running shoes are lighter, more flexible, and more breathable than hiking boots. If you know you'll be hiking in wet weather often, purchase boots or shoes with a Gore-Tex liner, which will help keep your feet dry.

When buying your boots, be sure to wear the same type of socks you'll be wearing on the trail. If the boots you're buying are for cold weather hiking, try the boots on while wearing two pairs of socks. Speaking of socks, a good cold weather sock combination is to wear a thinner sock made of wool or polypropylene covered by a heavier outer sock made of wool. The inner sock protects the foot from the rubbing effects of the outer sock and prevents blisters. Many outdoor stores have some type of ramp to simulate hiking uphill and downhill. Be sure to take advantage of this test, as toe-jamming boot fronts can be very painful and debilitating on the downhill trek.

Once you've purchased your footwear, be sure to break them in before you hit the trail. New footwear is often stiff and needs to be stretched and molded to your foot.

Hiking poles. Hiking poles help with balance, and more importantly take pressure off your knees. The ones with shock absorbers are easier on your elbows and knees. Some poles even come with a camera attachment to be used as a monopod. And heaven forbid you meet a mountain lion, bear, or unfriendly dog, the poles can make you look a lot bigger.

Backpacks. No matter what type of hiking you do you'll need a pack of some sort to carry the basic trail essentials. There are a variety of backpacks on the market, but let's first discuss what you intend to use it for. Day hikes or overnight trips?

If you plan on doing a day hike, a daypack should have some of the following characteristics: a padded hip belt that's at least 2 inches in diameter (avoid packs with only a small nylon piece of webbing for a hip belt); a chest strap (the chest strap helps stabilize the pack against your body); external pockets to carry water and other items that you want easy access to; an internal pocket to hold keys, a knife, a wallet, and other miscellaneous items; an external lashing system to hold a jacket; and a hydration pocket for carrying a hydration system (which consists of a water bladder with an attachable drinking hose).

For short hikes, some hikers like to use a fanny pack to store just a camera, food, a compass, a map, and other trail essentials. Most fanny packs have pockets for two water bottles and a padded hip belt.

If you intend to do an extended, overnight trip, there are multiple considerations. First off, you need to decide what kind of framed pack you want. There are two backpack types for backpacking: the internal frame and the external frame. An internal frame pack rests closer to your body, making it more stable and easier to balance when hiking over rough terrain. An external frame pack is just that, an aluminum frame attached to the exterior of the pack. An external frame pack is better for long backpack trips because it distributes the pack weight better and you can carry heavier loads. It's easier to pack, and your gear is more accessible. It also offers better back ventilation in hot weather.

The most critical measurement for fitting a pack is torso length. The pack needs to rest evenly on your hips without sagging. A good pack will come in two or three sizes and have straps and hip belts that are adjustable according to your body size and characteristics.

When you purchase a backpack, go to an outdoor store with salespeople who are knowledgeable in how to properly fit a pack. Once the pack is fitted for you, load the pack with the amount of weight you plan on taking on the trail. The weight of the pack should be distributed evenly and you should be able to swing your arms and walk briskly without feeling out of balance. Another good technique for evaluating a pack is to walk up and down stairs and make quick turns to the right and to the left to be sure the pack doesn't feel out of balance. Other features that are nice to have on a backpack include a removable day pack or fanny pack, external pockets for extra water, and extra lash points to attach a jacket or other items.

Sleeping bags and pads. Sleeping bags are rated by temperature. You can purchase a bag made of synthetic fiber, or you can buy a goose down bag. Goose down bags are more expensive, but they have a higher insulating capacity by weight and will keep their loft longer. You'll want to purchase a bag with a temperature rating that fits the time of year and conditions you are most likely to camp in. One caveat: The techno-standard for temperature ratings is far from perfect. Ratings vary from manufacturer to manufacturer, so to protect yourself you should purchase a bag rated 10 to 15 degrees below the temperature you expect to be camping in. Synthetic bags are more resistant to water than down bags, but many down bags are now made with a Gore-Tex shell that helps to repel water. Down bags are also more compressible than synthetic bags and take up less room in your pack, which is an important consideration if you are planning a multiday backpack trip. Features to look for in a sleeping bag include a mummy-style bag, a hood you can cinch down around your head in cold weather, and draft tubes along the zippers that help keep heat in and drafts out.

You'll also want a sleeping pad to provide insulation and padding from the cold ground. There are different types of sleeping pads available, from the more expensive self-inflating air mattresses to the less expensive closed-cell foam pads. Self-inflating air mattresses are usually heavier than closed-cell foam mattresses and are prone to punctures.

Tents. The tent is your home away from home while on the trail. It provides protection from wind, snow, rain, and insects. A three-season tent is a good choice for backpacking and can range in price from $100 to $500. These lightweight and versatile tents provide protection in all types of weather, except heavy snowstorms or high winds, and range in weight from four to eight pounds. Look for a tent that's easy to set up and will easily fit two people with gear. Dome type tents usually offer more headroom and places to store gear. Other tent designs include a vestibule where you can store wet boots and backpacks. Some nice-to-have items in a tent include interior pockets to store small items and lashing points to hang a clothesline. Most three-season tents also come with stakes so you can secure the tent in high winds. Before you purchase a tent, set it up and take it down a few times to be sure it is easy to handle. Also, sit inside the tent and make sure it has enough room for you and your gear.

Cell phones. Many hikers are carrying their cell phones into the backcountry these days in case of emergency. That's fine and good, but please know that cell phone coverage is often poor to nonexistent in valleys, canyons, and thick forest. More importantly, people have started to call for help because they're tired or lost. Let's go back to being prepared. You are responsible for yourself in the backcountry. Use your brain to avoid problems, and if you do encounter one, first use your brain to try to correct the situation. Only use your cell phone, if it works, in true emergencies.

Hiking with Children

Hiking with children isn't a matter of how many miles you can cover or how much elevation gain you make in a day; it's about seeing and experiencing nature through their eyes.

Kids like to explore and have fun. They like to stop and point out bugs and plants, look under rocks, jump in puddles, and throw sticks. If you're taking a toddler or young child on a hike, start with a trail that you're familiar with. Trails that have interesting things for kids, like piles of leaves to play in or a small stream to wade through during the summer, will make the hike much more enjoyable for them and will keep them from getting bored.

You can keep your child's attention if you have a strategy before starting on the trail. Using games is not only an effective way to keep a child's attention, it's also a great way to teach him or her about nature. Play hide and seek, where your child is the mouse and you are the hawk. Quiz children on the names of plants and animals. If your children are old enough, let them carry their own daypack filled with snacks and water. So that you are sure to go at their pace and not yours, let them lead the way. Playing follow the leader works particularly well when you have a group of children. Have each child take a turn at being the leader.

With children, a lot of clothing is key. The only thing predictable about weather is that it will change. Especially in mountainous areas, weather can change dramatically in a very short time. Always bring extra clothing for children, regardless of the season. In the winter, have your children wear wool socks and warm layers such as long underwear, a fleece jacket and hat, wool mittens, and good rain gear. It's not a bad idea to have these along in late fall and early spring as well. Good footwear is also important. A sturdy pair of high-top tennis shoes or lightweight hiking boots are the best bet for little ones. If you're hiking in the summer near a lake or stream, bring along a pair of old sneakers that your child can put on when he wants to go exploring in the water. Remember when you're near any type of water, always watch your child at all times. Also, keep a close eye on teething toddlers who may decide a rock or leaf of poison oak is an interesting item to put in their mouth.

From spring through fall, you'll want your kids to wear a wide-brimmed hat to keep their face, head, and ears protected from the hot sun. Also, make sure your children wear sunscreen at all times. Choose a brand without Paba—children have sensitive skin and may have an allergic reaction to sunscreen that contains Paba. If you are hiking with a child younger than six months, don't use sunscreen or insect repellent. Instead, be sure that their head, face, neck, and ears are protected from the sun with a wide-brimmed hat, and that all other skin exposed to the sun is protected with the appropriate clothing.

Remember that food is fun. Kids like snacks, so it's important to bring a lot of munchies for the trail. Stopping often for snack breaks is a fun way to keep the trail interesting. Raisins, apples, granola bars, crackers and cheese, cereal, and trail mix all make great snacks. If your child is old enough to carry her own backpack, fill it with treats before you leave. If your kids don't like drinking water, you can bring boxes of fruit juice.

Avoid poorly designed child-carrying packs—you don't want to break your back carrying your child. Most child-carrying backpacks designed to hold a forty-pound child will contain a large carrying pocket to hold diapers and other items. Some have an optional rain/sun hood.

Hiking with Your Dog

Bringing your furry friend with you is always more fun than leaving him behind. Our canine pals make great trail buddies because they never complain and always make good company. Hiking with your dog can be a rewarding experience, especially if you plan ahead.

Getting your dog in shape. Before you plan outdoor adventures with your dog, make sure he's in shape for the trail. Getting your dog into shape takes the same discipline as getting yourself into shape, but luckily, your dog can get in shape with you. Take your dog with you on your daily runs or walks. If there is a park near your house, hit a tennis ball or play Frisbee with your dog.

Swimming is also an excellent way to get your dog into shape. If there is a lake or river near where you live and your dog likes the water, have him retrieve a tennis ball or stick. Gradually build your dog's stamina up over a two- to three-month period. A good rule of thumb is to assume that your dog will travel twice as far as you will on the trail. If you plan on doing a 5-mile hike, be sure your dog is in shape for a 10-mile hike.

Training your dog for the trail. Before you go on your first hiking adventure with your dog, be sure he has a firm grasp on the basics of canine etiquette and behavior. Make sure he can sit, lie down, stay, and come. One of the most important commands you can teach your canine pal is to "come" under any situation. It's easy for your friend's nose to lead him astray or possibly get lost. Another helpful command is the "get behind" command. When you're on a hiking trail that's narrow, you can have your dog follow behind you when other trail users approach. Nothing is more bothersome than an enthusiastic dog that runs back and forth on the trail and disrupts the peace of the trail for others. When you see other trail users approaching you on the trail, give them the right of way by quietly stepping off the trail and making your dog lie down and stay until they pass.

Equipment. The most critical pieces of equipment you can invest in for your dog are proper identification and a sturdy leash. Flexi-leads work well for hiking because they give your dog more freedom to explore but still leave you in control. Make sure your dog has identification that includes your name and address and a number for your veterinarian. Other forms of identification for your dog include a tattoo or a microchip. You should consult your veterinarian for more information on these last two options.

The next piece of equipment you'll want to consider is a pack for your dog. By no means should you hold all of your dog's essentials in your pack—let him carry his own gear! Dogs that are in good shape can carry 30 to 40 percent of their own weight.

Most packs are fitted by a dog's weight and girth measurement. Companies that make dog packs generally include guidelines to help you pick out the size that's right for your dog. Some characteristics to look for when purchasing a pack for your dog include a harness that contains two padded girth straps, a padded chest strap, leash attachments, removable saddle bags, internal water bladders, and external gear cords.

You can introduce your dog to the pack by first placing the empty pack on his back and letting him wear it around the yard. Keep an eye on him during this first introduction. He may decide to chew through the straps if you aren't watching him closely. Once he learns to treat the pack as an object of fun and not a foreign enemy, fill the pack evenly on both sides with a few ounces of dog food in resealable plastic bags. Have your dog wear his pack on your daily walks for a period of two to three weeks. Each week add a little more weight to the pack until your dog will accept carrying the maximum amount of weight he can carry.

You can also purchase collapsible water and dog food bowls for your dog. These bowls are lightweight and can easily be stashed into your pack or your dog's. If you are hiking on rocky terrain or in the snow, you can purchase footwear for your dog that will protect his feet from cuts and bruises.

Always carry plastic bags to remove feces from the trail. It is a courtesy to other trail users and helps protect local wildlife.

The following is a list of items to bring when you take your dog hiking: collapsible water bowls, a comb, a collar and a leash, dog food, plastic bags for feces, a dog pack, flea/tick powder, paw protection, water, and a first-aid kit that contains eye ointment, tweezers, scissors, stretchy foot wrap, gauze, antibacterial wash, sterile cotton tip applicators, antibiotic ointment, and cotton wrap.

First aid for your dog. Your dog is just as prone—if not more prone—to getting in trouble on the trail as you are, so be prepared. Here's a rundown of the more likely misfortunes that might befall your little friend.

Bees and wasps. If a bee or wasp stings your dog, remove the stinger with a pair of tweezers and place a mudpack or a cloth dipped in cold water over the affected area.

Porcupines. One good reason to keep your dog on a leash is to prevent it from getting a nose full of porcupine quills. You may be able to remove the quills with pliers, but a veterinarian is the best person to do this nasty job because most dogs need to be sedated.

Heat stroke. Avoid hiking with your dog in really hot weather. Dogs with heat stroke will pant excessively, lie down and refuse to get up, and become lethargic and disoriented. If your dog shows any of these signs on the trail, have him lie down in the shade. If you are near a stream, pour cool water over your dog's entire body to help bring his body temperature back to normal.

Heartworm. Dogs get heartworms from mosquitoes, which carry the disease in the prime mosquito months of July and August. Giving your dog a monthly pill prescribed by your veterinarian easily prevents this condition.

Plant pitfalls. One of the biggest plant hazards for dogs on the trail are foxtails. Foxtails are pointed grass seed heads that bury themselves in your friend's fur, between his toes, and even get in his ear canal. If left unattended, these nasty seeds can work their way under the skin and cause abscesses and other problems. If you have a long-haired dog, consider trimming the hair between his toes and giving him a summer haircut to help prevent foxtails from attaching to his fur. After every hike, always look over your dog for these seeds—especially between his toes and his ears.

Other plant hazards include burrs, thorns, thistles, and poison oak. If you find any burrs or thistles on your dog, remove them as soon as possible before they become an unmanageable mat. Thorns can pierce a dog's foot and cause a great deal of pain. If you see that your dog is lame, stop and check his feet for thorns. Dogs are immune to poison oak but they can pick up the sticky, oily substance from the plant and transfer it to you.

Protect those paws. Be sure to keep your dog's nails trimmed so he avoids getting soft tissue or joint injuries. If your dog slows and refuses to go on, check to see that his paws aren't torn or worn. You can protect your dog's paws from trail hazards such as sharp gravel, foxtails, lava scree, and thorns by purchasing dog boots.

Sunburn. If your dog has light skin he is an easy target for sunburn on his nose and other exposed skin areas. You can apply a nontoxic sunscreen to exposed skin areas that will help protect him from overexposure to the sun.

Sasha (the authors' loyal trail companion) in the Mountain Lake Wilderness.

Ticks and fleas. Ticks can easily give your dog Lyme disease, as well as other diseases. Before you hit the trail, treat your dog with a flea and tick spray or powder. You can also ask your veterinarian about a once-a-month pour-on treatment that repels fleas and ticks.

Mosquitoes and deer flies. These little flying machines can do a job on your dog's snout and ears. Best bet is to spray your dog with fly repellent for horses to discourage both pests.

Giardia. Dogs can get giardia, which results in diarrhea. It is usually not debilitating, but it's definitely messy. A vaccine against giardia is available.

Mushrooms. Make sure your dog doesn't sample mushrooms along the trail. They could be poisonous to him, but he doesn't know that.

When you are finally ready to hit the trail with your dog, keep in mind that national parks and many wilderness areas do not allow dogs on trails. Your best bet is to hike in national forests, BLM lands, and state parks. Always call ahead to see what the restrictions are.

Off the Trail

(Events and Festivals throughout Virginia)

Eastern Virginia

Annual Pony Swim and Penning, July, Chincoteague, VA, (757) 787–2460. An event of national renown. Wild Chincoteague ponies are driven off the refuge, across a small water passage, and penned on Chincoteague Island for auction.

International Migratory Bird Celebration, May, and **Eastern Shore Birding Festival,** October, Chincoteague NWR, (757) 336–6122. Two major birding events held in conjunction with other wildlife refuges and state parks on the Eastern Shore.

March for Parks, Spring, First Landing State Park, Virginia Beach, VA, (757) 412–2300. Hikers obtain pledges to help support trail maintenance.

The Off-Road Duathalon (mountain bike/running), April, York River State Park, Don Peterson, (757) 486–4116.

The Pungo Strawberry Festival, May, Virginia Beach, VA, (757) 721–6001.

York River Fall Festival, October, Virginia Institute of Marine Science, (804) 684–7135.

Northern Virginia

Columbia Pike Blues Festival, May, the Sunday before Mother's Day, Columbia Pike, (703) 892–2776. One-day free music festival featuring national and local blues acts, food, and vendors.

Fairfax Chocolate Lovers Festival, first weekend of February, Old Town Fairfax, VA, (703) 293–7120.

Fairfax Cross-County Hike, National Trails Day, Fairfax County, VA, (703) 821–0975 (evenings only). Annual event raises awareness and support for a cross-county trail.

Taste of the Town, fourth weekend of June, Reston, VA, (703) 707–9045. Featuring two dozen or more restaurants, food kiosks, and some great eats.

The Annual Festival of Virginia Wines, August, The Plains, VA, (540) 253–5001. Admission charged.

The Cherry Jubilee, February, Dumfries, VA, (703) 221–3346. Celebrates George Washington's birthday.

The Occoquan Wine Festival and Craft Show, September, Occoquan, VA, (703) 491–1736.

The Virginia Gold Cup Races, May, The Plains, VA, (540) 347–2612. Horse races. Tickets must be purchased in advance.

Wolf Trap National Park for the Performing Arts, Vienna, VA, (703) 255–1860. National park dedicated to performing arts. Three different facilities offer year-round performances. The Theater in the Woods is especially geared toward children.

Central Virginia

Historic Appomattox Railroad Festival, second weekend of October, Appomattox, VA, (434) 352–2338. Food, music, craft, and antiques festival commemorating the donation of the Appomattox train depot to the town by Norfolk Southern Railroad.

James River Batteau Festival, mid-June, James River: Lynchburg to Richmond, (434) 528–3950, www.batteau.com. A weeklong celebration of a bygone era. Replicas of the batteau that transported commerce up and down Central Virginia rivers and canals in the 1800s travel from Lynchburg to Richmond, powered by volunteers in period costume. Picnics and parties are scheduled along the route in the towns of Columbia, Cartersville, and elsewhere.

Joel Sweeney Banjo Festival, each fall, Paradise Lake Family Campground, (434) 352–2621. Appomattox native Joel Sweeney was a nineteenth-century banjo maestro. He reputedly added the fifth string on the banjo. He toured Europe extensively and played for England's Queen Victoria. Admission.

Shenandoah National Park

Christmas Bird Count, December, National Audubon Society, Page County, (540) 999–3282.

Fall Foliage Celebration, Waynesboro, VA, (540) 949–8203. Craft show, theater, gem and mineral show, and a 10K run.

North American Butterfly Association Annual Count, July, Page County, (540) 999–3282.

The Virginia Mushroom & Wine Festival, third Saturday of May, Front Royal, VA, (800) 338–2576.

Wildflower Weekend, May, Shenandoah National Park, (540) 999–3582. Park hikes from Big Meadows led by volunteers from the Shenandoah National Park Association.

Valley and Ridge

CCC Reunion, September, Camp Roosevelt, VA, (540) 984–4101. Annual gathering of folks interested in the history of the Civilian Conservation Corps.

Fincastle Festival, September, Fincastle, VA. A street festival with arts and crafts, music, food, and live entertainment.

Heritage Days, July, Mount Jackson, VA, (540) 459–6220. A quaint Main Street affair with a can't-miss feature: homemade baked goods from the Mennonite church women.

Lauderdale Community Days, Third Saturday in October, Lauderdale, VA. A community apple-butter-making and craft sale.

The Highland Maple Festival, March, Monterey, VA, (540) 468–2550. Celebrates the county's status as Virginia's only producer of maple syrup.

The Virginia Garlic Festival, Rebec Vineyards, Amherst County, VA, (804) 746–5168. Food, wine tasting, music, arts and crafts.

Wintergreen Performing Arts Summer Music Festival, July, Wintergreen Resort, (434) 325–8292. Chamber and symphony music.

Southwest Highlands

Blue Ridge Highlands Storytelling Festival & Celebration of Homemade Pies, September, Tazwell, VA, (540) 988–6755.

Carter Fold Music Gathering, Saturday nights year-round, Hiltons, VA, (276) 386–9480.

Chautauqua Festival, June, Wytheville, VA, (276) 223–3355. Nine-day arts festival.

Coal/Railroad Days, August, Appalachia, VA, (276) 565–0055.

Festival in the Park, June, Pearisburg, VA, (540) 921–2955. Barbeque by the Lions Club and homemade arts and crafts.

Mountain Treasures Festival, July, Dungannon, VA, (276) 467–2306.

Oktoberfest, September/October, Mountain Lake Hotel, Mountain Lake, VA, (540) 626–7121.

Pembroke Heritage Days, September or October, Pembroke, VA, (540) 626–7772.

Radford Highlanders Festival, October, Radford, VA, (540) 731–9235.

Ralph Stanley Bluegrass Festival, May, Coeburn, VA, (276) 395–6318.

Summer Art Festival Concerts, Fridays in June and July, Blacksburg, VA, (540) 231–5921. Local artists featured in outdoor concerts.

Virginia Highlands Festival, two weeks in August, Abingdon, VA, (800) 435–3440, www.vahighlandsfestival.org. Southwest Virginia's premier event.

Mount Rogers

Appalachian Trail Days, third week in May, Damascus, VA, (276) 475–3542. Annual gathering of AT thru-hikers in the town dubbed "friendliest town on the AT."

Blue Ridge Backroads at the Rex Theater, Galax, VA, (540) 236–3862. Galax is about an hour-and-a-half east of Mount Rogers. Live radio music show every Friday from Galax's downtown theater. Programs air on 98.1 WBRC-FM.

Candlelight Christmas Tour of Homes, second Sunday in December, Abingdon, VA, (800) 435–3440.

Galax Old Time Fiddlers Convention, second week of August, Galax, VA, (276) 238–8130. Attracts national and international recording acts. Grayson Highlands State Park and the town of Fries also host bluegrass, old-time, and country music festivals every year.

Grayson Highlands Fall Festival, fourth weekend of September, Grayson Highlands State Park, Mouth of Wilson, VA, (276) 579–6061. Just one of many fall festivals in the area. Independence, Fries, Baywood, and Marion all hold fall festivals through September and October.

Naturalist Rally, Mother's Day Weekend, May, Mount Rogers, VA, (276) 783–2125.

Whitetop Mountain Ramp Festival, third Sunday in May, Whitetop, VA, (276) 773–3711. Ramps are a term for wild leeks, and this festival features an eating contest that can bring you to tears—from laughter or from the onion itself.

Contact Info

(Local and National Clubs and Organizations)

Statewide Information

State Travel Information, (800) VISIT–VA, www.virginia.org.
DCR - Division of State Parks, (804) 786–1712, www.dcr.state.va.us/parks.
DCR - State Park Reservation Line, (800) 933–PARK (7275).
DCR - Natural Heritage Program, (804) 786–7951,www.dcr.state.va.us/dnh.
Dept. of Game and Inland Fisheries, (804) 367–1000, www.dgif.state.va.us.
Dept. of Mines, Minerals and Energy, (276) 523–8146, www.mme.state.va.us.
Dept. of Forestry, (434) 977–6555, www.vdof.org/stforest.
　　　 ... Cumberland HQ, (804) 492–4121
　　　 ... Appomattox/Buckingham HQ, (434) 983–2175

National Forests

Supervisors Office, Roanoke, VA, (888) 265–0019, www.southernregion.fs.fed.us/gwj.

Ranger Districts
Clinch, Wise,VA, (276) 328–2931.
Deerfield, Staunton,VA, (540) 885–8028.
Dry River, Bridgewater,VA, (540) 828–2591.
Glenwood/Pedlar, Natural Bridge Station, VA, (540) 291–2188; Buena Vista, VA, (540) 261–6105.
Highlands Gateway Visitors Center, Max Meadows,VA, (800) 446–9670.
James River, Covington,VA, (540) 962–2214.
Lee, Edinburg,VA, (540) 984–4101.
Massanutten Visitors Center, New Market,VA, (540) 740–8310.
Mount Rogers National Recreation Area, Marion,VA, (276) 783–5196.
New Castle, New Castle,VA, (540) 864–5195.
New River Valley, Blacksburg,VA, (540) 552–4641;Wytheville,VA, (540) 228–5551.
Warm Springs, Hot Springs,VA, (540) 839–2521.

National Parks

www.nps.gov.
Blue Ridge Parkway, Ashville, NC, (828) 271–4779.
George Washington Memorial Parkway, McLean,VA, (703) 289–2500.
Great Falls Park, Great Falls,VA, (703) 285–2966.

Prince William Forest Park, (703) 221–7181.
Shenandoah National Park, Luray, VA, (540) 999–3500.

Hiking Clubs

Appalachian Trail Conference, P.O. Box 807, Harpers Ferry, WV, (304) 535–6331, www.appalachiantrail.org.

Local Chapters/Clubs:
Charlottesville: John Shannon, (434) 293–2953.

Regional Office for Central and Southwest Virginia, 1280 North Main Street, Blacksburg, VA 24060, (540) 961–5551.

Tennessee Eastman Hiking Club, P.O. Box 511, Kingsport, TN 37662, www.tehcc.org, (128 miles, Spivey Gap, TN [U.S. Highway 19 West] to Damascus, VA).

Mount Rogers AT Club, 24198 Green Spring Road, Abingdon, VA 24211-5320, www.geocities.com/yosemite/geyser/2539, (60 miles, Damascus, VA, to Virginia Route 670).

Piedmont AT Hikers, Piedmont Appalachian Trail Hikers, P.O. Box 4423, Greensboro, NC 27404-4423, www.path-at.org, (57 miles, Virginia Route 670 to Garden Mountain, Virginia Route 623).

Outdoor Club of Virginia Tech, P.O. Box 538, Blacksburg, VA 24060, filebox.vt.edu/org/outdoor, (36 miles, U.S. Highway 460 at Pearisburg, VA, to Pine Swamp Branch Shelter; Laurel Creek to Virginia Route 623.

Roanoke AT Club, P.O. Box 12282, Roanoke, VA 24024, www.ratc.org, (119 miles, Pine Swamp Branch Shelter to Blackhorse Gap; Virginia Route 611 to Virginia Route 608).

Natural Bridge AT Club, P.O. Box 3012, Lynchburg, VA 24503, www.nbatc.org, (90 miles, Tye River, Virginia Route 56 to Blackhorse Gap [Forest Road 186]).

Tidewater AT Club, P.O. Box 8246, Norfolk, VA 23503, www.tidewateratc.com, (11 miles, Tye River, Virginia Route 56 to Reeds Gap, Virginia Route 664.

Old Dominion AT Club, P.O. Box 25283, Richmond, VA 23260, www.odatc.org, (19 miles, Reeds Gap, Virginia Route 664 to Rockfish Gap, I-64.

Potomac AT Club, 118 Park Street SE, Vienna, VA 22180, (703) 242–0315/0693, www.patc.net, (240 miles, Rockfish Gap, I-64 to Pine Grove Furnace State Park, PA).

Conservation Organizations

Blue Ridge Parkway Foundation, P.O. Box 10427 Salem Station, Winston-Salem, NC 27103, (336) 721–0260, www.brpfoundation.org. Encourages bequests and conservation easements along parkway.

Chesapeake Bay Foundation, 162 Prince George Street, Annapolis, MD 21401, (888) SAVE–BAY, www.cbf.org.

The Conservation Fund, 1800 North Kent Street, Suite 1120, Arlington, VA 22209-2156, (703) 525–6300.

Friends of the Blue Ridge Parkway, Virginia Office: P.O. Box 20986, Roanoke, VA 24018, (800) 228–7275, www.blueridgefriends.org. Volunteers preserve and protect parkway.

Friends of the North Fork of the Shenandoah, P.O. Box 746, 122 South Commerce Street, Woodstock, VA 22664, (540) 459–8550.

Izaak Walton League of America, Inc., Virginia Division, 676 Ellen Drive, Front Royal, VA 22630, (540) 636–4019, www.iwla.org. Preservation and stewardship.

The Nature Conservancy Worldwide Office, 4245 North Fairfax Drive, Suite 100, Arlington, VA 22203-1606, (703) 841–5300, www.tnc.org; Virginia Office: 490 Westfield Road, Charlottesville, VA 22901-1633, (434) 295–6106.

Rail-to-Trails Conservancy, 1100 Seventeenth Street NW, 10th floor, Washington, DC 20036, (202) 331–9696, www.railstrails.org. Effort to convert old railroad beds to trail systems.

Shenandoah National Park Association, 3655 U.S. Highway 211, East Luray, VA 22835, (540) 999–3582, wwwsnp.org. Supports educational programs through sale of books and maps at visitor center.

Sierra Club (12 local groups), Six North Sixth Street, Richmond, VA 23219, (804) 225–9113, www.virginia.sierraclub.org.

Virginia Conservation Network, 1001 East Broad Street, Suite LL 35-C, Richmond, VA 23219, (804) 644–0283, www.vcnva.org.

Virginia Ducks Unlimited, 364 Shiloh Drive, P.O. Box 679, Windsor, VA 23487, (757) 242–3085, www.ducks.org.

Virginia Native Plant Society, 400 Blandy Farm Lane, Boyce, VA 22620, (540) 837–1600, www.vnps.org.

Virginia Outdoor Writers Association, www.vowa.org.

Virginia Outdoors Foundation, P.O. Box 322, Aldie, VA 20105, (703) 327–9777.

Virginia Wilderness Committee, Eleven East Monmouth, Winchester, VA 22601, (540) 662–7043, www.vawilderness.org. Publishes Virginia Wilderness newsletter.

Virginia Wildlife Federation, 1001 East Broad Street LL5, Richmond, VA 23219, (804) 340–1343.

The Wildlife Center of Virginia, P.O. Box 1557, Waynesboro, VA 22980, (540) 942–9453, www.wildlifecenter.org. Hospital for orphaned wildlife.

The Wildlife Society, Virginia Chapter, 1836 River Road, Farmville, VA 23901-3535, (804) 392–9645, www.wildlife.org.

Wintergreen Nature Foundation, P.O. Box 468, Nelysford, VA 22958, (434) 325–7451, www.twnf.org.

About the Authors

Bill and Mary Burnham live in the Chesapeake Bay region of Virginia, within easy reach of their sources of inspiration: ocean and mountains. Bill began hiking with friends in New York's Adirondack Mountains in the 1980s. Mary came aboard a few years later and together they have hiked and traveled America. Their first-ever trip as a couple came in Shenandoah National Park. After they married, they led adventure trips for youth in West Virginia. As full-time freelance writers, Bill and Mary will use any excuse to recruit friends, family—anyone who'll talk to them, really—for extended backpacking trips. A love of Virginia's mountains draws them year after year to favorite spots in far southwest Virginia and Alleghenies, while flatwater kayaking in eastern Virginia fills the winter months. Wherever they end up, they always seek out Virginia's renowned hospitality in the many wonderful bed-and-breakfast inns. Any inn, that is, that will also welcome Sasha, trail dog supreme.

Follow along the authors' adventures at www.BurnhamInk.com

WHAT'S SO SPECIAL ABOUT UNSPOILED, NATURAL PLACES?

Beauty   Solitude   Wildness   Freedom   Quiet   Adventure
Serenity   Inspiration   Wonder   Excitement
Relaxation   Challenge

There's a lot to love about our treasured public lands, and the reasons are different for each of us. Whatever your reasons are, the national **Leave No Trace** education program will help you discover special outdoor places, enjoy them, and preserve them—today and for those who follow. By practicing and passing along these simple principles, you can help protect the special places you love from being loved to death.

THE PRINCIPLES OF LEAVE NO TRACE

- 🐾 Plan ahead and prepare
- 🐾 Travel and camp on durable surfaces
- 🐾 Dispose of waste properly
- 🐾 Leave what you find
- 🐾 Minimize campfire impacts
- 🐾 Respect wildlife
- 🐾 Be considerate of other visitors

Leave No Trace is a national nonprofit organization dedicated to teaching responsible outdoor recreation skills and ethics to everyone who enjoys spending time outdoors.

To learn more or to become a member, please visit us at www.LNT.org or call (800) 332–4100.

Leave No Trace, P.O. Box 997, Boulder, CO 80306